To Charlotte and Harriet, and in memory of Ingrid Elisabeth Evans

CONTENTS

INTRODUCTION

Hi all,

After what has been an incredibly busy period, we thought it would be nice to make the most of this lovely weather and have some socially distanced drinks in the garden this evening.

Please join us from 6 p.m. and bring your own booze!

Martin.[1]

On 20 May 2020, at the height of the national lockdown – introduced by the Conservative government as part of its overall strategy for tackling the Covid pandemic – the above email was sent to all staff in No. 10, some 200 recipients, almost encouraging people to break the rules.

Many people might have assumed that the sender of this 'Partygate'* email was the Prime Minister's diary secretary, his office manager or even some kind of head butler in No. 10.

---

* The journalistic collective term for the series of parties at No. 10 and the centre of government, covered by the Sue Gray report.

In fact, the author and sender of the email was Martin Reynolds,[*] the principal private secretary to Prime Minister Boris Johnson. Reynolds was then a senior diplomat of director general rank on secondment to No. 10. A graduate of Cambridge University, a former UK ambassador to Libya and a Companion of the Order of St Michael and St George, he was the most senior civil servant in No. 10, and the private office which he headed represented a central plank of the machinery of UK government. Later, after the party had taken place with no journalists having picked up on this undoubtedly newsworthy story, Reynolds commented, 'We seem to have got away with it.'[2]

Reynolds's decision to take on the mundane task of issuing an invitation to drinks may have been an idiosyncratic one, but this action could easily have clouded the public's perception of the role of the principal private secretary in No. 10. The work of the Prime Minister's principal private secretary is not to be their social secretary but rather to manage the essential hub of support across the whole range of government activity, including advising on the appropriateness of events which the Prime Minister should attend. The job of the principal private secretary is also to run the equally prosaically titled 'private office'.

But it is not at all surprising that the public at large do not understand the dated and often obscure language used in Westminster and Whitehall, which often appears to delight in obfuscation, especially where job titles are concerned. How can the person on the street be expected to understand the difference between a principal private secretary and a parliamentary private secretary (both of which are referred to as 'PPS'), a permanent under-secretary of state

---

[*] Martin Reynolds CB CMG (1969–); principal private secretary to the Foreign Secretary (Philip Hammond, Boris Johnson and Jeremy Hunt) 2014–18; British ambassador to Libya 2019; principal private secretary to the Prime Minister 2019–22.

or even a special adviser? What exactly do they each do? Certainly, some strange job titles exist elsewhere in many professions – deputy pro-vice-chancellor, suffragan bishop, house officer (in medicine), for example – but only Whitehall seems to revel and delight in obscurity, and the ministerial private office is a choice example.

Obscure language can be a barrier to understanding. What is private about the private office? And where is the office, if there is one – or is it virtual? If there is a principal private secretary, is there also a secondary or subordinate private secretary? Who appoints these people and how? How are they trained for the role and to whom are they accountable? Perhaps, most importantly, what do they actually do?

Private office is, in fact, an essential part of our system of constitutional democracy and the civil service that supports ministers, who are accountable to Parliament. It is the interface between the elected politicians, the permanent apparatus of government and the civil servants in the government departments of state. Yet, despite its importance, private office is little known or understood – and little considered – by the media and by most academic studies. This book aims to fill that gap and seeks to shed a light on private office, what it does and how it has changed throughout history.

How was it that, during Partygate, the most senior civil servant in No. 10, responsible for maintaining standards and the integrity of the office of the Prime Minister, ended up proposing a social event that would drive a coach and horses through the national guidance then applying to the activities of every citizen in the country? The 20 May party was not even a unique event. The subsequent report conducted by Sue Gray,* a senior civil servant in the Cabinet Office,

---

* Sue Gray (1957–); director general and head of propriety and ethics, Cabinet Office, 2012–2018; Second Permanent Secretary Cabinet Office 2021–22. Subsequently left the civil service and was appointed, in 2023, as chief of staff to the Labour leader, Sir Keir Starmer.

identified sixteen such events that had taken place during the period of the Covid lockdown and that appeared to transgress the government's own regulations. Why was the authority of private office apparently diluted to such an extent that there was no voice to question the legality, let alone the wisdom, of holding parties at the height of lockdown? Why was Reynolds – whose key responsibility was to advise the Prime Minister on issues of propriety and ethics – seemingly so lacking in fulfilling that duty?

The shortcomings in the leadership and management of the No. 10 private office in 2020 were, however, not so much a one-off aberration in standards but rather they reflected part of a longer-term trend. Indeed, some politicians have argued that the support functions for ministers are not fit for purpose and need to be less the preserve of the civil service. Some want a more muscular, or even a more politicised, private office. Such an approach inevitably risks bringing the civil service – an organisation founded on the principles of independence and non-party politicisation – into conflict with government. Prime Minister Boris Johnson's principal private secretary – the head of his private office – appeared to be condoning, or even encouraging, rule-breaking. How had private office come to this?

This book explains what the ministerial private office is, what it does on a day-to-day basis and why it is so significant. Covering 200 years of political history, it highlights how the private office has played a prominent, if hidden, role in governance. It explores the vital role that some private secretaries have had at key events in British history, including how they interacted with ministers and political advisers. That great observer of the British constitution, Lord Hennessy, famously characterised the unseen elements that support the British political system as the 'hidden wiring' – by which he meant those structures, systems and people within, in particular, the civil service that collectively make the connections and ensure things happen smoothly, even though they themselves are usually invisible.[3] If the civil service, as a whole, represents the totality of the 'hidden wiring' in Hennessy's analysis, the private office represents the central junction box through which much political power and energy flows. Every minister, from the Prime Minister downwards, has a private office, whose job it is to ensure that business is transacted smoothly and efficiently, and yet usually out of sight of the media and the glare of publicity.

But, at times, the system has not always worked as seamlessly as it should. On occasion, the junction box has failed to make the right connections. This book traces the roots of the modern-day private office and its growth over the past two centuries, showing how it is now an established part of the hidden wiring and assessing the future of private office in the current political climate.

The title 'private secretary' and the functions of that role can be traced back some two centuries, although the term 'private office' is more recent. Originally, private secretaries were the officials attached to ministers and responsible for the conduct of managing ministerial business and ensuring the prompt receipt and despatch of ministerial business and correspondence. However, the modern-day private office plays a far more complex role than in the past. The role has, like that of ministers and Prime Ministers, expanded relentlessly. Today's private secretary to an energetic minister may well assist in the process of policy-making, help facilitate cross-Whitehall organisation, liaise with the royal households, get involved in crisis management and help handle the media and communications, all on top of managing the day-to-day transactions of government. They (or a deputy) may find themselves on call for twenty-four hours a day, seven days a week. A private secretary will accompany their minister to every official meeting.

Yet this role and the group of civil servants who work in private office have never been written about in detail. That is the gap which this book seeks to fill. Private secretaries are the characters who appear, sometimes only in passing, in biographies and memoirs; their roles have often been touched on but rarely in depth; and yet many ministers have testified as to how much they relied on them. Private secretaries have been, at times, some of the most powerful people in this country. Some have been colourful and controversial. Many have been brilliant minds and creative wordsmiths, well at-tuned to carrying out their political leaders' wishes. Some have had close relationships with their ministers and have become immense-ly influential. In particular, those officials who have worked within the Prime Minister's private office have contributed to, and helped to shape, history. These figures, while never household names – in modern times people such as Robert Armstrong, Robin Butler, Charles Powell, Kenneth Stowe, Alex Allan and Jeremy Heywood – were undoubtedly powerful and their role under-appreciated and under-chronicled. They were career civil servants and, for the most part, middle-class Oxbridge men in the traditional mould of the British administration. This is their story – warts and all. It is a history of a remarkable set of people who, while they may not have been well known, were close to, and even intimate with, the politicians who wielded power. At important junctures in our na-tional story – such as wars, crises and moments of great political change – it has often been the private office that has been the cen-tral body responsible for keeping the show on the road, whatever it takes.

Ministers and Prime Ministers have always had their favoured advisers. For example, in the late nineteenth century, Benjamin Disraeli, twice Prime Minister, was exceptionally close to his trusted private secretary Montagu Corry.* Disraeli famously described the relationship between minister and private secretary as second only to that between a man and his wife. By the time of the Second World War, the civil service had achieved a near monopoly in providing advice to ministers and Prime Ministers. Private offices were nearly always composed of only civil servants, albeit ones who had already formed close relationships with Prime Ministers, like Corry and John 'Jock' Colville,† who supported Winston Churchill during war and peace. While all Prime Ministers and ministers used informal sources of policy advice, including from Members of Parliament, there was, prior to 1964, no formalised process of special advisers providing political advice to ministers.

However, by 1964 and the election of Harold Wilson's Labour government, some voices had begun to question the dominance of the civil service, including within the ministerial private office. Labour intellectuals in the Fabian Society were sceptical about the establishment nature of the civil service, and some argued for a significant influx of political appointees and for the creation of more Continental-style 'cabinets' to support ministers, believing that breaking the monopoly of power that civil servants held in the private office would aid better decision-making. Wilson's Labour Party, when in opposition in the early 1960s, had toyed with the idea of establishing such a Continental 'cabinet'-type system alongside, or even in

---

* Montagu 'Monty' Corry (1838–1903); private secretary to Benjamin Disraeli 1866–81; created Baron Rowton 1880.

† Sir John 'Jock' Colville (1915–87); assistant private secretary to the Prime Minister (Neville Chamberlain, Winston Churchill and Clement Attlee) 1939–41 and 1943–45; joint principal private secretary to the Prime Minister 1951–55. Colville, unusually for a civil servant, published his diaries (*The Fringes of Power*) and they provide a unique insight into the workings of the No. 10 private office during the 1940s and 1950s as well as his relationship with the Prime Minister.

place of, private offices. Indeed, that had been the explicit aim of the Fabians in their influential 1964 pamphlet, *The Administrators*, which had argued that every Cabinet minister's private office should contain up to four political advisers.[4] In practice, Wilson was far less radical and appointed only five new special advisers across the whole of government. His most telling political appointee, however, was his new personal political secretary, Marcia Williams,[*] whose appointment, role and style were to create sharp tensions with the civil servants in Wilson's private office, and with whom she often clashed, during his eight years at No. 10. Even getting agreement to Williams's new title of 'political secretary' raised concerns within the civil service, not least from Wilson's principal private secretary, Derek Mitchell.[†]

Some twenty years later, a charge of politicisation was again raised within Margaret Thatcher's No. 10 private office. This time that charge was levelled against Charles Powell[‡] (her foreign affairs private secretary) and Bernard Ingham[§] (her chief press officer), both of whom heavily influenced Thatcher in her later years in power. Critics argued that they had effectively created a closed 'cabinet' of just two people – albeit both were career civil servants, not political appointees.

Under Tony Blair's New Labour government, elected in 1997, a different model emerged. For the first time, a new central post of chief of staff was created, working alongside the traditional civil service private office. Thatcher had dabbled unsuccessfully with the

---

[*] Marcia Williams (1932–2019); personal secretary to Harold Wilson 1956–64 and 1970–74; personal and political secretary to the Prime Minister 1964–70 and 1974–76; created Baroness Falkender 1974.

[†] Sir Derek Mitchell (1922–2009); principal private secretary to the Chancellor of the Exchequer (Reginald Maudling) 1962–64; principal private secretary to the Prime Minister (Alec Douglas-Home and Harold Wilson) 1964–66.

[‡] Charles Powell (1941–); private secretary (foreign affairs) to the Prime Minister 1984–91; created Lord Powell of Bayswater 2000.

[§] Bernard Ingham (1932–); chief press secretary to the Prime Minister 1979–90.

idea of such a new role, but under Blair the post was firmly established and ably filled by Jonathan Powell* over the whole decade of the Blair premiership. Powell's role entailed a reshaping of the private office. A political appointee (albeit, in Powell's case, a former civil servant) became a permanent feature at the centre of the No. 10 operation, capable of acting more politically than the traditional principal private secretary. That position, coupled with the dominance of Blair's new press secretary, Alastair Campbell,† gave No. 10 a more powerful cross-Whitehall clout than under previous regimes, although Blair still remained frustrated by what he called the lack of delivery. All subsequent Prime Ministers retained the position of chief of staff, and it is now an established role, although it has been occupied by a range of people from different backgrounds, including, exceptionally under Johnson, by a serving Member of Parliament in the House of Commons. The retention of the chief of staff position by all Prime Ministers from both political parties represents a good example of the organic development of private office over the past quarter of a century.

Another shift that has taken place over recent years has been in the balance between the role of the civil service and the influence of special advisers. Whereas half a century ago, the first special advisers concentrated on policy advice, more recently they have become far more interventionist on political issues, organisational questions and even appointments. The influence of special advisers – while never formal members of private office – on ministers has increased and deepened, while that of the civil service has declined. Indeed,

---

* Jonathan Powell (1956–); Foreign Office diplomat 1979–95; chief of staff to the Leader of the Opposition 1995–97; chief of staff to the Prime Minister 1997–2007.

† Alastair Campbell (1957–); former political journalist; chief press secretary to the Leader of the Opposition 1994–97; Prime Minister's chief press secretary and official spokesman 1997–2001; director of strategy and communications No. 10 2001–03.

the influence of special advisers on ministers during Partygate was considerable but under-reported, with most of the media's focus falling on the failings of the civil service.

Yet, despite these changes in culture and organisation, along with strictures from some ministers, the private office has survived and, for the most part, thrived. There was undoubtedly a body of opinion that sought to question the effectiveness of the traditional model of private office and to contrast it with the *'cabinet'* model and its greater blend of administrators and political advisers working in a single unit. But no Prime Minister or minister has yet come up with a better model. Rather, they have sought to adapt it. There is no evidence that a *'cabinet'* system is either more effective or more efficient than the private office. The traditional British model of the ministerial private office has existed broadly in its current format since the foundation of the modern system of Cabinet government at the end of the First World War. Many Prime Ministers sought to exert a greater level of scrutiny and control over the performance of government. This has led to periodic proposals for the establishment of a Prime Minister's department, although its structure and powers have never been fully articulated and no such department has ever been created. Its purpose would have been to bring together the functions of No. 10 with those of the Cabinet Office,* responsible for oversight of departmental policies and delivery.

When Edward Heath was Leader of the Opposition, before the 1970 general election, his advisers urged him to consider establishing such an office, but he rowed back from doing so. Margaret

---

* The Cabinet Office, headed by the Cabinet Secretary, has a responsibility to provide support and advice to the whole of Cabinet – not just the Prime Minister and No. 10. It is responsible, for example, for the structure of Cabinet committees which co-ordinate all cross-government policy and advice to the Prime Minister.

Thatcher and John Major did not see the need for such a body, preferring to keep No. 10 smaller and more focused. Tony Blair, both in the run-up to 1997 and once in office, considered the idea again but, like Heath, chose not to pursue it. Both Prime Ministers instead introduced structural changes at the centre to try to improve policy-making and delivery.

In the early 1970s, Heath created the Central Policy Review Staff (CPRS), based in Cabinet Office, to build capacity at the centre for longer-term strategic thinking. Wilson built on this model by establishing the Policy Unit at No. 10 to provide the Prime Minister with dedicated political capacity to concentrate on policy-making in priority areas. That unit has survived to this day, unlike the CPRS. Blair, during his second term, became frustrated by the lack of oversight of what he called the 'delivery' of the government's policies. That led him to establish the Prime Minister's Delivery Unit (PMDU) in No. 10, headed initially by an expert adviser, Michael Barber. Blair's view was that having a specific function focused on delivery of a more limited number of targets and with regular scrutiny and oversight by the Prime Minister made for a more effective premiership. Yet, while some of these initiatives over the past half-century or more could be said to reflect a frustration with the role of the traditional private office, it has survived in essentially its original form.

Which brings us back to the problems of the private office under Boris Johnson. The fundamental difference under Johnson's government was that the hidden wiring had become exposed, frayed and subject to extensive scrutiny, not least in the media. The 'good chaps theory of government', whereby things would be done and processes strictly followed as a result of the quality and integrity of people entrusted with power and its use within the organisation, no longer seemed to apply.[5] The constitution and long-standing conventions came under pressure soon after Johnson became Prime Minister in July 2019. The following month Parliament was prorogued illegally – as the Supreme Court of the United Kingdom subsequently declared.[6] The event undoubtedly also put the monarch in a difficult position. There is no evidence that the private office even warned the Prime Minister against this course of action. Later, Johnson's combative special adviser Dominic Cummings* sought, during the Covid lockdowns, to stretch the boundaries of credulity to the limit – arguing that a car journey to Barnard Castle in County Durham, allegedly to test his eyesight, was legitimate. Yet again, there appeared to have been no brake on the Prime Minister to rein in his and his adviser's potentially law-breaking tendencies. A number of public appointments were made which evaded 'due process' and showed the profound influence that some special advisers had begun to have, without clear oversight by the private office. When the first special advisers were appointed in 1964, their prime focus was on supporting policy-making. They had no role in public appointments, unlike nowadays.

Throughout all of these events, Johnson's private office and his special advisers were responsible for the overall operation for No. 10 and for advising Johnson on what he could or could not do. There is little evidence that they sought to counsel against such activities or that if they sought to do so and failed, they raised the issue higher up, for example with the Cabinet Secretary. While some of the most egregious examples may have been at No. 10, similar failings occurred in other ministerial private offices across Whitehall. In short, the system of checks and balances had failed to work.

---

* Dominic Cummings (1971–); special adviser to Michael Gove 2010–12; special adviser to Prime Minister Boris Johnson 2019–20.

LITERATURE ON THE PRIVATE OFFICE

The private office is one part of the mechanisms that help operate the unwritten constitution of the United Kingdom. It is a vital element in the 'hidden wiring' of government.[7] Surprisingly, though, in the existing academic literature, there has been no comprehensive study of the history of private office or the changing shape of that body, despite its importance. The subject has often featured in historical literature but usually only in passing, and it has rarely received detailed scrutiny. Biographies and histories are often written from the perspective of the politician or their political party and not the bureaucracy supporting ministers. While many politicians' memoirs pay generous tribute to the work of their private secretaries, few have focused on the tasks and characters of the private secretaries involved.

The diplomat Nicholas Henderson was an exception. Although not a politician, he wrote a book in 1984 on the Foreign Secretary's private office (which he subsequently updated in 2001). This volume, while of interest, was more a study of the Foreign Secretaries whom Henderson had observed and the ways in which they operated and engaged with their private offices.[8] He had served as private secretary to both Anthony Eden and Ernest Bevin, so had first-hand experience of the workings of the private office and powerful Foreign Secretaries. Henderson's book remains a useful memoir and source of anecdotes about how the private secretaries in the Foreign Office operated, but it is far from a systematic analysis of their work across Whitehall. There have been a small number of other academic studies of the private office. For example, Rod Rhodes devoted a chapter to what he describes as 'The Departmental Court' in his book *Everyday Life in British Government*.[9] Based on interviews with serving and former private secretaries, Rhodes documents the roles of, and relationships between, private secretaries, ministers and special advisers. His book provides a valuable addition to Henderson's. It is also more recent and covers three domestic departments.*

There have been a number of other studies of the role of the No. 10 private office and how it has changed over time. In 1988, George Jones wrote a chapter entitled 'The Prime Minister's Aides' in Anthony King's *The British Prime Minister*.[10] Jones describes the work of all Downing Street staff and not just the private office. Of the principal private secretaries, he says they can be categorised on a continuum:

> At one extreme are the 'smoothers', who regard their role as to pour oil on the system, to facilitate and expedite the flow of business. At the other extreme are those who see their role as being not just to smooth the passage of business for others, but to make their own contribution, injecting their own observations into the flow of business.[11]

As will be seen, in the No. 10 private office (as well as in other private offices) and among both principal private secretaries and private secretaries, there have been many examples of what Jones called 'smoothers', as well as what might be termed 'interventionists'. Other books and articles have also analysed aspects of the inner workings of the Prime Minister's office and its staff.[12] On the role of the private office, as a training ground for high office in the civil service, Kevin Theakston initially provided the best analysis of the background of

---

* Rhodes's analysis was based on interviews with the private offices of the Department for Environment, Food and Rural Affairs, the Department for Education and Skills and the Department of Trade and Industry.

senior mandarins, including their service in No. 10, the Treasury and private office.[13] More recently, Andrew Blick and George Jones have also explored the role of the private office in the wider context of the development of prime ministerial power.[14] Dennis Kavanagh and Anthony Seldon, in *The Powers Behind the Prime Minister*, also carried out more detailed analysis and looked at the operation of No. 10 from 1970 until the arrival of the New Labour government in 1997. Their book includes a valuable appendix on the staff of all the Prime Ministers from 1945 to 1999.[15] However, with the exception of that volume published in 1999, other studies of No. 10 have tended to focus on more political issues or the role of political advisers and accounts of the political power struggle between, for example, the Blair and Brown camps, as opposed to studying how administrative power operated and how the private office functioned.[16] More recently, Seldon has written, or co-written, histories of the Blair, Brown, Cameron, May and Johnson premierships, but, again, they are more studies of politicians, policies and events and not of the systems of governance and administration that supported them.[17] The private office gets only a passing mention, rather than being a central theme in these volumes.

An exception to this is a book by Jonathan Powell, who served as chief of staff to Blair throughout his decade as Prime Minister. *The New Machiavelli* (which is partly a memoir of Powell's time at No. 10) contains many references to the organisation and operation of No. 10, including the way in which he, as a special adviser, worked effectively alongside the permanent civil servants within the No. 10 private office.[18] The book also provided Powell's justification for the new post of 'chief of staff to the Prime Minister', which was introduced with his arrival in No. 10 and which has existed ever since. The chief of staff, a political appointee, now works closely alongside the No. 10 private office. The most senior civil servant within private office during Powell's time was Jeremy Heywood,* who was to remain in or close to No. 10 for around a quarter of a century. Powell paid particular tribute to Heywood, calling him 'an outstanding civil servant for whom the word "Stakhanovite" might have been invented'.[19] Andrew Holt and Warren Dockter's more recent work focused mainly on the foreign affairs private secretaries at No. 10.[20] However, in the final chapter of their collection, Anthony Seldon analyses the background and the different styles of principal private secretaries in No. 10.[21]

There have also been attempts to explain the specific role played by the private secretary. For example, in 1980, Gerald Kaufman† wrote *How to Be a Minister*, a light-hearted yet valuable study of the way in which the power around ministers operates.[22] While it is often more in the tone and style of the *Yes Minister* television series, it offers a helpful perspective on the way in which ministers operated in the second Wilson government and on the systems surrounding them, including the private office and the private secretaries.‡ Kaufman commented that, for a minister, the private secretary

> is in charge of your personal domain, ready to anticipate and pander to your every whim and also to keep a sharp eye on you in case you show signs of getting out of line ... Your Private Secretary, or one his assistants, will accompany you to all your

---

* Jeremy Heywood (1961–2018); private secretary to the Financial Secretary to the Treasury 1986–88; principal private secretary to the Chancellor of the Exchequer (Norman Lamont and Kenneth Clarke) 1991–94; private secretary (economic affairs), subsequently principal private secretary, to the Prime Minister (Tony Blair) 1997–2003; principal private secretary to the Prime Minister (Gordon Brown) 2008–10; Permanent Secretary No. 10 2010–12; Cabinet Secretary 2012–18; created Lord Heywood of Whitehall 2018.

† Gerald Kaufman (1930–2017); political assistant to the Prime Minister and parliamentary liaison officer, No. 10, 1965–70; MP 1970–2017.

‡ *Yes Minister* was the satirical BBC television series written by Antony Jay and Jonathan Lynn and based around the workings of a Cabinet minister's office, including the relationship with his Permanent Secretary and his principal private secretary.

engagements except Cabinet Committees, take a note of all your meetings, listen in to all your telephone conversations, travel with you at home and abroad. He will get to know you better than anyone except your close relatives.[23]

A more recent book, in the style of Kaufman, is *How to Be a Minister: A 21st-Century Guide* by John Hutton and Leigh Lewis.[24] This is a guide to being a Cabinet minister, which touches on how a minister can make the best use of their private office. Hutton and Lewis worked together as Secretary of State and Permanent Secretary in the same department.* They state authoritatively that 'to be a successful minister you need to have a good private office. It is as basic as that.'[25] They go on to explain recruitment to private office, the pivotal role of the principal private secretary ('the most important person in the private office') and the skills that are required to fulfil the role.[26] Hutton and Lewis also emphasise:

> Private secretaries are not there to be your cheerleaders. And they are not part of your party political support team either, however close you might get to them as colleagues. Private offices can provide something much more important than support. The best private offices should be able to provide engaged objectivity, a sound source of additional advice and pointers to you so that you [as a minister] can make the right decisions.[27]

Of course, Hutton and Lewis's book, like Powell's and Kaufman's, was written by insiders and they are therefore all partially witness accounts. Such accounts can bring great insight and expertise to

---

* Hutton served as Secretary of State for Work and Pensions from 2005–07, while Lewis was his Permanent Secretary at that time.

the question of what happens within the private office. However, they may also, at times, be less detached in scrutinising their subject matter.

Beyond the literature on private office itself, there is a wealth of sources on wider political history and political science which refer to the power and influence of the Prime Minister, the Prime Minister's office and the development of the civil service. The two most detailed volumes are both by Peter Hennessy. *Whitehall*, first published in 1989, focused on the role of Whitehall departments and the Cabinet Office, but has a substantial section on the operation of the centre of government and the part played by private office.[28] *The Prime Minister: The Office and its Holders Since 1945* carries out an examination of the operation of the office of each Prime Minister from Attlee to Blair, including references to the working of, and officials within, the No. 10 private office.[29] In addition, there is the wider context of the history of the civil service and reform.[30]

SOURCES AND METHODOLOGY

This book has relied on a range of sources, not just the above literature, and is based on research conducted over the past decade. These include files from the National Archives (TNA), the traditional repository for much research material. However, those files and others from similar archives, such as the Margaret Thatcher Foundation (MTF), offer relatively limited access to the past for any study of the private office or of private secretaries in the period covered here. There are three reasons for that. First, there is no single archive holding for private offices, since their records were not habitually kept as a whole or even in part. The traces of their work and that of private secretaries can be found in files at TNA, and to a lesser extent the MTF, but they are disparate and incomplete. Second, many TNA records for the period beyond the thirty-year rule covered in this book, namely after 1990, remain closed. Third, even if full papers were filed at TNA for private offices since 1964, the nature of government papers would mean that their activities, and especially those of private secretaries, would probably not be captured. That is because the purpose of private office is not to dominate decision-making but to enable its processes and actions. Moreover, and critically, government records do not chronicle the personal interactions and human relationships that have existed between ministers and private secretaries and that have been vital to the function of government.

Consequently, I sought to get first-hand testimonies on the role and work of private office, drawing on thirty-six original interviews (the full list is contained in the bibliography) and associated correspondence with former private secretaries and other officials and ministerial advisers of the past fifty years. Those testimonies included interviews with all the four living Prime Ministers (John Major, Tony Blair, Gordon Brown and David Cameron) covering the main period I studied. I am very grateful to them and their offices for the time they devoted to helping me. Major and Brown, of course, came to No. 10 with many years of ministerial service and knowledge of the working of private offices, whereas Blair and Cameron became Prime Minister with no prior ministerial experience.*

---

* Although Cameron did have experience of working in the Treasury as a special adviser at the time of 'Black Wednesday' and therefore knew many of the key figures then working in No. 10 and the Treasury, including Gus O'Donnell and Jeremy Heywood (both future Cabinet Secretaries).

I also interviewed eight principal private secretaries to the Prime Minister, from Robert Armstrong,* who served in No. 10 from 1970 but had far wider private office experience going back to the 1950s, up to Simon Case,† the current Cabinet Secretary, who was one of David Cameron's principal private secretaries. I interviewed many other private secretaries and officials who had worked at No. 10 and elsewhere in a range of Whitehall private offices, and who regularly interacted with the No. 10 private office. I spoke to five other former Cabinet Secretaries. In order to gather evidence from the private offices on the handling of specific events, I interviewed David Omand‡ (the Falklands), Richard Mottram§ and Charles Powell (Westland), Jeremy Heywood (Black Wednesday and many other events of the past two decades), Jonathan Powell and Alex Allan¶ (the transition to New Labour in 1997), James Bowler (the Brown–Cameron transition in 2010) and Caroline Slocock** (on being the first female private secretary in No. 10). I consulted advisers who had worked at No. 10 such as Bernard Donoughue,†† who served from 1974 to 1979 in the No. 10 Policy Unit under Wilson and Callaghan, and

---

* Robert Armstrong (1927–2020); private secretary to the Economic Secretary to the Treasury 1953–54; private secretary to the Chancellor of the Exchequer (R. A. Butler) 1954–55; joint principal private secretary to the Chancellor of the Exchequer (Roy Jenkins) 1967–68; principal private secretary to the Prime Minister (Edward Heath and Harold Wilson) 1970–75; Permanent Secretary to the Home Office 1977–79; Cabinet Secretary 1979–87; created Lord Armstrong of Ilminster 1988.

† Simon Case (1978–); civil servant, Permanent Secretary No. 10 2020; Cabinet Secretary 2020–.

‡ David Omand (1947–); private secretary to the Secretary of State for Defence 1973–75; principal private secretary to the Secretary of State for Defence (Francis Pym and John Nott) 1979–83. Later Permanent Secretary Home Office and security and intelligence adviser to the government.

§ Richard Mottram (1946–); assistant private secretary to the Secretary of State for Defence 1972–73; private secretary to the Permanent Secretary (Sir Frank Cooper) 1979–81; principal private secretary to the Secretary of State for Defence (John Nott and Michael Heseltine) 1982–86; later Permanent Secretary in five departments, including the MoD. He ended his career as the government's chief intelligence and security adviser.

¶ Alex Allan (1951–); principal private secretary to the Chancellor of the Exchequer (Nigel Lawson) 1986–89; principal private secretary to the Prime Minister (John Major and Tony Blair) 1992–97; high commissioner to Australia 1997–99; e-Envoy 1999–2000; Permanent Secretary Ministry of Justice 2004–07; chairman of the Joint Intelligence Committee 2007–11.

** Caroline Slocock (1956–); private secretary to the Prime Minister (home affairs) 1989–91.

†† Bernard Donoughue (1934–); head of the Downing Street Policy Unit 1974–79.

David Lipsey,* who worked for Callaghan from 1976 to 1979. I also interviewed people who worked in the communications function in government, notably Joe Haines† and Alastair Campbell. The choice of officials to interview was mainly based on the level of engagement that they had had with private offices in their careers. I sent them questions in advance, held face-to-face (or occasionally telephone) interviews and followed up with further questions via correspondence, as necessary. Only one former adviser – the late Marcia Williams (Baroness Falkender) – refused to be interviewed.

A combination of these interviews and correspondence plus research in official papers and other historical sources has enabled me in this book to faithfully portray the operation of the private office and how private secretaries worked and behaved over the past half-century. Inevitably, oral history has some shortcomings, because individuals' memories may be partial and/or fragmentary. In addition, some participants in past events or during crises may recall what they wished they had done rather than precisely what they had done. That said, oral history is a vital component of contemporary history, and the triangulation of different memoirs collectively can usually be held to clarify exactly what happened at any time.

My research methodology has therefore had three distinct elements. First, this is a work of political history drawing on the traditional tools of such historical research as described above, using archival material and the rich vein of primary and secondary sources written by politicians and others of the era, together with the perspectives of modern political historians and commentators.

Second, the methodology is informed by my career, my

---

* David Lipsey (1948–); special adviser to Anthony Crosland MP 1974–77; special adviser to the Prime Minister 1977–79; created Lord Lipsey 1999.
† Joe Haines (1928–); chief press secretary 1969–70, 1974–76.

perspective and, also perhaps, my prejudices. I worked for over twenty years in the senior civil service from 1993 to 2015. During that time, for almost four years, I was a principal private secretary to three different Cabinet ministers in two different departments.* I ran the private office of those Cabinet ministers and managed junior ministerial offices. Those duties gave me direct experience and understanding of the role of the principal private secretary as well as the relationships between ministers and their private offices. I witnessed first-hand how the machinery worked at many critical moments, including the transition following the general election of 1997. I saw how the institution helped to support, or hinder, the political process. Following my service in private office, I worked at No. 10 when Tony Blair was Prime Minister and then for the office of the Deputy Prime Minister.

Third, I used the documentary and archival evidence to help create a narrative of what happened in private office during some critical moments of history over the past fifty years. I analysed specific events when the private office played a prominent role to illustrate the operation of that body at such times. Two case studies show the private office as policy-makers (at the time of Britain's accession to the European Community in 1972 and during the negotiations with the International Monetary Fund in 1976). One case study shows the operation of private offices during a military conflict (the Falklands War in 1982), while another shows the private offices of two different departments effectively at war with each other (during the West-land affair in 1986). More recently, a series of events showed private office in response to crises (during the New Labour era from 2000

---

* Alun Evans (1958–); civil servant; principal private secretary to the Secretary of State for Employment 1994–95; principal private secretary to the Secretary of State for Education and Employment (Gillian Shephard and David Blunkett) 1995–98; head of the Strategic Communications Unit, No. 10, 1998–2000.

to 2003) and a final brief study shows how private office responded, at short notice, during the financial crash of 2008. These case studies were not meant to be comprehensive in coverage but rather to show how private secretaries acted and functioned in response to different historical circumstances. They have helped to build up a strong evidence base of how decisions were taken and the influence of the private office at such critical times. To tell this narrative, my research had to go beyond the official records at the National Archives and elsewhere. While private secretaries often record the outcome of a meeting, or note the discussions and positions taken, they very rarely discuss their role, or that of the private office, in these events. Hence the need to rest on original oral testimony.

Chapter 1 introduces and explains the structure of the private office, as well as the roles and responsibilities of its members. These include the principal private secretary who, in any government department, acts as the key channel of communication between the Secretary of State (the political head of a government department) and the Permanent Secretary (the administrative head of a Whitehall department). Chapter 1 also dissects the tasks performed by the private office and explains how those tasks have changed over time, including, for example, as a result of the growth of new technology. It categorises the twelve essential functions of the private office in a more systematic way than has ever been done before. The work of private office has increased over the period studied and the functions are now far more complex and interdependent than they were in 1964. Chapter 2 then examines the changing make-up of private offices, including the background of the principal private secretaries in No. 10.

Chapters 3 to 10 present a history of the private office from its origins in the seventeenth century up until the present day, including case studies that illustrate when the private office played a major role in British governance. These chapters follow a broadly chronological approach to show how the role of the private office has and has not changed during that period, and the factors that underlay such changes.

I start before the office of the Prime Minister even existed. Chapter 3 begins with an analysis of the origins of the concept of private secretaries – or 'clerks', as they were then termed – in the seventeenth century up until the fall of Chamberlain at the start of the Second World War. This was the period that saw the emergence of the first people who could be classed as 'private secretaries', albeit ones who were then political adherents of the ministers for whom they worked, many of whom later became politicians themselves. In the mid-nineteenth century, the Northcote–Trevelyan report laid out the principles of recruitment on merit to the civil service. However, many Prime Ministers during the late nineteenth century continued to recruit personal supporters. It was only at the end of the First World War that, with the establishment of the Cabinet Office and the greater formality of Cabinet government, the private office became independent. That moment was marked because private secretaries at No. 10 emerged as independent of their Prime Minister, as exhibited by the fact that when there were changes of Prime Minister, the private office remained to manage the support of the incoming premier. This was a fundamental change in terms of the party political neutrality of private secretaries.

Chapter 4 shows how private office operated in the war years up until 1964. Churchill's key private secretaries – not least Jock Colville – became extremely powerful in terms of both the personal support they offered the Prime Minister and their influence on policy development.

Chapter 5 then examines in depth private office during the first Wilson premiership, a turbulent period of political flux and of relative economic decline. The chapter describes the private office which Labour inherited and charts how Wilson developed his own and brought in the first formal special advisers to enhance the political capacity of his government, especially on economic policy and, later, on communications.[31] Chapter 6 assesses how private office changed when Wilson lost the 1970 general election and Edward Heath proceeded to reinstate a far more traditional form of private office, relying more on established civil servants. Wilson's chief press officer was replaced by a civil service press officer and Heath's new political secretary, Douglas Hurd,* with a diplomatic background, assimilated well into the atmosphere at No. 10. That was in contrast to his predecessor, Marcia Williams, who did not fit with the 'good chaps theory of government' as described by Peter Hennessy, whereby politicians and their advisers were expected to 'behave themselves' and abide by and adhere to 'unwritten rules'.[32] Private office evolved again with a return of the Wilson entourage in 1974 and the expansion of special advisers in No. 10 and elsewhere. The No. 10 Policy Unit, established in 1974, worked alongside the private office. Chapters 5 and 6 also highlight the role of the private office in providing stability in the period between 1964 and 1979, when there were five different political administrations and four changes of government all within fifteen years. The general election in which the private office played its most significant role was that of February 1974. As principal private secretary at No. 10, Robert Armstrong was central to facilitating the transition between Heath as Prime Minister and Wilson's return to Downing Street.

Chapters 7 and 8 cover the years of Conservative rule from 1979 to 1997, which were dominated by Margaret Thatcher. She had strong

---

* Douglas Hurd (1930–); Foreign Office diplomat 1952–66; political secretary to the Prime Minister 1970–73; Conservative MP 1974–97; Home Secretary 1985–89; Foreign Secretary 1989–95; created Lord Hurd 1997.

views about the ways in which she managed her office and, according to some of the civil servants who worked for her, the private office was at its most effective in terms of organisation and efficiency when Thatcher was in power and at her most decisive. Chapter 7 examines how the No. 10 private office developed during the later Thatcher years and how, for much of that time, it came to be identified with two people, neither of whom was its head, namely Charles Powell and Bernard Ingham. Powell was the Prime Minister's private secretary for foreign affairs from 1984 to 1991 and became one of the most powerful officials in Britain, operating with the full authority of the Prime Minister. Ingham, another career civil servant (although not part of Thatcher's private office), was her chief press secretary and managed all No. 10 relations with the media. By contrast, Chapter 8 shows how, under John Major's seven-year premiership, the private office reverted to a far more traditional role.

Chapter 9 then examines the period from 1997 to 2010 – the New Labour years and beyond. It begins by analysing the approach of the 1997 general election and the way in which New Labour prepared for government. It considers how the private offices prepared for transition and change while, at the same time, supporting the Major administration during a period when it was widely expected to lose the forthcoming general election. This chapter also shows how the Blair government grew in confidence and competence and how private office itself evolved and connected with the wider network of support and advice on which Blair and his advisers tended to rely. The chapter also analyses the continued rise of special advisers in British politics and their influence on the functions of the private office, including the roles and powers of two No. 10 special advisers, Jonathan Powell and Alastair Campbell. Powell's new role as chief of staff bridged the civil service and political worlds and meant that a political appointee became formally a part of the private office, while Campbell was Blair's all-powerful chief press secretary and official spokesman. The Cabinet Secretary was concerned about their likely powers. Gordon Brown, and subsequently David Cameron, despite initial protestations that they wished to reduce the size of the No. 10 machine, both sought to strengthen the centre to enforce their policies and their influence across Whitehall. In practice, Brown's premiership became dominated by the economic crisis of 2008–09, and he became ever more reliant on his private office, led by Jeremy Heywood, whom Brown persuaded to return to the role he had left in 2003.

Chapter 10 begins with reflections from the incoming Prime Minister David Cameron in May 2010 about what he took from his experience as a special adviser and observing the workings of No. 10 prior to his entering Downing Street, including what he and his advisers learned from private office in the New Labour years. It then examines how, under Cameron's premiership, with Nick Clegg as his deputy, there was a large increase in the total number of special advisers working for the Prime Minister and Deputy Prime Minister. The process of decision-making became a much more contested area than under New Labour, with new forms of governance emerging for managing interministerial coalition discussions, including via a process known as the 'quad'.* Finally, with the Brexit referendum of June 2016 and the fall of Cameron, the nature of British politics changed and the process for 'getting Brexit done' came to dominate all aspects of politics, including the role of private offices. Theresa May's chief of staff Gavin Barwell† has related how, throughout the three years of May's premiership, that policy area

---

* The 'quad' was the mechanism which developed during the coalition for resolving disputes between the two parties.

† Gavin Barwell (1972–); chief of staff to the Prime Minister (Theresa May) 2017–19.

became his sole focus. Finally, with the Johnson premiership, many of the most basic principles of good governance – including those of the private office and No. 10 – began to fall apart. There was no process to flag up these failings and, seemingly, no one to caution the Prime Minister and other senior ministers about what they were doing. Chapter 10 concludes with some wider thoughts on the role and effectiveness of private offices, as well as some reflections about the context in which private offices now operate.

This book tells the history and story of private office, from its origins in the seventeenth century to the far more complex and yet still relatively small and intimate body that it has become. There is a central, and essential, role in the civil service for such an impartial body to support all ministers and, in particular, the Prime Minister, working with and alongside political advisers. The case for a more politicised private office has not been made and, indeed, it would be a constitutional upheaval with enormous implications were it ever to happen. That said, the failings of private office that have been witnessed over recent years need to be addressed urgently. The private office needs to change with the times. Its integrity needs to be restored and restated. Private secretaries should not be cheerleaders for their ministers, still less should they be routinely in the public eye. The role and powers of special advisers need to be more clearly and closely defined. They have a responsibility to remain in the background, away from the public eye, but to resume their function as an essential and central part of the hidden wiring of our constitution. That is a challenge for Prime Ministers, ministers and private secretaries themselves to seek to achieve in future.

1

THE JUNCTION BOX OF GOVERNMENT: WHAT IS PRIVATE OFFICE AND WHAT DOES IT DO?

In 1880, Prime Minister Benjamin Disraeli reflected on his relationship with his private secretary Montagu Corry, highlighting that

> the relations between a minister and his secretary are, or at least should be, among the finest that can subsist between two individuals. Except the married state, there is none in which so great a confidence is involved, in which more forbearance ought to be exercised, or more sympathy ought to exist.[1]

In the 1970s, Labour politician and former Foreign Secretary Anthony Crosland commented, 'I think of Private Office as family,' meaning that 'with them he could show himself: he didn't mind if they knew he was vulnerable, though there was still a great deal of privacy and reserve about him.'[2] More recently, Prime Minister Boris Johnson's close adviser Dominic Cummings said, 'Trust private office – they're the only reliable thing between you and disaster.'[3] So, what precisely is the private office which made such an impression on completely different people from across the political spectrum 150 years apart?

A private office is the group of officials that works in support of the leader or leadership team of any major organisation. Private offices exist in a range of organisations, including the military, the church, universities, royal households, banking and in business. While the precise term may not be used, private offices are common across a varied range of bodies, providing the function that manages the interface between the leadership of the organisation, or its executive body, and the wider organisation. Within government, the Permanent Secretary (the most senior civil servant in any government department) will have a private office, as will the heads of non-ministerial departments (such as His Majesty's Revenue and Customs) and holders of specific senior posts (such as the chief medical officer). Increasingly, other senior officials, including many directors general, have private offices. However, the most well-known and most consequential of private offices are those of government ministers and it is these private offices – their functions, characteristics and the people who work within them – that are the subject of this book.

What exactly does the ministerial private office do? What tasks take place within a ministerial office and what responsibilities must be fulfilled – in any private office – for the minister and the department to be able to operate effectively? For while principal private secretaries and private secretaries appear regularly in the political history of Britain, often via walk-on parts in biographies and memoirs, their actual roles have rarely been set out and dissected. One commentator has rightly written that the private office 'has not attracted much attention' in literature.[4] And yet a more recent study by the Institute for Government, based on its many interviews with former ministers from 2015 to 2019, together with a book by its former director, Peter Riddell, underlines how critical the private office is in the life of a minister.[5]

For many people, their only knowledge about private office comes from the BBC comedy programmes *Yes Minister* and *Yes, Prime Minister* from the 1980s. David Cameron, in paying tribute in the House of Commons to his principal private secretary Chris Martin,* who died from cancer in 2015, said:

> Everyone in this House and many people watching at home will know from *Yes, Prime Minister* the central role that Bernard, the Prime Minister's principal private secretary, plays in the life of the Prime Minister and of No. 10 Downing Street. This morning, my Bernard, my principal private secretary, Chris Martin, died of cancer. Chris Martin was only forty-two. He was one of the most loyal, hard-working, dedicated public servants that I have ever come across. I have no idea what his politics were, but he would go to the ends of the earth and back again for his Prime Minister, for No. 10 and for the team he worked for … [The wider No. 10 family is] a bit like a family and we feel we have lost someone between a father and brother to all of us.[6]

Cameron's tribute captured well and movingly much of the essence of the best private secretaries (including their party political neutrality), and probably conveyed more than any dry academic study could do.

Private office exists to manage the flow of information to and from ministers. This chapter analyses how it does that, the specific tasks it performs on a day-to-day basis and how advice and support to ministers are managed, all within the wider context of the civil service's commitment to party political independence and supporting the government of the day, and specifically within the private

---

* Chris Martin (1973–2015); Treasury civil servant; principal private secretary to the Prime Minister (David Cameron) 2011–15.

office context – where close proximity to political power may heighten the chance of politicisation. That risk has been mitigated, to some extent, by the introduction of special advisers into the system of government, one of the most significant alterations to the private office over the past fifty-plus years. However, while special advisers and other factors – including the rise of new technology and modern communications – have changed private secretaries' methods of operating, it is nevertheless still possible to discern twelve common and discrete functions of the private office.

The private office is the body of civil servants which supports a minister and includes a principal private secretary and a team of private secretaries. It is central to the operation of the British political system. Private secretaries' perspectives and their recollections are therefore valuable to historians. They have been, at times, both participants and witnesses, and sometimes the only witnesses, to events. Their evidence can help explain how decisions were made and why. Yet the private office has received surprisingly little detailed historical analysis, even though many ministers have often testified to the contribution of their private secretaries and how much they trusted them.

The private office matters because, in any department and especially in No. 10, it is the central point through which all governmental work is transacted. The only business that would not be carried out through private office would be personal or entirely political material, although even some of that would be within the private office traffic. For all aspects of official work, it remains the ever-present element in the life of a government minister. The private secretary can be both a player in their own right and a witness of the politician at close quarters, especially when a minister is under pressure or in the media limelight. Although the private secretary's authority stems only from the minister's, they can wield considerable influence. The private office is one of the main instruments for ensuring that the political wishes of the government and its ministers are carried out. In practice, how that is done is often up to the individual minister. They must choose how to use their private office and the level of trust and authority that they invest in their individual private secretaries.

There is no commonly accepted definition of the term 'private office'. The phrase is imprecise and may be interpreted in different ways and in different contexts. In other organisations (business, local government, the military, the church or foreign administrative systems), the concept of the private office does not always exist or, if it does exist, it may go under a different name and operate in a different way. In several other walks of life in which a senior figure has a supporting aide or cadet, the junior partner would usually aspire to the job of the principal for whom they were working. For example, in business, a chief executive officer might often have an up-and-coming executive member of staff as the head of their private office. In the armed forces, the Chief of the General Staff and the chiefs of each service all appoint young officers, destined for rapid promotion, to support and possibly emulate them. However, nowadays such a career aspiration would be very unlikely to happen in the British civil service, in the sense that civil servants are required to be politically impartial, and their career progression would not therefore lead into a career in politics. It is rare, but not unknown, for officials to quit the civil service in order to enter politics. In the post-Second World War era, only one person (Andrew Lansley) has been both a principal private secretary and then a Cabinet minister later in life. Such is the level of separation between politicians and officials in Britain.*

---

* It is worth noting that Hugh Gaitskell (later Labour Chancellor of the Exchequer) was principal private secretary and 'chef de cabinet' to the wartime Labour Cabinet minister Hugh Dalton. Gaitskell, however, had been a temporary civil servant and was plucked by Dalton to perform the new role in 1940.

The term private office is not clearly and authoritatively defined as it relates to its modern-day function within the public administration in government departments. Even that ubiquitous encyclopaedia of the present day, Wikipedia, only refers its readers to a useful guide to private office written by a former senior civil servant.[7] The website politics.co.uk gives the following definition:

> All Ministers, of whatever rank, have a Private Office of four or more civil servants assigned to him or her on appointment. The lead figure in the Private Office is the Private Secretary who works closely with the Minister in discharging all his or her functions. The Private Office is responsible for the Minister's diary and work programme, including the content of the famous red boxes.[8]

The private office is almost always situated physically next to, or very close to, the minister's office, and it is usually housed in a room or open-plan area adjacent to the minister's office. The words private office themselves conjure up the notion of something both secretive and bureaucratic, while the term private secretary may imply the idea of a supportive staff member with a primary loyalty to their minister. The definition used in this book is that the ministerial private office is the co-ordinating body within government that provides the immediate support system to the Prime Minister and all Cabinet ministers, as well as to each departmental junior minister.

In British government, the private office is rooted in the independence of the civil service. In 1854, the Northcote–Trevelyan report (a document of only twenty-three pages) was the foundation of establishing an impartial administrative system to support ministers.[9] Such independent and impartial civil servants have, at least since the First World War, been the predominant members of every ministerial and prime ministerial private office. Traditionally, the private office was composed almost exclusively of career civil servants. The modern private office nowadays often contains a richer mix of civil servants, depending on the department, including some with frontline delivery experience (for example, from the Prison Service in the Ministry of Justice, or from Jobcentres in the Department for Work and Pensions). However, the important point to stress is that it is not a party political body and does not routinely contain political appointees.[*] However, it has to work closely with political players, including special advisers and some other political advisers on communications. One of the key challenges therefore for a private office is to ensure a good working relationship with the party political elements of a minister's work – including their duties in Parliament – while protecting the impartiality of civil servants and the integrity of the civil service. In that sense, the private office is fundamentally different from the Continental *cabinet* system which includes both non-party political officials and political advisers within a single unit.[10]

While all ministers have a designated private secretary, the key person supporting a Cabinet minister is referred to as the principal private secretary. In No. 10, the holder of that post is one of the most important officials in Whitehall. Peter Hennessy, in *The Hidden Wiring*, cites the analysis of Ken Stowe,[†] principal private secretary to three Prime Ministers in the 1970s, who explained that the holder of that post (together with the Cabinet Secretary and the monarch's private secretary) can find themselves at the centre of three 'interlocking circles', namely command of a political party,

---

[*] The significant exception to this is the existence, since 1997 to the present day, of the post of chief of staff to the Prime Minister, which was held for nearly all of that period by a special adviser/s appointed by the Prime Minister to oversee the working of No. 10, including the private office.

[†] Kenneth Stowe (1927–2015); principal private secretary to the Prime Minister (Harold Wilson, James Callaghan and Margaret Thatcher) 1975–79; Permanent Secretary Northern Ireland Office 1979–81; Permanent Secretary DHSS 1981–87.

command of a majority in the House of Commons and command of the executive.[11] It is particularly in those circumstances when there is a prime ministerial transition, and not just after electoral defeat, that Stowe's three circles and the No. 10 principal private secretary play important roles in assuring a smooth transfer of prime ministerial power and thus assume such constitutional significance.[*] The principal private secretary of a Cabinet minister is also their main confidant. Andrew Cahn[†] served as both a principal private secretary in the UK civil service and as a '*chef de cabinet*' in the European Commission. He described the role as follows:

> The principal private secretary probably finds himself as the one person in the department who the minister can trust almost absolutely and who knows things that nobody else knows. He or she is discreet and loyal. Of course, the private secretary has a dual loyalty both to the minister and to the civil service as well as the Crown. But the primary loyalty is to the minister. That is who you spend most of your time supporting. The other loyalties may constrain that first loyalty.[12]

Yet, while each private office is different and responds to the needs and personal styles of the relevant minister and department, they all carry out certain essential and universal functions. Understanding the workings of private office therefore helps to unravel the nature and working of British government. The private office may be considered akin to a 'junction box' of government, which transmits

---

[*]   For example, at the time of the resignations of Prime Ministers Wilson (1976), Thatcher (1990), Blair (2007), Cameron (2016) and May (2019).

[†]   Andrew Cahn (1951–); UK civil servant; principal private secretary to the Chancellor of the Duchy of Lancaster (William Waldegrave) 1992–95; *chef de cabinet* to the European Commission vice-president (Neil Kinnock) 1997–2000.

each minister's wishes to ensure that the government machine is well co-ordinated, smoothly managed and as efficient as possible.

The private office and its role will be shaped by the Prime Minister and ministers of the time. However, from my consideration of the history of private office, there has always existed what may be termed a 'pendulum effect' whereby, under different Prime Ministers, the No. 10 private office has become more or less political – and even, at times, politicised. This can then be reflected in the ways in which the whole government operates. This is not to imply that the private secretaries have themselves become party political, but rather that the style and approach of the Prime Minister has become more political. Changes of Prime Minister have accentuated or diminished the level of politicisation within the office of the Prime Minister. This pendulum effect has been a feature of post-war history. The introduction of special advisers, for example, was an explicit desire by Wilson to have greater political input to his government and policy advice, without necessarily compromising the civil servants.[13]

THE OPERATION OF UK GOVERNMENT AND THE MAKING OF PUBLIC POLICY

While Cabinet government and the notion of collective responsibility predated the Cabinet system, the processes of making government policy and assuring the cross-government agreement to policies became far more formalised from 1916 onwards. But what exactly is 'policy', what do we mean by the 'policy-making process' and how does the work of the private office fit within that overall framework?

In government, 'policy' and 'policy-making' have always been widely used but often imprecisely defined terms. In opposition, politicians seek to articulate their policies to appeal to the public and so win power. In government, ministers and departments are constantly developing, refreshing and changing policies in response to events, emerging evidence, examples of best practice or even media demands. Ministers may clash or argue about policies in general or the more specific aspects of them. Prime Ministers may impose their will and demand changes in policies from departments or they may seek more conciliatory approaches and look to agree compromises. Policy as a concept may never have been perfectly defined, although Herbert Morrison's, no doubt apocryphal, statement that 'socialism is what a Labour government does' is a useful indication of where certain politicians may be coming from in terms of what policy means to them.

Within departments of state, the Secretary of State sets the strategic direction of policy, and their civil servants are responsible for supporting the process, including, for example, by drafting White Papers or helping to shape major policy announcements. In No. 10, the Policy Unit, established in 1974, nowadays also helps the Prime Minister set and co-ordinate the overall shape and direction of government policy and advises on individual policies, working with ministers and government departments. Departments also have an important role in the policy process. As the closest advisers to ministers, private secretaries will always have a responsibility for ensuring that the business of policy-making within government is transacted smoothly and efficiently, and they will also work with departmental officials and those in No. 10 on how to achieve this. The more interventionist private secretaries, as will be seen, have sought, on occasion, to become personally more involved in helping shape and make policy on behalf of their minister.[14]

All government ministers are bound by the Ministerial Code, which sets out the 'standards of conduct expected of ministers and how they discharge their duties'.[15] This code was originally a secret

Cabinet document known as *Questions of Procedure for Ministers* until John Major renamed it and made it public in 1991.[16] Since then, it has been updated regularly by Prime Ministers and the most recent version dates from December 2022.[17] However, in terms of the tasks of the private office, the current code has only two specific references to private secretaries. Both refer to the taking of notes of meetings. Paragraph 8.14 states that 'a private secretary or official should be present for all discussions relating to Government business'.[18] Paragraph 10.5 states that 'when holding meetings overseas with Ministers and/or officials from overseas governments, or where official business is likely to be discussed, Ministers should always ensure that a private secretary or Embassy official is present'.[19] However, while those are the only two explicit points that mention the role of the private office, there are many more ministerial duties and responsibilities identified in the code which, in practice, fall to the private office to deliver. Civil servants themselves, in turn, are bound by the Civil Service Code, which dates from 1996.

HOW BIG IS PRIVATE OFFICE?

Most private offices of Secretaries of State now have over a dozen staff, whereas fifty years ago they were, on average, half that size. The sizes of the private offices of middle-ranking ministers (those at Minister of State level) and of more junior ministers (those at parliamentary under-secretary of state level) have also swollen. For example, when Robin Butler* was private secretary to the Financial

---

* Robin Butler (1938–); private secretary to the Financial Secretary to the Treasury 1964–66; private secretary (economic affairs) to the Prime Minister (Edward Heath and Harold Wilson) 1972–75; principal private secretary to the Prime Minister 1982–85; Second Permanent Secretary to the Treasury 1985–87; Cabinet Secretary 1988–98; created Lord Butler of Brockwell 1998.

Secretary to the Treasury (a Minister of State-level post) in the run-up to the 1964 general election, he had a staff of two and a half posts – himself, a junior private secretary plus a shared typist.[20] Almost half a century later, in 2010, the equivalent Treasury private office (of the Financial Secretary to the Treasury) had a team of five members. The average junior minister's private office in the 1980s would normally have had two members of staff (the private secretary and one other assistant, sometimes shared between offices). Now even the smallest private offices tend to have three or four members of staff, again representing a rough doubling in size. This pattern of growth has been replicated across nearly all Whitehall departments.

In 2010, there were a total of seventeen departmental ministerial private offices in government departments headed by a Cabinet minister.* On average, those Cabinet ministers' private offices had 8.9 staff members, ranging from five in the Department for Culture, Media and Sport to twelve the Home Office and the Ministry of Justice.[21]† In all junior ministerial offices, the average size of private office was 4.9 members of staff, ranging from two to seven people.‡ By comparison, in 1964, the average size of ministerial private offices was much smaller. Insofar as valid comparisons can be made,

---

* These figures include the private offices of the two Treasury Cabinet ministers. A small number of departments are not headed by a politician (for example His Majesty's Revenue and Customs – which reports to Treasury ministers). Such departments are excluded from this analysis (as are the offices of the Secretaries of State for Scotland, Wales and Northern Ireland). Figures include only core private office staff – not parliamentary or correspondence teams.

† A similar analysis, based on data from answers to parliamentary questions about the private offices of fifteen Cabinet ministers, and published by the Institute of Government in 2013, showed that the size of private offices in 2010 ranged from five staff in the smallest case (the Department for Culture, Media and Sport) to eighteen in the largest office (that of the Foreign Secretary). However, the latter figure clearly included some staff carrying out work which was outside the core private office tasks for the Foreign Secretary.

‡ This information is derived from Cabinet Office private office staff statistics. These figures show those members of staff actually working within the private office. While some roles and functions will always be counted within private office staff numbers, others may not be. For example, in some departments, the management of correspondence and the organisation of email traffic are often handled separately from the core work of the private office – that of providing advice and support to the minister. That may account for some of the differences in size.

they ranged from about two members of staff in a junior minister's office up to six in a Cabinet minister's office.[22]*

Some, but not all, of the increase in the seniority and numbers of private office staff may be accounted for by changes in workload, the speed of transaction of business and the greater focus on communications. On the positive side, the volume of work may be managed more smoothly and efficiently, and ministers may feel better supported. As a result, some private secretaries may not be required to work the excessively long hours that many used to (although they would certainly be expected to be available on the phone at most times). A potential downside could be that more decision-making, or even the development of independent policy advice to ministers, may become handled by the private office rather than managed within the department. If this happens, it is a failing of the private office and of the minister if they have encouraged such independent thinking. As one observer of private office has commented, 'Sometimes, encouraged by their ministers, [some private secretaries] start acting as alternate policy advisers, commenting freely on the merits of [civil servants'] work ... Something has gone badly wrong if a minister prefers to hear the advice of his private secretary to that of the responsible official.'[23]

Over the past half-century, the idea of establishing more of a Continental *cabinet*-type system in place of, or even alongside, private office has emerged at a number of points. It was the explicit aim of the Fabians in their 1964 pamphlet, *The Administrators*, as will be discussed in Chapter 5.[24] The charge levelled against Charles Powell and Bernard Ingham during their dominance of the Thatcher administration, as discussed in Chapter 7, was that they had effectively created a *cabinet* of just two people. Most recently, at the start of

---

* For example, the Chancellor of the Exchequer's immediate private office in 1964 contained five members of staff.

the coalition government of David Cameron, some of his ministers, such as Francis Maude,* argued strongly for the partial replacement of the private office by the establishment of 'extended ministerial offices' (EMOs). This short-lived initiative was a further attempt to establish what would have been akin to a UK *cabinet* system for ministerial support on the European model.[25] In the event, only five EMOs were established before Theresa May abolished them all in July 2016.[26] One former Conservative minister even went so far as to describe them as 'bonkers', because EMOs would create 'a second structure of mini experts within your own private office' which would isolate ministers from their departments.[27] (Nevertheless, there has been a trend in some departments to appoint 'policy advisers' within private offices. Such advisers provide specific policy support to ministers and work within the private office, often on fixed-term contracts. However, they are not special advisers but civil servants and so are subject to civil service impartiality rules.)

WHAT DOES THE PRIVATE OFFICE DO?

The private office has been ever-present in the lives of ministers, and private secretaries have helped to ensure that the multi-faceted business of government has been managed as efficiently as possible. A private secretary will attend practically every official meeting that their minister attends. Collectively, they are and always have been the junction boxes of Whitehall, making connections and ensuring the business flows effectively.

Just as every Prime Minister is different, so too do different private

---

* Francis Maude (1953–); Conservative MP 1983–92 and 1997–2010; Paymaster General and minister for the Cabinet Office 2010–15.

offices have their own distinctive characteristics. To a large extent, these are inevitably shaped by the departmental Secretary of State, their political priorities, the departmental workload and the ways in which they have chosen to engage across Whitehall, together with how they communicate and use the media. However, the nature of private office has also, at times, been determined by the personality and style of individual private secretaries. To take what was perhaps the most striking example, and as discussed in Chapter 7, Charles Powell defined the way in which the No. 10 private office operated in the later Thatcher years because of his personal relationship with her and his force of personality. He did so even though he was not the principal private secretary.

There have been few codified cross-Whitehall guidelines for the workings of private office, other than the two specific references contained within the Ministerial Code. Only in the early part of the new millennium did the civil service even produce a cross-government handbook on ways of working with ministers, including a chapter on the role of private office.[28] Yet despite this lack of codified guidance, there have always been a number of essential functions carried out by the private office. Taken together, these comprise the overall role and purpose of the private office.

By way of comparison, the political historian Peter Hennessy explained how the functions of the Prime Minister were first codified by the Cabinet Office in the late 1940s, and he has subsequently updated this list on several occasions.[29] Hennessy identified six broad functions of the premiership and, within those categories, catalogued the discrete activities that fall to the Prime Minister to manage.[30] When he last updated this list, during the period of the coalition government, there were no fewer than eight broad categories and forty-seven separate functions, up from twelve tasks in

1947.[31] It is also possible to catalogue the functions of the private office, using a framework similar to that used by Hennessy, when he sought to answer the question 'What is a Prime Minister for?' This chapter seeks to answer the related question 'What is the private office for?'

Recognising that there may be differences of emphasis within some departments, and certainly there have been such variants at No. 10 under different premierships, there are, nevertheless, three broad categories and twelve distinct functions that characterise the work of the private office. As with the activities of the Prime Minister, these have grown over time. First, there are those functions which might be termed transactional tasks carried out by the private office, or, in other words, those tasks which are essential in order to ensure the efficient day-to-day management of departmental and government business. Second, there are those functions which are about relationship management within the department and across Whitehall more widely, and the role which the private office may play to support the minister and so ensure that their work has greater impact. Finally, there are those functions which fall within the field of personal support to, and the handling of sensitive issues for, the minister. These functions will often depend on the strength of the personal relationship that has developed between the minister and the private secretary, including how long they have worked together.

THE FUNCTIONS OF PRIVATE OFFICE

TRANSACTIONAL FUNCTIONS
1. Managing departmental governmental business efficiently
Managing the essential business of government is, and has always

been, the central and most vital function of every private office. It involves managing the smooth day-to-day running of the minister's work and the efficient co-ordination of all their departmental activities. The function includes ensuring the provision of clear advice on ministerial views about critical issues and tasks, such as the strategic direction of a department; overseeing the communication of the Secretary of State's views and wishes to the department (in consultation with the Permanent Secretary – or with the Cabinet Secretary in the case of No. 10); and handling specific policy issues. Traditionally, every private office has managed business by presenting a range of papers, usually daily, in the minister's red box. Private secretaries prepare these ministerial red boxes at the end of most days for the minister's attention and then, usually the next day, will report back the minister's views to the department and to the individual authors of papers. The private secretary will put the papers in the box in the order which they believe they should be read, prioritising and annotating them as needed and identifying which have to be read by the next morning, as a bare minimum. Papers are usually flagged as 'urgent', 'routine', or 'for information'. (Some private offices now sometimes seek only very short papers – typically 150–200 words – so as to secure faster ministerial approval, especially if sent electronically.)

Alistair Darling served in five different Cabinet posts between 1997 and 2010.* Of the red boxes, he said, 'It is very often the piece of paper at the bottom of the box, which does not seem important at the time, that can come back to haunt you. In my experience, it is worth ministers reading everything that is put in front of them.'[32]

---

* Alistair Darling (1953–2023); Labour MP 1987–2015; Chief Secretary to the Treasury 1997–98; Secretary of State for Work and Pensions 1998–2002; Secretary of State for Transport 2002–05; Secretary of State for Trade and Industry 2006–07; Chancellor of the Exchequer 2007–10; created Lord Darling of Roulanish 2015.

A private secretary will often attach personal notes to much of the material in the red box. Such covering 'box notes', many of which are preserved in the National Archives and elsewhere, can become the stuff of history. The more confident a private secretary, and the closer their relationship with their minister, the more direct and frank the box notes tend to be. Ministerial red boxes and the process of handling papers in this way dates back well over a century. The most famous red box was that used by the Chancellor of the Exchequer on Budget days and manufactured for William Gladstone when he delivered his first Budget in 1853. Within No. 10, there has always also been a further box which is blue with a red stripe around it which is used for the highest security papers and those on intelligence matters. This secure box was nicknamed 'old stripey' by Harold Wilson when he was Prime Minister.

The private office of the Secretary of State is responsible for ensuring that Cabinet ministers attend meetings of Cabinet (and get permission to be absent when necessary), as well as the attendance of junior ministers at Cabinet committees and other cross-departmental meetings. The role also includes managing external engagements with a wide range of stakeholders and with the other parts of government, No. 10, the Deputy Prime Minister's office and the royal households.

Most formal ministerial business handled by the private office has always taken the form of what are called submissions. A submission is a document produced by a civil servant and sent to a minister for information, action or decision. Submissions can cover a whole range of issues and may be short, related to a specific departmental issue on which the minister's views are sought, or more wide-ranging. More often, submissions will be more complex and involve input from different sections of the department and may also reflect the views of other departments. For example, any submission involving possible increases to public expenditure would need to reflect the views of the Treasury. A submission with implications for other parts of the United Kingdom would need to consider the likely views of the appropriate devolved administrations. Departments have often produced guidance for civil servants to explain how to write a submission, and private offices used to lay on training sessions for their officials on working with ministers and ministerial preferences for submissions and briefings.[33][*]

Today, with far more ministerial business conducted by email, text, WhatsApp messages or by mobile phone, there is a risk that the 'paper trail' or audit trail may become less robust or comprehensive than it used to be. Nevertheless, many ministers still prefer paper copies. Even David Cameron, the youngest and one of the most technologically aware Prime Ministers, who conducted much business by email or mobile phone, still preferred to see hard copies of documents. 'There was a collision of the paper and digital worlds that hasn't quite been resolved ... I insisted on seeing everything in paper in my box so that there was a single record of my views.'[34] So Cameron, while technologically 'savvy', wanted to rely on a hard copy of advice. Boris Johnson, when he was Prime Minister, was not so punctilious.

Ministers will often gain a reputation for how efficient they are at 'doing their red boxes'. Some ministers were renowned for their effectiveness at managing and completing the box. Harold Wilson and Margaret Thatcher were two such Prime Ministers. Other ministers' performances have been more variable. The Labour minister

---

[*] An example of departmental-specific guidance was that produced by the DTI in the 1980s by Norman Tebbit's then private secretary, Andrew Lansley, who later left the civil service and himself became a Cabinet minister in 2010.

Tony Crosland would only ever take one red box per evening and, as a result, his private office had to extract all non-essential papers and cram it full of the essential ones. Occasionally, a minister would refuse to take any red boxes at all and insist on doing all the work while in the office. Such ministers could be the bane of a private secretary's life, in that one member of the private office always had to arrive very early or stay very late at the office while the box work was completed. Ken Clarke,* who entered the Cabinet in 1986, was usually assiduous in doing his red boxes overnight. Occasionally, however, he would visit Ronnie Scott's Jazz Club in Soho and the red box would come back unopened the next morning.[35] Thatcher, with her ability to survive on as little as four hours' sleep a night, was usually able and willing to turn around material very quickly at any time. It was her determination to read a relatively unimportant government paper at 3 a.m. that, just possibly, even saved her life during the Brighton bombing in 1984 (see Chapter 7).[36]

One of the key questions about private office concerns the influence that private secretaries have over shaping ministerial responses to submissions, by amplifying the points made or seeking to reinterpret or even reject them on behalf of their minister. Private secretaries will routinely enforce their ministers' preferred formats and written style, but some private secretaries have gone further and, by a variety of ways, have been able to influence the development of government policy. Robert Armstrong, for example, as principal private secretary to Heath, undoubtedly influenced the overall policy of the UK government in relation to joining the

---

* Kenneth Clarke (1940–); Conservative MP 1970–2019; junior ministerial posts 1972–74 and 1979–85; Paymaster General and Minister for Employment 1985–87; Chancellor of the Duchy of Lancaster and Minister for Trade and Industry 1987–89; Secretary of State for Health 1988–90, for Education and Science 1990–92; Home Secretary 1992–93; Chancellor of the Exchequer 1993–97; Lord Chancellor and Secretary of State for Justice 2010–12; Minister without Portfolio 2012–14; created Lord Clarke of Nottingham 2020.

European Community (as will be seen in Chapter 5). Similarly, in the early 1990s, Jeremy Heywood helped shape the government's macro-economic policy in his role as principal private secretary to Chancellors of the Exchequer Norman Lamont and Ken Clarke, especially in terms of policy on the European Exchange Rate Mechanism (see Chapter 8). How much of a free hand a minister gives their private secretary to respond on their own initiative, without reference back, has always depended on the relationship and degree of trust between minister and private secretary. Sometimes, especially in junior ministers' offices, the private secretary's role may be limited to writing 'Do you agree?' on a submission and then putting it in the minister's box. However, where any private secretary is more confident, understands the subject matter and has the authority of the minister to do so, they may well suggest a different course of action than that proposed by officials, particularly when they feel confident that they can predict the minister's view.

A core task of the private secretary has always been to keep a true record of all official meetings and to agree the actions decided. Such meetings may well be generated from reading a submission on which the minister asks for a meeting. Every official ministerial meeting will be recorded by the private secretary present. There is a convention that the private secretary of the more senior minister present should take the minutes and produce the record of the meeting. No. 10 meetings are always recorded by the relevant No. 10 private secretary. However, there can sometimes be some 'behind-the-scenes negotiations' between the respective private offices, to confirm exactly what was agreed and by whom, before the final and agreed note of the meeting is published. It is rare for an official meeting not to have a private secretary present and that would only happen, exceptionally, if the issue were so sensitive that the Prime Minister or minister agreed that it should not be recorded. Action points of meetings are then circulated, ideally by the end of the day on which the meeting takes place. A key private secretary skill has always been to be able to produce, often at very short notice, a succinct note of any meeting, including action points, which the minister has attended. In recent times, there have been some criticisms of the lack of robust recording of certain decisions such as during the Iraq War of 2003, when the charge of decision-making by a 'sofa government' was made (see Chapter 9). These are rare exceptions. Only if meetings are genuinely personal or wholly political between ministers would there be no private secretary (or possibly only a special adviser) present.

For some political meetings, a private secretary may well attend but not take an active part or fully minute the meeting. However, in such circumstances, it has always been the responsibility of a private secretary attending to provide a note of any meeting, the governmental decisions taken and the government actions agreed. Any political actions are for the special advisers present to pursue, as appropriate. If a private secretary has not attended for whatever reason, any actions which emerged from the meeting should be captured in writing and then pursued. This may involve the private secretary specifically asking their minister if there are any departmental points that should be pursued. Occasionally, there can be potentially embarrassing moments when a minister or a Prime Minister fails to make the points they had planned to do in a meeting or even says nothing at all. And, of course, ministers are not infallible. In the words of the famous aphorism, even Homer sometimes nods. If so, the private office can often rectify that problem. For example, Margaret Thatcher – usually an efficient and alert minister – had occasional lapses of concentration, as detailed by Jonathan Powell, the brother of Thatcher's private secretary:

On one memorable occasion, at a meeting with FitzGerald [the Irish Prime Minister] after a particularly long and tiresome [European Community] meeting, Thatcher fell asleep soon after sitting down with him. FitzGerald looked at … Charles Powell, Thatcher's foreign policy aide, to ask what they should do. Charles suggested that FitzGerald carry on making all the points he intended to make and Charles would dutifully note them down. They could then wake her up to agree the joint press statement.[37]

All private offices of Cabinet ministers must also be available, at short notice, to discuss issues with the No. 10 private office. For events such as preparation for the weekly session of Prime Minister's Questions (PMQs), which nearly always focus on topical issues, it is essential. Departmental parliamentary teams also typically sit within or very close to the private office and play a significant role in parliamentary matters, particularly in legislation and select committee matters. The private office is the link between the Prime Minister's office and the relevant department. Until 1997, PMQs took place for fifteen minutes twice a week on Tuesday and Thursday afternoons when the House of Commons was sitting. This brief encounter consumed much of the time of the No. 10 private secretary for parliamentary affairs for the day leading up to PMQs, as well as the time of those private offices and departmental staff whose policies or activities were in the news. In May 1997, Tony Blair changed PMQs to a thirty-minute session once a week every Wednesday at 12 noon when Parliament was sitting. Despite initial criticism of that move, it has survived in that same format ever since.

Private office must therefore be familiar with, and well briefed on, at least in general terms, all the main items of business of the department, not just those that may come up in PMQs. One of the private secretaries needs to be available at any time of day (or night) if required. No. 10 will often judge how effective a private office is by how effective their private secretaries are, especially when contacted out of hours.[38]

Efficient working and, if necessary, long hours have always been the hallmarks of the best private secretaries. Over the past half-century, working hours have increased. In the Wilson era of the 1960s, many private secretaries, even at No. 10, could often get home by 7.30 p.m. during the weekdays and sometimes not be disturbed at the weekend.[39] However, that was partly because Wilson's then principal private secretary Michael Halls took it upon himself to work such long hours and found it very difficult to delegate to other private secretaries (see Chapter 5). By the time of Thatcher's premiership, the pressure was more demanding. Robin Butler recalled that, when he was her principal private secretary, 'the hours were horrendously long: I was never home before 10 p.m., and sometimes did not finish until 3 a.m., 4 a.m. or even 5 a.m. I always then went home. I would be back in for 8 a.m. and she would be fine.'[40] Private secretaries have always had to be efficient in their ways of working, but the job, especially at No. 10, cannot be done without such long hours. For example, David Cameron observed private office first when he was a special adviser to Chancellor Norman Lamont and again when he became Prime Minister. Of Jeremy Heywood, who had been principal private secretary to Lamont and in charge at No. 10 when Cameron became Prime Minister, he commented that:

[Jeremy Heywood] was outstanding. He had this enormous capacity for hard work. I have never seen anyone work so hard. Jeremy was at his desk when I arrived first thing in the morning and still at his desk when I left last thing at night. If I had forgotten some papers and turned up in the middle of the night, he would probably still have been there. He just never seemed to sleep.[41]

2. Managing the minister's diary

It has always been the case, and certainly since the modern private office was introduced during David Lloyd George's premiership, as part of a drive for greater administrative efficiency during the First World War, that effective management of a minister's diary has been essential for making the best use of their time. This function will usually be managed by one member of the private office, the diary secretary, although the principal private secretary will also wish to be kept abreast of key meetings and to review the forward diary of events on a regular basis. The diary secretary manages internal and external appointments and will also liaise with the minister's parliamentary and constituency secretaries. The diary secretary has also, at many times in history, often acted as a 'gatekeeper' to the minister and can therefore become an influential figure in the department, in their own right, by managing access to the minister. Some diary secretaries have earned a fearsome reputation and develop strong personal relationships with their minister, staying a long time in the post. (Few, though, have taken that personal relationship to quite the extremes that John Prescott's diary secretary did when, as Deputy Prime Minister in 2006, he admitted that he had had a two-year affair, which was well publicised in the media, with Tracey Temple.) It is hard to overstate the importance of diary management and the diary secretary to a minister. It is the diary secretary who ensures that the minister will be in the right place at the right time with the right briefing. Mistakes in this area and the associated reputational damage are very visible. There are many 'war stories' among private offices about a minister being sent to a Cabinet committee meeting at 9.30 a.m. only to find that the meeting started at 9 a.m.; or about the senior Cabinet minister who arrived at a black tie dinner in a lounge suit; or about the trade minister who arrived at the start of an overseas tour to find that the embassy had only realised that he was to be accompanied by his wife as they walked off the aeroplane to be greeted by the ambassador. A recent study by the Institute for Government of the role and work of private office has simply served to underline how much importance many ministers attach to efficient diary management.[42]

The order in which ministers prioritise their work depends on their individual style and preferences, their appetite for work and the balances that they choose to make between the administrative, political and media-related roles as well as their personal lives. Nevertheless, a rough order of priority for a typical Cabinet minister has usually been as follows:

1. Attending meetings of Cabinet (an essential task) and of key Cabinet committees. All Cabinet ministers want to attend meetings of Cabinet. In Heath's day, there were often two Cabinet meetings a week, and in Callaghan's time (such as during the International Monetary Fund crisis throughout the autumn of 1976), they regularly lasted well over three hours. Therefore, the meetings and preparations for them were then a larger part of the ministerial week's work than they are today. Nowadays, the Cabinet tends to meet weekly and meetings are more routine, rarely lasting much beyond an hour. Absences from Cabinet meetings have always been acceptable, but only with the agreement of No. 10, as set out in the Ministerial Code.* Deputies have never been allowed

---

* Paragraph 2.5 of the Ministerial Code covers ministerial absences from Cabinet meetings.

to attend full meetings of the Cabinet.[43] The Cabinet agenda has always been sent in advance to all private offices by the Cabinet Secretary, although it is usually brief and with little detail. It is then the job of the private office to ensure briefing on all the issues, particularly if the department has a locus of responsibility for any item under Cabinet discussion. The private office would always wish to ensure that there was briefing and possible lines to take (the departmental shorthand for their position on any issue of the day that may be raised) should their minister wish to intervene during the Cabinet meeting.

2. Attending meetings with the sovereign or meetings with other members of the royal family. For Cabinet ministers, this includes meetings of the Privy Council. Only the staunchest republican minister would choose to alienate the palace by not accepting a royal request. Meetings of the Privy Council take place monthly and are usually completed quickly (not least because they always take place standing up).* Ministers may also be invited to banquets for state visits and, again, the majority of ministers would wish to attend such events.

3. Working on major political and departmental speeches on policy and strategy – including visits and the accompanying communications activities. Most ministers (particularly those who seek a high profile in the media and to be noticed) will prioritise speeches and ensure enough time is freed up by the private office for preparation and full briefing. Speeches are the mechanism by which many ministers, including the Prime Minister, try to shape the political agenda, and they will often use a speech to make a major new announcement and seek media coverage.

---

* This procedure represents a throwback to Victorian times when Queen Victoria wanted a means of ensuring quick meetings with her ministers.

Speechwriting can be one of the most frustrating or rewarding aspects of a private secretary's life. Many departments now have a dedicated speechwriter or speechwriting teams, who will work closely with the special advisers and officials from the relevant policy team. Some private secretaries have been naturally gifted writers and communicators who, through long association with their minister, know how to craft phrases which their minister will favour and wish to use. Charles Powell, for example, knew exactly which words to offer Thatcher and had what one of his contemporaries called a 'golden pen'.[44]

4. Working on core departmental policy priorities and interministerial meetings on such issues.

5. Attending less important Cabinet committee meetings. These meetings can cover anything from legislation to home affairs or even crisis management – the domain of the COBRA committee meeting, which can be convened at any time and in the light of any major crisis. Depending on the nature of the subject matter, these meetings might be delegated to a junior minister, although it is the job of the private office to assess the importance of such meetings and to ensure that a junior minister or, where acceptable, a departmental official should attend.

6. Working on correspondence and, in particular, constituency correspondence. This does not merely mean letters received from a minister's constituents but rather any item of correspondence received by a Member of Parliament and forwarded to the relevant departmental minister for their comments and reply. Managing the correspondence function well and on time is a key role of private office but one which rarely reaches the public eye. So, while this may often have been seen as a less-than-urgent task, it has always been one to which ministers pay great attention. Ministers

tend to have a favoured style to use with their constituents and will want to ensure that the private office knows that and that their department provides sufficient resources to any letter of a constituency nature.

3. Supporting the minister in their parliamentary work

Parliament has always mattered to ministers for three main reasons. First, because it is and has always been the forum where Members of Parliament are democratically held accountable and, at critical points – such as the 1940 Norway debate, the 1956 Suez crisis or the 1982 Falklands War – it can become the central focus of political attention. Second, because Parliament is the place in which the executive (i.e. a government minister) has to defend its policies. Third, Parliament is one of the places where a minister's reputation and political capital are judged by their performance at the despatch box.

The parliamentary function of the private office involves overseeing the minister's role in all parliamentary business, including the handling of legislation, ministerial participation in debates, written and oral parliamentary questions, appearances before, and the provision of information to, parliamentary select committees and more besides. The main prime ministerial parliamentary event has been and remains the weekly session of PMQs. Similarly, the key parliamentary event which every departmental private office manages has been the regular (usually monthly) day when the department is 'first for questions' (FFQs) in the House of Commons.[45]* In this process, every department has to face around fifteen oral questions in the House of Commons and be prepared for any challenges that

---

* 'First for questions' refers to the monthly occasion when all ministers from a department answer questions on their area of responsibility.

may be raised. Secretaries of State and junior ministers have to be well prepared for this, and they all know that their performances at FFQs will reflect well, or badly, on them and their private offices. In addition, ministers may have to make speeches associated with taking laws through the parliamentary process, providing speakers on government days (those days which are allocated for government business in the House of Commons) and responding to opposition debates. Since 1997, there has been a steady increase in the number of urgent questions (UQs, previously known as private notice questions) that the Speaker may accept if they consider that an important topical issue in the day's news requires an immediate government response or a debate.[46] If the Speaker agrees to this, a statement is required at short notice (three or four hours). The private office would be heavily involved in this process and could even draft the whole statement to ensure speed and to provide a first draft that fits the minister's style.[47]

Parliamentary work also entails additional private office tasks, such as checking that the minister has not, inadvertently, said anything inaccurate. If so, a letter of correction has to be provided to Parliament so that the official parliamentary record (Hansard) can record accurately what the minister has said, along with responding to any commitments that they have made to fellow MPs. A private secretary will wait to receive the first draft from the Hansard reporter to ensure that their minister's words are correctly recorded. One of the minister's private secretaries will always sit in the officials' box in the chamber of the House of Commons (or Lords) and be responsible for the two-way traffic of notes between the minister and their official during a debate or a speech. There is a certain political theatre involved when the notes are passed back and forth between the minister and the private secretary (via the parliamentary private secretary or a parliamentary messenger), all during the course of a debate or when answering a parliamentary question. At times a minister may even say something like 'the answer to the Hon. Member's question evades me for the moment, but I feel sure that inspiration will arrive shortly'. The overseas visitor watching from the gallery of the House of Commons will have no idea that the minister is simply 'buying time' to await a message from their private secretary to give them some plausible-sounding words to say in response to the question. (However, this process has recently tended to be overtaken by sending messages via mobile phones which, since 2011, have been allowed to be used in the chambers of the Houses of Commons and Lords, subject to certain rules.)

4. Crisis management

This function which, by definition, is hard to predict or define, involves the private office responding to all manner of crises, usually at very short notice and at speed, often working outside normal office hours and, on occasion, well beyond the normal remit of the departmental brief. The number of crises that seem to take place at the weekend can appear disproportionate to the unprepared private secretary.* From the human health implications of animal diseases to volcanic eruptions and their effects on air traffic movements; from a mass prisoner escape or a terrorist attack to a financial crisis; such events are unexpected and require agile, confident responses, and often in the context of limited information about what is happening on the ground.

During many such events, the management of the crisis and its aftermath will be conducted between the private office of the

---

* For example, the critical House of Commons debates on Suez and the Falklands both took place on a Saturday.

responsible department and that of No. 10, which may have equally limited information. The Permanent Secretary of each affected department will also take a close interest and might even choose to attend every meeting. At such moments, the private office can again best be considered as the essential junction box, making (or sometimes failing to make) the right connections and ensuring that the flow of work is properly managed, even though the private office would not be the place in which all the work was done. A private secretary will often have to contact external organisations, some of which they may well never have dealt with before and which may have no previous experience of dealing with government departments or ministers. All the time, the private office must seek to protect the minister's and departmental interests.

Crisis management is time consuming and can be stressful. For example, during the critical stages of the banking crash of 2008, the private offices of No. 10 and the Chancellor of the Exchequer worked throughout the night to put together the respective financial packages. During many crises, the private office has often had to become knowledgeable, and in short order, on subjects which may have been completely unknown beforehand. In 1995, when I was principal private secretary to the Secretary of State for Education and Employment, I had no knowledge of the animal disease BSE (which suddenly broke out unexpectedly), but I had to find out about it rapidly to support my Secretary of State, who had been a former agriculture minister and knew far more about the subject than I or my then department did. As one former principal private secretary told me, 'The instinct of the principal private secretary, at time of crises, should be to march towards the sound of gunfire. That is quite a good metaphor for the role.'[48]

RELATIONSHIP FUNCTIONS

5. Providing advice and challenge, if required, to the department

All ministers may, at some point, be wary of departmental opinion and may seek clarification of recommendations they have received. Some ministers may wish to challenge such departmental advice on a more regular basis. For example, Ken Clarke for the Conservatives and David Blunkett for the Labour Party were always quick to challenge any submission which referred to 'the departmental line', as if that was something separate from ministerial or government policy. The No. 10 private office will certainly look to departmental private offices for quick interpretations or elaboration of material it has received, as well as to challenge the robustness of the departmental arguments. The private office has always therefore had to provide both advice and challenge on behalf of their minister, balanced with representing the department, as appropriate, to the minister or to No. 10. So, private secretaries have often had to be able to face different directions at the same time.

As part of their work, the private secretary needs to be able to summarise, interpret and sometimes amplify or even tone down departmental advice, although they would rarely do the latter. Charles Powell did admit that, at one time, he held back submissions to Thatcher from her Foreign Secretary Geoffrey Howe, because Howe's views would have only served to irritate her. He even excluded Howe from relevant meetings.[49]* A minister may wish to challenge or amend so-called departmental lines to make them more consistent with their political views. Ministers of all parties

---

* See, for example, how Powell alone worked with Thatcher on nuclear defence policy and suppressed Howe's input to decision-making. Powell also admitted that he held back some documents from departmental private offices.

can develop reputations for challenging conventional policies and seeking to change departmental lines. As Prime Minister, Margaret Thatcher certainly did so, though she appears to have been far less willing to intervene in that way as Education Secretary in Heath's government. Other Labour ministers, such as Richard Crossman, were consistently frustrated by the departmental advice they received and challenged many of the conventional civil service briefings with which they were provided. David Blunkett, for example, was irritated to have been told in an early briefing on becoming Home Secretary in 2001 what 'Home Office policy was'.[50] He expressed his deep frustration and pointed out that there was no such thing as an independent Home Office line. The only policy was that of the government of the day and/or the policies of the Home Secretary.[51] Those private secretaries who have felt that they understand their minister's mind, style and prejudices may well have been emboldened to challenge departmental advice, on behalf of the minister, but such an approach is never risk free. Some departmental officials may resent their advice being ignored or downplayed. Yet it can often fall to the private secretary to handle some of the trickiest situations quickly and perhaps personally to revise a speech or letter on behalf of the minister, rather than to commission something from within the department.

A few notable private secretaries have developed a skill in interpreting their minister's or their Prime Minister's views better than their departments. For example, Jock Colville for Winston Churchill, Tim Bligh* for Harold Macmillan or David Dowler for Roy Jenkins. Robert Armstrong developed a very close relationship with Edward Heath, including leading negotiations on his behalf

---

*   Sir Tim Bligh (1918–69); principal private secretary to the Prime Minister (Harold Macmillan and Alec Douglas-Home) 1959–64.

on Europe and other matters. Charles Powell's relationship with Margaret Thatcher allowed him to act in a way which, at times, implied that he, rather than the Foreign Secretary, was in charge of foreign policy. Jeremy Heywood wrote many of the speeches and statements made by Norman Lamont and some officials in No. 10 and the Treasury saw him as the real power behind the Chancellor.[52] However, and importantly, Armstrong, in retirement, stressed the critical point that a private secretary alone has no power and no authority whatsoever: 'In yourself, you are nothing. You are a representative of the Prime Minister or your minister. You should never allow yourself to nurture yourself. As a private secretary, you are only of any interest precisely because you are a representative of the minister or of the Prime Minister.'[53] Many private secretaries have sought to represent their minister. The skill has always been to do so without being susceptible to the charge of politicisation.

6. Acting as an 'early warning system'

A private secretary is the eyes and ears of a minister and can often provide an 'early warning system' about forthcoming risks or potential emerging tensions. Such foresight can certainly help diffuse or lessen a crisis when one happens. A No. 10 private secretary needs to be able to spot when a department is underperforming or not being wholly open with the centre. If there are differences of approach over a particular policy, or if problems are looming, it is the job of the private secretary to try to smooth things over in advance of them escalating, including by liaising with relevant senior officials and the departmental Permanent Secretary as necessary. Such policy differences may sometimes emerge via the process of seeking collective ministerial agreement to policies through the so-called write-round process, whereby decisions made at Cabinet committee

level are then confirmed or amended following an exchange of letters between relevant departments.* In general, such differences do
not emerge from the formal processes of government but, rather,
may reflect political or policy tensions between ministers.

Throughout history there have often been tensions between No.
10, departments and the Treasury over economic policy. There
have also, at many times, been policy differences within ministerial teams, such as happened in 1997 in the Department of Social
Security when the Secretary of State (Harriet Harman) and her
deputy (Frank Field) had fundamentally contrasting approaches
to the issue of welfare reform. There were also, inevitably, policy
divisions during the Conservative–Liberal Democrat coalition.
Paradoxically, though, the very existence of the coalition, by definition, required greater consultation and there were more administrative negotiations, which the civil service and ministerial private
offices were well placed to provide. Many Prime Ministers have
often relied on their private secretaries to spot problems in advance
and to broker deals with the key officials and advisers. Both Blair
and Cameron, as Prime Minister, relied heavily on their principal
private secretaries to do this.[54] Jeremy Heywood was the master of
spotting departmental failings and then helping to broker often innovative solutions.[55]

7. Advising on communications issues

The importance of effective communications and engagement with
the media has grown enormously since the 1960s. More recently,
with the growth and development of the 24-hour news cycle and

---

* In those circumstances where a Cabinet minister wants to clear a document or change some policy, they
write rounds to all departmental ministers for authority for the change of advice. Cabinet Office co-
ordinates this process, working with the relevant departmental private offices.

the rise of social media, communications have become an ever-present element of ministerial and private office life. For most ministers, speeches were always an essential part of their armoury, dating back to at least Victorian times. The great political orators (from William Gladstone and David Lloyd George, through Winston Churchill and up to Aneurin Bevan) made speeches both as rhetoric but also to advance their thinking on key policy issues. Nowadays, politicians will make speeches at a range of venues, such as at conferences, to trade associations, trade unions, think tanks, universities and learned societies. However, unlike fifty years ago, ministers today would be most interested in how the speech was communicated, how it was presented in the media and what coverage it received. This is a vital part of the role and life of private office, working alongside communications officials and special advisers. In the 1960s, if necessary, a private secretary would routinely liaise with the departmental head of information, who would manage most media contacts. Some thirty years later, and because of the influence of New Labour's approach, understanding communications became a major task for every private office and it has remained so, especially nowadays in the era of social media. The rise of communications was something that defined New Labour and this aspect is explored further in Chapter 9. Joe Haines, Harold Wilson's press secretary, recalled that when he arrived at No. 10, the No. 10 principal private secretary did not allow him sufficient access to the Prime Minister, and he often had to bypass the private office in order to get direct contact with Wilson.[56] It is inconceivable that such a situation would happen now.

An essential skill of the private secretary is therefore to have, or to develop quickly, good news judgement and a keen eye for the communications angle of departmental business. Depending on the personalities involved, there may also be a need for the private office to smooth the workings of the relationships between ministers, the press office and special advisers. Many special advisers focus specifically on the media and therefore the private office must be attuned to their mode of operation on behalf of the minister. Of the two special advisers allowed now to every minister, one will often focus solely on media relations. Private secretaries have often helped develop lines quickly for the press office to use (or 'knocking copy', as Charles Powell used to call it), and often have to work with the press office and special advisers to communicate with the media.

8. Making space for the minister's role as a constituency MP

Most ministers are also members of the House of Commons. So, just as all ministers have concentrated on their parliamentary work, nearly all members of the House of Commons have always taken a strong interest in their constituency and constituency matters, not only the formal official process of constituents' correspondence. Most ministers who are MPs may wish to spend time regularly in their constituency, attending events which may have no relevance to departmental business. Increasingly, therefore, the private office has had to ensure sufficient time is reserved for their minister's role in their political party and to maintain effective relationships with those working in the constituency. The private office must judge the various tasks of the minister, and to balance them, in order to ensure that constituency work is not seen as secondary to the departmental role. Inevitably, MPs will tend to see much of their work through the lens of their constituents and their constituency parties. Many ministers will judge their private offices by how well they ensure enough time is allocated for constituency business. That, in turn, may well affect the way in which they ask their department to oversee particular issues and to handle items of correspondence. Private offices have always sought to handle such concerns sensitively and increasingly so in recent years, given the enhanced level of scrutiny of MPs' constituency activities.

PERSONAL SUPPORT FUNCTIONS

9. Advising on issues of propriety

Most ministers are usually assiduous in following the rule book, although, as the parliamentary expenses scandal of 2009 showed, as well as some well-publicised more recent examples, there is always the potential for MPs and ministers to transgress or even to exploit the rules.[57] However, it is important to stress that many of these issues are not clear-cut and some minor transgressions can be or can appear to be inadvertent. For example, in terms of using government cars, any minister can use a government car when on departmental business – but not when on party political business. That sounds straightforward. However, often a minister may take a red box in their car en route to a party political event and claim that they are 'working all the time on government business'. The private secretary is usually the first port of call for a minister to use in ensuring due propriety, and to advise if they think the minister may have overstepped the mark. Cases such as use of ministerial cars are very hard to call. Occasionally, ministers have been known to ask for a red box specifically in order to get a government car to take them to a party event. A senior Cabinet minister once deliberately made himself late for a trip to the USA, for which he had been booked on a standard transatlantic flight, so that, in order to catch up on time, he had to be transferred onto the far quicker Concorde flight, a plane on which he had never previously flown. It is the role of a private secretary to ensure their minister is fully aware of the

Ministerial Code, and the private office would always raise such cases with their Permanent Secretary, as soon as possible, if there were any doubts. However, many new ministers may be unaware of the code on arrival in office so, 'for new ministers not used to government it is essential reading, not least because breaking any of the rules can lead to an early departure'.[58]

Prime Ministers are not immune from such scrutiny, and it is the job of the No. 10 private office to advise the Prime Minister if their integrity is questioned in any way. The whole Johnson premiership underlined that. The Ministerial Code was predicated on the fact that the final arbiter in the case of potential transgression of the code by any minister would be the Prime Minister. In fact, the first paragraph of the code states: 'Ministers of the Crown are expected to maintain high standards of behaviour and to behave in a way that upholds the highest standards of propriety.'

That is followed shortly afterwards by: 'It is of paramount importance that Ministers give accurate and truthful information to Parliament, correcting any inadvertent error at the earliest opportunity. Ministers who knowingly mislead Parliament will be expected to offer their resignation to the Prime Minister.'[59]

The Ministerial Code now covers the role of special advisers and some prominent cases in recent years have considered whether special advisers have acted with due propriety. Special advisers were first introduced in 1964, yet regulation of their activities and being brought within the ambit of the Ministerial Code did not occur until over a quarter of a century later in 1991.[60*]

Sadly, the authors of the code clearly never, for an instant,

---

* Since special advisers are civil servants, albeit temporary ones, they are ultimately responsible to the Permanent Secretary of their department.

considered that the main transgressor might be the Prime Minister themself.

10. Providing support to the minister and acting as a personal confidant

As with crisis management, this function has never been easy to characterise or define precisely, but it is one that has always proved invaluable to a minister, particularly when under pressure. Roy Jenkins recognised the value of his totally loyal private secretary David Dowler but also his downsides in terms of relationships across Whitehall, when he described Dowler as 'a wonderful private secretary to me, but I suppose not altogether easy to work under'.[61] Having a good personal relationship built on trust means that a private secretary can become more of a personal confidant to a minister. They can act as a sounding board, offer a second opinion or even provide a, metaphorical, shoulder to cry on. Private secretaries have often seen more of their minister's personal life than anybody other than the minister's spouse. While Disraeli's view may not be entirely accurate, it underlines the point well. When Margaret Thatcher threatened to resign if her private secretary, Charles Powell, was moved from No. 10, it was a sign of just how dependent she had become on him (see Chapter 7). A private secretary is also there to support a minister if they are sacked, helping while they wind up their departmental responsibilities and hand over to their successor.

Many private secretaries will take some personal secrets if not to their grave, then certainly well beyond their career in the private office. At other times, their recollections have put the work of their minister in perspective. For example, in 2017, when the Wiltshire Police concluded their investigations into allegations of child abuse against a former Prime Minister – the late Edward Heath – it was members of his former private office who defended him. Robin Butler, a former private secretary to Heath, pointed out that it was 'improbable that, while in office, Heath would have been able to avoid the constant supervision of friends, protection officers, and his private office whether he was at No. 10 or on his yacht'.[62] As a private secretary, Butler knew Heath well and had relevant expertise from observing Heath as Prime Minister. Butler's view was that, certainly for the period he worked in his private office, Heath simply could not have been responsible for the posthumous allegations made against him. That was a brave statement to make from a loyal and impartial civil servant.

11. Advising on sensitive matters of appointments or financial issues

In every department, there are, and have always been, public appointments that require the approval of the relevant Secretary of State. In 1964, there was no proper or consistent regulation of public appointments. However, in 1994, the Committee on Standards in Public Life (also known as the Nolan Committee – named after its first chair) was established. It proposed that ministerial appointments should be overseen by a commissioner for public appointments. In 2001–02, there were 3,506 public appointments, although a decade later that figure had fallen to 1,740.[63] The number of public appointments declined as a result of reductions in the number of public bodies and on account of devolution. In the most recent year that figures are available, there were 1,844 new public appointments and reappointments.[64] The Prime Minister is personally responsible for a swathe of public appointments. While the process is overseen by the commissioner, all ministers from the Prime Minister downwards have always taken a close interest in appointments and some seek to influence the choice of appointments to certain posts. However, increasingly, journalists and the media have sought to highlight appointments that appear not to have been made on merit or which have not followed due procedure. In such cases, there will often be a reputational risk to the department and the minister, of which the private office will need to be aware.

Equally important is the management of departmental or cross-government financial issues. On matters of the Budget and the department's finances, including when major Budget negotiations or spending review discussions with the Treasury are underway, the principal private secretary would be the private office member responsible for negotiations below Secretary of State level. They would work in tandem with the departmental accounting officer, the Permanent Secretary. The ability to negotiate well with the Treasury, and to be successful in such negotiations, will often be a sign of success for the department and therefore the minister will put a lot of weight on this aspect of the principal private secretary's performance.

12. Managing the transition to a new minister

Finally, one of the most critical roles performed by a private secretary is the management of transition and ministerial succession. The task tests agility, political judgement and skills. While the department is responsible for briefing a new minister, it is almost always the principal private secretary who welcomes the new minister to the department, often even by waiting at the door of the department following a general election or a ministerial reshuffle. The way in which that process is handled and whether the new minister feels able to 'hit the ground running' has always depended to a large extent on how the private office performs on that first day. In the post-Second World War era, there have been eighteen prime ministerial transitions and those of 1945, 1951, 1964, 1970, 1974, 1979, 1997 and 2010 involved a change of political party. In such cases, the challenge for the private office has been even greater to help ensure a smooth and efficient handover of power. It is usually a matter of some personal pride for a principal private secretary to be able to ensure a seamless transition between Prime Ministers or Cabinet ministers from different political parties. It also shows the benefits of the politically impartial British civil service in the best possible light.

In additional to their constitutional role, it is at such moments that private secretaries can become witnesses to history while not players with any formal role. In 1955, Jock Colville, who developed a close bond with Winston Churchill while being his private secretary, wrote on the evening before Churchill left No. 10 that:

> I went up with Winston to his bedroom. He sat on his bed, still wearing his Garter, Order of Merit and knee-breeches. For several minutes he did not speak and I, imagining that he was sadly contemplating that this was his last night at Downing Street, was silent. Then suddenly he stared at me and said with vehemence: 'I don't believe Anthony can do it.' His prophecies have often tended to be borne out by events.[65]

Only a private secretary as close to the Prime Minister as Colville was could witness such a moment. In February 1974, Robert Armstrong wrote a detailed account of how he handled the final days and hours of Heath's premiership. Armstrong admitted that he personally was close to tears as Heath prepared to resign (see Chapter 6). Similarly, Andrew Turnbull[*] witnessed Thatcher's resignation in

---

[*] Andrew Turnbull (1945–); private secretary (economic affairs) to the Prime Minister 1983–85; principal private secretary to the Prime Minister (Margaret Thatcher and John Major) 1988–92; Cabinet Secretary 2002–05; created Lord Turnbull of Enfield 2005.

1990 and wrote a full narrative of the events (see Chapter 7). Those tasks that fall to the private secretary would have been repeated in many different contexts and transitions of ministers at all levels.

The process of the handover of power can be quick and dramatic. It is the private office which will guide the former minister out of the door whether they are demoted, promoted, sacked or even ejected by the electorate. It is the same private office workers who will welcome the new minister. The civil servants who clap out the old Prime Minister and those who clap in the new Prime Minister an hour or so later are the very same people. Civil servants have a clear and unambiguous role to play. Ministers (at all levels) often remember the nature of their welcome. First impressions can shape the relationship between a minister and their private office for a long time. Even Gordon Brown, who rarely displayed emotion, said of his welcome by the Treasury staff on 2 May 1997:

To my surprise I [entered the Treasury building] to a warm and enthusiastic reception from civil servants lining the lobby, the stairways and landings above. TV cameras showed me shaking hands with my new officials and acknowledging the cheers of a normally reserved group of economic experts. Within minutes of arriving at my new office, accompanied by Ed Balls, I met Terry Burns, the Permanent Secretary and Nick Macpherson, now my principal private secretary and later to hold Terry's job.[66]

Private offices, and most private secretaries, will treat how well they can manage a change of minister, both at an election or following a ministerial reshuffle, as a test of their competence, impartiality and professionalism. The integrity of the civil service relies on the independence of civil servants and their support for the government of the day and for the individual ministers who form that government. James Bowler, who handled the transition from Gordon Brown to David Cameron in 2010 (and who, in 2022, was to become Treasury Permanent Secretary), commented that the transition was most immediate in No. 10, where the private office staff had 'to manage the transition hand-to-mouth and in real time'.[67] By contrast, departments may have slightly more time to prepare and discuss arrangements. Bowler also commented:

> I managed Gordon Brown's last PMQs and David Cameron's first PMQs. One of the proudest things in my whole civil service career was that I ran the No. 10 private office and that [after the 2010 general election], I ran the exact same private office, and each member of that private office team was in-situ a year later. Yet the same private office had served two such completely different Prime Ministers. Cameron could have been suspicious of our loyalty to him but, to his great credit, he was not.[68]

It is, of course, the constitutional duty of the private office to support their minister to the best of their ability. That is why this twelfth function is so vital. While there have been a small number of examples of private secretaries who left or who chose to leave private office shortly after a transition, many private secretaries remained, bridging the change in political leadership and so providing administrative continuity at a time of political change. Robert Armstrong gained the trust of Wilson despite having been personally close to Heath for over three years, and notwithstanding the stiff opposition from Wilson's personal aide, Marcia Williams. Alex Allan was described by Tony Blair as 'so professional' and 'invaluable' in the handover from Major in 1997, whom he had served loyally for five years previously.[69] Jeremy Heywood served as principal private secretary or Permanent Secretary at No. 10 for three different Prime Ministers, two Labour and one Conservative. He later became Cabinet Secretary to David Cameron and Theresa May.

THE STRETCHING OF THE PRIVATE OFFICE

Taken together, these twelve functions sum up the core purpose and work of the private office. Ministers and their priorities drive the political and policy agendas of governments, but it is the private secretaries and, collectively, the private office that have helped to interpret those agendas, to transact the essential tasks and to support ministers in ensuring that they operate as efficiently as possible and help get the best from the civil service. Over the past half-century, the private office's remit, scope and size have expanded, but it remains a vital part of the administrative landscape of the civil service, providing continuity during change. While there have been, at times, clashes and tensions between some private secretaries and ministerial special advisers, the private office has usually been the junction box of government, managing the traffic smoothly, seeking to avoid clashes, brokering compromises, responding to crises and helping departments and Prime Ministers set their future direction. The private office, with some exceptions, has remained non-politicised and worked well with the growing number of special advisers in the civil service. That said, it has become stretched over the past half-century, in five distinct ways which have certainly led some observers to question whether it remains fit for purpose in its current form.

First, the workload of private office has expanded. Just as the range of issues handled by the Prime Minister, as chronicled by Peter Hennessy, grew from only twelve tasks in 1947 to forty-seven in 2010, so, inevitably, over that same period a greater number of administrative tasks fell to private offices. The workloads of the private offices of all ministers, but especially those of Cabinet rank, expanded considerably, especially from 1964 onwards.

Second, the speed of transaction of much private office work has increased. The vast majority of issues, fifty years ago, were safely handled by paper-based submissions and put to ministers via their daily red box for decision overnight. Nowadays, the demands of the 24-hour media, and the increasing volatility of, for example, financial markets, means that the handling of many decisions and the work of the private office has to be far more agile than that of its counterparts in the pre-internet age. For example, the International Monetary Fund (IMF) crisis in the second half of 1976 lasted for three months and spanned twenty-seven meetings of Cabinet and Cabinet committees. By way of contrast, during the critical moments of the financial crisis in October 2009, the Chancellor and his private office were given only three hours to save the then largest bank in the world, RBS.[70]

Third, communications have become an increasingly important, and time-consuming, aspect of the work of departments, the civil service and the private office. While the arrival of New Labour in 1997 represented a step change in this aspect of the private office's work, it was part of a growing trend dating back at least to Wilson's era as Prime Minister. By comparison, Attlee, in 1945, paid little attention to the media. He only agreed to the installation of a telex machine in No. 10 because he was told that it also provided regular updates of the cricket score. Today, the additional pressures from modern communications and the 24-hour news cycle have only been exacerbated by the vast expansion in the number of news outlets and the impact of the internet and, subsequently, of social media.

Fourth, technology and the ways in which it has been used have reshaped the work of the private office. In 1964, all submissions were paper-based, typed in a typing pool and with limited numbers of carbon copies. Domestic phone calls could not all be dialled; international calls had to be pre-arranged. Innovations such as the photocopier and the fax machine had not then reached the civil service. In those days, international and diplomatic work was mainly conducted using hard copies of Foreign Office telegrams. All of this made for slower processes but ones which would nearly all be transacted via the private office. (Even in Blair's era, nothing ever went to Blair himself by email and he never sent any emails.)

Today all ministers have access to mobile electronic devices which can deliberately, or by mistake, mean that private office may be bypassed. In the 1980s, the growth in the use of faxes and computer technology, and increasingly mobile data, also transformed the work of private office. Finally, the rapid expansion in the new millennium of other technologies, and specifically the rise of social media, has transformed ministerial work, including that of private office and the communications function. Many ministers today have active social media presences as well as far more efficient mobile telephony and will wish to respond to a range of stories breaking on the internet at all times of day and night and at the weekend. Similarly, much private office activity today relies far more on new technology. Business is transacted via mobile phone, video conferencing and email even though submissions and correspondence may well still take the form of hard copies in the daily red boxes, depending on a minister's personal preferences. In the early years of the Wilson government, one of the tasks of the private secretary who accompanied the Prime Minister on his holidays to the Scilly Isles was to pay a daily visit to the islands' coastguard station to contact the Land's End coastguard and receive a daily report on the balance of payments to pass to Wilson at his holiday home.[71] The past does indeed resemble a different country.

Finally, the stretched private office of the 2020s has been forced to be far better attuned to the political dimension of the work of government than its antecedents. The more that a private secretary can employ political antennae, without becoming politicised, the more effective they are likely to be in serving politicians and defending their departmental interests. At No. 10 or in the Chancellor's private office, this is even more significant. Since 1964, there has been a large growth in the number of special advisers from zero prior to the general election in 1964 to over 100 today, forty-one of whom work in No. 10.[72] This has had a direct effect on the private office. Private secretaries must be able to work well alongside special advisers, often within highly political atmospheres, yet without themselves becoming politicised.

Private offices have had to be able, individually and collectively, to adapt to the warp and weft of changing policies and day-to-day events and to deliver as many of these twelve functions as efficiently as possible. Private secretaries have had to carry out those ever-increasing tasks, provide a strong intellectual input and, when needed, personal support, yet without becoming politicised. The private office in British political history has evolved greatly since 1945, and yet it has often still been the private offices – and those key private secretaries who have served within them – who have helped steer No. 10 and ministerial offices through high-profile events and crises as well as through the day-to-day life of ministers and their departments. In that sense, and despite the massive technological changes of today, their role is just the same as it was some eighty years ago.

2

A MIXTURE OF LEPORELLO AND MEPHISTOPHELES: WHO ARE THE PRIVATE SECRETARIES AND WHERE DO THEY COME FROM?

In 1964, Denis Healey* joined Harold Wilson's Labour Cabinet as Secretary of State for Defence. Healey had no experience of government, ministerial office or the workings of the civil service. He very soon came to rely on his private secretary, Patrick Nairne,† who had served as a civil servant in the Admiralty since 1947 and who ran Healey's private office from shortly after the election until 1967. As Nairne departed, Healey wrote a letter of farewell and thanks to him which reveals just how vital he had been:

> It did not take me long to learn that my Private Secretary was the most important man in the department – a mixture of Leporello and Mephistopheles, the fulcrum or axle of the whole operation, responsible for lubricating himself! I have no expectation of

---

* Denis Healey (1917–2015); Secretary of State for Defence 1964–70; Chancellor of the Exchequer 1974–79; deputy leader of the Labour Party 1980–83.

† Sir Patrick Nairne (1921–2013); principal private secretary to the Secretary of State for Defence 1965–67; Permanent Secretary to the Department of Health and Social Security 1975–81.

coming across anyone in the rest of my career who combines all the desirable qualities even half as well.[1]

It was perhaps typical of the cultured Healey that he should make such literary comparisons to both Leporello – Don Giovanni's faithful servant in Mozart's opera of that name – and Mephistopheles, the devil to whom Faustus sells his soul! However, Healey's description of Nairne's administrative abilities and commitment underlines his significance to Healey and to the fulfilment of his ministerial duties:

> Your wisdom, experience and imagination were invaluable. Most of all, perhaps, in retrospect, I value the indefatigable stamina which enabled you to force me to think things through when my own energies were flagging. Management has always been uniquely a Nairne forte – here again you showed your extraordinary ability to follow through a decision and programme the handling of a problem, so that the solution was achieved on time. What little I have learnt about administration – a closed book to me in 1964 – I owe overwhelmingly to you.[2]

On a cold, wet morning in January 2015, almost fifty years after he wrote that letter, I interviewed Healey in his East Sussex home. He was, by then, physically frail and somewhat deaf, yet his critical faculties were attuned and alert. I asked him who, in his opinion, was the best private secretary he had encountered or with whom he had ever worked in Whitehall. Without a moment's hesitation he answered, 'Pat Nairne.'[3] By then, Healey had already paid a far fuller tribute to Nairne's outstanding qualities when he wrote, in his autobiography, that his former private secretary had been 'the perfect choice for the most difficult two years of my service as defence secretary, when I was taking my most important decisions on equipment, commitments and strategy … He was a glutton for work … Unfailing courtesy and a pretty wit made him a joy to work with.'[4] A new minister, such as Healey in 1964, coming into a department as its political leader may know nothing about the department or its subject area. And, as Healey made clear, new ministers will often know nothing of the way in which their department is administered. The role of the private secretary and the private office is to help ministers understand their responsibilities and navigate their way around the department in which they may find themselves deposited at short notice. But who are those people who perform that role? What is their background and how are they chosen? That is what this chapter seeks to answer.

A VITAL PART OF THE CAREER LADDER

Service in private office has, traditionally, been a route to the top. Historically, the majority of Permanent Secretaries have spent time as ministerial private secretaries. Most aspiring young 'high-flyers' – the administrators most likely to be the future leaders of the civil service – will know that they are expected at some point in their career to work in private office. For many of them, it will be a central aim of their early careers. For example, an analysis of the background of Permanent Secretaries from 1945 to 2020 shows that having worked in a private office provided valuable experience and was a clear indicator as to who might reach the most senior departmental roles. There is a greater correlation than either service in No. 10 or in the Treasury, two of the other main traditional routes to civil service success.

Background of UK departmental Permanent Secretaries 1945–2020[5*]

	1945	1960	1970	1980	1993	2010	2020
Private office experience?	18	12	10	16	15	12	10
	64%	46%	59%	76%	75%	71%	56%
Treasury experience?	9	10	8	7	9	8	6
	32%	39%	47%	33%	45%	47%	33%
No. 10 experience?	1	1	0	4	3	3	6
	4%	4%	0%	19%	15%	18%	33%
Oxbridge?	22	19	15	14	14	13	14
	79%	73%	88%	67%	70%	77%	78%
Female?	0	2	0	0	1	4	6
	0%	8%	0%	0%	5%	24%	33%
Total	**28**	**26**	**17**	**21**	**20**	**17**	**18**

Nowadays, with more direct external recruitment to senior White-hall posts, the proportion of senior figures in departments who have served as private secretaries has decreased slightly. That said, service within private office remains an important element in the recruitment of many of the current leaders of the civil service, with some 56 per cent of the current cadre having served in such roles.

Traditionally, many aspiring young civil servants planning their careers have been the 'high-flyers' – the future leaders of the civil service – who, at a relatively early stage in their careers, will un-doubtedly look to gain private office experience, along with a range of other development options (such as working in the Treasury or No. 10, taking a secondment or gaining operational experience). Taken together, such experience would help to establish their rep-utation and to rise further up the ladder. As shown above, many

---

* The table refers to the Permanent Secretaries who headed the major Whitehall departments in the year featured and does not include data on Second Permanent Secretaries or their earlier equivalents or other Permanent Secretary-ranking posts. Data for 2010 is from the period after the general election of that year.

Permanent Secretaries were private secretaries earlier in their careers, sometimes both to a junior minister and then to a Cabinet
minister, or to the Prime Minister. At the very least, that will get
them noticed by more senior officials. It also gets them direct access
to, and experience of the interface between, politicians and the civil
service. Such young officials, early in their career, may find themselves working closely with senior ministers and officials and handling enormously sensitive issues. The theme of career progression
of private secretaries and the benefits such experience can bring
means that often service in private office can be part of a 'golden
ladder' to success, although possibly less so now than in some previous era, when for many civil servants it was a 'career anchor' to
which they could, and often would, return. For example, Robert
Armstrong was a private secretary to a Treasury junior minister
early in his career before becoming one of the Chancellor of the
Exchequer's private secretaries in the early 1950s. In the following
decade, he was principal private secretary to the Chancellor of the
Exchequer and, subsequently, held the same role for two Prime
Ministers (Heath and Wilson) before ending his career as Cabinet
Secretary serving Thatcher when she was Prime Minister. Robin
Butler was initially a private secretary to the Financial Secretary
to the Treasury in the early 1960s. He was later one of the private
secretaries to Edward Heath, working for Robert Armstrong from
1972–75 and then became principal private secretary to Thatcher in
the following decade. He too ended his career as Cabinet Secretary
to Thatcher, Major and Blair. Andrew Turnbull followed a similar
route to the top. The former Cabinet Secretary Jeremy Heywood
was initially private secretary to Norman Lamont when he was Financial Secretary to the Treasury. Heywood subsequently became,
aged only twenty-nine, principal private secretary to Lamont when

he was promoted to become Chancellor of the Exchequer. Heywood went on to serve as first private secretary and then principal private secretary to Prime Ministers Blair, Brown and Cameron. Heywood was also made the first ever Permanent Secretary at No. 10. Of the thirteen Cabinet Secretaries, ten served in private office; only Maurice Hankey, Edward Bridges and Gus O'Donnell did not.[*]

Some civil servants have become very attached to private office and stayed in the role for a long time, often at the behest of their minister. This can be because either the minister feels very comfortable with their private secretary – increasingly so, as the private secretary comes to understand their minister's personal style and preferences. Or it can also be because the private secretary enjoys the role and the sense of personal loyalty and authority that it can confer. The more both of these aspects pertain, the greater the likelihood that the minister and private secretary will want to stay together. This is not always a healthy phenomenon if the minister becomes over-reliant on the private secretary who, in turn, is unwilling to leave private office. In addition, it can also be the case that more junior staff in private office, below private secretary level, may choose to stay for many years in private office, sometimes moving between ministerial offices in the same department. It may well be that they enjoy the status, the allowances and overtime that they can earn and that they might therefore find it difficult to return to less prominent roles elsewhere in their department.

While the average spell as principal private secretary to the Prime Minister since the Second World War has been just under three years, two occupants of the post stayed for over five years. Robert

---

[*] O'Donnell did, however, serve as chief press secretary to John Major when he was successively Chancellor of the Exchequer and Prime Minister.

Armstrong served Heath as principal private secretary for nearly all his premiership and his role was pivotal. Wilson retained Armstrong in that role when he returned to No. 10 in 1974. From 1992 to 1997, Alex Allan also served for over five years, having also previously been principal private secretary to the Chancellor of the Exchequer for over three years. Of No. 10 private secretaries, Charles Powell fulfilled a highly significant function as private secretary for foreign affairs to Margaret Thatcher and remained at No. 10 for seven years. Notably, Powell was never principal private secretary, and his No. 10 posting was the only ministerial private office job in his career. Yet he was one of the most influential private secretaries ever. Armstrong and Powell were both kept in No. 10 on the direct orders of the Prime Minister of the day when their senior managers wanted them to return to their home departments. Powell became so loyal to his boss that, at times, he crossed the line between civil service impartiality and party political support for a politician (see Chapter 7).[6] More recently, Jeremy Heywood became one of the most indispensable of private secretaries to Prime Ministers of different party political persuasions, although he was never accused of politicisation in any of his posts. Heywood was, for over twenty-five years, at the heart of British government, mostly behind the scenes and out of sight of the cameras, and he managed to cope with the styles and varied modes of operation of four Prime Ministers, all of different political persuasions. The No. 10 private office was, though, for nearly all the period covered, a male-dominated organisation. The first female private secretary at No. 10 (Caroline Slocock) was not appointed until 1989, although over the next twenty years many more women served in that role. There had never been a female principal private secretary at No. 10 until 2022, when Rishi

Sunak brought Elizabeth Perelman[*] to No. 10 from the Treasury (where she had been his principal private secretary). In Whitehall, more generally, there is far better gender diversity. For example, in 2023, just over 50 per cent of principal private secretaries were women.

THE PRIVATE OFFICE OF THE SECRETARY OF STATE AND OF JUNIOR MINISTERS

Private office experience can take several different forms. At the lowest rungs of the ladder are the offices of junior ministers, all of whom will have a private secretary and perhaps one or two assistant private secretaries. The Permanent Secretary of the department will also have private offices. But within a department of state, every Secretary of State has a private office which is the most significant private office in the department. Through it will flow all significant policy, financial and administrative material – hence its role as the junction box of government, and of every department. While the Permanent Secretary is, as the name suggests, the most senior official responsible for administering the work of the department, the political head of the department – the Secretary of State – will always wish to be kept apprised of all the main developments and senior appointments in their department. That is where the private secretary and, in particular, the principal private secretary play a pivotal role acting as the link and main channel of communication between the political and administrative parts of the system. Within a Secretary of State's private office in the second half of the

---

[*]   Elizabeth Perelman (1980–), civil servant; principal private secretary to the Chancellor of the Exchequer (Sajid Javid and Rishi Sunak) 2020–22; principal private secretary to the Prime Minister (Rishi Sunak) since 2022.

twentieth century, there may have been perhaps four or five immediate members of staff – the private secretaries and the diary
secretary. Today that number is closer to double that, depending on
the political significance of the department. For example, in 2023,
many departments had as many as ten private secretaries. Even the
smallest department – the Welsh Office – had five.*

The private office of every Cabinet minister will certainly contain the following posts. First, the principal private secretary is the
head of the private office.† They are the most senior member of the
private office and are jointly responsible to the Secretary of State
and to the Permanent Secretary of the department.‡ That position is
almost always held by a senior civil servant, at either deputy director level (formerly called Grade 5 or assistant secretary) or, in more
recent years, at director level (formerly called Grade 3 or under-
secretary). In recent years and certainly in some departments, there
has been a so-called grade drift upwards, whereby the same post has
been occupied by a civil servant of a higher grade. (Similarly, in No.
10 and for most of the period covered, the office was traditionally
headed by a director general-level senior civil servant, at Grade 2 or
deputy secretary level, although for brief periods it was headed by
an official at Permanent Secretary level.)

In most departments, the principal private secretary will be a
'high-flyer',§ who has impressed ministers and senior civil servants

---

* These figures include only the principal private secretary and other private secretaries. They do not include
the other administrative and support staff in the private office.

† The principal private secretary (PPS) should not be confused with the parliamentary private secretary
(often also called a PPS). That role – a political appointment – will be held by a Member of Parliament and
they provide political support to their allocated Cabinet minister by, for example, feeding back views from
the House of Commons and from the party.

‡ Although only the Permanent Secretary, or another senior civil servant, would be the formal 'line manager'
of the principal private secretary.

§ A 'high-flyer' is a shorthand phrase used in the civil service for those civil servants who come through
the competitive administrative exams and tests – the fast stream – and are then put on an accelerated
promotion route. They are also sometimes called 'fast-streamers'. These civil servants will therefore often
reach senior posts within government departments at a far younger age than most other civil servants.

by their managerial and administrative skills, coupled with a political sensitivity.[7] Any principal private secretary must be able to
work effectively with their Secretary of State and so, normally, the
Secretary of State would make the final selection from a shortlist
of candidates as recommended by the Permanent Secretary. The
Permanent Secretary will always take a keen interest in ensuring a
strong shortlist, and very possibly put their most-favoured candidates prominently on the list. The biggest test of the ability of any
principal private secretary is that they can maintain the full trust
and confidence of the Secretary of State. Douglas Hurd, who served
for over eleven years in three different Cabinet posts, explained that
having confidence in your principal private secretary at moments
of crisis was, for him, the best single test of their ability.[8] So, the
most important abilities and skills for a principal private secretary
to have often been personal and diplomatic, rather than just administrative and strategic. A principal private secretary without the full
support of their Secretary of State is likely to find that they have a
short career in private office.

The private office of a Secretary of State will also contain two,
three or four other private secretaries or assistant private secretaries, depending on a range of factors, including the importance of
the department, its size and the scope of its responsibilities. These
are graded at a range of levels. They may be Grade 7s (formerly
called 'principals') or junior fast-streamers. Increasingly, recently,
there has also been a tendency for many private offices to introduce new posts, such as a deputy principal private secretary, so as
to reduce the overall burden on the principal private secretary. This
accretion of roles has been mirrored more widely in departments
with the creation of many 'Second Permanent Secretaries', where
previously there had been only one head of department. However,

it is certainly not yet clear whether such upward 'grade drift' has led to better governance or the better functioning of private offices. For example, as something of a workaholic, Thatcher's charismatic foreign affairs private secretary Charles Powell liked to reflect, somewhat waspishly, that 'in the No. 10 private office, under Blair, there were six people providing foreign affairs advice. I did that by myself.'[9]

Every ministerial private office will also have a diary secretary, often responsible for acting as 'gatekeeper' to the minister plus a range of support staff. Insofar as there is evidence, ministers are clear that they put a large emphasis on the ability of diary secretaries and the vital importance of that function.[10] Some ministers even describe the diary secretary as the most important person in their private office.[11] The selection of officials to fill these posts below principal private secretary level will usually be made in the following way. A selection process will be held involving the personnel or HR function of the department, identifying potential candidates who the principal private secretary and/or one of the more senior private secretaries will interview. The Permanent Secretary may also be consulted and may even have a view on the shortlist. The Secretary of State is then almost certainly asked to make the final choice of candidate, given the need for the two people to be able to work closely together.

The process for identifying and selecting potential candidates to serve as private secretaries to junior ministers is similar to that for Secretaries of State, although the departmental Cabinet minister would rarely be involved in such appointments. The principal private secretary does usually play a leading role in identifying potential candidates and, once again, the final decision will be made on the merits of candidates by the relevant junior minister. The process does not always go smoothly. For example, a prominent Conservative minister in the 1990s refused to accept any of the candidates put forward for interview, although many of them had excellent credentials and backgrounds. The minister asked for another shortlist, all of whom were also rejected. In the end, the minister demanded that every one of their existing private office be promoted and only the most junior post could then be filled through open competition. This virtually unprecedented event caused a stand-off which was escalated to the Permanent Secretary. Both sides dug in, and the matter was finally resolved only when the minister involved was moved to another department in a ministerial reshuffle.[12] That story is testament to how attached some ministers can become to their private offices. Rarely would such a stand-off happen, although there are often examples of ministers who insist that their private secretary accompany them to whatever new ministerial post they get, even within a different department.

RECRUITMENT TO THE NO. 10 PRIVATE OFFICE

A similar process takes place in selecting the most senior officials to serve in No. 10. The Cabinet Office will be involved in identifying some of the best potential candidates from across Whitehall. Some posts – such as the economic affairs private secretary to the Prime Minister – will almost certainly come from the obvious economic department which is the Treasury. Similarly, the foreign affairs private secretary will almost certainly come from the Foreign Office. The other private secretaries may come from a range of departments and be interviewed by the principal private secretary. The Prime Minister will nearly always be involved in the choice, and the interviewing, of candidates to serve as their principal private secretary and possibly also as the supporting private secretaries. However, that is not always the case. Heath made an inspired choice of Robert Armstrong as his principal private secretary based on his reputation and reports, having never even met him (see Chapter 6). The head of the home civil service, Sir William Armstrong,* felt that their shared love of music would help their working relationship – and it did. This criterion was, to put it mildly, a bizarre factor to use in the selection of the person to fill such a critical post.

At No. 10, there is also always a diary secretary and often someone who can best be called a 'gatekeeper' to the Prime Minister. Indeed, these two functions can often be combined in one person, as usually happens in Cabinet ministers' private offices. This gatekeeper function can become very influential in that the post-holder often controls access to the relevant minister or to the Prime Minister on a day-to-day basis. Over recent years, gatekeepers have become vital to managing a Cabinet minister's time and access. The concept of the gatekeeper first gained significance when it was fulfilled from 1964 by Marcia Williams, who was brought into No. 10 by Harold Wilson on becoming Prime Minister. Her role and interventions brought her a fearsome reputation among ministers and civil servants alike and she was viewed as a ruthless gatekeeper on Wilson's behalf (see Chapters 5 and 6). Many subsequent Prime Ministers have also had gatekeepers, although not all in the Marcia Williams mould. Interestingly, many of them have been women. These include Arabella Warburton (for John Major), Anji Hunter

---

* Sir William Armstrong (1915–80); civil servant; private secretary to the Cabinet Secretary (Sir Edward Bridges) 1943–45; principal private secretary to the Chancellor of the Exchequer (Stafford Cripps, Hugh Gaitskell and R. A. Butler) 1949–53; Permanent Secretary to the Treasury 1962–68; head of the home civil service 1968–74.

(for Tony Blair), Sue Nye (for Gordon Brown) and Kate Fall (for David Cameron).[*]

Private secretaries will take great care to remain detached from the party political aspects of their minister's work and there should never be any doubt about the political independence of the civil servants in a private office. Although many of them, especially the principal private secretary, will need a well-honed understanding of the wider political world and to be alert to the context in which their ministers operate, they will avoid crossing the line into party political support. Such transgression undermines one of the central tenets of the apolitical British civil service, dating back to the time of Northcote–Trevelyan. That said, there have been several examples of ministers, both at Cabinet and junior ministerial level, who have been so impressed by, and attached to, their private secretaries that they have taken them with them when they have been promoted or moved department. However, that does not, in itself, imply that the individual private secretaries have become politicised.

In addition, the relationship between the private offices of the Prime Minister and the Chancellor of the Exchequer is always critical because of the central role of government spending in politics and, therefore, the power of the Chancellor. The tensions between Prime Ministers and Chancellors (such as those between Callaghan and Healey, Thatcher and Lawson or Blair and Brown) were often played out by their respective private offices. Solutions to political tensions between No. 10 and No. 11 were often brokered by the relevant private secretaries.

However, despite the importance of private secretaries in departments, it is those within the Prime Minister's private office who play

---

[*]   Arabella Warburton (c. 1955–). Anji Hunter (1955–); assistant to Tony Blair in opposition 1987–97; head of government relations 1997–2001. Sue Nye (1955–). Kate Fall (1967–).

the most significant and most consequential roles of any Whitehall private office. Clearly, No. 10 has the highest profile and so, obviously, regularly attracts some of the most talented officials from across the civil service. It is also of a qualitatively different nature, being far larger than any other Whitehall private office. Only the private office of the Chancellor of the Exchequer, and then only at some specific points in history (such as during the financial crash of 2008–09), has ever had anything near approaching the power or influence that the No. 10 private office maintains.

There have been some occasions, such as under Prime Ministers Heath and Blair, when the idea of transforming the office of the Prime Minister into a self-standing government department was considered (see Chapters 6 and 9). Some of Heath's advisers in opposition urged him to do this, but he decided instead to retain the existing small, high-powered unit around him. Blair, too, having toyed with other configurations, was eventually not convinced that the upheaval it would cause would be worth the benefits it might bring.[13] Despite the accretion of power within No. 10, the British system of government remains a system of Cabinet government, not a presidential system as occurs, for example, in the USA or France where the presidential offices are far larger than that of the UK Prime Minister.

The principal private secretary to the Prime Minister is the most senior private secretary in Whitehall. In the period from the Second World War until 2020, there have been thirty incumbents.[14] The post of principal private secretary had never been held by a woman until Rishi Sunak became Prime Minister in 2022, underlining the fact that, despite the advance in gender diversity within Whitehall over the past quarter of a century, No. 10 has often remained more traditional in its appointments policy and practice. Indeed, it was not even until 1989 that the first female private secretary (Caroline Slocock) was appointed at No. 10, a decade after the first female Prime Minister.[15] Slocock was told that, prior to her appointment, there was a belief in No. 10 that Margaret Thatcher did not want women appointed to the private office and that 'Whitehall had been discouraged from putting them forward'.[16] Whether that was a true reflection of Thatcher's views on women at No. 10 is not clear, but Slocock's appointment broke the dam and she was the first of many female private secretaries appointed in the following thirty years.

From 1945 to 2024, there were thirty holders of the post of principal private secretary to the Prime Minister, one of whom (Heywood) served for two separate spells. The following table lists those thirty civil servants, noting their university education and the department from which they came, their age on appointment and their next position on leaving No. 10. It also summarises their experience after leaving No. 10. From this information, it is possible to draw some general observations of those people who have held office, since the Second World War, as the most important private secretary in the United Kingdom.

Principal private secretaries to the Prime Minister 1945–2024[17]

Name	Period in No. 10	University	Home department	Age on arrival	Next posting	Prior experience		
						As private secretary	In Treasury	In No. 10
Leslie Rowan	1945–47	Cambridge	Treasury	37	Second secretary, Treasury	Yes	Yes	Yes
Laurence Helsby	1947–50	Oxford	Treasury	39	Deputy secretary, Ministry of Food	No	Yes	No
Denis Rickett	1950–51	Oxford	Cabinet Office	43	Washington embassy	Yes	Yes	No
David Pitblado	1951–56 (1951–55 joint)	Cambridge	Treasury	39	Treasury	Yes	Yes	No
John Colville	1951–55 (joint)	Cambridge	Foreign Office	36	Private sector	Yes	No	Yes

Freddie Bishop	1956–59	London	Cabinet Office	40	Deputy secretary, Cabinet Office	Yes	No	No
Timothy Bligh	1959–64	Oxford	Treasury	41	Private sector	No	Yes	No
Derek Mitchell	1964–66	Oxford	Treasury	42	Deputy secretary, Department of Economic Affairs	Yes	Yes	No
Michael Halls	1966–70	King's College London	Board of Trade	51	Died in post	Yes	No	No
Alexander Isserlis	1970	Oxford	Ministry of Housing and Local Government	47	Assistant secretary, Home Office	Yes	No	No
Robert Armstrong	1970–75	Oxford	Treasury	43	Deputy secretary, Home Office	Yes	Yes	No
Kenneth Stowe	1975–79	Oxford	Department of Health and Social Security	47	Permanent Secretary, Northern Ireland Office	No	No	No
Clive Whitmore	1979–82	Cambridge	Ministry of Defence	44	Deputy secretary, Ministry of Defence	Yes	No	No
Robin Butler	1982–85	Oxford	Treasury	44	Second Permanent Secretary, Treasury	Yes	Yes	Yes
Nigel Wicks	1985–88	Cambridge	Treasury	45	Second Permanent Secretary, Treasury	Yes	Yes	Yes
Andrew Turnbull	1988–92	Cambridge	Treasury	43	Deputy secretary, Treasury	Yes	Yes	Yes
Alex Allan	1992–97	Cambridge	Treasury	41	High commissioner, Australia	Yes	Yes	No
John Holmes	1997–99	Oxford	Foreign Office	46	Ambassador to Portugal	Yes	No	No
Jeremy Heywood	1999–2003	Oxford	Treasury	37	Private sector	Yes	Yes	Yes
Ivan Rogers	2003–06	Oxford	Treasury	43	Private sector	Yes	Yes	No
Oliver Robbins	2006–07	Oxford	Treasury	31	Director, Cabinet Office	No	Yes	No
Tom Scholar	2007–08	Cambridge	Treasury	38	Deputy secretary, Treasury	Yes	Yes	No
Jeremy Heywood	2008–10	Oxford	Treasury	46	Permanent Secretary, No. 10	Yes	Yes	Yes
James Bowler	2010–11	Oxford	Treasury	40	Director, Treasury	Yes	Yes	No
Chris Martin	2011–15	Bristol	Treasury	37	Died in post	Yes	Yes	No
Simon Case	2016–17	Cambridge	Cabinet Office	37	Director general, Department for Exiting the European Union	Yes	No	Yes
Peter Hill	2017–19	N/A	Foreign Office	N/A	Foreign Office	Yes	No	No
Martin Reynolds	2019–22	Cambridge	Foreign Office	49	N/A	Yes	No	No
Peter Wilson	2022	Oxford	Foreign Office	53	N/A	Yes	No	No
Nick Catsaras	2022	N/A	Foreign Office	N/A	Foreign Office	Yes	No	No
Elizabeth Perelman	2022–	Cambridge	Treasury	42	N/A	Yes	Yes	No

In summary, over the past half-century, the background of the most senior official adviser to the Prime Minister has had a relatively narrow profile. He (and there has only been one 'she' – the current incumbent) was likely to have been Oxbridge educated (89 per cent). The median age on arrival in post was forty-two. Indeed, apart from three holders of the post (Halls, Robbins and Wilson), every principal private secretary to the Prime Minister was, on taking up post, between thirty-seven and forty-nine. Over the past three quarters of a century, the average length of stay in post was 2.7 years. No fewer than twenty-six out the thirty holders of the post (87 per cent) had previously served in a private office, and nineteen of them (63 per cent) were either Treasury officials or had worked in the Treasury at some stage in their career. Indeed, nearly all of the men who held the most senior post in No. 10 had previous experience of working in No. 10, in the Treasury or as a private secretary. Only one of them, Kenneth Stowe, arrived in Downing Street with none of those three critical experiences. Ironically, that was the very argument Stowe made to Wilson as to why he was not a good choice for the job, and yet those were the same reasons why Wilson wanted him to take on the role.[18*] So, the 'gene pool' for this critical civil service posting has remained consistently narrow over the period covered by this book and beyond. Yet, by all accounts and with few exceptions, the quality of the people appointed has been very high. The testimonies of most Prime Ministers in their memoirs confirm this.

With the massive changes that have happened in technology and communications, can the private office still play the comprehensive co-ordinating role acting as the junction box of government that it

---

* Stowe had working-class origins in Dagenham, east London, which undoubtedly endeared him to Wilson.

has done in the past? In the current media-driven world, does the traditional private office, staffed almost entirely by impartial civil servants, still have the same role to play? If so, how does it need to adapt? Can the traditional model still support ministers who may be more politically driven than some of their predecessors? How might private offices adapt to these new challenges? Can the private office and the civil servants who are the private secretaries of today still play the multi-faceted role of Leporello and Mephistopheles, identified and praised by Denis Healey over fifty years ago?

3

GENESIS OF AN INSTITUTION: THE ORIGINS AND GROWTH OF PRIVATE OFFICE

It is not entirely clear when the terms 'private office' and 'private secretary' were first used. In their work on the history of prime ministerial aides, Andrew Blick and George Jones comment that it was only in the 1920s that the career officials who were the private secretaries were first collectively known widely as 'the private office'.[1] The concept, though, is not a new one and has its genesis in the late seventeenth and early eighteenth centuries, when the scope of government and the associated workload of government ministers increased, leading, in turn, to a requirement for more efficient support systems. As government grew, so did the need to manage the wider administrative processes more effectively and systematically, and not just in terms of raising revenue, a core function of government.

The title 'private secretary' has a far longer provenance than the term 'private office' but an equally imprecise origin. Ministers often employed 'clerks' to manage their business and such officials best represented the origins of the modern private secretary. The first references to anybody akin to the private secretary are perhaps those described by Samuel Pepys* in his diary. From 1660, when he was appointed as Secretary to the Admiralty, Pepys often referred to his loyal member of staff William Hewer,† whom he employed as his servant and clerk in the same year. Hewer accompanied Pepys on travels, carried out administrative tasks and supported him on much official and personal business. After Pepys's death, Hewer was even the executor of his will.² (In something of a repeat of history, some 300 years later, Robert Armstrong, who had been Edward Heath's loyal and devoted private secretary, also acted as executor for the former Prime Minister's will after his death in 2005.)

Hewer, though, as well as being clerk to Pepys, had political ambitions of his own and, in later life he too became a successful politician, becoming an MP. In the pre-Northcote–Trevelyan era, many private secretaries would have been given jobs on account of their political loyalty to their patron. This was therefore a career path that the early 'private secretaries' could follow, given it was before the days of the non-party political civil service.

Some sixty years after Pepys, Sir Robert Walpole,‡ generally acknowledged as the first Prime Minister, was also the first to have an official designated as his secretary. However, according to Blick and Jones, 'the precise genesis of the role of private secretary to the Prime Minister is uncertain'.³ They argue that only from the premiership of Henry Pelham (who became Prime Minister in 1743) onwards is it 'possible to identify those individuals who might be termed a Prime Minister's private secretary'.⁴ Moreover, they highlight that 'unlike his successors, Walpole did not have a private secretary attached to him in his capacity as First Lord of the Treasury. But

---

*   Samuel Pepys (1633–1703); naval administrator and diarist.
†   William Hewer (1642–1715); clerk to Samuel Pepys; MP for Yarmouth, Isle of Wight, 1685–89.
‡   Sir Robert Walpole (1676–1745); Prime Minister and Chancellor of the Exchequer 1721–42.

debate exists about whether Henry Bilson-Legge supported him in his role as emergent Prime Minister.[5] There is a strong argument to be made that Bilson-Legge* was, in fact, the first official who was consistently referred to as a ministerial private secretary. Walpole served as premier from 1721 to 1742 and Bilson-Legge appears to have served the Prime Minister in that role for three years from 1736 to 1739, after which point Walpole made him a minister.[6] Today, there is a painting of Bilson-Legge, sitting alongside Walpole, displayed in the Cabinet Office meeting room which was for many years the location of the weekly Wednesday morning meeting of all departmental Permanent Secretaries. Given that many Whitehall Permanent Secretaries today would have been private secretaries earlier in their civil service careers, it is fitting that the painting is located where it is. However, the delineation in Pepys's and Walpole's time between political activities and administrative functions was not nearly as precise as it was to become. Private secretaries themselves often went on to have subsequent political careers. Bilson-Legge, like Pepys's clerk Hewer before him, became a Member of Parliament and later served three separate terms as Chancellor of the Exchequer. Similarly, Edmund Burke,[†] who would later achieve great fame as a pamphleteer, polemicist and politician, originally achieved notice as a private secretary. He was private secretary to the Whig Prime Minister Lord Rockingham and 'an astonishing sequence of events over a few months in 1765 saw Burke appointed as Rockingham's private secretary, Rockingham made prime minister and Burke himself elected to Parliament'.[7] Rockingham was briefly Prime Minister for a year from 1765 to 1766, and Burke was

---

*   Sir Henry Bilson-Legge (1708–64); private secretary to Robert Walpole 1736–39, later Chancellor of the Exchequer.

†   Edmund Burke (1729–97); philosopher and politician; MP and private secretary to the Prime Minister (the Marquess of Rockingham).

his principal adviser and was especially influential on tax matters. Rockingham lost office but returned to No. 10 in March 1782 and made Burke a minister. Burke was devastated when Rockingham died in office only three months after becoming Prime Minister for the second time. Burke's ease of movement between being a private secretary, an MP and then a minister again showed the fluidity that existed in the days prior to the emergence in the nineteenth century of the party politically neutral civil service.

By the late eighteenth century, the office of the Prime Minister was firmly established and, from this point onwards, it was separate from the office of the Chancellor of the Exchequer, though some Prime Ministers did later combine the two roles. However, even after 1854 when Northcote–Trevelyan laid the foundations of the non-party political civil service, many private secretaries continued to be appointed on the basis of patronage. Stafford Northcote[*] himself had been private secretary to Gladstone when the latter was president of the Board of Trade, between 1843 and 1845. However, Northcote too became a politician and ended up on the opposite side of the House of Commons from Gladstone, as Chancellor of the Exchequer in Disraeli's second government of 1874–80.

Gladstone expanded the number of private secretaries employed at No. 10, partly because, during some of his premiership, he 'foolishly doubled up' the job of Prime Minister and Chancellor of the Exchequer and so his workload was exhausting.[8] In 1861, he appointed Algernon West[†] as his private secretary. West was 'reputedly the last Civil Service recruit never to have taken an examination of any kind', and he worked for Gladstone in and out of government

---

[*] Stafford Northcote (1818–87); joint author, with Charles Trevelyan, of the Northcote–Trevelyan report. Later MP and Chancellor of the Exchequer 1874–80; created Earl of Iddesleigh 1885.

[†] Sir Algernon West (1832–1921); private secretary to William Gladstone 1861–94.

from 1861 to 1894.[9] West had dropped out of university and, in 1851, aged nineteen, was offered a job in the civil service in the Admiralty. He later became private secretary to the Secretary of State for India and then Gladstone asked him to become his private secretary. West recalled his interview for the post with the Grand Old Man as follows:

I was kindly received in the hall [of Gladstone's home at 11 Carlton House Terrace] by Mrs Gladstone, who at once ushered me into Mr Gladstone's library, and I then had my first interview with him. He was sitting, as I see him now, at his writing-table, wearing a dark frock-coat, with a flower in his buttonhole; a pair of brown trousers with a dark stripe down them, after the fashion of twenty years earlier; a somewhat disordered neckcloth and large collar ... He was surrounded with a mass of accumulated correspondence, which added to my involuntary awe in approaching him; but he at once in a flattering way asked me to be his Private Secretary. I cannot describe the delight with which I accepted his offer.[10]

The scrutiny of West before getting such a senior post working with the Prime Minister appears to have been limited and minimal – based more on patronage and personal recommendation rather than competitive interview. West, though, proceeded to serve Gladstone in different roles during a period of some thirty-three years, both as private secretary when Gladstone was Prime Minister but also when he was in opposition. West became chairman of the Inland Revenue, but in 1892, he agreed to return to No. 10 for a final time at the start of Gladstone's fourth term as Prime Minister. Having been chairman of the Inland Review, 'it would clearly have been impossible for West merely to resume his old post of Private Secretary ... Gladstone was desirous that it should be known that West was his chief of staff, and a notice to this effect was thereupon duly inserted in the *Pall Mall Gazette*.'[11] That was some 100 years before the job title and role of 'chief of staff to the Prime Minister' was finally firmly established when Tony Blair appointed Jonathan Powell to the role (see Chapter 9). Gladstone also appointed his son Herbert as one of his private secretaries, for a brief period, underlining that he was not as committed to free and fair competition as he might have made out. (Gladstone's son later went into politics and rose to be Liberal Home Secretary between 1905 and 1910.) The relative inefficiency of the administrative system then in operation was perhaps best illustrated by the fact that, as late as the 1870s, Gladstone was said to be doing his own correspondence. In the words of his biographer Roy Jenkins, 'Gladstone kept no secretary during the second half of the 1870s. This meant that he spent much of his time grappling with and complaining about the "chaos" created by his incoming correspondence.'[12]

By contrast, Disraeli relied, throughout most of his political career, on just one loyal private secretary – Montagu Corry. Corry became a combination of friend, aide, confidant and political adviser. Disraeli had first met Corry when the latter was only twenty-seven and was apparently impressed by, among other things, his dancing skills: 'Recognising his qualities and beguiled by his attractive personality, it was not long before Disraeli – still susceptible as always to the charm of handsome men younger than himself – asked him to become his private secretary, a position he was to occupy, as a lifelong bachelor, until his master's death.'[13]

Corry took up his duties in 1866 and 'in a very short time the relations between the two men had become of the most intimate and confidential character, and so they remained until Disraeli's death fifteen years later'.[14] Disraeli would undoubtedly not have been the effective Prime Minister he was without the contribution played by Corry who was, at least in part, responsible for negotiating the successful outcome of the Treaty of Berlin in 1878, one of Disraeli's most notable achievements. This included negotiations behind the scenes with Otto von Bismarck. It also included providing considerable support at the conference to the ailing Disraeli who, by then aged seventy-four, was 'constantly ill and hobbled about on the arm of Monty Corry'.[15]

What precisely was Disraeli's relationship with Corry, and how close were they? Some commentators have even suggested that there might have been a sexual relationship between the two men. However, there is no real evidence of this. What is clear though is that Corry had absolute loyalty to Disraeli and that he 'was the ideal private secretary – [in that] he never wanted anything for himself, and he was always content to remain behind the scenes. He exercised enormous power, but he never made the least parade of it.'[16] For example, Corry was even said to have vetted potential Conservative parliamentary candidates on Disraeli's behalf.

When Disraeli finally left office, he 'shocked the sticklers for precedent' by asking the queen to give Corry a peerage, which she duly agreed.[17] Queen Victoria had enormous affection for both Disraeli and Corry. As late as 1900, nineteen years after the death of Disraeli and less than a year until Victoria died, it was to Corry (by now ennobled as Lord Rowton) that Victoria would turn and ask him to express her concerns over foreign policy to the then Prime Minister, Lord Salisbury. Corry's peerage was unprecedented and remained the only example of a private secretary to the Prime Minister being given a peerage solely on account of service in No. 10

until 1963, when John Wyndham was given a peerage by Harold Macmillan. Later, in 2000, Charles Powell was awarded a peerage partly in recognition of his service as a private secretary, although, in Powell's case, it was ten years after Margaret Thatcher had left office.

By the turn of the twentieth century, the post of private secretary to the Prime Minister was firmly established, as was the same role in supporting other Cabinet ministers. The existence of the modern-day system of Cabinet government dates from the First World War and was the brainchild of David Lloyd George, who became Prime Minister in 1916. He was determined to create a more effective mechanism for decision-making and managing government business, in support of the war effort. That system was introduced by the first Cabinet Secretary Sir Maurice Hankey.[18]* The Cabinet Office itself was established in December 1916 and the War Cabinet first met on 9 December in that year. It had five full members and four others in attendance with Hankey as secretary and, from the outset, operated with formal agendas and minutes of proceedings.[19]

In Lloyd George's first Cabinet of his coalition (which lasted from 1916 until 1922), there were twenty-two members, each of whom would have had at least one member of staff or larger teams, the equivalent of the modern private office, to support them in their ministerial duties.† By way of comparison, and a century later, the 2020 Cabinet also had twenty-two full members with four others in attendance, although nowadays there are far more junior ministers.[20] Only after the First World War did the independence of the No. 10 private office became firmly established. Increasingly, the

---

* Sir Maurice Hankey (1877–1963); civil servant and first Cabinet Secretary; created Baron Hankey 1939.
† The private secretaries and other members of staff of private offices are recorded in the *British Imperial Calendar and Civil Service List*, which was published every year from 1809 until 1972, when it was replaced by the *Civil Service Yearbook and Diplomatic List*.

private secretaries were not politically aligned and the best evidence of this was that they remained in office when there was a change of Prime Minister. A. J. Sylvester* was a private secretary to the Liberal Prime Minister David Lloyd George, yet subsequently served Andrew Bonar Law and Stanley Baldwin, both Conservatives, thereby underlining his party political independence as a civil servant, despite his enormous personal regard for Lloyd George.[21] When the Prime Minister resigned in 1922, Sylvester commented that:

> I was a civil servant and, as such, could be employed in virtually any capacity. I had grown to admire and love Lloyd George … Now all this was to end. I would revert to the position of a civil servant and possibly have to leave Downing Street, with others, for undoubtedly the new Prime Minister would bring with him his own secretariat … [However,] rather to my surprise when Mr Bonar Law came to Downing Street, he asked me to remain on as one of his secretaries … I was, however, always on the best terms with the new Prime Minister and enjoyed his complete confidence.[22]

Sylvester's comments underline that it was at about this time that a critical feature of the private office emerged, namely that civil servants could, and often did, continue in post, working in the ministerial private office, regardless of the political affiliations of their minister. It was effectively the practical realisation of the principles of party political impartiality, established by Northcote–Trevelyan over half a century previously. In a similar way to Sylvester, Sir Patrick Gower served successively as principal private secretary

---

* A. J. Sylvester (1889–1989); civil servant; private secretary to the Prime Minister (Lloyd George, Bonar Law and Baldwin) 1921–23.

to Bonar Law, Ramsay MacDonald and Baldwin, although he later resigned from the civil service, becoming chief publicity officer for the Conservative Party in 1928. That caused the Labour politician Philip Snowden to ask the Prime Minister if there was 'any precedent for a civil servant who has acted as a principal private secretary to successive Prime Ministers accepting a responsible position in the headquarters of a political party'.[23] Baldwin's answer was instructive in that he said he could not recall 'any precedent for a civil servant having acted as principal private secretary to successive Prime Ministers in the past, but [that a civil servant was], of course, at liberty at any time to resign from the service and take up outside work whether commercial, professional, or political in character'.[24] Blick and Jones argue that it was not until 1929 that the convention was finally established that the private secretaries at No. 10 were career officials and therefore would continue to serve the Prime Minister even if he were of a different political party.[25]

SIR HORACE WILSON

Nevertheless, and despite this convention, there were some civil servants who were not afraid to deploy their own personal political views in helping to shape government policy and none more so than Horace Wilson.[26*] Throughout the late 1930s, Wilson became an increasingly pivotal figure and one of the most powerful advisers to successive Prime Ministers. He was a civil servant who served both Baldwin and Chamberlain, although, when he first worked at No. 10, he was not formally within the private office and took

---

* Horace Wilson (1882–1972); Permanent Secretary Department of Labour 1921–30; later chief industrial adviser to the Prime Minister (Neville Chamberlain) 1930–39; head of the home civil service 1939–42.

the unusual title of 'chief industrial adviser to the Prime Minister'. When he left No. 10, he was all-powerful and very influential. Wilson assumed what would now be called a policy advisory role, including challenging the orthodoxy of the Foreign Office.[27] As Blick and Jones highlight:

> Baldwin made Wilson his most important personal aide at No. 10 – where he had an office – in practice supplanting the Principal Private Secretary. In one account his stature was akin to that of the head of a Whitehall department, a permanent secretary to the premier, though no such title formally existed.[28]

In fact, Wilson appears to have been acting like a chief of staff, and with wide-ranging influence, some fifty years before such a post was formalised. He was, for example, central to the negotiations with Buckingham Palace over the abdication of Edward VIII, and he appears to have taken a particular dislike to Wallis Simpson, whom the king wished to marry.[29] On behalf of the Prime Minister, Wilson even 'went so far as to authorise the Home Secretary to arrange for the bugging of Edward VIII's telephone calls'.[30] And he went further still: 'Wilson was particularly influential during the abdication crisis, stoking up fears of mob riots and violence. He and Baldwin's private secretary, Tommy Dugdale, "did much delving into the gangster side of the affair; the seamy side not politic for the Prime Minister to know about".'[31]

Yet there is no evidence that anyone sought to restrain Wilson. If anything, his powers increased when Chamberlain became Prime Minister in 1937 and he became more active in foreign affairs. He was certainly more influential than the Prime Minister's official private office:

Under Chamberlain ... his role expanded yet further and it was not long before the softly spoken civil servant was recognised as the Prime Minister's closest confidant on all matters, including foreign policy. That Chamberlain trusted Wilson's judgement and relied on his counsel to an inordinate extent is clear. 'He is the most remarkable man in England. I couldn't live a day without him,' he told the art historian Kenneth Clark, who admired the civil servant's 'supple ... Jesuitical turn of mind'. Wilson's room adjoined the Prime Minister's and every day the two men would walk together in St James's Park.[32]

One critic described Wilson as being in a 'more powerful position than that held by "almost anybody since Cardinal Wolsey"'.[33] He was a strong supporter of Chamberlain's appeasement policy, at a time when the Permanent Secretary of the Foreign Office, Sir Robert Vansittart, was generally believed to be opposed to the government's strategy.[34]

Wilson, who had little policy expertise in foreign affairs (as was clear from his formal title of chief industrial adviser), had apparently expected to return to his home department, the Board of Trade, when Baldwin retired. 'In the event, Chamberlain kept him in the same wide-ranging role as he had had with Baldwin, but with an increased emphasis on foreign policy, reflecting the new Prime Minister's interests.'[35] Wilson's role would become pivotal within a year when he became Chamberlain's central source of advice on foreign policy in the run-up to the Munich crisis and was described by one close observer, Sir John Colville (who later became Churchill's most trusted private secretary), as Chamberlain's 'alter ego' without whose advice the Prime Minister rarely acted.[36] Wilson also became 'Chamberlain's confidant in political matters. For example, in April

1939 the Prime Minister discussed with him the pros and cons of bringing Churchill into the government.'[37] Wilson also sought to influence the BBC and generate support from the media for the government's appeasement strategy and became 'the person who was called upon to give advice on, and act as the Prime Minister's agent in, any matter in which Chamberlain was interested'.[38]

What is perhaps most striking about the relationship between Chamberlain and Wilson, his de facto chief of staff, is the extent to which the Prime Minister effectively delegated foreign policy to Wilson and used him as an alternative source of foreign policy advice from that offered by his Foreign Secretary, Anthony Eden, thereby effectively bypassing the Foreign Office. For example, in relation to Italy and Benito Mussolini's hostility to Eden, Wilson took it upon himself to change Foreign Office advice. 'Chamberlain wrote a personal letter to Mussolini ... [on 27 July 1937] ... Wilson made sure it was sent without Eden having a chance to comment on it, because Wilson knew that, had the Foreign Office seen the letter, it would not have been sent.'[39] This was a classic example of the most senior member of Chamberlain's private office effectively rewriting the policy of the Foreign Secretary and Foreign Office. This foreshadowed by some fifty years some of the criticisms made of Thatcher's loyal private secretary Charles Powell and the way in which he sought to influence government policy (see Chapter 7). Ironically, the criticism of Wilson was that his expertise was in industrial policy whereas he was effectively steering the government's foreign policy. In the case of Powell, and certainly at the time of the Westland affair, the criticism was that he was the Prime Minister's foreign policy adviser extending his remit into industrial policy.

When Churchill succeeded Chamberlain, he stipulated that he did not want Wilson in No. 10 ever again.[40] He was alleged to have threatened 'to make him Governor of Greenland if he ever saw him in Downing Street again'.[41*] Churchill was supported in his view of Wilson by the Deputy Prime Minister, Clement Attlee, whose view was that Wilson was a hindrance to good government:

> On entering the War Cabinet [Attlee] conducted a review of Cabinet machinery, and cut down the number of ministerial and official committees, in the process getting rid of Chamberlain's trusted adviser, Sir Horace Wilson. ('He had a hand in everything, ran everything. We got rid of him at once. It was essential.')[42]

Attlee's specific criticism of Wilson was that, within a year of joining the coalition, he had identified Wilson as 'resisting decisions reached by the coalition on [economic] planning. Indeed, [Attlee] believed that resistance to reforming the state was "not only wilful but instinctive and habitual in the ranks of higher Civil Servants".[43] He thought that Wilson was central to this blocking process, hence the need to remove him. It is perhaps a tribute to the influence wielded by Wilson over Chamberlain that he so effectively unified the Prime Minister, the Deputy Prime Minister and the incoming coalition government in their determination to get rid of Wilson as soon as Chamberlain left office.

On the day after Churchill became Prime Minister, Wilson walked into No. 10 and to the office he had occupied since 1935:

> Sitting in his chair was Churchill's henchman, Brendan Bracken. As usual, his red hair was askew and there was a malicious glint in his eye. The new Prime Minister's most loyal follower, Bracken had

---

[*] The historian Peter Hennessy believes that Churchill meant to say the Falkland Islands – a UK territory – rather than Greenland, which was then part of Denmark.

spent the last nine months intriguing shamelessly on Churchill's behalf against Chamberlain. Many people claimed to see a physical resemblance between the Irish-Australian newspaper owner and his hero. A scurrilous (and false) rumour had it that Bracken was Churchill's illegitimate son. Next to him lounged Churchill's actual offspring, Randolph. There was no mistaking whose child he was. They had come to tell Wilson to clear out.[44]

Wilson did indeed leave No. 10 that day, never to return, although he was not sacked. Churchill wanted to do so but was reluctantly persuaded otherwise by Kingsley Wood, the Chancellor of the Exchequer.[45] Wilson reverted to the Treasury as Permanent Secretary and retired two years later.

With Chamberlain and Wilson gone, the coalition government could focus on its key strategic objective of winning the war. Both Churchill and Attlee were united on the need for an effective machinery at No. 10 to organise the central civil service operation. Private office was central to that process throughout the war.

4

GOVERNING IN WAR AND PEACE: PRIVATE OFFICE 1940–64

When Winston Churchill succeeded Neville Chamberlain on 10 May 1940 following the latter's resignation, Churchill inherited the private office of his predecessor. Horace Wilson had been summarily ejected by Brendan Bracken and Randolph Churchill, and his all-purpose roving brief as adviser to the Prime Minister was abruptly ended. Winston Churchill brought no new personal staff into No. 10, as might happen nowadays. At a time when Churchill was being called on to save the nation in its hour of need, it is perhaps strange that he chose not to have any genuinely personal staff around him. He did, though, have the support of the colourful Bracken (his parliamentary private secretary) to rely on as his 'political fixer', alongside his traditional private office. Harold Macmillan said of Bracken:

> Brendan was no yes-man. Because he understood Winston's mind better than anyone, he was well able to stand up to him and to say exactly what he thought. His language could be most abusive, too, yet Churchill often took it calmly. The only way I can describe

their disagreements is to say that when the two men quarrelled, they quarrelled like husband and wife.[1]

The small private office was headed by the principal private secretary Eric Seal* with four other private secretaries – Anthony Bevir, John Peck, John Martin† and John 'Jock' Colville. Both Martin and Colville were later to serve as principal private secretary to the Prime Minister – Martin during the war years and Colville from 1951–55 during Churchill's second premiership. Colville went on to become one of Churchill's closest confidants, serving him during both his premierships, but Colville was initially somewhat unimpressed by Churchill's style and manner. Showing, perhaps understandable, loyalty to the previous Prime Minister, Colville's first comments about Churchill were that he was 'a stronger, more colourful personality than any of [his Cabinet colleagues]'.[2] However, he added that 'many of his colleagues, and most senior civil servants, regarded him with suspicion, an attitude reflected by the staff at 10 Downing Street'.[3]

Despite these early strictures, the No. 10 private office came to enjoy the camaraderie and thrill of working with Churchill. Martin described it thus:

It is all tremendously exciting, and the stimulus of the excitement seems to make up for lack of sleep … I enjoy it all enormously and have got over the complete funk with which I began. There are three of us working in the room next to the Cabinet Room – Seal,

---

* Sir Eric Seal (1898–1972); civil servant; principal private secretary to the Prime Minister (Winston Churchill) 1940–41.
† Sir John Martin (1904–91); principal private secretary to the Prime Minister (Winston Churchill) 1941–45.

Bevir and myself, while there are two younger secretaries in another room [Peck and Colville] and also Miss Watson, so we are
quite a crowd; but with the stream of phone calls and alarms and
excursions everyone is needed, particularly while the PM alter-
nates between Admiralty House (where he still lives) and No. 10.[4]

Colville too came to find working for Churchill far more stimulating
than when performing the same role for Chamberlain. Comparing
the two premiers' ways of working, Colville noted:

Chamberlain was austere, and he seldom said to me anything not
strictly related to business. At weekends he retired to Chequers,
where there was only one telephone (and that in the pantry). He
disliked being disturbed, telephonically or otherwise, at weekends or after dinner at 10 Downing Street. He never took a Private Secretary with him to Chequers; nor did he ever invite the
members of his staff to lunch or dine with Mrs Chamberlain and
himself. That was in marked contrast to Winston Churchill, who
treated his Private Secretaries as part of the family, and indeed
to Clement Attlee. Yet this austere man had such integrity, such
devotion to duty and such high ideals and standards, that if it was
at first difficult to feel affection for him it was impossible not to
feel esteem.[5]

It is remarkable to think that, at the time of the Munich crisis and in
the run-up to the outbreak of war, at weekends the Prime Minister
was unaccompanied by any of his private office team and that the
only way of contacting him was via the catering staff at Chequers.

One interesting member of the Churchill wartime private office team was Edith Watson* – although she was always referred to simply as 'Miss Watson'. As far back as 1914, she had been Bonar Law's personal secretary and was brought in to support him as Prime Minister in 1923. She remained in No. 10 for over twenty years and served six Prime Ministers. By 1945, she was given the title of private secretary for parliamentary affairs, although it was then a smaller portfolio than the formal private secretary role and the title was essentially honorific in recognition of her long service. Watson was, nevertheless, the only woman to have held the title of 'private secretary' until Caroline Slocock was appointed as private secretary for home affairs in 1989. In January 1940, Colville recorded in his diary that 'Miss Watson, who had been a typist at No. 10 since the days of Lloyd George and Bonar Law, was promoted to the rank of Private Secretary and dealt conscientiously and well with the preparation of replies to Parliamentary Questions'.[6] He added, somewhat patronisingly, that while she was 'not over-endowed with brain-power and her incurable tendency to make a fuss could be exasperating', she did, however, have considerable political acumen in predicting over twenty years before it happened that Lord Dunglass (Alec Douglas-Home) would become Prime Minister one day.[7]

By all accounts, not least those of Martin and Colville, the private office at No. 10 operated well in wartime. However, when the Labour Party won the 1945 general election by a landslide, some members of Churchill's private office might have had some concerns about whether the new Prime Minister would accept his predecessor's team. If so, such forebodings were entirely misplaced. Clement Attlee was a firm believer in the integrity and impartiality of the civil service. So as Attlee began his premiership, he made it very

---

* Edith Watson (c.1895–1953); personal secretary to Andrew Bonar Law 1914–23; personal and private secretary, No. 10, 1923–45.

clear that, while his policies were far removed from Churchill's, he was a supporter of the civil service and of the private office which he inherited. Colville, who moved seamlessly from being Churchill's private secretary to serving Attlee, praised the new Prime Minister's 'virtues of total honesty, quickness, efficiency and common sense'.[8] A more recent commentator has described the transition from Churchill to Attlee as follows:

> As Attlee took the helm, all of the prime-ministerial staff noticed a great contrast in approach by the new chief. Much of the glamour, dynamism and excitement were now missing, but there were compensations in more normal hours and swifter decisions. Attlee once said that 'a sense of urgency, of dispatch' was a central quality needed in a Prime Minister, and he lived up to that precept. The change from Churchill's more colourful, discursive approach was noticed immediately by Downing Street secretary Marian Holmes, who wrote in her diary for 1 August: 'Working for the new PM is very different … No conversation or pleasantries, wit or capricious behaviour. Just staccato orders. Perfectly polite and I am sure he is a good Christian gentleman. But it is the difference between champagne and water.'[9]

No doubt many of Attlee's private office staff appreciated his more effective ways of working and the benefits for what would now be called their 'work–life balance'.

The post-war private office of the Prime Minister began to resemble more closely its modern-day equivalent, albeit on a smaller scale. It was headed by a career civil servant, Leslie Rowan, who had served both Churchill and then Attlee after the latter's victory in the 1945 general election, thus underlining the political neutrality of the role. As principal private secretary, Rowan was supported by private secretaries who held separate portfolios, covering foreign, economic and parliamentary affairs, and the office reported formally to the Cabinet Secretary, Sir Edward Bridges, who had served in that role since 1938. The staff were all employed as civil servants, although the press secretary, Francis Williams, was a known Labour supporter but one who had served in the Ministry of Information throughout the war, when 'the boundaries between the Civil Service and the outside world became more porous'.[10]

Attlee, notoriously, had little interest in the communications side of his role. This was in stark contrast to modern-day politics and the No. 10 'spin machine'. Williams wanted to change that, if only to a limited extent. He wanted to install a telex machine to get the most up-to-date news from around the world. Attlee was unimpressed by the idea until Williams pointed out that it would provide up-to-date cricket scores. Williams got his machine.

Elsewhere in Whitehall, Labour politicians worked extremely well alongside their private offices. For example, Hugh Gaitskell, who became Chancellor of the Exchequer at the end of the Attlee premiership, said how sad he was to be leaving his private office and his principal private secretary, William Armstrong, who later became head of the home civil service. Speaking of his private office, Gaitskell commented, 'Civil Servants in this country, thank goodness, have to be hardened to changing Governments and changing Ministers. It is rather remarkable what close and intimate relations one manages to develop despite this.'[11]

The No. 10 private office under Attlee remained relatively small, and it continued that way when Churchill returned to office in 1951. Subsequently, there was a period of a joint principal private secretaryship between David Pitblado,* who had served at the end of the Attlee premiership, together with Colville, Churchill's favoured private secretary, who had worked for him in the war and who Churchill wanted to be his sole principal private secretary.

The compromise of the joint role, proposed by Bridges (by now head of the home civil service), worked well, and in Colville's words, 'I became a frequent channel of [Churchill's] communication with other Ministers, many of whom I already knew well. Pitblado for his part handled with exemplary skill the Treasury, the Civil Service and economic affairs.'[12] The Colville–Pitblado experience was the only time when the post of the principal private secretary to the Prime Minister was held jointly, and the arrangement appeared to have been successful, especially during the period in 1953 when Churchill suffered a stroke which left him substantially incapacitated. It is arguable that Colville and Pitblado, working alongside some political players, including Churchill's son-in-law Christopher Soames, kept the government of the country going and acted as surrogates for the Prime Minister.[13]

Churchill had, by the summer of 1953, been Prime Minister again for almost two years. However, he was aged seventy-nine and his lifestyle was certainly such that it would have been unsurprising were he to suffer a stroke, a heart attack or worse. But what was striking, certainly by today's standards, was the way in which his private office and close political advisers sought, and managed, to keep his condition private from the media. On 23 June 1953, after

---

*   David Pitblado (1912–97); civil servant; principal private secretary to the Prime Minister (Clement Attlee) 1951; joint principal private secretary to the Prime Minister (Winston Churchill) 1951–55; principal private secretary to the Prime Minister (Anthony Eden) 1956; Permanent Secretary Ministry of Power 1966–69, Ministry of Technology 1969–70 and civil service department 1970–71; comptroller and auditor general 1971–76.

a dinner for the Italian Prime Minister, Churchill suffered a very severe stroke. As Roy Jenkins notes, 'The Italians and others were quietly hustled away. The next day he managed a sadly drooping nominal chairmanship of a Cabinet. Then he departed for Chartwell, where he remained for a full month.'[14]

In the words of Martin Gilbert, Churchill's biographer:

> During the drive to Chartwell, Churchill gave Jock Colville 'strict orders not to let it be known that he was temporarily incapacitated and to ensure that the administration continued to function as if he were in full control'. By the evening, however, as Colville later recalled, 'his physical powers had deteriorated considerably and, if I remember right, he was more or less paralysed in the whole of his left side. By the following day, Friday, he was almost completely paralysed.' Lord Moran [Churchill's doctor] was so alarmed when he came down to Chartwell later that day that he told Colville 'he did not think the Prime Minister could possibly live over the weekend'.[15]

And yet, remarkably, Churchill did survive and over the coming days his health stabilised and then began slowly to improve. Colville followed to the letter Churchill's instructions that the nature and severity of his illness should be concealed from all but a small number of trusted friends, family and very close advisers, including his private office. It is remarkable that the ruse worked as well as it did, and Churchill recovered after a month's absence. Jenkins explains:

> Colville stayed at Chartwell for two weeks, and also on the spot and in more or less constant attendance were Clementine [Churchill's

wife], Moran, Christopher and Mary Soames [Churchill's son-in-law and daughter respectively], two secretaries for typing and dictation (although for once there was not much of the latter) and soon a couple of nurses.[16]

However, what Churchill did not know was that Colville, as well as doing the Prime Minister's bidding in ensuring his illness remained a secret – and certainly from Fleet Street – was also making other contingency plans. Had Churchill died, there would have been an immediate question as to who would be his successor as Prime Minister. The obvious choice was the Foreign Secretary and de facto Deputy Prime Minister, Anthony Eden. However, Colville knew that Eden was at that time in the United States, undergoing abdominal surgery and so would have been unable to take over immediately as Prime Minister. Colville accordingly contacted Tommy Lascelles, the Queen's private secretary, to put contingency plans in place for Churchill's death:

> In defiance of the Prime Minister's orders, I rang up Sir Alan [known as Tommy] Lascelles ... on the telephone on the scrambler and told him what had happened. I said that the Queen must be prepared, so shortly after her Coronation, to be faced with the necessity of appointing a new Prime Minister on Monday morning.[17]

Colville was here exercising the vital constitutional role of the No. 10 private office – as part of the so-called golden triangle* of advisers (the principal private secretary to the Prime Minister, the

---

* The 'golden triangle' is Peter Hennessy's phrase.

monarch's private secretary and the Cabinet Secretary – then Sir Norman Brook) to prepare for the handling of a possible change of Prime Minister.[18] They concocted a contingency plan whereby Lord Salisbury would take over the premiership, on a temporary basis, until Eden was well enough to take over as Prime Minister. Yet, remarkably, it was not necessary. Churchill recovered within a month or so, and the whole episode was kept hidden from the press and the wider world.

Martin Gilbert summarised this remarkable episode of British political history thus:

> The speed with which Churchill was able to regain his grasp of events, and to attend to the problems which were most pressing and urgent, was remarkable. In this, he was helped by the discretion and skill of three men, his Principal Private Secretaries, Jock Colville and David Pitblado, and his son-in-law Christopher Soames. It was the 33-year-old Soames, the only Member of Parliament of the three who, quite unobtrusively, took a hundred decisions in Churchill's name, without once breaching the trust which such a heavy responsibility involved.[19]

The contingency plan worked. Churchill survived and retired almost two years later, to be replaced by Eden, who in 1955 finally achieved the job of Prime Minister which he had so long coveted. Churchill was to live for a further ten years.

Following Eden's brief premiership, Harold Macmillan became Prime Minister in January 1957, and he was determined to set a new direction. He wanted his small private office to be the nucleus for overseeing his government's policies and priorities. Under Macmillan, a number of powerful private secretaries began to emerge and have more direct influence over the policy agenda, which Macmillan appears to have encouraged. These included Freddie Bishop,* who had previously served Eden first as foreign affairs private secretary and then as principal private secretary in 1956, and Philip de Zulueta,† who was foreign affairs private secretary from 1956 until 1964. De Zulueta became deeply involved in foreign policy-making and, in a similar way to Charles Powell who held the same post some thirty years later, became 'over-identified' with Macmillan such that, like Colville before him and Powell after him, he resigned from the civil service on leaving No. 10.[20]

In addition, Macmillan broke with the then well-established principle that the private office should contain only permanent civil servants by appointing his friend John Wyndham,‡ with whom he had worked during the war. Wyndham took the title 'political and personal private secretary'. It was the equivalent of a modern special adviser role and Wyndham was richly rewarded in 1963 when Macmillan's 'resignation honours list had raised eyebrows with – shades of Disraeli and Monty Corry – its peerage for John Wyndham'.[21] So, despite the trend towards an impartial private office staffed by civil servants, as established during the immediate post-war years, Macmillan certainly favoured either loyal private secretaries who were close to him such as Bishop and, to a greater degree, de Zulueta or, in the case of Wyndham, openly political appointees. It was, in some ways, a taste of what was to come with the appointment by Harold Wilson of the first formal special advisers.

Wyndham was a key figure in the private office. He had previously

---

* Freddie Bishop (1915–2005); civil servant; private secretary (foreign affairs) to the Prime Minister 1955–56; principal private secretary to the Prime Minister (Anthony Eden and Harold Macmillan) 1956–59.

† Philip de Zulueta (1925–89); civil servant; private secretary (foreign affairs) to the Prime Minister (Anthony Eden, Harold Macmillan and Alec Douglas-Home) 1956–64.

‡ John Wyndham (1920–72); political and personal private secretary to the Prime Minister 1957–63; created Baron Leconfield and Egremont 1963.

been a civil servant and had known the new Prime Minister since he served as his private secretary, aged only twenty, when Macmillan was parliamentary secretary in the Ministry of Supply. Wyndham moved with Macmillan as his private secretary when the latter transferred to the Colonial Office in an early but rare example of a minister insisting on taking his private secretary to his new department. In 1943, Macmillan was posted to Algeria as the minister resident at Allied Force Headquarters in Algiers. Again, Wyndham went with his boss. Wyndham left the civil service after the war and joined the Conservative Research Department. Then, in 1957, some four months after Macmillan became Prime Minister, he wrote to Wyndham, enquiring if he would be 'willing to rejoin the old firm'.[22] Macmillan expressed his personal doubt that his administration would succeed, but 'having managed to pull the old mare through the brook and somehow got to the other side with the same jockey up', he was taking the plunge to ask Wyndham for his service once more: 'I know our team at No. 10 would like very much to have you with them.'[23]

Wyndham described this letter, unsurprisingly, as 'one of the most remarkable letters I have ever received'.[24] The Prime Minister was confessing that he would not have survived in office for more than a few months and was now pleading with his young friend to return to work for him. Wyndham took the job and remained by Macmillan's side until he left office six years later.

Wyndham provides a detailed explanation of how the No. 10 private office operated in the early days of the Macmillan government. It is remarkable as his description of the work patterns are so similar to those described by Andrew Turnbull, who some twenty years later was to serve as Margaret Thatcher's private secretary (see Chapter 7). In many ways, and notwithstanding the increase in material dealt with electronically, the system for managing government business in today's private office was shaped by Macmillan and his small team, and it now remains much as it was over sixty years ago. In Wyndham's words:

> The Prime Minister himself used to wake up early in the morning and straight away he would attack a huge box of papers consisting of submissions put up to him by his private secretaries the night before. The box had stood on a table in the private secretaries' room the day before, and the private secretaries during that day had dropped their submissions into it. As the day wore on, the box got fuller. The great crime was not to know what was in the box. The box was closed at the end of business by the private secretary on late duty and given to a messenger, who then put it in the Prime Minister's bedroom.
>
> When we came in next morning the box would be back downstairs with succinct comments by the Prime Minister on each submission. We all got to know Mr Macmillan so well that the shortest of notes by him would often suffice. For example: 'Tell him No. H.M.'[25]

Inevitably, the leeway that Macmillan gave to his small team of trusted private secretaries in interpreting his scant comments ran the risk of politicisation. In particular, Macmillan's principal private secretaries were very close to him. When Freddie Bishop left private office in 1959 and returned to the Cabinet Office, his replacement, Tim Bligh, became even closer to Macmillan and undoubtedly was to cross the boundary between a trusted principal private secretary and a politicised supporter of the Prime Minister.

For example, Bligh was not averse to briefing the media himself directly.[26] He was involved in the aftermath of the Profumo affair of 1963. He personally carried out the security interview with John Profumo* when the latter finally confessed to having had an affair with a model, Christine Keeler, at the same time as she had been having a relationship with the Russian naval attaché Yevgeny Ivanov.[27] While it was not improper for a civil servant to have carried out this interview, the fact that the Prime Minister entrusted the task to Bligh is testament to his remarkable high standing, influence and discretion. In February 1963, Bligh also briefed the media, notably the *News of the World*, about the Profumo affair.[28]

Such tasks nowadays would not be carried out by a private secretary to the Prime Minister, however senior. Bligh effectively played four separate roles at the same time: principal private secretary and senior adviser to the Prime Minister; adviser on ethics and propriety; security investigator; and press officer. His political briefings for the Prime Minister in 1962 about who to sack in Macmillan's so-called Night of the Long Knives ministerial reshuffle – regarded as one of the most brutal Cabinet reorganisations in British political history – were further evidence, if needed, of his lack of impartiality.[29] Bligh appears to have crossed the line of political impartiality for any private secretary, from being a loyal and robust defender of the government and government policy to being a cheerleader for the Prime Minister as a politician.

The feeling that the No. 10 operation may, to some extent at least, have been politicised had a profound effect on the Labour opposition. Harold Wilson, based on his views dating back to his wartime service in the British administration system, was known to be sceptical about the civil service and, in particular, the dominance of the

---

* John Profumo (1915–2006); Secretary of State for War 1960–63.

Treasury. He wanted to be assured that he would be fully in control of No. 10 if and when he became Prime Minister.

By the time Macmillan was replaced as Prime Minister by Sir Alec Douglas-Home in the autumn of 1963, it was obvious that there was a strong possibility that the Conservatives could lose office the following year. In recognition of this and the need for a smooth transition were Labour to come to power, the new Prime Minister, soon after he took office, established what became known as the 'Douglas-Home rules'. These rules, which exist relatively unaltered to this day, permitted opposition parties' spokespeople to meet departmental Permanent Secretaries, up to a year in advance of a general election, to discuss their plans for government should they win the election.[30] Similarly, the arrangements at No. 10 provided for the opposition leader's staff to meet No. 10 staff, and so Wilson had arranged for Marcia Williams to meet Alec Douglas-Home's principal private secretary, Sir Tim Bligh. The pair had several lunches and a dinner. Williams was known to have a strong scepticism about the civil service and, in particular, those civil servants in No. 10 whom she thought had either been there too long or were, in some ways, politicised.[31] Her discussions with Bligh were based on his assumption that he would be continuing in that role. Unsurprisingly, these initial talks did not go well. Bligh was very much a traditionalist and, as she later related, he had made it clear that 'the Civil Service considered that there was no place for me, or my office colleagues, at Number 10'.[32] So, as Kavanagh and Seldon observe, 'battle lines were being drawn, and the Private Office was not considered an appropriate base for her'.[33]

Williams reported Bligh's views back to Wilson and they jointly decided 'to disagree with Sir Timothy'.[34] She later described Bligh as 'elegant, charming and amusing'.[35] He had also invited her to No.

10 to meet some of the Downing Street staff and insisted she have tea with all the private secretaries. She commented, 'It was a rather curious meeting. They were not the sort of men I had envisaged as serving Harold Wilson in action.'[36] For all the conviviality, it was not a meeting of minds or sympathies. To Williams, the senior echelons of the civil service at No. 10 appeared overwhelmingly male, lacking in dynamism and full of upper-middle-class officials who seemed ill at ease with a 31-year-old builder's daughter from Northampton-shire representing the potential next Prime Minister.

The prospect of Williams and Bligh working together at the heart of Wilson's government was averted when Bligh was reluctantly persuaded to step down from the role he had held since 1959. Burke Trend (the Cabinet Secretary and head of the home civil service) decided in late 1963 that it was time for Bligh to move on but not before there was a bizarre stand-off between Bligh and his chosen successor, Derek Mitchell, who had been recruited from the Treasury by Trend. Mitchell's obituary in *The Times* in 2009 recalled how Bligh had

adamantly refused to vacate his post for the position on offer. He seemed to regard himself as indispensable to the new Prime Minister, Sir Alec Douglas-Home, and even talked of staying on for the widely expected transition to a Labour government. A frustrated Mitchell ... moved into the Private Secretaries' inner room and sat at a desk opposite Bligh. While the latter despatched business and guarded access to the Prime Minister, Mitchell read novels and sometimes went to the cinema in the afternoon. This bizarre situation continued for nearly four months and was never made public.[37]

Bligh subsequently left the civil service. He attempted, unsuccessfully, to become a Conservative politician and he died relatively young. His obituary in *The Times*, in 1969, said that it was 'one of the tragedies of life that it was difficult for him to combine his strong views on the conduct of affairs with the neutral attitude which seems necessary for the civil servants under our present system.'[38]

However, the tensions – bordering on aggression – between Bligh and Mitchell meant that they undoubtedly took their eyes off the ball. They should have been properly focused – at that stage in the electoral cycle – on contingency planning for a possible transition and a change of Prime Minister. Bligh had met Marcia Williams but, for a range of reasons – class, gender, 'establishment' – had been unable to engage with her in anything approaching a constructive way to prepare for the evident possibility of a Labour government and how such a transition might be managed smoothly. When Bligh eventually, and grudgingly, exited No. 10 to hand over to Mitchell, and with the Douglas-Home rules by now in place, it is very surprising that Mitchell did not do more to seek to build bridges with the Labour leader's entourage – especially Marcia Williams. In fact, Mitchell never met Williams until after Wilson became Prime Minister.

5

REFORM AND THE ARRIVAL OF SPECIAL ADVISERS: PRIVATE OFFICE 1964–70

Between the summer of 1964 and that of 1979, the British parliamentary system and the civil service underwent a phase of political turmoil unprecedented in the post-war era. Over a period of
just fifteen years, there were six general elections, seven different
administrations, five Prime Ministers and four transitions. In 1964,
Harold Wilson's Labour Party narrowly defeated the Conservatives
under Alec Douglas-Home and Wilson entered No. 10 in October
of that year. Wilson intended to make major changes in the management of the government machinery, including the civil service.
He was the first Prime Minister systematically to bring in outsiders
to help advise his administration and expand the sources of advice
open to government. Wilson also established the most fundamental inquiry into the workings of the civil service which, in 1968,
produced the Fulton report.[1] He and his successor, Edward Heath,
focused on making changes to structures and systems to try to improve the operation of government, in the belief that they could
use greater centralisation to enhance the efficiency of Whitehall.
Wilson's second term in office, beginning with his election victory in February 1974 and concluding with his resignation two years

later in April 1976, saw a noticeable waning of his appetite for civil service reform. His successor, James Callaghan, saw his administration beset by economic difficulties and the loss of its parliamentary majority in March 1977, which left little time or energy to devote to administrative change.

This period has generated a large body of political and social literature.[2] There has also been some more specific work on the relative economic decline of the UK during this period.[3] A number of authors have examined the progress of reform within the civil service,[4] as well as examining the genesis of the role of special advisers in government, beginning with their introduction under Wilson in 1964, which represented the start of a structural change that endures to this day.[5] This period is also rich in political memoirs: Wilson published two volumes covering his terms in office as well as a book on the governance of Britain which contains his analysis of the role of private office.[6] Three major biographies of Wilson have been produced and a collection of essays reappraising his reputation was released to coincide with the centenary of his birth.[7]

In addition to the memoirs and autobiographies of his colleagues,[8] Wilson's first premiership is also notable for producing the first major modern political diarists in the form of Richard Crossman,[*] Barbara Castle[†] and Tony Benn.[‡] Between them, they published eight volumes covering this period.[9] Crossman's diaries are particularly significant for their observations on the workings of

---

[*] Richard Crossman (1907–74); MP for Coventry East (1945–74); Minister for Housing and Local Government, 1964–66; Lord President of the Council and Leader of the House of Commons 1966–68; Secretary of State for Social Services 1968–70.

[†] Barbara Castle (1910–2002); MP for Blackburn (1945–1979); Minister for Overseas Development 1964–65; Minister of Transport 1965–68; First Secretary of State and Secretary for State for Employment and Productivity 1968–70; Secretary of State for Health and Social Services 1974–76; created Baroness Castle 1990.

[‡] Anthony Benn (1925–2014); MP for Bristol South East 1950–60 and 1963–83 and for Chesterfield 1984–2001; Postmaster General 1964–66; Minister for Technology 1966–70; Secretary of State for Industry 1974–75; Secretary of State for Energy 1975–79.

the private office. Other key advisers have also written about their time working in government, one of whom, Marcia Williams (Lady Falkender), will be discussed in greater detail since her role, as Wilson's personal and political secretary, saw her rise to a position of controversial eminence within No. 10 and across Whitehall.[10] Williams was one of the first external individuals brought into Downing Street on day one of the Wilson administration and, being a powerful adviser who had the ear of the Prime Minister, frequently clashed with many of the more traditional senior male civil servants as well as other members of Wilson's staff.

Taken together, these form part of a rich seam of historical sources. The literature covering the terms in office of Wilson's successors, Heath (1970–74) and Callaghan (1976–79), is slimmer given their shorter period in office. Heath published his autobiography in 1998, and two other major biographies have been produced.[11] The record of his government, its approach to policy-making and Heath's reputation as a moderniser within Whitehall have also been analysed by a number of historians.[12] Callaghan's autobiography was released in 1987, followed, a decade later, by Kenneth Morgan's biography, which remains the only major study of his life.[13]

In the considerable upheavals from 1964 to 1979, the private office was one of the few consistent factors in Whitehall, and this gives rise to three questions. First, what was Wilson's thinking (if any) prior to his becoming Prime Minister and what was the nature of the structure and purpose of the private office during that turbulent period? Second, how did its form and function change in response to the forces acting upon it? Finally, what part did it play in the execution of government policy in relation to delivering the different Prime Ministers' policies and in respect of the machinery and structure of government?

The two dominant political figures of this period were Wilson and Heath. Although political opponents, they had a great deal in common and so comparing and contrasting their approaches to the civil service and private office are instructive. Born in the same year (1916), both were grammar schoolboys who excelled academically and attended Oxford University before seeing different types of wartime service.* They had short careers as civil servants (Wilson during the war and Heath at the Ministry of Civil Aviation following his demobilisation) and then enjoyed rapid advances up the parliamentary ranks.† They shared a strong interest in the processes of administration and the machinery of government, unmatched by the interests of any other post-war Prime Ministers. Wilson's views were shaped by his wartime experience of the civil service and his distrust of the Treasury, whereas Heath had a more abstract interest in the principles of 'modern management', including how to create conditions for greater well-informed strategic thinking by ministers.[14] Yet, as Prime Minister, neither man was particularly good at managing his immediate No. 10 private office team.

WILSON AND THE CIVIL SERVICE

Reform of the civil service was at the heart of Labour's plans to transform Whitehall into the 'powerhouse' of the new Britain Wilson wished to create once in office.[15] As has been seen, Wilson had formed strong views during his time in the 1940s as president

---

* Heath was an officer in the Royal Artillery, and Wilson was research assistant to William Beveridge and, later, was the director of economics and statistics in the Ministry of Fuel and Power.

† Wilson rose more quickly, becoming the youngest Cabinet minister of the twentieth century, aged thirty-one, when he was appointed president of the Board of Trade in September 1947, two years after entering Parliament. It took Heath longer to make his mark, becoming government Chief Whip in December 1955, aged thirty-nine, five years after he took his seat on the back benches.

of the Board of Trade on how such change could be achieved, both by reducing the overall power of the Treasury and by importing outside talent to develop policy and challenge the orthodoxy of the permanent civil service. He was heavily influenced in his views by Thomas Balogh,[*] a Hungarian émigré and economist at Balliol College, Oxford, who corresponded regularly with Wilson in the run-up to the 1964 election. Balogh's essay 'The Apotheosis of the Dilettante', which had appeared in 1959, had launched an outright attack on what he perceived as the amateurism of the civil service and the lack of access of outsiders to decision-making while advocating 'the increasing use of experts in the regular Civil Service'.[16] This particularly applied to ministers in charge of large departments who, he argued, 'must at least be armed with private offices and experts recruited from outside and dependent on the ministers'.[17]

Both Balogh and Wilson believed that Whitehall 'was excessively dominated by an upper middle-class mandarinate'[18] formed from a narrow Oxbridge clique. According to Tony Benn, Wilson charged Balogh 'with the task of planning the division of the Treasury and turning half of it into an independent Ministry for Expansion'.[19] Balogh, for his part, urged the Labour leader to consider putting a 'limited number of political appointments in the Chancellor's Private Office' to ensure that reform was carried out.[20] Balogh was also a member of the Fabian group on civil service reform, chaired by the Cambridge economist Robert Nield,[†] who later became a special adviser at the Treasury under Wilson's Labour government, and whose other members included Tony Crosland[‡] and Shirley

---

[*]   Thomas Balogh (1905–85); economist and Cabinet Office special adviser 1964–68; created Lord Balogh 1968.

[†]   Robert Neild (1924–2018); economist; economic adviser to the Treasury 1964–67.

[‡]   Anthony Crosland (1918–77); MP 1950–55 and 1959–77; Secretary of State for Education 1965–67; president of the Board of Trade 1967–69; Secretary of State for Local Government and Regional Planning 1969–70; Secretary of State for the Environment 1974–76; and Foreign Secretary 1976–77.

Williams,* together with some senior civil servants, among whom were two future permanent secretaries.[21]

In June 1964, three months before the general election, the Fabian group published *The Administrators*, calling for a root and branch overhaul of the civil service and making eight fundamental proposals for reform.[22] The main thrust of this pamphlet was that the civil service, and specifically the 2,500 civil servants who formed the most senior administrative class within it, was an elite organisation and one that was overdue for reform. One of the proposals referred to private office, arguing 'for a far greater influx of specialists into the civil service – either subject experts or political advisers', as 'ministers, especially those in charge of major departments dealing with a wide range of policy issues, may feel the need to have near them persons whose personal and political judgment, as well as expertise they trust'.[23] This could be done, they stated, by introducing

> something akin to the Continental system of ministerial *cabinets* … That is to say, a Minister would be able to make a number of outside appointments – up to say, three or four, as assistants in his private office. They would have direct access to him and all the information in the department; they would not make administrative decisions; they would be there to assist the Minister in making use of the machine to formulate policy.[24]

This represented an important shift towards constructing a new form of private office, as well as ending the monopoly of civil service advice that had existed since the foundation of the Cabinet system of government.

---

* Shirley Williams (1930–2021); general secretary of the Fabian Society 1960–64; MP 1964–79 and 1981–83; Secretary of State for Prices and Consumer Protection 1974–76; Secretary of State for Education 1976–79; created Baroness Williams 1993.

Balogh and the Fabians were not alone in identifying the Continental approach as a possible solution to countering the inertia of Whitehall. The economist and journalist Samuel Brittan* was another 'outsider' who would join the new Labour government as an adviser at the Department of Economic Affairs in 1965. In his book *The Treasury Under the Tories*, published in 1964, Brittan had argued that ministers should be provided with '*cabinets* or "brain trusts" of technical experts and political advisers, to help them challenge the assumptions underlying official advice'.[25] The establishment of the Department of Economic Affairs, on which Brittan was brought in to advise, was another keystone of Labour's plans to adjust the balance of power in Whitehall by reducing the influence of the Treasury. Under these proposals, responsibility for the long-term planning of the economy and industry would rest with the new department, while the Treasury would remain in charge of raising revenue and financial management. Wilson was deeply suspicious of the Treasury's influence and blamed 'Britain's economic failure on [its] lack of regard for expertise and training and – above all – on its supremacy over other departments'.[26]

But *The Administrators* was not without its critics. At the time, Brittan thought it was not strong enough and, more recently, historian Rodney Lowe has argued that it failed to engage the support of many of the leading Labour politicians of the time and focused too narrowly on the top echelons of the civil service dealing 'almost exclusively with the Treasury and economic policy'.[27] Some figures in the civil service also thought it was not a work of high standard.[28] Civil service reform did not feature heavily in Labour's manifesto for the 1964 general election, *The New Britain*, which spoke only

---

* Samuel Brittan (1933–2020); economist and journalist.

in general terms of the need to modernise the machinery of government by introducing 'new techniques' and 'new kinds of skill and experience', if it was to manage successfully the increasingly numerous and complex tasks of government.[29] These 'new kinds of skill and experience' would be essential to the Wilsonian vision of transforming No. 10 from a 'failed monastery' into 'a powerhouse', but, as will be seen, in terms of the private office, it too often resembled something closer to a madhouse. [30]

THE 1964 TRANSITION, MARCIA WILLIAMS AND THE 'KITCHEN CABINET'

When Labour came to power in 1964, initially the most eye-catching reforms were the first appointments of new special advisers together with changes to the departmental structure of Whitehall. Five new departments of state were created – the Department of Economic Affairs, the Ministry of Technology, the Ministry of Land and Natural Resources, the Ministry of Overseas Development and the Welsh Office. However, it is not possible to understand the handling of the 1964 transition, or the way in which Wilson and his private office subsequently operated, without understanding the role and influence of Marcia Williams (Lady Falkender).

As Wilson's personal and political secretary, Williams soon assumed a powerful and influential position for three reasons.[31] First, because she was a determined woman in the male-dominated echelons of the senior civil service, many mandarins simply did not know how to deal with her. Second, because she knew she acted with the full authority of Wilson. And third, because she deliberately set out to ruffle Whitehall feathers – something in which she succeeded.

Since 1956, Williams had been Wilson's personal secretary. In 1964, at the age of thirty-two, she also became his political secretary at No. 10 following Labour's general election victory. Their relationship was unusually close; it may have been based on an 'intellectual and psychic intimacy', or even a physical one.[32] Joe Haines, who later served Wilson twice as his chief press officer, believed there had been an affair between the two of them in the late 1950s and because of it she often claimed she had material which could 'ruin him'. Whatever the truth, Williams became a central figure during Wilson's tenure as Prime Minister. In the words of Wilson's biographer, 'When she shouted, he listened.'[33]

Williams initially struggled to carve out a secure niche for herself in No. 10. Her arrival had been met with a mixture of suspicion and political contempt in Whitehall. This was due in part to the fact that her position heralded something of an innovation in the architecture of central government but also because the precise nature of her responsibilities was never clarified or set out formally (except in respect of what security material she could see).[34]

When Wilson arrived in No. 10, Derek Mitchell was firmly established as the principal private secretary. At that time there were only four private secretaries: Mitchell (head of the office), Oliver Wright (foreign affairs), Philip Woodfield (parliamentary affairs) and Malcolm Reid (home and general affairs).[*] Mitchell had not managed to see Williams before the election, although she later described him as 'one of the most brilliant civil servants I encountered'.[35] They first met on Friday 16 October, the day after the general election, and there was an early indication of the problems that lay ahead when

---

[*] All of whom, except Reid, went on to become Permanent Secretaries.

discussion turned to the job title that Williams wished to adopt. She had proposed 'private secretary', but this was not possible given that this was the title used by the civil servants in the private office. In the end, it was agreed that her title would be 'personal and political secretary to the Prime Minister'.

However, Mitchell did not believe there was 'any administrative point to Williams' role beyond personal and spiritual support to the Prime Minister'.[36] This, however, ignores the importance that Wilson placed on having such individuals at the heart of Downing Street in order to share the burden of the premiership. As he told Sir Laurence Helsby,* the head of the home civil service, 'No. 10 is an office, not a Government Department; it is also a small and necessarily intimate community'.[37] Loyalty and trust were assets to be prized and Williams embodied them to the highest degree. As his closest adviser, she had his absolute confidence and could speak frankly to him in terms which few others would dare to do. As Joe Haines has argued, '[any] future historian's appraisal of Harold Wilson's role as Prime Minister and Leader of the Opposition will be incomplete unless he comprehends the full extent of her sway'.[38] While Haines's views might not be entirely unbiased, given the level of animosity between him and Williams by the time Wilson left office, his first-hand observations are testament to the power that she wielded. She saw her principal task as keeping Wilson in touch with the party in Parliament and in the country.[39] According to Roger Dawe,† who joined No. 10 in 1966 as the private secretary responsible for home affairs:

---

* Laurence Helsby (1908–78); Joint Permanent Secretary to the HM Treasury and head of the home civil service 1963–68.
† Roger Dawe (1941–); civil servant; private secretary (home affairs) to the Prime Minister 1966–70; principal private secretary to the Secretary of State for Employment 1972–74.

Wilson trusted Marcia most of all … She got rid of the people she wanted to get rid of. Her role was on the personal side and seeing political plots [against Wilson] all the time. Defending his personal position in the party but with no real focus on longer-term strategy.[40]

Moreover, Dawe says that Williams's power was based on determining 'who [Wilson] should and should not trust. The party dimension was very important to her and nobody at that time in the Labour Party trusted anybody. Significantly, she did not involve herself heavily in policy issues.'[41]

Williams also possessed, in the judgement of Joe Haines, 'the best political brain of any women (and many men) I knew. She attended Wilson's speech-writing sessions. She had a gift for the ordering of speeches … She was a highly intelligent political animal.'[42] Her political antennae were also acutely sensitive and attuned to picking up any hints of disloyalty not only from the party but also from within the civil servants at No. 10. She took a particular dislike to some of the 'garden room girls',* the typists who supported the Prime Ministers and private office and whom she believed were unsympathetic to the incoming Labour administration. Many of the No. 10 staff had not been appointed by anything approaching free and fair competition and it is likely that, in the previous thirteen years, some staff with a distinctly Conservative outlook had been recruited.[†43] Dawe recalled:

Marcia didn't like the garden room girls because a) they were

---

* The 'garden room girls' was the term given to the shorthand typists who supported the Prime Minister and private office. They were based on the lower ground floor of No. 10, next to the garden.
† Even Wilson at one point expressed doubts about whether private secretaries in the previous decade had been entirely politically unbiased.

very attractive, and b) they were Conservatives. She couldn't take six-foot ferocious girls from an agency in Kensington. She soon persuaded the private secretary for domestic affairs [Derek Andrews], to trawl openly for the best candidates competitively. This led to a far better mix of staff, with some East End girls coming into the Downing Street team.[44]

The private office, in order to ensure that the business got done and the process of government was transacted smoothly, did finally come to something of an accommodation with Williams. Dawe, the most junior private secretary, developed a better working relationship with Williams and he held regular meetings with her to discuss diary matters and other business.[45] Yet she would still often get her way and later still, when Mitchell left the post of principal private secretary in early 1966, it seems there was nobody senior willing to challenge her.[*]

Notwithstanding the idiosyncratic style of Williams, the private office was responsible for the day-to-day business of government and ensured it was well transacted, but it was predominantly an administrative function. It did not have what might be termed a policy development function as some future No. 10 private secretaries were to assume. Dawe has argued that it was 'highly influential as an efficient machine to ensure the Prime Minister's wishes were carried out across Whitehall as a whole' but that it 'did not initiate policy in the way it might do now', confining itself to 'liaising closely with departments'.[46] Most significantly, it did not have to contend with 'conflicting advice from, for example, special advisers'.[47] This last point is critical to understanding the way in which the private office supported Wilson. Unlike some future Prime Ministers,

---

[*]   Marcia Williams was the only person who did not agree to take part in an interview in preparing this book.

Wilson explicitly did not want or seek policy input from his private secretaries. His No. 10 civil servants ran no risk of politicisation because he relied on his fellow politicians and a small number of special advisers to provide him with such ideas. As a result, the boundaries between private office and political advice were more clearly defined and less blurred than they were to become under some future administrations.

The private office was also a much smaller and less frenetic operation than it is now. Wilson was punctilious in completing the red boxes prepared for him overnight by his private office. One No. 10 official was quoted as saying, 'His conduct of business was efficient and clear … Decisions were made very precisely, with a brief indication of what to do and how to do it.'[48] Looking back on an era that existed long before technology and the internet transformed the way government functions, Dawe recalled:

> The pace of life was different. There were no special advisers (at least none operating as they do in the modern-day sense). A duty rota operated for late nights and weekends. If you were not on duty, you could get off by about 7.30 p.m. There were, of course, no mobile phones. Whole weekends could go by with nothing happening. 'Switch" would link you in with any phone call that happened and to which you needed to listen.[49]

Wilson, while always convivial, open and trusting of his private secretaries, did not seek their personal views.[50] The job of the private office at that time was to ensure that ministers' wishes were carried out and that the business of government was efficiently transacted.

---

* 'Switch' is the shorthand term for the No. 10 Switchboard. Manned twenty-four hours a day, 365 days a year, it now has a reputation of being able to get hold of anyone, at any time and anywhere in the world.

There was never the type of relationship between Harold Wilson and his private secretaries that developed in the 1970s between Edward Heath and Robert Armstrong, in the 1980s between Margaret Thatcher and Charles Powell or at the turn of the century between Tony Blair and Jeremy Heywood. Wilson, as a former civil servant, was very proper in delineating what advice he got from the civil service and what policy advice he got from his political network. Ben Pimlott's conclusion was that Wilson actually 'liked advice coming to him from different angles' and appeared to relish the competition of those sources, 'playing off one against another' while often 'frustrat[ing] both and remain[ing] his own man'.[51]

The figure in Whitehall who, arguably, had the greatest influence on Wilson was his Cabinet Secretary, Burke Trend.* Wilson came to rely on Trend greatly and he became his 'favoured civil servant for informal advice'.[52][†] Trend was the archetypal mandarin, 'academically distinguished, cool and reserved, omniscient, with sound judgement and total calm in the face of crisis'.[53] Wilson often sought his counsel at their private weekly meetings.[54]

Wilson also liked to discuss ideas with a small set of loyal political supporters. This close group of advisers became known as his 'Kitchen Cabinet'. It was a phrase that stuck, even though Wilson tried to distance himself from it.[55][‡] As ever, Marcia Williams was essential to the process and became both the official and non-official conduit for access to Wilson, filtering which political allies he saw. Though the Kitchen Cabinet's name may have implied a coherent group with a fixed membership that met regularly, this was not the

---

* Burke Trend (1914–87); Cabinet Secretary 1963–73.
† In his biography of Wilson, Philip Ziegler describes Trend as 'the man who influenced Wilson most during his first administration' and 'the best civil servant he had ever known'.
‡ In an article in *The Times* in January 1967, Wilson argued against the Labour Party's submission to Fulton that every Cabinet minister should have a Kitchen Cabinet. He is quoted as saying, 'If I thought this was necessary, I would have done it in government.'

case. Roger Dawe more accurately described it as 'not a collective but rather a bunch of individuals, with different roles, and giving advice [to Wilson] separately and not *en masse*'.[56]

In addition to Williams and Wilson's two close Cabinet allies, Richard Crossman and Barbara Castle, there were perhaps four other regular confidants. Wilson relied heavily on George Wigg, a 'somewhat sinister and weird operator' according to Dawe, with close links to the security services, who would use Williams to gain direct access to the Prime Minister, thus bypassing the private office.[57] Wigg's self-determined role was to cover Wilson from supposed political plots and he would also send private, cryptically worded notes to Wilson. For example, on 17 July 1966 – a year before the sterling devaluation crisis – Wigg wrote Wilson a five-page letter marked 'personal and top secret', which ran over options for a possible devaluation (which he called the 'D' operation rather than name it).[58] None of this went via the private office, thereby underlining how, at times, it was excluded from some of the policy-making process.

Other members of the Kitchen Cabinet included Gerald Kaufman, who ran Wilson's small political office, an innovation that formalised the existence of a small retinue of party political staff to No. 10.[59] Press issues were handled by Trevor Lloyd-Hughes[*] until he was replaced by Joe Haines, who had a good rapport with the civil servants in the private office but always had a tense relationship with Williams.[60] However, despite the media fascination with it, the Kitchen Cabinet made little overall difference to the policies of the Wilson government. Its main impact on the work of private office seems to have been making its members' lives more complicated by

---

[*] Trevor Lloyd-Hughes (1922–2010); chief press secretary to the Prime Minister 1964–69.

the failure to share information relevant to government decision-making and not just party matters.[61]

THE IMPACT OF THE FIRST SPECIAL ADVISERS

A more significant and long-lasting formal structural change introduced by Harold Wilson was the appointment, with the agreement of the Cabinet Secretary, of the first special advisers in government. Andrew Blick has identified the five initial appointments during Wilson's first administration: John Allen, Thomas Balogh, Nicholas Kaldor, Robert Neild and Michael Stewart.[62]* All were appointed at the beginning of the Wilson government and were described as 'special advisers to the Prime Minister'. Of the five, Balogh was perhaps the most significant. He was certainly the most voluble in his belief that the civil service needed radical reform and argued that 'the solution to the problem of the Establishment was to replace it with a new socialist one', since 'so long as Labour hankers after being accepted by the old "Establishment", instead of creating its own, so long will it be in an awkward position, forced mainly on the defensive'.[63]

Balogh and Kaldor achieved a certain notoriety, in part because they were both Hungarian émigrés (and jokingly nicknamed 'Buda' and 'Pest' by the Labour politician Denis Healey). They were Jewish and suffered, at times, from antisemitic criticisms.[64] It is clear, from the papers in the Wilson Archives at the Bodleian Library which contain personal advice from Balogh to Wilson, as well as from both Ben Pimlott's and Philip Ziegler's biographies of Wilson, just

---

* Blick analyses the terms of their appointment and whether they were successfully integrated into the civil service.

how central a role Balogh played, especially in the early years of the administration. His notes for the Prime Minister on economic policy were usually handled directly by Marcia Williams in order to bypass standard civil service channels. Ziegler captures the nature of Balogh's influence on the Prime Minister:

> Wilson admired [Balogh], shared his expansionist ideas and was ready to endure the storm clouds which so often seemed to herald Balogh's arrival for the sake of the stimulation and intellectual challenge which he provided. Sometimes he was provoked almost beyond endurance by an act of churlishness of some outrageous demand – 'Those awful Europeans', he would say, 'and intellectual Europeans are the worst of all!' – but he could endure almost endless affront if he thought the offender basically well disposed and worth listening to, and he remained loyal to Balogh for many years.[65]

The new advisers worked with officials in No. 10 and at the Treasury and had good access to Wilson when required, but it was a haphazard and fairly ad hoc system running in parallel with the formal administrative operation of the No. 10 private office. In this initial period of their existence, special advisers were not formally responsible to a minister and there was no management structure. Of the five, Balogh, Allen and Stewart were assigned to the Cabinet Office, while Kaldor and Neild were attached to the Treasury.[66] They concentrated on making proposals and responding to ideas from elsewhere in government. There certainly does not appear to have been any real tensions between the private office and the new advisers, although Blick does refer to 'some obstructing from career officialdom, presumably motivated by a desire to preserve the position of the Civil Service'.[67] There were no accusations of alleged 'interference' by such advisers, either by overstepping the mark in influencing policy-making or in trying to direct civil servants. In addition, the first special advisers had little or no role in communications and media matters, as was to become far more common thirty years later.

Balogh's hopes that Wilson might introduce more radical far-reaching reform of the civil service, for which he had been ardently pressing for many years, were ultimately disappointed. The effect of the 'significant constitutional innovation' brought about by bringing the modern special adviser into Whitehall was also mitigated by the fact that there were only five initial appointments.[68]* While Wilson might have baulked at the prospect of a mass clearout of existing official staff, he was not dissuaded from his belief that the service needed to be opened up to encourage new talent to enter its ranks.[69]

These hopes of Wilson were embodied in the remit of the Fulton Committee, the creation of which was announced by Wilson in the House of Commons on 8 February 1966.[70] It was tasked to examine the 'structure, recruitment and management, including training, of the Home Civil Service', and it reported in June 1968.[71] Wilson regarded the Fulton Committee as fundamental to the achievement of lasting reform. The committee received submissions from a wide range of contributors, including the Fabian Society which proposed radical reforms based on the arguments it had set out in *The Administrators*. The Labour Party's submission to Fulton was similarly based on Fabian arguments.[72] Two key points relating to private office appeared in the final report. First, in considering the relationship between ministers and civil servants, it rejected the case

---

*   Recent governments have employed over twenty times that number. In 2019, there were 108 special advisers.

for 'a personal *cabinet* on the French model'.[73] Instead, it argued for a stronger departmental policy adviser to ministers which would therefore mean there was 'no need for ministerial *cabinets* or for political appointments on a large scale'.[74] Second, Fulton stated that:

> Because of the nature of the Private Secretary's duties, he must be personally acceptable to the Minister; there should therefore, in our view, be no obstacle in the way of a Minister's selecting from within the department, or on occasion more widely within the Service, as his Private Secretary the individual best suited to his ways of working; no stigma should attach to a person who is moved out of this job.[75]*

Wilson himself welcomed the report and its findings yet, in essence, Fulton had shied away from radical reforms to the system of ministerial support.[76] While some of the other Fulton proposals were quite radical, no changes were proposed in the structure or organisation of private offices.[77]†

PRIVATE OFFICES ACROSS GOVERNMENT

Elsewhere in Whitehall, new Cabinet ministers, often with no ministerial experience, inherited private offices without knowing how to get the best out of them. Denis Healey, for example, was adamant that he should initially keep the private secretary whom he inherited from his predecessor as Defence Secretary: 'I won my essential

---

* Unsurprisingly, the Fulton Committee, all twelve of whom were men, assumed all private secretaries would also all be men.

† Rodney Lowe characterises the report as 'flawed' and Fulton as a poor chairman. Peter Hennessy, by contrast, describes the Fulton legacy as 'mixed'.

first battle with the bureaucracy by refusing to accept a new Private Secretary in place of the able Arthur Hockaday, who had been working for my Conservative predecessor, Peter Thorneycroft.'[78] In his autobiography, Healey recalled that 'to run the ministry the way [he] wanted', his 'most essential need was for a first-rate private secretary – a clever young man with experience of defence and a knowledge of the key civilian and military personalities'.[79] Judgement and discretion, in Healey's opinion, were particularly valuable assets as a minister's private secretary was 'not only his eyes and ears' but also the one who decided what reached 'the minister personally out of the hundreds of men and thousands of documents always clamouring for his attention'.[80] Hockaday became the 'ideal man' to help Healey in those early stages.[81] There was no hint that he might not have been impartial on account of his having served the Conservative administration previously. Hockaday soon moved on and was replaced as Healey's private secretary early in 1965 by Patrick Nairne – whom Healey rated the best civil servant he ever worked with.[82]

By contrast, Richard Crossman became Minister for Housing and Local Government and, also having no prior ministerial experience, was initially less enamoured with his civil servant inheritance in the shape of George Moseley,* who had served under Crossman's Conservative predecessor, Keith Joseph. While acknowledging that Moseley was 'extremely efficient and pertinacious to the last degree' and 'desperately anxious to prevent me from doing things wrong', Crossman admitted that he would have preferred 'a livelier, more vital young man in whom I could confide'.[83]

Crossman later came to have a much warmer appreciation of

---

*   Moseley later rose to become Permanent Secretary in the Department of the Environment.

Moseley's abilities. However, he had even greater praise for Moseley's successor, John Delafons.* For Crossman, Delafons represented the ideal of the 'livelier, more vital young man' that he was looking for and, within a week of his appointment, Crossman wrote in his diary that Delafons 'has wholly transformed the Private Office ... I now know I am all right. I have somebody who can talk to me ... somebody enormously ambitious who also thinks it exciting to work with me, and, above all, somebody who knows his way about the Department.'[84] It was the efficiency with which Delafons ran the private office that most impressed Crossman. Comparing the two, he said of private office that, 'under George Moseley it was a good solid Rover of a Private Office [whereas] under John Delafons it was a Rolls-Royce.'[85]

One of the most interesting characters to emerge from private office in this period was David Dowler.† Dowler was a career civil servant whose loyalty to a single politician (in his case, Roy Jenkins) was a precursor to the sort of relationship Charles Powell would enjoy with Margaret Thatcher in the 1980s. Jenkins had met Dowler when he was appointed as Minister of Aviation in 1964 and was so impressed by his knowledge of the department's work that he asked for him to be made his principal private secretary. Dowler repaid this confidence with unswerving loyalty until his untimely death in 1970, aged only thirty-nine. In 1972, when Michael Heseltine became Minister of State for Aerospace and Shipping (a successor to the Ministry of Aviation, which was part of the new Department of Trade and Industry, created by Edward Heath), he received some

---

* John Delafons (1930–2007); civil servant; principal private secretary to the Secretary of State for Housing and Local Government 1965–66.

† David Dowler (1930–70); principal private secretary to the Minister of Aviation 1965–66; principal private secretary to the Home Secretary 1966–67; joint principal private secretary and subsequently sole principal private secretary to the Chancellor of the Exchequer 1967–70.

advice. Tam Dalyell, who had been Crossman's parliamentary private secretary and who understood the private office system well, advised the new minister to

> surround yourself, if you can, with some really astringent civil servants who will brief you properly on the minefield work of aviation. Roy Jenkins is the first to admit that his success in your department was due, at least in part, to the remarkable capacities of the late David Dowler who subsequently went with him to the Home Office and the Treasury.[86]

In 1965, Wilson replaced Sir Frank Soskice as Home Secretary with Roy Jenkins in an early Cabinet reshuffle.[87] Jenkins wanted to take Dowler with him to the Home Office and additionally requested that John Harris, who had spent two years as Labour's director of publicity before going to the Foreign Office as an adviser to Patrick Gordon Walker and Michael Stewart, be transferred to handle his media relations. Such a demand was almost unheard of. The formidable Permanent Secretary of the Home Office, Sir Charles Cunningham,* fiercely resisted the proposal. He always 'expected things to be done his way' and 'strongly defended all the officials whom Jenkins wanted to replace, asserted that moving Dowler was contrary to civil service rules; and objected to the secondment of Harris.'[88] Jenkins persisted and, eventually, got his way. Dowler and Harris both joined him at the Home Office and Cunningham took retirement soon after. The Dowler incident was significant in that it was one of the first examples, and certainly the most prominent, of a Cabinet minister insisting his principal private secretary

---

* Sir Charles Cunningham (1906–98); Permanent Secretary Home Office 1957–66.

should transfer with him when he moved job. Dowler made no secret of where his loyalties lay. He argued, terrier-like, for his minister come what may. Some fifty years on, Roger Dawe still recalled that Wilson distrusted both Dowler and Harris.[89] Dawe continued:

> Dealing with [Dowler] was quite different from dealing with other private secretaries in Whitehall. He wasn't like them. He was almost a political animal and only working for Jenkins personally. You could be pretty frank with other private secretaries, but I was always cagey with Dowler. It was more like dealing with a special adviser nowadays.[90]

According to this view, Dowler combined the roles of private secretary and political adviser in a way which was rare and represented an early example of politicisation within the private office world. Dowler was protected in that he knew that Jenkins would always back his position if ever criticism of him were made.

Philip Allen, who had succeeded Cunningham as Permanent Secretary at the Home Office during Jenkins's first tenure as Home Secretary, recalled that Dowler 'had an instinctive understanding of Roy's thinking and likely reaction, and although he was not conciliatory in dealing with people and identified himself with his minister to an extent unusual for a private secretary, he came to be respected in the Department for his ability, intelligence and sharp wit'.[91]

In Dowler's obituary, Jenkins wrote:

> He had one of the most consistently alert critical minds that I have ever encountered. He could, of course, always spot the weak point in an argument when he was looking for it. But that is not a unique gift. What was almost unique was that he hardly ever

failed to register the weak point even when he was not conscious-
ly looking for it ... He knew instinctively what was important and
what was not: he was always looking for a solution and not an impasse. Combined with these gifts he had an exceptional devotion
to duty, persons and causes.[92]

Jenkins was the first to admit that his successes were built on the
support, skill and insights of his private secretary who supported
him throughout his early government career. He described Dowler
as 'my closest possible confidant'.[93] Unlike in Wilson's private office,
Jenkins relied heavily on his private secretary to help him shape
policy, by arguing his minister's case with No. 10 and others, by
crafting speeches for Jenkins as well as doing 'the dirty work for
him'.[94] It that sense, he was more like Charles Powell became for
Thatcher rather than any of Wilson's private secretaries.

There had also been changes in the No. 10 private office. Derek
Mitchell, who had never found the relationship with Marcia Williams
easy, left No. 10 and returned to the Treasury in the spring of 1966.
In selecting his successor, Wilson put strong emphasis on recruiting
someone he had worked with before and, as ever, he remained ill-
disposed to taking anyone with a Treasury background. As a result
of these prejudices, Wilson made a very unusual choice and, against
the official advice he received, selected Michael Halls[*] as his new
principal private secretary. Halls was then aged fifty-one (relatively
old to take on that post) and had previously worked for Wilson for
two years from 1948 to 1950 as his private secretary at the Board of
Trade. Since serving Wilson in the late 1940s, Halls had worked in

---

[*] Michael Halls (1915–70); private secretary to the president of the Board of Trade 1948–50; principal pri-
    vate secretary to the Prime Minister 1966–70. Prior to Halls's appointment, all eight No. 10 principal
    private secretaries since the Second World War had been aged between thirty-six and forty-three on their
    appointment to the post.

middle-ranking jobs in the Board of Trade (including as the board's Midlands regional manager) and in a post at the Imperial Defence College, neither of which required him to report directly to ministers.

Halls was not the preferred choice of the civil service, which feared the job would prove to be beyond his capabilities. Laurence Helsby, the head of the home civil service, warned Wilson that appointing Halls in this manner would be an improper use of prime ministerial patronage (and asked him to consider a list of five other possible candidates, whom Wilson duly interviewed but remained committed to his original decision).[95] In a minute to Helsby, Wilson revealed the strength of his frustration with Whitehall, arguing that if it was a question of choosing between 'Prime Ministerial patronage and patronage exercised by a small, self-perpetuating oligarchy of Permanent Secretaries, I have no alternative but to say that patronage, if patronage it be, must be exercised by me'.[96] Wilson also stressed that he wanted the appointment made because he regarded it 'as the means of ensuring that my office will work ... as efficiently, smoothly and agreeably as possible. What I want is a Private Secretary, not either a Presidential Assistant, nor a Permanent Secretary, actual or in embryo.'[97] The Prime Minister was within his rights to choose whomever he thought best for this most sensitive of posts and one where personal chemistry mattered. Overriding civil service advice has always been the prerogative of any minister, if deployed cautiously. Yet that presupposed Wilson's choice would be the equal of, or better than, the other candidates on offer. In the case of Halls, this proved not to be the case.

Halls himself apparently did not even particularly want the job, but Wilson persuaded him to take the post. Halls's widow later sued the government, arguing that the stresses placed on her husband contributed to his premature death.[98] From the start, Halls could not delegate and took on far too much of the work himself. According to Dawe, 'unfortunately, he simply wasn't up to it'.[99] Robert Armstrong also doubted Halls's fitness for the post. 'He was very conscientious, a great worrier, and he was not good at delegating to his fellow private secretaries. He worked punishingly long hours, both in the office during the day and when he went home at night.'[100] Even Wilson allegedly said of him 'I know he's second rate, but I can trust him.'[101] In addition, there was what could only be termed the 'Marcia Williams issue'. Halls could not engage effectively with Williams and so that liaison role was often delegated to the more junior private secretary, Dawe.[102] Williams took precedence in access to Wilson and often it was not until around midnight that Halls could even sound out the Prime Minister on government business after Williams had dealt with personal, political and party matters. As his widow said:

> [Halls] was called upon continually to placate Mrs Williams in order that Mr Wilson could do his own work. My husband was therefore having to stay later and later every evening at the office and work at the weekends to get his normal work done. The head of the civil service was kept aware of all these circumstances.[103]

By the end of Halls's time in Downing Street, this pressure was clearly getting too much for him, and yet a combination of duty and his loyalty to Wilson kept him going. He also became quite obsessed with ensuring the findings of the Fulton report were carried through, thus underlining, as Armstrong noted, that he was temperamentally not able to delegate.[104] The implementation of Fulton was a task for the Cabinet Office and Treasury, overseen by the Cabinet Secretary and the head of the home civil service. It was not the role of the No. 10

principal private secretary and yet Halls took it on himself. He died, tragically, aged fifty-five in April 1970 of a heart attack, and the matter caused Wilson a considerable sense of guilt.[105] He had witnessed the strains that the job had put on him, he knew the difficulties that Williams could cause and yet Wilson did nothing about it. As Ziegler explains, 'He knew Halls had been promoted beyond his proper level and that the strain this had imposed upon him had contributed to his fatal heart attack. It was an appalling blow for him.'[106] In his autobiography, Wilson commented that 'the news of his coronary, still more the news of his death, created an atmosphere of utter gloom and sympathy for his widow, Marjorie Halls', and said that nothing 'could begin to assess his dedicated contribution to the public service; and to me personally'.[107]

Wilson may have felt some direct personal responsibility. He persuaded the reluctant Halls to take the job in the first place and yet, when it became obvious that he could not cope, there was no mechanism to reduce the stress. And so, the fact that, when his widow subsequently sued the government, the civil service did not accept any responsibility for her husband's death must have been a bitter pill for her to swallow.*

Halls's time as head of the No. 10 private office coincided with deepening economic crisis. Despite having won the 1966 general election with an overall majority of ninety-eight seats, economic pressures soon began to take their toll on Wilson's government.[108]† In the autumn of 1967, following a long sterling crisis, pressure on the pound became so intense that Wilson agreed to devaluation, representing a major political climbdown for him. Following

---

* Marjorie Halls eventually settled out of court and was given an *ex gratia* payment but without any admission of guilt by the civil service department.

† Labour won 364 seats compared to the Conservatives' 253 seats.

devaluation, Wilson moved Callaghan from the Treasury, replacing him with Jenkins. At the Treasury, Robert Armstrong was proposed as the new principal private secretary to the Chancellor.

Armstrong was one of the most significant civil servants and private secretaries of the twentieth century.[109]* In a career spanning over forty years, culminating in serving for seven years as Cabinet Secretary under Thatcher, he held a range of private secretary posts. After Jenkins had replaced Callaghan, Armstrong was 'summoned to see the Chancellor … I only realised later that I was being interviewed to be his new principal private secretary.'[110] The Treasury had wanted Armstrong to get the post and had therefore asked Jenkins to meet him, but Jenkins had other ideas. Again, he demanded to bring Dowler with him to the Treasury from the Home Office. There was something of a stand-off and the issue was eventually, and extraordinarily, referred up to the Prime Minister, who ruled that the Chancellor should have both men as joint principal private secretaries. So, the two of them worked together in a somewhat tense, and certainly unusual, relationship. Dowler tended to liaise with Jenkins, and Armstrong with the Treasury official team. Of the bizarre arrangement, Armstrong commented, 'Dowler was a decent man but a bit prickly. However, we made it work.'[111] Jenkins's views of the arrangement, which he acknowledged was seen as 'an affront to the Treasury', was that the two officials were like 'two very senior airline captains both trying to fly the same plane'.[112] However, 'amazingly, it worked well for nine months … which was a tribute primarily to the balance of Armstrong's personality'.[113]†

---

* The *Daily Telegraph* once described him as 'the greatest "Mandarin" of his generation'.
† This whole episode did Armstrong no harm in one key respect, in that Jenkins respected him for having accepted the strange dual posting with Dowler. As Home Secretary in Wilson's second administration from March 1974, Jenkins had to recommend a new Permanent Secretary for that department. He proposed Armstrong.

6

GOVERNING IN HARD TIMES: PRIVATE OFFICE 1970-79

British politics throughout the 1970s was dominated by three politicians – Edward Heath, Harold Wilson and James Callaghan. They were Prime Ministers in a decade marked by vast political and industrial upheavals. In parallel, three private secretaries were the dominant figures of that same period: Robert Armstrong, Robin Butler and Ken Stowe. This chapter assesses how they sought to support their political masters in keeping the ship of state on course during a period of steady economic decline.

Heath's victory in the general election of 1970, held on Thursday 18 June, was unexpected. Despite the difficulties of the Wilson government since devaluation in 1967, there had been a recovery in the polls, the economy was stronger under the chancellorship of Roy Jenkins and Wilson was more popular than the Conservative leader.[*] However, Heath won a majority of thirty and entered No. 10 as Prime Minister of one of the best-prepared governments, at least in terms of policy and plans, of any post-war administration. Nowhere was this clearer than in his proposals for reform of the

---

[*] In May 1970, Labour overtook the Conservatives in the Gallup opinion poll for the first time since February 1967. By 1970, GDP was at its highest level ever, having grown 18 per cent since 1963.

civil service – something which Wilson had planned, but failed, to achieve. Heath was deeply interested in the management and the machinery of government issues and had developed policies well in advance of the election. As Leader of the Opposition since 1965, he had given considerable thought to how he might reform the machinery of government should he enter No. 10.[2] There had even been an argument, in some quarters, that government was simply becoming unable to manage events and was suffering from what later became known as 'overload'.[3] Many thought the central 'machine' was in need of radical reform. Heath argued, instead, that there was a need 'to change the structure of government, based upon the thorough examination we had carried out in opposition'.[4]

Heath was not a traditional politician, being more a technocrat than a politically driven party leader. Indeed, he had initially wanted to be a civil servant and had passed the civil service exams before becoming a Conservative candidate in 1947. He was 'happier in the company of permanent secretaries than he was with his ministerial colleagues'.[5] One of his obituarists neatly captured this element of his nature, writing that 'in some respects Heath was a permanent secretary manqué, more at ease with civil servants than with his own Cabinet'.[6] As his biographer John Campbell wrote, Heath was, 'from the beginning, determined not to surround himself with a Wilsonian Kitchen Cabinet of cronies', in order to avoid the chaos and dysfunctionality that had characterised his predecessor's running of his private office.[7]

In assessing how Heath, once Prime Minister, subsequently shaped and used his private office, three broad questions emerge. First, what were the major managerial changes that he introduced in the civil service, why did he think they were so essential and how effective were they? Second, how did Heath change the role of No.

10 and his private office during his premiership, including its contribution to policy-making, and who were the key people supporting him in that task? Third, what was the impact of his most striking move, carried out within only two weeks of becoming Prime Minister, when he effectively sacked the principal private secretary he had inherited from Wilson and replaced him with Robert Armstrong?

Wilson's broad strategy for the civil service had been based around two basic tenets: to reduce the power of the Treasury and to inject greater external political advice and advisers into the system. Heath, by contrast, believed in the benefits of 'managerialism', tackling bureaucracy, the greater use of business techniques in government and the freeing up of ministerial time for more strategic thinking. In opposition, he had established a committee of former civil servants chaired by the formidable Baroness Sharp,* whose clashes with Richard Crossman were infamous. Heath also sought political advice on the future of the civil service from David Howell[†] and Mark Schreiber.[‡] They had helped him shape his Whitehall reform policies via the Public Sector Research Unit (PSRU) established within the Conservative Research Department in 1967.[8] Their proposals even mooted creating a Prime Minister's department, which would certainly have been a very radical departure, although Heath eventually rejected that idea.[9§] Howell and Schreiber had also urged him to develop a policy unit in No. 10 which could serve him personally, but 'Heath's concern was with widening the range of advice available to the Cabinet as a whole'.[10] After the 1970 election,

---

* Baroness Sharp (1903–85); civil servant; Permanent Secretary Ministry of Housing and Local Government 1955–66.
† David Howell (1936–); MP for Guildford 1966–97; Secretary of State for Energy 1979–81; Secretary of State for Transport 1981–83; created Lord Howell 1997.
‡ Mark Schreiber (1931–); Conservative Research Department adviser to Edward Heath 1967–70; member of the CPRS 1970–74; created Lord Marlesford 1991.
§ Rodney Lowe argues that the creation of a Prime Minister's office after 1970 'was never a practical proposition'. Heath himself confirmed this in an interview with Anthony Barker in 1978.

Heath brought Howell into the then civil service department, as junior minister for the civil service, with responsibility for Whitehall reform.

The 1970 Conservative Party manifesto, while not detailing the proposed reforms, stated that 'the Government in Whitehall is overloaded'.[11] Heath believed in smaller and more efficient government and found the debates about how to structure government 'of extraordinary interest'.[12] He was concerned that ministers 'spent too much time on day-to-day matters, instead of on strategic thinking'.[13] Accordingly, after the general election, Heath moved quickly on this theme. On becoming Prime Minister, he reduced the size of the Cabinet to eighteen members (the smallest since Churchill's 1951 Cabinet) and Cabinet often met twice weekly, as opposed to the previous norm of once a week. In turn, their meetings tended to discuss more weighty policy papers rather than merely focus on day-to-day politics. Within four months, the government published a radical White Paper on reform of Whitehall entitled 'The Reorganisation of Central Government'.[14] Peter Hennessy described this initiative as 'the most systematic attempt to reform the mechanics of Cabinet government since Lloyd George'.[15] It set out to: create fewer and bigger ministries; slim down the Cabinet and ensure that it had better briefing; 'hive-off' certain departmental executive functions to agencies; improve the information flow to ministers (including via a new central body under the Prime Minister but providing information for all ministers); and examine departmental programmes for their utility and efficiency.[16]

Historians of the Heath government have concentrated on the changes related to the machinery of government – including the creation of so-called mega-departments, the introduction of Programme Analysis and Review (PAR) and the establishment of the

Central Policy Review Staff (CPRS) in 1971. The structural changes were substantial and of the five new departments created by Wilson only one – the Welsh Office – survived in the same format under Heath.[17] Yet how effective the Heath reforms were is a different matter. John Campbell, Jon Davis, Peter Hennessy, Rodney Lowe and Kevin Theakston all argue that, possibly with the exception of the CPRS, they promised much but delivered far less.[18] Campbell argues that 'the [civil service reform] programme was neither sufficiently precise nor, in practice, all that radical'.[19] Davis points out that, in general, 'Heath's Government's extensive ambition was dashed so quickly … and it remains the biggest failure to carry out a programme in the post-war period'. He describes the Programme Analysis and Review as 'the key disappointment'.[20] Theakston similarly states that, overall, the reforms

> turned out to be something much less than the 'new style of government' so optimistically talked about in 1970. The new giant departments were broken up or lost major functions within a few years. PAR was a damp squib. Little was hived-off. Only the CPRS stands out as a really successful innovation and even its lustre had faded some time before it was axed in 1983.[21]

Lowe analyses the reasons for the failures of the reforms in detail, arguing that they were brought down, at least in part, by a lack of consistent support from politicians and civil servants alike.[22] Even the CPRS, which generated considerable interest at the time and subsequent enquiry by historians, survived for only twelve years.[23] These changes had the potential, if successful, to be more far reaching than Wilson's organisational changes. In practice, they made little difference to the overall functioning of government.

Davis argues that 'the White Paper degenerated into a dry list of machinery-of-government changes bereft of the philosophy that had given birth to them'.[24] In a similar vein, Theakston comments that 'like Wilson, Heath seems to have lost interest in his reforms after their initiation and his attention was diverted away from re-shaping Whitehall'.[25]

As co-authors, Kavanagh and Seldon and, in particular, Baston and Seldon consider the way in which Heath used his private office and did so more effectively than Wilson.[26] The latter comment that 'Heath's No. 10, as was intended, was a significant improvement on Wilson's in 1964–70'.[27] However, they also conclude that, by rejecting early on the notion of a Prime Minister's department, Heath 'preserved the rather ramshackle Number 10 machine. Heath's path of cautious reform, which he inherited from Wilson, has been followed by all his successors to date.'[28] Indeed, since Heath's time, no Prime Minister has tried to carry out a wholesale reform of the private office but has retained it as a relatively small, high-powered body and made only minor reforms to its mode of operation. In his autobiography, Heath described his approach to the machinery of government questions and the use of his private office.[29] Learning from the Wilson experience, he pointedly stressed the need to 'avoid friction between the civil service team and the political team'.[30]

Heath's private secretaries and his political appointees such as Douglas Hurd, William Waldegrave and Timothy Kitson all had a similar class and cultural backgrounds. All were men and most were Oxford educated. Of them collectively, Heath commented:

The subsequent careers of these individuals bear witness to the quality of the team I had working for me at 10 Downing Street. I had complete confidence in their intellectual abilities, their competence, their commitment, their loyalty and their discretion. No Prime Minister could ask for a better or more agreeable team to support him in No. 10 … They were not just colleagues but friends, on my own as I was, a kind of extended family.[31]

Why, though, did Heath not make any substantive structural changes in the shape and size of the No. 10 private office? Partly it was because he was opposed to big government in general and, having rejected the idea of a Prime Minister's department, he was keen to keep the centre of government as small as reasonably possible, 'signalling a change of style and tone from the Wilson "Kitchen Cabinet" regime'.[32] He wanted to mark a break from Wilson's approach of using political advisers in a somewhat ad hoc way. Heath believed that Wilson's approach of bringing in outside policy-makers undermined the role of the civil service, and he was far more comfortable with getting first-rate civil servants around him. He liked the more structured and small-scale approach. Nevertheless, as Hennessy has commented, it is surprising that 'Heath did not reshape the Prime Minister's Office. He just got on with what he found.'[33] The real reason Heath did not make any significant changes to private office, after the initial change of leadership, may be that the organisation that emerged was what he needed, and it was one that worked well for him. Heath, as a single man, had no close relatives or 'confidants' to whom he could turn for advice and so his close-knit private office really became, as he himself acknowledged, like the family he didn't have. The team that was eventually built around Heath at No. 10 believed in what they were doing and felt, in Robin Butler's words, 'that we were part of an elite organisation heading a serious government'.[34]

Heath had made one significant decision on personnel very early on, when he decided that he would not retain Alexander 'Sandy' Isserlis* as his principal private secretary. Heath retained the other members of Wilson's private office that he had inherited, namely Peter Moon (foreign affairs), Christopher Roberts (parliamentary affairs), Peter Gregson (economic affairs) and Alan Simcock (home affairs).[35†] Isserlis had replaced Michael Halls and had only been in the position for a little over two months before the change of government. Heath's memoirs recall their first day working together when, after having kissed hands at the palace, he arrived back in Downing Street with Willie Whitelaw and Francis Pym to begin work as Prime Minister. Heath asked if the private office could provide them with some food, and Isserlis announced its arrival by poking his head through the half-open door and shouting 'Grub's up!', sending Whitelaw into 'paroxysms of fury' and demanding that he be sacked at once.[36] Isserlis's dismissal a few weeks later provoked a brief flurry of press comment questioning whether the new Prime Minister was deliberately seeking to remove officials appointed by his predecessor.[37] It was, and remains to this day, the only post-war example of a No. 10 principal private secretary being replaced by the incoming Prime Minister, either after an election or when the office changed hands – ostensibly on the grounds that the Prime Minister simply did not rate him.‡ An article in *The Times*, however, rebutted the view that this was outside the normal course of events, noting: 'At the level of private secretary it is said to be fully accepted that when there is a change of Government, Ministers – because of the personal relationship involved – are free either to

---

*   Alexander 'Sandy' Isserlis (1922–86); principal private secretary to the Lord President of the Council and Minister for Science 1960–61 and to the Minister of Housing and Local Government 1962; principal private secretary to the Prime Minister (Harold Wilson and Edward Heath) 1970.

†   Heath later said that he was 'exceptionally well supported by [his] private office team'.

‡   Recent Prime Ministers (Johnson, Truss and Sunak) have imported their previous principal private secretaries but have not 'sacked' the incumbents.

keep or change the men whom they "inherit" from the previous Administration.'[38] It was accompanied by a statement from Isserlis supporting the decision.[39]

Isserlis's replacement was Robert Armstrong, who had built a strong reputation in the civil service principally through his time at the Treasury, where he had served as private secretary to two Chancellors, R. A. Butler and Roy Jenkins. Armstrong later recalled how, on 1 July 1970, he had been summoned by the Permanent Secretary to the Treasury, Sir Douglas Allen, and told that he was to become principal private secretary to the new Prime Minister: 'I had no interview with Mr Heath. I had met him at Balliol and he knew my father well.'[40] Armstrong's father, Sir Thomas Armstrong, was a former principal of the Royal Academy of Music and had not only interviewed Heath for the prestigious organ scholarship at Balliol College but conducted him as a member of the Oxford Bach Choir. Armstrong said, 'It was known that I had an interest in music and Sir William Armstrong [head of the home civil service and no relation] thought I might therefore get on well with Heath. Heath himself just wanted someone appointed by merit not by Wilson.'[41] Armstrong started in No. 10 on 6 July and Isserlis, according to Armstrong, 'showed no signs of resentment; on the contrary, he was friendly and helpful. I had the impression that he was not sorry to be leaving No. 10.'[42] The belief that Heath and Armstrong would bond over their shared love of music proved to be justified. Their relationship became 'exceptionally close – almost paternal/filial … which further contributed to the warmth and camaraderie of the team in Downing Street.'[43] Armstrong was to stay almost five years at No. 10 and, 'by common account, performed superbly'.[44]

Heath was renowned as something of a loner in politics, as in life. Robin Butler, who joined No. 10 from the CPRS in 1972, said of

Heath that he 'was not "chummy" [but that] he was in many ways touchingly dependent on us [the private office] and we responded to that'.[45] Unmarried, and with few friends, even Heath's close colleagues would not claim to understand him fully. The same was true of his private secretaries. Heath described Armstrong as a 'superb private secretary, skilful, sympathetic and famously discreet' and yet Heath apparently found it hard to give him any personal feedback.[46] 'He was simply unable to say thank you or well done,' Armstrong recalled.[47] He admitted that, even some two years into his tenure at No. 10, he had no idea how well Heath felt he was performing:

> In 1972, after having spent two years at No. 10, William Armstrong contacted Heath to say that he wanted me to return to the Treasury and be promoted to deputy secretary. Heath said that I could not leave, adding that if they wanted to promote me, it was fine by him, but I was to stay at No. 10. It was the first time I had received any feedback at all from the Prime Minister on my performance to date. As a result, I also got promoted in post to deputy secretary.[48]

Despite Heath's miserliness in parting with praise, the pair grew to admire each other and their respective talents.[49]* Heath's memoirs praised Armstrong's 'first-rate mind, his remarkable skill as a draftsman and his ability concisely to state an argument'.[50]

Heath had never been a minister in the Treasury but had seen the economic problems Labour had faced, and so having good links to the Treasury, via his principal private secretary, was both important

---

* Armstrong later became executor of Heath's will, taking on responsibility for preserving his house in Salisbury as a museum and a tribute to the former Prime Minister. Armstrong also robustly defended Heath, who died in 2005, from accusations that he was involved in child abuse, and 'he generally helped look after the often-difficult former Prime Minister until his death in 2005', according to the *Daily Telegraph*.

and useful. Armstrong knew all the key officials in that department from the Permanent Secretary downwards and had served alongside William Ryrie,* who was principal private secretary to the Chancellor. In addition, Heath could also use Sir William Armstrong for personal advice, thereby bypassing the Treasury, if he wished.[51]

Private office under Heath was a stimulating place to work and, most significantly, Heath gave the office greater authority than it had previously had. The small team was well led by Armstrong, who ensured that the political and official parts of the office co-operated well. Increasingly, as Heath focused on the policy issues associated with European accession, he became ever more reliant on Armstrong who led on this work. Heath empowered his private office, and in particular Armstrong and Butler, to take the lead on specific issues and so represent the Prime Minister externally. As a result, Heath's private office became far more powerful as it took on more of a policy-focused role, which Harold Wilson had never encouraged. Ziegler, Heath's biographer, captures well the atmosphere at No. 10 which developed during this period:

> It *was* hard work but immensely rewarding and, thanks to the friendly atmosphere in Number 10, to which both Heath and Armstrong signally contributed, enjoyable as well. He could not have supported the demands of the job, Armstrong believes, if it had not also been enormous fun. He became far more than a private secretary; Heath told Anthony Seldon that he 'became devoted to Armstrong and found him one of the most intelligent, and companionable officials he encountered in his career'.[52]

---

*   Sir William Ryrie (1928–2012); Treasury civil servant; principal private secretary to the Chancellor of the Exchequer (Roy Jenkins, Iain MacLeod and Anthony Barber) 1970–72.

Despite appearing to be 'personally stiff and diffident' at times, Armstrong found Heath to be 'a good man and an honourable man'.[53]

Official speechwriting was mainly handled by the private office with input from Douglas Hurd on the political side.[54] (Hurd was effectively operating as a modern-day special adviser would.) Butler thought Hurd a 'great speechwriter' and one who 'understood and respected fully the distinction between party and official work'.[55] As a result, the whole atmosphere of No. 10 was more positive than under Marcia Williams's interventionist style during the Wilson era. Heath was less efficient than Wilson in managing business, which again enhanced the private office role. As Robin Butler recalled, 'There were difficulties in getting [Heath] to work through his boxes of official papers and even greater difficulties in preparing speeches for him. He contributed nothing himself and [unlike Wilson] no one could describe him as creative.'[56]

The CPRS was at the time an important innovation. When the Conservatives were in opposition, there had been a proposal to create what would have been a Policy Unit in No. 10, but that idea came to nothing and the CPRS was housed, following advice from Burke Trend, in the Cabinet Office.[57] According to historian Rodney Lowe, despite initial advice from the civil service department that the CPRS might work out of Downing Street, Trend argued strongly that, constitutionally, it should be housed in the Cabinet Office.[58] Dr Jon Davis's view is that Trend could not countenance Heath becoming 'more than *primus inter pares*' and insisted that the new unit be a resource for the whole Cabinet and that it should be formally called the CPRS, not the 'Think Tank'.[59] The No. 10 private office, therefore, effectively assumed the role of a mini Policy Unit inside No. 10, and Heath worked closely with Robert Armstrong, in particular on Europe, and with Butler – who was the lead private secretary for the critical Northern Ireland negotiations of 1973 – as well as with Sir William Armstrong in the Cabinet Office.[60] Heath also reduced the number of political posts at No. 10. He made two important appointments in Douglas Hurd and Donald Maitland.* Heath was determined to keep the office as small as possible and the team he assembled at No. 10 – composed of predominantly civil servants but with one full-time political appointee (Hurd) – worked very well, as he had hoped. In his autobiography, he explained, 'I kept my Private Office as small as possible, retaining Douglas Hurd as my political secretary and sharing Michael Wolff, an excellent speechwriter, with Willie Whitelaw.'[61] Butler's memory supports Heath's:

> The private office was very harmonious and worked well under Heath. Robert Armstrong, Douglas Hurd and Donald Maitland got along very well together and their teams – civil service, political and press office – followed the lead ... We all felt that it was a privilege to be working in No. 10.[62]

Hurd had joined No. 10 on the day after the election, succeeding Marcia Williams, and he rapidly developed a far better relationship with the private office than existed between Williams and Wilson's officials. For a start, Armstrong had known Hurd from their Eton schooldays and they developed a strong working relationship. Armstrong recalled, 'He was a good friend, going back to schooldays. He clearly knew where to draw the line between what was appropriate for civil servants to do and what was political activity which he should handle.'[63] Hurd had been a Foreign Office diplomat for fourteen years and so knew how government, No. 10 and the

---

* Sir Donald Maitland (1922–2010); FCO diplomat; principal private secretary to the Foreign Secretary (Michael Stewart and George Brown) 1967–69; chief press secretary to the Prime Minister 1970–73.

private office worked. He was of the same background, mould and class as Armstrong. By comparison with Marcia Williams, Hurd did not have to prove himself. He did not have to establish a new role for himself or justify his access to the Prime Minister. He certainly did not have to put up with the sexist attitudes with which his predecessor had to contend. On the other hand, he did not make enemies in the way Williams seemed to do, and nor did he seek to intervene unnecessarily or meddle in the way in which she often did. He agreed early on that the private office, and not the political office, 'should have the main responsibility for the Prime Minister's diary, for answering letters from MPs, for editing and drafting official speeches, for the choice of guests at official receptions and for a number of other minor matters'.[64] He focused on his central task of providing political advice to Heath and building a strong relationship with private office. Hurd had the great advantage of having worked inside the civil service, albeit on the diplomatic side, but had then left to go into politics. As a result, he knew both the political and the administrative sides of the coin and was perfectly placed to manage the interface smoothly, using his diplomatic skills to ensure feathers were not ruffled.

Armstrong was also central to building a strong relationship in a way that Williams and Wilson's private office never managed. Hurd describes how Armstrong

let me look through his pending tray, which usually held the minutes of the latest Cabinet and Cabinet Committee meetings. These arrangements would never have been possible if everyone had stood on their constitutional rights. I was probably helped by the fact that I had been a government servant myself for fourteen years, so that I spoke the language. But overwhelmingly this easy co-operation came about because of the understanding attitude of the civil service private secretaries, and in particular of Robert Armstrong ... They expected in return only that I would not complicate their lives unnecessarily. With different individuals and in more difficult circumstances we re-created the easy informality of Harold Macmillan's Private Office. That is the only spirit in which Number Ten can be run.[65]

The relationship between Armstrong and Hurd was crucial to re-establishing a climate of trust at No. 10 and for giving a clear sense of direction and purpose across Whitehall more generally. It was quite unusual in the history of the private office for the principal private secretary and the Prime Minister's lead political adviser to get on this well. It says much about their shared education, culture and background. Heath recognised this:

I had, in Douglas Hurd, only one political adviser in Number Ten. Of course, I had an advantage because Douglas Hurd had been in the Foreign Service as a permanent official. He had been in the Private Office of Sir Derek Hoyer-Millar when he was Permanent Under-Secretary of the Foreign Office, so he had Private Office experience in government. It was therefore very easy for him to get on with the civil servants who were in my Private Office at Number Ten. They always worked extremely harmoniously together.[66]

Heath also needed a new chief press secretary and, wanting fewer political appointees, he deliberately chose a career civil servant to replace Joe Haines. Donald Maitland was a Foreign Office diplomat with whom he had worked closely during Macmillan's government, including during the UK's first attempt to join the Common

Market, when Heath had been the lead minister. According to a 2010 obituary of Maitland:

> In three years at Number 10 Maitland became one of Heath's most trusted advisers, notably on industrial relations and Northern Ireland, where he kept a line open to Catholic opinion. Critics blamed him for what they saw as Heath's presidential style of government, and Labour grew frustrated at his skill in getting Heath on to current affairs programmes – to which they had no right of reply – rather than ministerial broadcasts, for which they would be guaranteed equal time.[67]

So the body of staff that Heath brought into No. 10 was based on a familiar pattern: all were male, of a similar outlook and background; three were educated at Oxford while Maitland had attended Edinburgh University. However, the key to the overall success of the private office was undoubtedly Armstrong. The fact that he remained in post for five years, and was then retained by Wilson, was a tribute to his skills and also demonstrated a key criterion for a private secretary, namely the ability to work loyally with different Prime Ministers of different political persuasions and styles. Theakston referred to him as a 'mandarin's mandarin', underlining both Armstrong's reputation across all departments but also his ability to protect and promote the interests of the civil service while simultaneously loyally serving his political masters.[68]

ROBERT ARMSTRONG AND THE COMMON MARKET NEGOTIATIONS

Heath's main political achievement as Prime Minister was to take

Britain into the Europe Economic Community (EEC). From his first day in office, he took a close interest in the negotiations. The day after his general election victory, Heath had received a 'top secret' document from the Cabinet Office proposing a potential negotiating strategy for Europe. This focused, in particular, on how to handle discussions with the French, since UK officials advised that they would be critical to achieving entry to the EEC, given that France had previously blocked Britain's accession application. Once Armstrong became principal private secretary in early July, he soon became one of the conduits for liaising with French President Pompidou's chief negotiator and secretary-general to the Élysée, Michel Jobert.[69] As a result, eventually all decisions had to be filtered on the UK side via Armstrong, who came to know Heath's mind so well that he often did not even feel the need to refer certain decisions back to him.[70] It helped that, fortuitously, Heath knew Jobert well since they had met when they were both on holiday in Spain ten years previously.[71] According to Heath, he and Jobert 'spent many hours on the beach in the intervals between bathing, discussing European politics and the part Britain would play in them', and Jobert displayed considerable sympathy for Heath's position.[72] So Jobert often liaised with Armstrong or with the UK ambassador to France, Christopher Soames, who could report directly to Armstrong and Heath, thereby bypassing the Foreign Office.[73]

Many of the negotiations had to be conducted secretly on account of tensions between the Foreign Office and No. 10, since, according to Heath, 'some officials in the Foreign Office wanted to isolate the French by working with the Five [other members of the European Community] against them'.[74] The negotiations were also kept secret because of the sensitivity of some of the policy issues under discussion. For example, Heath's initial briefing noted (some thirty years before the adoption of the euro) potential difficulties, including on 'the Community's development toward full monetary and economic harmonisation'.[75] Heath and his close advisers believed that an early Anglo-French summit was essential in order to get French support for the UK's entry to Europe. They believed, correctly, that the French would be the 'real masters of the outcome'.[76]

The strategy paid off, and by early 1971, arrangements were in hand for a summit between Heath and Pompidou. The initial arrangements were made by Soames and Jobert and then 'the final stage of preparation was the visit to Paris on May 15 by Robert Armstrong, accompanied by Peter Thornton [from the Cabinet Office] and Douglas Hurd to discuss the agenda with Jobert'.[77] The summit between Heath and Pompidou proved to be a success and helped smooth the route to British membership of the Common Market.

Again, Heath used his principal private secretary as his most senior policy adviser in a way Wilson never did. The arrangement was done formally with the agreement of the Cabinet Secretary, Burke Trend, who, as a result, became more distant from the Prime Minister. Trend had been a close confidant of Wilson, but he never developed a similar relationship with Heath. According to Armstrong:

> I got particularly involved in the European negotiations. It was Heath's key ambition. Burke Trend was an old friend and my mentor. Yet he was more of an Atlanticist and Commonwealth man. As a result, Ted [Heath] used me more, with Burke's complete agreement. I therefore took on some of the role of the Cabinet Secretary.[78]

Heath specifically used his principal private secretary as his lead

broker to help deliver his most important political priority. He trusted Armstrong totally to perform that task. Trend, who had been as
close to Wilson as any civil servant, was effectively sidelined from
the Europe debate and 'Heath's disillusion with Trend was becoming common knowledge'.[79] Heath's biographer says that, put simply,
Heath found Trend 'too correct, too objective, too detached [and]
too non-committal'.[80] Trend retired in 1973 and was succeeded by
Sir John Hunt. On 28 October 1971, the House of Commons voted
in favour of joining the EEC on the basis of the negotiated arrangements, and on 1 January 1973, the United Kingdom joined the EEC.[81]

Following British accession to the European Community, Armstrong continued to play a central role for Heath in liaison with the
French officials, including Jean Monnet and, once again, Michel
Jobert, who by April 1973 became French Foreign Minister. Armstrong met him that month for discussions about whether Britain
would join the European monetary system, which 'was a matter
of great importance to the President'.[82] At their private lunch, and
with no other officials present, Armstrong asked about the future
of direct contacts between the staff of No. 10 and the Élysée Palace.
Jobert reported that the French President thought the contacts had
worked well and that he wanted Jobert, now as Foreign Minister,
'to be his Kissinger' and to continue to liaise directly with Armstrong.[83] In passing, Jobert also commented that he had heard that
Armstrong might be leaving No. 10 and was relieved to find that the
rumour was incorrect. When Armstrong reported this latter point
to the Prime Minister, Heath's only comment was to ask, jokingly,
'Has the Civil Service Department been penetrated? Or No. 10?'[84]
Heath would not be letting Armstrong leave No. 10 so long as he
remained Prime Minister.

Even in the autumn of 1973, Pompidou was still using Armstrong as a conduit to contact Heath, without Foreign Office knowledge. At another private lunch with Jobert, in September, Armstrong reported back to Heath with 'two messages which Jobert asked me to convey to the Prime Minister, for his eyes and ears only'.[85] The first message concerned Pompidou's views on a proposition that the European Community might nominate a spokesman (first German Chancellor Willy Brandt, then the UK Prime Minister and then Pompidou) to deal with the United States.[86] The second point concerned Pompidou's request that Heath support him in opposing direct elections to the European Parliament. As Armstrong reported, Jobert stressed that both messages from the President were 'for the Prime Minister only and were on no account to be passed to the Foreign and Commonwealth Secretary or to the Foreign Office. He said that, once anything got into the hands of the diplomats, it was halfway across Europe before you knew where you were.'[87] Negotiations were between Pompidou and Jobert on the French side and only Heath and Armstrong on the British side. The UK Foreign Secretary was excluded. (In many ways, this presaged the way in which Margaret Thatcher would use Charles Powell during the latter part of her premiership. Powell, like Armstrong, used to pride himself on being able to read the Prime Minister's mind and therefore felt able to speak on Thatcher's behalf without always referring issues back to her. Armstrong often did the same with Heath.)

Despite the political difficulties of his administration, Heath had, in his relatively short time as Prime Minister, been a radical reformer of Whitehall. He had introduced a broad slew of managerial changes, one of which at least, the CPRS, felt like a powerful tool for enhancing longer-term strategic thinking in government, which had been his aim. The other Whitehall changes had proved far less successful. The No. 10 machine was working more efficiently than when he became Prime Minister, and the private office was central to that. There were fewer political advisers and nothing approaching a 'Kitchen Cabinet'. Rather, there was a small private office and an even smaller political presence which worked in tandem, thanks in large part to the similar backgrounds of the two principal figures, Armstrong and Hurd. The decision by Heath, within a fortnight of becoming Prime Minister, to sack Wilson's principal private secretary and to replace him with Whitehall's nominated choice, Robert Armstrong, certainly paid dividends. Armstrong became Heath's indispensable and trusted adviser, negotiating on his behalf at the highest levels in Europe. Ironically, by the end of Heath's time in office, the No. 10 private office was working at its most efficient, just as the government's fortunes went into decline.

Throughout 1973, the political storm clouds had been brewing. The Heath government's agenda soon became dominated not by Europe but by a combination of the search for a settlement of the Northern Ireland issue and, increasingly, the growing economic crisis. By the end of 1973, Heath was 'exhausted … He was facing the crisis of his government.'[88] Battered by the imposition of a three-day week to save energy supplies and then with a national miners' strike, Heath called a general election on 28 February and lost his working majority. Although the results gave the Conservatives a greater share of the popular vote, the Labour Party under Wilson won four more seats.[89*] The next four days were to be important for the nation and critical for the private office. Armstrong, as principal private secretary, was to play a central role.

---

* The final results were as follows: Labour 301 seats, Conservatives 297, Liberals fourteen, SNP seven and others sixteen.

THE 1974 TRANSITION AND THE ARMSTRONG MEMORANDUM

In 1974, the private office had given little thought as to planning for a hung parliament. Unlike nowadays, there was no blueprint for Cabinet Office or the No. 10 private office and as Armstrong recalled:

> I do not remember that either Sir John Hunt [the Cabinet Secretary] or I had done much by way of preparation for a hung parliament before 1 March 1974. It was very many years since there had been such an electoral outcome, and we were too preoccupied with the current [economic] situation.[90]*

Indeed, even on election night, the private office officials thought that Heath was likely to be returned to No. 10 as Prime Minister. They were all attending a party at Robin Butler's south London house. When the first constituency result came in, Armstrong realised that the outcome was going to be far closer than they had thought, and he hurried back to Downing Street.[91]

Armstrong had to manage much of the transition process almost single-handed. However, he took contemporaneous notes of all the meetings he attended and later recorded what he had done, when and why. This chronology provides a detailed overview and explanation of the role of the private office during a transition. His memorandum, entitled 'Note for the Record: Events Leading to the Resignation of Mr Heath's Administration on 4 March 1974', chronicles Armstrong's activities as well as those of Heath, Hunt, other members of the private office, Buckingham Palace officials

---

* The last hung parliament had, in fact, been in 1929 – forty-five years previously.

and the key politicians during the period between Friday 1 March to Monday 4 March.[92]*

Armstrong noted that on 1 March, the morning after the election, Heath held a meeting with Chancellor Anthony Barber, Home Secretary Robert Carr, Lord President James Prior and Energy Secretary Lord Carrington. Hunt and Armstrong were also present. After ruling out any form of coalition with the Labour Party, the meeting identified 'three possible courses open to the Government':

1. to resign forthwith;
2. to continue in office until Parliament met, and then to resign if defeated in a vote on the Address in reply to the Queen's Speech;
3. to try to come to some kind of understanding with the Liberal Party, as a basis either for a Conservative administration with Liberal support or for a Conservative–Liberal coalition.[93]

According to Armstrong, Heath's view the previous day had been to try to stay in office and wait until Parliament met, but only if the Conservatives had more seats than Labour. In fact, the Conservatives ended with four fewer seats. Following their discussion, the meeting agreed that the Prime Minister 'should put the options to a meeting of the Cabinet later that day ... with an indication of their inclination towards an attempt to come to some arrangement with the Liberal Party'.[94] Armstrong spent the afternoon keeping the Queen's private secretary, Sir Martin Charteris, fully informed, and later that day Cabinet agreed the approach. Heath also met the Queen that evening.

The Armstrong note goes on to record the faintly amusing

---

* Curiously, the final paragraph of Armstrong's memorandum is retained and has not been released by the National Archives.

attempts to contact Jeremy Thorpe,* the leader of the Liberal Party, who claimed he had waited over one and a half hours by his phone for a call from the Prime Minister, but his phone was out of order. He agreed to meet the Prime Minister on Saturday at 4 p.m. In the afternoon, Thorpe saw Heath and, although their personal accounts differ, Thorpe clearly pressed for the job of Home Secretary, but nothing was offered. However, as Heath himself noted before any discussion with Thorpe, 'I had been made aware that there were matters in Thorpe's private life, as yet undisclosed to the public, which might make this a highly unsuitable position for him to hold.'[95]† Their talks continued over the weekend and it is clear from the Armstrong memorandum that the Conservatives were looking for a formal coalition to provide greater stability for whatever government might be formed, and that the Liberals would not accept that. The Liberal Party's demands for electoral reform were unacceptable to the Conservatives and, in Armstrong's words, the most the government could offer would be 'to support the setting up of a Speaker's Conference to examine the matter and make recommendations which could then be the subject of a free vote in Parliament.'[96]

The other options, including a possible approach to the Scottish National Party (SNP), came to nothing. Perhaps that was an error by Heath. Both the Liberals and the SNP believed strongly in greater devolution to Scotland and might have agreed a package that would provide at least short-term support to a minority Heath government in exchange for greater autonomy north of the border. According to Armstrong, no such overtures to the SNP were made.[97] However,

---

* Jeremy Thorpe (1929–2014); leader of the Liberal Party 1967–76.

† Thorpe did not say whether he was ever offered the post of Home Secretary by Heath. (In correspondence, I asked Armstrong specifically about the information provided by the security services to Heath on Thorpe's private life. Unfortunately, Armstrong died before replying to my email.)

by the lunchtime of Monday 4 March, Armstrong's memorandum makes clear that there was no scope for an agreement with the Liberals, and so the rest of the day focused on the arrangements leading up to Heath's resignation. Heath met his Downing Street staff to say goodbye and to offer them a drink at about 5.40 p.m., and then Armstrong had to leave the party 'to ring Mrs Marcia Williams, to warn Mr Wilson that he could expect a telephone call from Buckingham Palace at about 7 p.m. or soon thereafter, and to find out where Mr Wilson would be'.[98] Finally, 'at 6.25 p.m. the Prime Minister left 10 Downing Street for Buckingham Palace. I went with him; and on the drive we neither of us said a word. There was so much, or nothing, left to say'.[99] Armstrong admits that, in accompanying Heath to the palace, he 'nearly broke down in tears'.[100]

By this time, Armstrong had been Heath's principal private secretary for all but twelve days of his three and a half years as Prime Minister and, by all accounts, had run the private office effectively during that period. Armstrong's memorandum is probably the best recorded example of the critical role principal private secretaries play during the transition. It shows Armstrong's role in supporting Heath and managing the overall process, advising on options, keeping the palace and other players fully involved, overseeing the press releases on progress and, all the time, remembering that, at the end of the process, he might well have to serve a new Prime Minister. It remains a rare example of how to handle a complex transition.[101]*

Armstrong's memorandum does, however, expose the lack of planning within private office prior to the election. The possibility of the first hung parliament for forty-five years was a very real one. The fact that Armstrong and Hunt had not given much thought

---

* In 1990, Andrew Turnbull made a similar record of the Thatcher–Major transition (see Chapter 7).

as to how to handle that possibility was clearly an oversight. The opinion polls had suggested a strong possibility that there might be a hung parliament and that the Liberals might have considerably more seats in the new Parliament than the six they held in the outgoing one.[102]* At general elections nowadays, the Cabinet Secretary and the No. 10 principal private secretary are far better prepared for all eventualities.

PRIVATE OFFICE AND THE RETURN OF LABOUR

Armstrong recorded his narrative of the events following the general election on 16 March, by which time Wilson was firmly reinstalled in No. 10. How did the private office operate during Wilson's second term as Prime Minister and what were the differences by comparison with his first administration? And what happened during the administration of James Callaghan, who succeeded Wilson as Prime Minister in 1976? That later period was dominated by the country's continuing economic challenges. How did private office exercise its authority throughout these difficult times?

Wilson re-entered No. 10 on Monday 4 March with Marcia Williams and Joe Haines returning to their previous roles. He completed his team of senior external advisers with the appointment of Bernard Donoughue to head a new team in the Prime Minister's office called the Policy Unit. Donoughue, an LSE academic, had impressed Wilson in the opposition years and had worked for the Labour Party during the February 1974 election campaign, after

---

* Half of the opinion polls conducted throughout the campaign predicted that the gap between the two main parties would be 4 per cent or less. Of the final seven polls conducted for election day, the average percentage prediction for the Liberal Party was over 22 per cent. The final difference between the two parties was 0.8 per cent and the Liberals in fact polled 19.8 per cent.

which Wilson invited him to join No. 10. Donoughue's diary entry at the time described himself as a 'new boy in Whitehall' who 'was urgently required to create a new institution in central government, against the scepticism and occasional hostility of some of the regular civil servants'.[103]

Donoughue's view was that Wilson wanted him to provide more integrated policy analysis across the broad political agenda:

> Previous Prime Ministers had employed individual advisers. However, until Harold Wilson created the Policy Unit there was no systematic policy analysis separate from the regular civil service machine and working solely for the Prime Minister ... This strengthening of the supportive mechanisms serving the Prime Minister has proved an important reform among the several contributions Harold Wilson made to the effectiveness of British central government.[104]

As described by Donoughue, the establishment of the Policy Unit provided the Prime Minister with independent advice from a formal source in No. 10 outside his private office and yet which worked closely alongside it. It was different from the approach Heath favoured and his use of Armstrong as his policy lead, especially on Europe. The Policy Unit represented a distinctive new approach to policy-making in No. 10 in a way that had never previously happened. It also meant that more resources could be devoted to policy in No. 10, and Donoughue initially appointed some six to eight policy experts together with two supporting research assistants.[105]

The logic of why Wilson created the Policy Unit was clear. In his first administration, on many of the major policy challenges – including the economy and devaluation, trade union reform, Fulton and, arguably, even Europe – he did not have vast policy resources at his own disposal in No. 10. This was something he wished to rectify. The CPRS, which Wilson retained on returning to Downing Street, provided him with some capacity for longer-term strategic advice, and the private office, under Armstrong's leadership, worked well. Wilson wanted the Policy Unit to support him with stronger political advice on the day-to-day policy issues facing the government. In his book *The Governance of Britain*, Wilson commented that he set the Policy Unit up in order to 'advise on, propose and pursue policies to further the Government's political goals. For policies without politics are of no more use than politics without policies.'[106] Every subsequent Prime Minister has retained the No. 10 Policy Unit.

Donoughue's diary charts the, often tense, atmosphere over the following two years as he attempted to forge good relations with the private office while, at the same time, having to engage with the Prime Minister and manage Williams's temper. Fortunately for him, relations between Donoughue and Haines on the political side and Armstrong and Butler (who stayed in No. 10 as the economics private secretary) on the official side, remained positive throughout.[107] The major policy focus of the unit from 1974 to 1975 was on economic policy and developing an active interventionist industrial strategy. Donoughue worked closely with Butler on this and described him as 'the most outstanding civil servant with whom I ever had to deal, at any level'.[108] However, the looming economic crisis and the growth of inflation meant that by 1976, the Policy Unit had to turn its mind to how to cut government expenditure.[109]

Marcia Williams's increasingly idiosyncratic behaviour was also putting additional pressures on the No. 10 private office. Her unpredictability had become more acute. She did not turn up at No. 10 on a regular basis and, when she did, she tried to give orders in the way she had done a decade previously but now with far less authority. According to Butler, it was, at times, 'bedlam'.[110] For example, Williams 'would use Wilson's official car to go shopping and you could never get away with that now. She deliberately made engagements that clashed with those the private office made.'[111] She took against Armstrong and Butler, claiming they were biased. Her distrust of Armstrong appears to have been because he had served Heath loyally for three and a half years but also because he personally supported Common Market entry. In his recollection:

> When Harold Wilson came back to No. 10 on 4 March 1974, I knew that Marcia Williams wanted me out. After the first few days, during which Wilson was concentrating on appointing his team of ministers, I said to him that I had been at No. 10 for three and a half years and had been known to be a supporter of our accession to the EEC, and that I should quite understand – no skin off my nose – if he wanted a change of principal private secretary. He said that he did not want me to go: 'You and I are getting along well together, and the office is working far better than when I was here last time. You stay around.'[112]

Wilson's emphasis that the private office was, by this time, more effective than under his first administration also showed that, by inference, Williams was less influential than she had been when Derek Mitchell had headed private office ten years earlier. It was also probably a tacit recognition by Wilson that the private office for most of his first administration, under principal private secretaries chosen by him, had not been well led. Armstrong, and in due course Stowe, were to provide No. 10 with a quality of leadership and ballast that had been lacking during Wilson's first term. As Pimlott highlights, 'Armstrong's high Whitehall reputation and diplomatic skills ensured that Wilson got the best the Civil Service could offer: this was all the more welcome, because he followed two disastrous choices, Michael Halls and (briefly) Sandy Isserlis, in the 1966–70 administration.'[113]

Marcia Williams also wanted Robin Butler removed from No. 10, for two reasons. First, that he had attended the Trades Union Congress, entirely legitimately, to support the Prime Minister when Wilson spoke there, and it is not clear why she took offence to this. Second, and possibly with slightly more justification, Williams was irritated that Butler had attended one of the regular monthly lunches organised by *Private Eye*. On this occasion, Joe Haines and Bernard Donoughue both came to his rescue and 'took Butler's side so strongly against her – a fact which [Butler] has publicly acknowledged – that Wilson kept him in place, removing a threat to his subsequent career'.[114]

Butler, for his part, found the transition from Heath back to Wilson frustrating. Despite Heath's style, his private office had a unity of purpose and professionalism, whereas Wilson's second administration

> was quite different. The atmosphere was conspiratorial with different factions within the office, principally between Marcia Williams on one side and Bernard Donoughue and Joe Haines on the other. Harold Wilson almost seemed to encourage these internal civil wars ... The private office was the meat in the sandwich between the warring factions.[115]

Butler was neatly expressing a far wider problem with Wilson's No. 10 private office, in that the Prime Minister was often so focused on politics that he could lose sight of the business of government. The No. 10 machine was far less efficient than in Heath's day, when there had been unity of purpose across the politicians and private office. Butler even felt that Wilson almost enjoyed this disruption, as it allowed him to practise manipulating the factions in the Labour Party. As a result, in Butler's opinion, the business of private office, which was simply 'doing its best to keep the show on the road, suffered'.[116] Butler had expressed the frustrations felt by the civil service at a time of ever-growing economic crisis and the seeming impotency of the private office, which appeared to be having no effect. With the private office reverting to a more traditional role of simply managing the day-to-day business, it was far less influential than it had been when Heath was Prime Minister.

Armstrong eventually left No. 10 at a time of his own choosing: 'Wilson said he wanted me to stay, and I did so until April 1975.'[117] He moved to the Home Office, where he joined his former political master Roy Jenkins, to spend two years as deputy secretary prior to becoming its Permanent Secretary. Butler, too, left No. 10 in 1975, to return to the Treasury. Following Armstrong's departure, Wilson remained sceptical about appointing someone from the Treasury as his principal private secretary and decided instead to choose a senior official from the Department of Health and Social Security (DHSS), Ken Stowe. Stowe was surprised to have been offered the job because he was not from the Treasury and had never been a private secretary before. Those qualities were precisely what endeared him to Wilson, as did the fact that he had been brought up on a Dagenham council estate where he had attended the local school. As before in the 1960s, Wilson opposed the original 'Treasury-dominated list of candidates' proposed by Sir John Hunt as Armstrong's successor and alighted instead on Stowe who was proposed as an alternative. According to his *Times* obituary, 'the more Stowe argued [with Wilson] that he was a peripheral official, and had never been a private secretary before, the more Wilson wanted him.'[118] It turned out to be an inspired choice and the mild-mannered Stowe remained at No. 10 for five years, loyally serving three very different Prime Ministers. His *Guardian* obituary highlights that '[Stowe] was modest, soft-spoken, direct, discreet and motivated by a commitment to public service. There was an acute sense of crisis in British government in the 1970s; at times various administrations seemed barely able to cope and some in Downing Street lost their heads. Stowe, however, was never flustered.'[119]

The choice of Stowe once again underlined Wilson's scepticism of the Treasury and what he saw as a civil service establishment view. He always had more empathy with outsiders, favouring non-Treasury types, and, as was the case with Stowe, looked for officials who had no predetermined thoughts as to how the job might be done. Given the economic pressures that were about to engulf the government at the end of 1976, Stowe's calmness and administrative skills were to prove invaluable during the IMF crisis. Donoughue described him as one of the best private secretaries he encountered.[120] In comparison with Armstrong, whom Donoughue also admired, he commented:

> [Stowe] was an easier and simpler man, entirely without side. He gave the Policy Unit every possible assistance and we worked closely and comfortably together. His great virtues were his calmness, his openness and his directness. Mr Callaghan thought the world of him, and I could quite see why. He was a marvellous team member.[121]

Similarly, Haines rated him, saying that 'Ken Stowe was an excellent man. Very much on our side in the Marcia business. Robert

[Armstrong] sometimes found it difficult to tell us what was happening, whereas Ken Stowe was always very good at doing so.'[122] Finally, David Lipsey, who joined No. 10 when Callaghan succeeded Wilson, described Stowe as 'very straight, if not all that imaginative' but someone who 'ensured everything was done correctly'.[123] In other words, Stowe was a private secretary in the traditional mould, which suited both Wilson in this later phase of his premiership and certainly Callaghan who succeeded Wilson in April 1976. The new, and for its time unusual, three-way relationship which developed between the private office (led by Stowe), the press operation (led by Haines) and the policy-making process (led by Donoughue) for the final two years of Wilson's premiership provided a strong degree of collective ballast at No. 10 as the economic crisis grew.[124] The Policy Unit gave the Prime Minister access to high-quality independent economic advice from Donoughue's team, Haines continued to manage communications robustly and the private office, led by Stowe, supported and managed the overall process but without any risk of politicisation.

However, Wilson now was not the Prime Minister he had been. He was drinking more and so became increasingly reliant on his private office to manage his administration and No. 10. According to Anthony Seldon:

> His ailments were in part alcohol-related. Kenneth Stowe ... said that 'it could be pointless [because of drink] to get a decision out of him after 6 p.m.' Another aide [Bernard Donoughue] said that PMQ days were the worst, when he needed brandies to fortify him before, and more brandies to celebrate after.[125]

Stowe also played a key role for Wilson as he prepared to leave No.

10. After the October 1974 general election, Wilson told Haines that he would leave office after two further years as Prime Minister. A year later, at the October 1975 Labour Party conference, he again confirmed to Haines that he would step down early in 1976.[126] Haines recalled:

> Wilson told me to draw up a timetable and a resignation plan ... and then to go through the procedures for his departure. He told me to work with Ken Stowe and to tell no one, to make only one plan and to take no copies. So Ken and I worked on this together.[127]

They were able to keep the secret of Wilson's intended announcement from leaking to the press or the wider political world. Haines noted: 'Harold told Marcia eventually. Various other people got to know. Harold let it slip more or less to Jim Callaghan on a trip to Brighton. But, in the end, I reckon there were only twenty people who knew.'[128]

The ability of Stowe and Haines to work together in planning Wilson's exit from Downing Street was an example of the relative harmony that existed in his private office during his second administration. It also shows how Haines recognised the value of the civil servants in private office and the benefits of their close working relationships.[129] Private office from 1964 to 1970, with its weak leadership, did not cope well. From 1974 to 1976, and by the end of the Wilson premiership, it was to become a part of his political life-support system. By 1976, Wilson was ailing physically, he had only a very slim parliamentary majority and the economy was approaching a crisis. In those circumstances, he chose to resign. As ever, it was the task of the private office 'to keep the show on the road'.

PRIVATE OFFICE AND THE CALLAGHAN PREMIERSHIP

Harold Wilson left No. 10 on 5 April 1976. His successor, James Callaghan, was a different type of politician. He saw his role very much as '*primus inter pares*'. According to his special adviser David Lipsey, Callaghan was 'the last of the old-fashioned Prime Ministers. Included in this creed was that Secretaries of State were important people who on the whole should be left to get on with their jobs to which they were appointed.'[130] Callaghan, therefore, tended to rely on the Cabinet Secretary (John Hunt) plus his private office and a very small number of close advisers. As historian Kenneth O. Morgan highlighted, 'like Attlee, Callaghan linked a collective delegative style of management with areas of personal authority. On economic policy, he adopted his own separate approach, through talented advisers in his Policy Unit headed by Bernard Donoughue.'[131] Joe Haines left when Wilson did and was replaced by 'the quiet-spoken Scot, Tom McCaffrey [who], as press secretary, was far removed from the empire of spin in the Alastair Campbell era twenty years later'.[132] McCaffrey was a permanent civil servant which also underlined that Callaghan (who himself had been a civil servant before the war) had greater trust in the civil service as an institution than did his predecessor.

Within his Cabinet, Callaghan had some strong intellects (including Tony Benn, Tony Crosland, Michael Foot, Denis Healey, Peter Shore and Shirley Williams), but he also had access to powerful minds in the CPRS, in the Policy Unit as well as 'the formidable Private Office line-up he enjoyed of Ken Stowe, Nigel Wicks, Tim Lankester and Patrick Wright'.[133] Evidence of the sheer quality of Callaghan's private office is that all four of those private secretaries went on to hold Permanent Secretary positions later in their civil service careers (at the DHSS, the Treasury, the Department for Education and the Foreign Office, respectively). So, there was no shortage of intellectual firepower at the centre of government as the country approached what was to be one of the deepest economic crises since the Second World War.

PRIVATE OFFICE AND THE IMF CRISIS OF 1976

During the summer and autumn of 1976, Britain was plunged into a most serious economic crisis regarding the International Monetary Fund (IMF). The handling of that crisis has been related elsewhere in many books and articles.[134] The discussions were handled at the political level and Callaghan managed, via an 'arduous' series of 'twenty-six ministerial meetings (nine of them full Cabinets), to talk it out over two months'.[135] Skilful though this was on one level, it was also an example of almost dysfunctional government. At various points in the crisis, ministers, officials and political advisers all felt excluded from decision-making. At No. 10, the two most important official advisers were Hunt and Stowe, showing how much Callaghan trusted his Cabinet Secretary and the principal private secretary, both of whom he had inherited from Wilson.

Before Callaghan became Prime Minister, the economy had already taken a turn for the worse. In January 1976, the Treasury had pressed for a package of cuts, which had been agreed, but nevertheless sterling remained under pressure by the time Callaghan reached No. 10.[136] There was growing pressure on the pound such that, by the summer, Callaghan and Healey were seeking a further package of cuts and authorised the Bank of England to spend reserves in order to support sterling on the international markets up to a limit of £500 million. However, the No. 10 private office was frustrated by what it saw as the Treasury not telling them what was happening. In August, Patrick Wright, the foreign affairs private secretary, complained to Stowe that the Treasury would not tell him how much of the £500 million had been used up. In a private note to Stowe, he said that, unless the Chancellor had told the Prime Minister confidentially how much of the money had been spent, 'the Treasury should be hung, drawn and quartered'.[137] Tensions between No. 10 and No. 11 were high.

Callaghan's strategy was complex. He had to gain agreement to further cuts, ensure that there was not a split in his Cabinet and secure the wider support of the Labour Party for his approach. He also had to garner international support for his strategy from world leaders. As early as 22 September, the Chancellor of the Exchequer told his Cabinet colleagues that an application to the IMF for financial support was inevitable.[138] On 28 September, Healey dramatically turned back from attending the annual meeting of the IMF in Manila to address instead the Labour Party conference about the crisis.[139] However, it was clear by now that the IMF would inflict strict borrowing conditions on the government as part of any loan, and that such conditions would be hugely painful and unpopular.

On 6 October, Healey wanted to increase interest rates from 13 per cent to 15 per cent and, uncertain of the Prime Minister's support, threatened to take the issue to Cabinet, where he would be bound to lose and would therefore resign. Before that could happen, though, Healey recalled that 'the door opened and in came the Prime Minister's principal private secretary, Ken Stowe. "Excuse me, Chancellor," he said, "the Prime Minister has asked me to tell you that he was only testing the strength of your conviction. Of course, he will support you."'[140] It was perhaps a sign of the regard in which Callaghan already held Stowe that he used him as his messenger on a personal and political issue that was so sensitive.

Callaghan was very cautious and wanted to keep matters as secret as possible, including concerning whom he consulted. When he met the German Chancellor Helmut Schmidt at Chequers the weekend after Healey's threatened resignation, seeking German support for sterling, he would not even let Stowe, his closest aide, into the bilateral meeting and instead dictated afterwards an account of his conversation. As a result, Stowe's note for the record may not be entirely accurate, as opposed to recording what Callaghan wished had been agreed.[141] Callaghan was clearly determined to keep discussions at a political level and not let Treasury officials know what was going on. Later in the autumn, Callaghan met the IMF's chief negotiator with Stowe as the only official present. 'Meetings were kept totally secret,' notes Kenneth O. Morgan.[142] Donoughue felt he was not fully involved and, in his memoirs, complained about 'decisions being taken which could decide the fate of this Labour Government. Yet the Labour members of it are frozen out of the decision making. Apart from the Prime Minister and the Chancellor only civil servants are informed'.[143] Those officials were Hunt and Stowe. Donoughue had to resort to 'asking Ken Stowe direct questions which he generally answers, partly because he has always preferred to be open and helpful, mainly because it would be ridiculous not to'.[144]

At one point, Callaghan asked Hunt to consult a slightly wider group of Permanent Secretaries about the potential for introducing import controls as part of the overall package, but there was little appetite for that.[145] It was striking once again that the two people who Callaghan worked closest with, Hunt and Stowe, were both officials in what was essentially a political crisis. By way of contrast, that would never happen today.

After almost three months of Cabinet discussions, the Cabinet backed the package of spending cuts and the IMF loan – the largest it had then ever granted – was finally agreed. The process was handled traditionally and, once again, with Hunt and Stowe firmly in charge of the civil service side of the operation. In many recent crises, the role of the No. 10 private office has been much reduced and the influence of special advisers, and other political advisers, far higher. Under Callaghan, the stature and influence of the principal private secretary was paramount. Stowe was the only official with the full picture. When, two years later, the Callaghan government was finally facing electoral defeat as a result of the so-called Winter of Discontent, it again was to Stowe that Callaghan confided: 'I let the country down.'[146]

From 1970 to 1979, private office had to cope with changes of Prime Minister and the accompanying policy adjustments. Wilson and Heath both sought to make interventions from the top to re-shape the processes of government. These included changes to the structures of departments and the machinery of government, the introduction of managerial initiatives to address government processes and wider civil service reform. Throughout this era of relative economic decline, crises and political change, it was often the private office that provided the unseen junction box and ensured that the business of government continued.

Overall, the fifteen-year period covering Wilson's, Heath's and Callaghan's administrations may perhaps be best characterised as the start of a 'pendulum effect', whereby the role and functions of the Prime Minister swing back and forth between being more or less forceful and interventionist, and whereby the civil service, and in particular the private office, flips between holding greater or lesser influence. Prior to the 1964 election, Whitehall had tried to ensure that Wilson would be well supported by installing Derek Mitchell as the No. 10 principal private secretary. As Prime Minister, Wilson never looked to his private office for policy advice but relied instead on his political advisers, his 'Kitchen Cabinet' and, on occasions, the Cabinet Secretary. Information was not always shared fully with the private office, thereby making its task harder. The private office's power and position was tested early on by the dominant role played by Marcia Williams and the influence which she sought to exert over officials, together with the influence of some of Wilson's newly appointed special advisers. All of these outsiders wanted to see a more political dimension from the government, fearing that, otherwise, the civil service could block reform. Mitchell tried, but failed, to reach an accommodation with Williams, and Wilson's next two appointments to that key post were simply unable to provide the level of leadership required. This underlines a recurring theme of the central importance of the principal private secretary to the smooth and efficient functioning of No. 10.

Heath, though, adopted a different administrative approach to his style of governing. He was certainly more innovative in terms of introducing new systems for the provision of advice to ministers, including via the Central Policy Review Staff, albeit far less political in his outlook and the way he used advisers. But he was not an innovator in the private office. Under Heath, the central role of the permanent civil service was restored and much of the credit for that must go to Robert Armstrong, who served Heath throughout his premiership as principal private secretary and took on a considerable policy role on Europe. The pendulum swung back towards the traditional civil service and permanent officials. Because of the similar outlook and background of private secretaries and political appointees under Heath, this process was far less fraught than under Wilson. However, it underlines the benefits that can accrue when the No. 10 private secretaries are seen to be working in harmony with the political side.

Notwithstanding the severity of the economic crises which punctuated the 1970s, the leadership of Armstrong and his successor Ken Stowe brought an authority back to the No. 10 private office which had been singularly absent during Wilson's first administration. Armstrong and Stowe were from different social and departmental backgrounds, but both were good leaders of people, respected by politicians and civil servants alike and both managed the complex business of No. 10 in an efficient manner. Crucially, both men were calm at times of crisis. In addition, Armstrong and Stowe were to serve well different Prime Ministers of different parties as principal private secretary – one of the criteria for judging the effectiveness of a private secretary. By contrast, officials such as Tim Bligh under Harold Macmillan, David Dowler under Roy Jenkins and, later, Charles Powell under Thatcher became either politicised or too closely associated with just one politician. Armstrong and Stowe proved their ability to serve a range of different political masters.

Under Wilson, the private office offered less by way of policy support and challenge. By contrast, during the Heath and Callaghan administrations, Armstrong and Stowe respectively became almost indispensable to their political masters. Stowe was to consolidate private office's role as the central junction box of government, choreographing access and the provision of advice to the Prime Minister, usually working smoothly if not always seamlessly with the political advisers in No. 10. He played one of the central administrative roles in the IMF negotiations in the autumn of 1976. The Policy Unit, established in 1974 under the leadership of Bernard Donoughue, was a valued innovation and became a permanent fixture at the centre of government.

At the start of his second term as Prime Minister, Wilson made a significant decision by retaining Armstrong following his years of service to Heath (in the face of opposition from Marcia Williams), thus recognising the value of the seasoned Whitehall mandarin by comparison with the two outsiders he had chosen for that role in his first term. He acknowledged that the system was working far better when he returned for his second stint as Prime Minister than it had been when he left office in 1970. Indeed, the No. 10 private office in the 1960s and 1970s worked at its best under Heath and with the team led by Armstrong. Four elements of an effective private office came together: clear political direction from the Prime Minister; strong civil service leadership from the principal private secretary; a team of excellent private secretaries; and an authority that was respected Whitehall-wide. Yet, paradoxically, the private office excelled at about the same time as, politically, Heath's government had come under pressure and finally crumbled in the face of the second miners' strike. Similarly, five years later at the end of Callaghan's premiership, the private office was working well under firm leadership and the private secretaries were of a high calibre, but the Winter of Discontent battered Callaghan's popularity. So, a good private office does not guarantee a successful administration, but for a Prime Minister to succeed, they must have an effective private office.

From 1964 to 1979, while ministers, Prime Ministers and at times governments were seemingly at the mercy of events and, in Peter Hennessy's words, simply 'muddling through' as best they could, the constant ballast of government at No. 10 was provided by the permanent civil service and, more specifically, the private office.[147] Some of the most prominent private secretaries of the era emerged and became key players in No. 10 and, at least in part, shapers of policy and makers of history. Robert Armstrong and Robin Butler both went on to serve with distinction as Cabinet Secretary for a period lasting, between the two of them, over eighteen years. However, following the 1979 general election, a fundamentally new type of politics would emerge which, in due course, would also have implications for the operation of private office and the type of private secretaries who served within it.

7

PERSONALITIES AND WARS: PRIVATE OFFICE 1979–90

On Monday 27 January 1986, Margaret Thatcher gathered a small group of her closest advisers in her study at No. 10 Downing Street to continue her last-minute preparations for the third debate in the House of Commons on the Westland crisis. There was only one hour until the debate was due to start at 3.30 p.m. In her autobiography, she explained that she had already spent the previous day 'with officials and speechwriters ... clarifying in [her] own mind what had been said and done, by whom and when', and yet she still felt far from confident.[1] Turning to Charles Powell, her loyal and trusted private secretary for foreign affairs, and Sir Geoffrey Howe, her (perhaps, less trusted) Foreign Secretary, she said simply, 'I may not be Prime Minister by six o'clock tonight.'[2]* How had the Prime Minister who had been in office for almost eight years, won two general elections and already established her reputation as a radical and effective premier managed to get dragged into a crisis of her and her private office's making which now threatened her very survival as Prime Minister? By this time, two of her Cabinet ministers

---

* Charles Moore, Thatcher's official biographer, also says that she used the same phrase, or variants of it, to other private secretaries and to the Cabinet Secretary, Sir Robert Armstrong.

THE INTIMACY OF POWER

had already resigned over the crisis (about the future direction and funding of Westland, a medium-size helicopter company in south-west England), one of whom – Leon Brittan, her former Trade and Industry Secretary – even went so far as to say that she had 'plotted by underhand means against her own ministers [notably Michael Heseltine] … That is what she had done.'[3]

How had Thatcher, having assumed office in 1979 as the inexperienced first female Prime Minister, become so dominant and powerful that she ignored all but a few ministers who stood up to her? How did she manage to make such an enemy of Michael Heseltine? And why, by 1986, did she rely increasingly on only a small number of trusted officials in No. 10? Indeed, how did two key members of her staff eventually become politicised in such a way that, by the end, they were operating effectively as a mini '*cabinet*' within No. 10? This chapter explains how that process happened and how the private office transformed throughout the decade of 'Thatcherism'.

The general election of 1979 has been seen by many contemporary political historians as a watershed, with Margaret Thatcher's victory marking the beginning not only of a new political era but also of a radically different type of politics.[4] The consensus nature of the British system of government, dominant for most of the period since 1945, was coming to an end. Certainly, for the next two decades, the relatively regular transfer of power between the two main parties turned out to be over. The style of government which Thatcher increasingly pursued over her eleven-year period as Prime Minister was of a more idealistic, dogmatic and, at times, confrontational nature than anything seen since 1945. Accordingly, the private office that supported her in No. 10 had to reflect that changed style of political leadership, while – at the same time – upholding the traditions and practices of the impartial British civil service.

Because of its almost revolutionary aspects and political upheavals, the Thatcher era has attracted much attention. Contemporary
historians and journalists began by attempting to capture her impact
while she was still Prime Minister.[5] Following her departure from
Downing Street, a number of significant biographies of Thatcher
were published, including two volumes of autobiography which
stand alongside numerous memoirs written by her contemporary
Conservative politicians.[6] More recently, a new wave of historical
research has begun to use archival and other primary sources to
ask fresh questions and revise earlier accounts of Thatcherism.[7] This
body of literature has focused on Thatcher's record in government,
examining the core elements of her political philosophy (privati-
sation, the belief in free markets, limiting the power of the trade
unions, anti-communism and, in her later years, an increasingly
growing Euroscepticism). The literature also focuses on her style
of leadership, especially in moments of controversy and crisis, and
how this affected the social, economic and political development of
the United Kingdom in her period in office and beyond.

Many political historians have examined how, over time, Thatcher adapted the machinery of government to suit her personal preferences. Yet, the role of her private office during her premiership
has remained a neglected area of study. There has been no systematic exploration of the work of the private office under Thatcher,
although its influence on her was, at times, profound.[8] Those years
were also significant in the evolution of British political history,
particularly in terms of changes in the power and relative influence
of the civil service and private office. But how, under Thatcher, did
private office change and operate and how did she use private office
to drive Whitehall departments to help deliver her agenda?

This chapter examines how Thatcher's private office functioned, from her first days in power following her election triumph, and how it then came to be shaped by her own disciplined management of government business. It focuses in detail on the private office during two moments of supreme crisis in the history of her administration, the Falklands War of 1982 and the Westland affair of 1986. The chapter highlights the role played by two key advisers, Charles Powell, her foreign affairs private secretary, and Bernard Ingham, her chief press secretary, and the tensions that their powerful positions created within the hierarchy of the civil service. It considers the extent to which their increasing influence caused profound unease among ministers, MPs and officials. According to one observer, Powell's politicisation, 'his closeness to the Prime Minister and his influence with her, his willingness to venture into the political world, came to seem a threat to the balance between No. 10 and Whitehall'.[9]

The chapter also explains the ways in which private office changed during the Thatcher years and assesses how it almost came to resemble a Continental-style '*cabinet*'. Finally, the chapter examines Thatcher's downfall and how both Powell and Ingham remained with her at the end.

THE 1979 TRANSITION AND THATCHER'S PRIVATE OFFICE

The private office that Thatcher inherited in May 1979 was in the traditional mould – small, staffed only by male civil servants and with a structure largely unchanged over several decades. The principal private secretary, Ken Stowe, was responsible for ensuring the transition tasks were completed, and the Cabinet Secretary, Sir

John Hunt, oversaw the whole process.* Stowe had already served the two previous Labour Prime Ministers, Wilson and Callaghan, for some four years and was a consummate professional in the role. His professionalism extended to sensitivity about Thatcher's gender. He advised the new Prime Minister to sit behind the driver in the official car on return from the palace so that 'she could get out ... at the door of 10 Downing Street without the waiting press and photographers seeing her legs first'.[10]

Margaret Thatcher's next task was to form her Cabinet and, again, it was to her principal private secretary that she turned: 'Stowe led Mrs Thatcher to the Cabinet room ... At the door, she turned to Stowe and asked him, "Ken, what do I do now?" "You might want to speak to John Hunt, Prime Minister," said Stowe. "You've got to form an administration."'[11]

According to Charles Moore, Thatcher's biographer, this exchange was 'heartening' for Stowe and the private office in that it showed, early on, that the new Prime Minister was willing to take the advice of her immediate civil servants.[12] It also reveals a slightly less decisive image of Thatcher, at this initial stage, than she was later to present. In her autobiography, she praised the 'sheer professionalism' of the civil service, 'which allows governments to come and go with a minimum of dislocation and maximum of efficiency', adding that it is 'something other countries with different systems have every cause to envy'.[13]

The immediate team of private secretaries was five strong – the principal private secretary (Stowe) and the private secretaries for foreign affairs (Bryan Cartledge), economic affairs (Tim Lankester),

---

* Lord Hunt of Tanworth (1919–2008); Cabinet Secretary 1973–79.

home affairs/correspondence (Michael Pattison) and parliamentary affairs (Nick Sanders).[14]* No. 10 then only comprised some seventy members of staff. Charles Powell, who was to join the team five years later, recalled that it was of a similar size to the No. 10 private office under Neville Chamberlain in the late 1930s.[15] That was a remarkable fact given the increased workload of the Prime Minister over that period.

Thatcher accepted the No. 10 model she inherited. This was, perhaps, surprising. As a former Secretary of State for Education who had served in the Heath government, she knew how a Cabinet minister's private office operated and, had she wished, could have made changes. It is striking though that, in the section of her autobiography covering her three and a half years as Education Secretary, she makes no reference at all to her private office and its role or that of her private secretaries. As she approached the job of Prime Minister, she does not appear to have thought through, in advance, the organisation of No. 10 and how she might use it to best effect. For example, on arrival, she did not even have a chief press secretary. Bernard Ingham, who was eventually to fulfil that role, did not join her until October 1979.[16] The dominance of Thatcher and the power of her trusted No. 10 officials were nowhere near as evident as they later were to become. While, by instinct, she was sceptical of the civil service, in practice she proved 'at first surprisingly innocent' about the central functions of government that she would inherit as Prime Minister.[17] According to one of the private secretaries she inherited from Callaghan, 'She loved us, but she loathed civil servants at large.'[18]

Had Thatcher wished to reinvigorate her No. 10 office with

---

* An updated list of the key private secretaries and other officials who served at No. 10 since 1945 is included in Appendix 2 of this book.

outsiders, she could have done so by making more appointments to her Policy Unit. In fact, she did the opposite and, as a result, had to rely more on her private office. The Policy Unit, being a relatively new construct, created by Wilson five years previously and maintained under Callaghan, did not immediately appeal to her as a way of managing change across Whitehall. It had been staffed by Labour political appointees, all of whom left after Thatcher's victory. She was slow to realise the potential benefits that a strong unit might bring in terms of independent policy advice separate from that of the traditional civil service. By comparison with her successors as Prime Minister, she was underpowered on the policy front from day one. Her Policy Unit initially contained only three members of staff. By comparison, today it has well over twenty special advisers to provide such policy expertise.

John Hoskyns, a businessman, was appointed in May 1979 by Thatcher as the new head of the Policy Unit, but he accepted that it was to have a far smaller remit and his influence would be commensurately less than that of her private office. He later commented:

> I wanted a much smaller unit [than Callaghan's] … concentrating solely on 'stabilising the economy', the central objective of the new government's first term … As I was taken round Number Ten, I could sense in the very air of the large private office adjoining the cabinet room the unspoken pressure on any newcomer, especially from outside, to conform … An incoming adviser knew – if he was wise – that he would be seen as at best, an irrelevance.[19]

Unlike nowadays, the power resided far more with civil servants than with advisers. Elsewhere across Whitehall, the transfer of power happened smoothly. The civil service remained broadly in charge. The most recent transition between parties had been in 1974. Civil servants, including close ministerial aides – the officials serving in private office – understood the process well. At the Treasury, for example, the new Chancellor of the Exchequer, Sir Geoffrey Howe, inherited his predecessor Denis Healey's team. The journalist Peter Riddell recalled that he had been at the autumn 1978 Commonwealth finance ministers' meeting in Montreal and the International Monetary Fund meeting in Washington early in 1979, when Healey was Chancellor.[20] Riddell attended the same meetings a year later in Malta and Belgrade, by which time Howe was Chancellor. The only difference in personnel was the change of Chancellor, whereas the supporting entourage of private secretaries and officials remained the same as the previous year.[21]

By 1979, special advisers were becoming an established part of No. 10 and government departments, although none were members of Thatcher's private office. Stowe oversaw all No. 10 appointments, thus underlining how the process was then firmly controlled by the permanent civil service, a fact that would change over time. Three days after Thatcher became Prime Minister, Stowe wrote to all private offices to stipulate the procedures to be followed by Cabinet ministers who wished to appoint special advisers, reminding them that all such appointments required prime ministerial approval, via him.[22] Thatcher eventually appointed ten special advisers to her No. 10 office.

Thatcher did, however, make one innovation in the structure of her office. She created a new position of chief of staff and appointed the businessman David Wolfson* to the role. In practice, however, and despite the impressive nature of his title, the role appeared

---

*   David Wolfson (1935–2021), chief of staff, No. 10, 1979–85; created Baron Wolfson of Sunningdale 1991.

curiously ill-defined. He was not in charge of anything, had no staff at his disposal and did not manage the private office. It is not even clear to whom he reported. According to Charles Moore, Wolfson saw it as his job 'to be aware of the few things that mattered and to make sure that she saw the right people at the right time'.[23] By contrast, Dennis Kavanagh and Anthony Seldon argue:

> Wolfson had no job description but saw himself as 'essentially being responsible for anything that nobody else was doing'. His task was not helped by his office being placed in a small room opposite the door to the Cabinet Office, away from the Prime Minister's office ... He was a sounding-board with considerable potential to affect her future; but both officials and ministers rapidly came to regard him as having no influence on policy.[24]

Despite its apparent triviality, the point about physical proximity to the Prime Minister is an important one. All ministers, including the Prime Minister, want their key advisers close at hand, but this can lead to their dealing with minor administrative tasks if they become the first port of call.[25]* Wolfson was not a permanent civil servant and was paid by the Conservative Party.[26] There is no evidence that he played a significant advisory or executive role, and so the chief of staff initiative was not a great success. The private office operated effectively without a chief of staff and Wolfson, with no clear role or distinct area of responsibility, had little if any value to add to the overall No. 10 operation. Thatcher appears finally to have realised this as Wolfson left No. 10 quietly in 1985 and was not replaced. By

---

* This was certainly the case when Gordon Brown initiated his central core team working in a 'horseshoe' design around him based in No. 12 Downing Street (see Chapter 9).

that time, Charles Powell was already emerging as the key player in her private office.

Andrew Turnbull, who was Thatcher's private secretary for economic affairs in 1983 and later became her principal private secretary, recalled Thatcher as being very hard-working and meticulous. Her working style and the way in which she used her private office were both efficient and effective. He described the mode in which the Prime Minister's office then operated as the classic example of the private office working at its best (and it mirrored John Wyndham's description of the workings of the Macmillan private office, some two decades previously):

> The private office was a well-run and disciplined operation around the flow of paper and red boxes. The content of [Thatcher's] boxes usually consisted of four key elements:
>
> 1. Briefings for meetings the following day (e.g. with a Secretary of State) which would usually have a proposition from the Cabinet member; a note from the Cabinet Office; a brief, if required, from the Policy Unit;* together with a covering overview note from the relevant private secretary to pull together all the documents and to offer a handling strategy for the meeting;
> 2. Correspondence to note what had come in and on which the Prime Minister might wish to comment;
> 3. Items for signature; and
> 4. Background reading material.[27]

---

* The Policy Unit which under Callaghan was headed by Bernard Donoughue was under Thatcher led by John Hoskyns (1979–82), Ferdinand Mount (1982–83), John Redwood (1983–85) and Brian Griffiths (1985–90).

The most important material was in the first category. Thatcher would use meetings with Cabinet colleagues to try to shape departmental policies and to impose her thinking on the Cabinet. The private office was the conduit to enforce that objective and to pursue actions. She was, according to Turnbull, extremely decisive. For example, Turnbull, who served both Thatcher and Major, judged that over 95 per cent of material seen by Thatcher would be actioned and resolved without further requests for information or discussion. For Major, he judged that figure to be 75 per cent. Major, therefore, required many more follow-up meetings, and decisions tended to take longer to be reached.[28] The pace and overall efficiency of the system were reduced as a result.

According to Turnbull, the practical process for managing private office business was as follows:

> At the end of the day, the red boxes were assembled in the private office and sent up to Mrs Thatcher in the flat above 10 Downing Street. The first one would go up at about 7.30 p.m. and the second one at about 9.30 p.m. I would go up to her flat, ring the bell, then leave the box and go without seeing her. You didn't want to have to talk to her about it.[29]

The inference in Turnbull's final comment, no doubt, reflected Thatcher's appetite for robust discussion with her close advisers at whatever time of day or night. Private secretaries would usually avoid that opportunity if they could. The boxes would be collected early the next morning by either the duty clerk or the first private secretary to arrive at No. 10. Then the relevant private secretary for each item of business would dictate action notes, based on Thatcher's comments. So, in summary, according to Turnbull, 'Something which left a government department at, say, 5.30 p.m. one afternoon was turned around with a decision and actions the following morning by around 10.30 a.m.'[30] According to Turnbull, this efficiency in the management of private office business under Thatcher would not be maintained under future occupants of No. 10.

As Prime Minister, Thatcher moved swiftly to establish a well-managed private office system, and in this first phase of her premiership, she still relied on the full range of support from all members of her private office. The private office had strong civil service leadership; it was given clear political direction by the Prime Minister; it had an excellent team of private secretaries; and its authority was widely respected across Whitehall. Those four elements of a private office rarely come together as effectively as they did in Thatcher's first term of office. That smooth operation was soon to be tested to its extreme during the most unexpected crisis to hit the Thatcher government – the Falklands War.

PRIVATE OFFICE DURING THE FALKLANDS WAR

Had it not been for the invasion of the Falkland Islands by Argentine forces on 2 April 1982, life would have been very different for Defence Secretary John Nott. Shortly before the invasion, he had decided not to stand again for Parliament and had informed, in confidence, his private office. With the invasion, his retirement plans were put on hold and the upcoming announcement was cancelled. The fortunes of Margaret Thatcher might also have been dramatically different. The Conservative Party was trailing in the opinion polls, reaching a depth of unpopularity around the July 1981 Budget. By spring 1982, economic growth was beginning to pick up, albeit slowly, but there was only limited improvement in the Conservatives' standing.[31]* Their electoral chances and the prospect of Thatcher herself retaining power were far from favourable. Victory in the Falklands War, after three months of conflict, irrevocably changed the trajectory of her entire premiership. Her overall management of the crisis, including the effective operation of her private office, undoubtedly contributed to the final outcome.

Much has been written about the Falklands and the way in which Thatcher used the War Cabinet to good effect.[32] Yet in the literature, there is hardly any comment on the role of private office. Lawrence Freedman's official history of the war has only one reference to the No. 10 operation.[33] The parts played by other private secretaries across Whitehall do not feature. Freedman's focus is mainly on military operations and intelligence. Similarly, Lord Franks's official inquiry report makes no mention of private office. Indeed, the only witness who spoke about the role played by private office was the Prime Minister herself in giving evidence to the Franks Committee on 25 October 1982.

The two most significant private offices involved in the Falklands crisis were those of No. 10 and the Ministry of Defence (MoD). At No. 10, the private secretary for foreign affairs was John Coles,† who was overseen by the principal private secretary, Clive Whitmore,‡ whose MoD background (dating back to when he had joined the then War Office in 1959) would be crucial. The principal private secretary to John Nott, the Defence Secretary, was David Omand.

---

* The 'poll of polls' for March 1982, one month before the outbreak of the Falklands War, put the Conservatives on 32 per cent, up from a low point of 25 per cent in December 1981. Labour was on 35 per cent (compared to 26 per cent in December 1981) and the SDP–Liberal Alliance was on 31 per cent (compared to their high point of 47 per cent in December 1981).

† John Coles (1937–); private secretary (foreign affairs) to the Prime Minister 1981–84.

‡ Clive Whitmore (1935–); principal private secretary to the Prime Minister 1979–82; Permanent Secretary MoD 1982–88; Permanent Secretary Home Office 1988–94.

The private offices were small. Coles was the only No. 10 private secretary working full-time on the Falklands, while at the MoD the private office had only four private secretaries (three of whom were relatively junior), and not all worked on the Falklands.[34]

Thatcher relied heavily on her private office to support the overall effort. Coles and Omand developed a good working relationship. Private offices need to be agile in their response to unforeseen events. If they do not co-operate, they are far less effective. However, they are not trained to prepare for war and the Falklands War posed a unique challenge, threatening one of the United Kingdom's last remaining overseas territories. There was no immediate blueprint to which the government, or the private offices, could turn. Private offices were to become part of the machinery – the junction boxes – that made the connections and so helped join up government.

Omand recalled that on 31 March 1982, just days before the full invasion, he and Nott were drafting an important speech to be delivered by Nott in the House of Commons, announcing the decision to acquire the Trident D5 strategic missile system from the USA.[35] While working on the speech, they received information (from GCHQ signals intelligence on Argentine naval communication in the South Atlantic) that Argentina was preparing to invade the Falkland Islands. They immediately contacted No. 10 and discovered that the Prime Minister was in her office at the House of Commons.* When they rushed down the corridor to meet her there, they showed her the intelligence reports and briefed her on the conclusion they had drawn, namely that an all-out invasion of the Falkland Islands was imminent. Coles and Omand then gathered together as many of the key advisers as were available for the

---

* Margaret Thatcher rarely worked in her House of Commons office and, usually, only when she had parliamentary business.

crisis meeting in her Commons office (the Foreign Secretary was on a visit to Israel and the Chief of the Defence Staff was in New Zealand). While this immediate change of priority would have been second nature, given the level of threat, there was also the political imperative that the government had to be seen to grasp the issue and give strong leadership. For that to happen, the effectiveness of the private offices in supporting ministers would be vital. Thatcher knew that failure would end her political career.

Sir Henry Leach, the First Sea Lord and Chief of the Naval Staff, still in his full dress uniform, had been at a naval ceremony and heard of the meeting on his return to the ministry. But given the exceptional secrecy of the meeting, he had great difficulty gaining access and persuading House of Commons security staff to admit him.[36] When he finally arrived, he found ministers wringing their hands. As Charles Moore has commented, the meeting has acquired 'mythical status in the history of the Falklands War'.[37] This was because Thatcher's

> instincts told her to fight, but she could not do so in defiance of all expert advice. Leach gave her the necessary countervailing expertise … [Nott's] private secretary, David Omand, who was at the meeting, noted that Mrs Thatcher's very inexperience emboldened her: 'She was placing the entire trust of the government in the navy'.[38]

Freedman later stated the critical nature of this point in the whole Falklands story: 'By being able to report that a Task Force was being prepared and ready to sail … [Thatcher] was able to provide a rallying point for Parliament'.[39]

The key contribution of Thatcher's private office in those early, traumatic hours of the conflict was to help convey the message behind which she sought to unite Parliament and the British public.

As Freedman has shown, in his only reference to her private office, 'the speed of events meant that her speech [for the debate in the House of Commons on Saturday 3 April] had been written by her two private secretaries – Clive Whitmore and John Coles – the previous night'.[40] While private secretaries will usually help in the drafting of any major government speech, the intensity of events that weekend after the Argentine invasion were of a qualitatively different nature. Hence, Whitmore and Coles did the job pretty much by themselves that weekend.[41] That was highly unusual for a speech of such political significance.[42] The speech itself was, as Freedman underlines, part of the overall 'rallying point' behind which the House of Commons could unify.

Omand's role, subsequently, as principal private secretary to the Defence Secretary, was also significant in that he personally had to ensure that MoD ministers and officials were fully briefed. As he put it, 'The rhythm of the day was that the chiefs of staff would meet early every morning. I would attend every chiefs of staff meeting and I could then report back to the Secretary of State. I would also tell the chiefs what was on his mind.'[43] Omand would then relay the information back to Nott and the MoD Permanent Secretary, Sir Frank Cooper. Omand recalled, 'In that period, I saw the Permanent Secretary probably three or four times a day. Everything else was delegated elsewhere. And then the trio of us [Nott, Cooper and Omand] worked on the Falklands.'[44]

Omand was a pivotal part of that 'battle rhythm'. Thatcher, with no military expertise, was reliant on the Cabinet Office for co-ordination and on the MoD to lead the war effort. The Prime Minister emphasised just how few resources she had to call on when giving evidence to the Franks Committee. She said:

We work only really with a private office, five private secretaries, and I have no separate sources of information save those that come to me from the departmental office – one has one or two private contacts – or those that come to me through Sir Robert Armstrong [the Cabinet Secretary] … My private secretary, John Coles, looks at everything that comes in for me and will usually mark up the relevant parts and put it in my box in the evening.[45]

Although Thatcher had, theoretically at least, the full weight of the civil service and the MoD at her disposal, in practice she had just one person in her private office working full-time for her on the Falklands (Coles), together with support from her principal private secretary (Whitmore) and the Cabinet Secretary (Armstrong). Coles, the private secretary closest to the Prime Minister, was also in the rare position of observing the personal strain on her. He recalled, for example, that 'she felt it badly. I remember South Georgia when one of our helicopters crashed. Margaret Thatcher broke down. She actually cried and, in a way, she was on a very rapid learning curve.'[46] Few people, outside her private office, would have seen the intense stresses faced by a Prime Minister at such a time. Few people outside her private office, other than her husband Denis, could offer her that type of close support.

Looking back, Coles commented that, while Thatcher was initially totally inexperienced in fighting a war, she learned quickly:

It was absolutely all-consuming. From the time the Argentines invaded until the time they surrendered, very little else was done in Downing Street. We were at it all day, every day, so my experience was quite unlike that of any other foreign affairs private secretary, before or after, in that this international issue took the Prime Minister's time all the time.[47]

After the military victory in the Falklands, the political fortunes of Thatcher and her party were transformed.[48*] Emboldened by this triumph and the improving health of the economy,[49†] she called a general election in June 1983 and, having won a 144-seat overall majority, returned to Downing Street in triumph. Most outside observers would have concluded that she was at her political height at this stage. However, Coles witnessed a different side of the Prime Minister:

> During the period 1983–1984 a decline in her energy became apparent. I date it from her successful re-election in June 1983. Some of us noticed that it was not quite the same Margaret Thatcher who returned to No. 10 … Why? Partly, I think, because the exertions of 1979–1982 had begun to take their toll on a woman who was not young … For many Prime Ministers it is a sufficient ambition, having been elected once, to lead your party to triumph a second time. I recall my surprise when she said to me, just two or three days after the Conservative victory of June 1983, 'I have not long to go.' For someone who had just won a majority of [over] 140 seats this was a remarkable statement.[50]

That Thatcher was willing to confide in her private secretary in such terms was, again, a reflection of the level of trust that had developed between them. Coles, discreet as ever, did not reveal what she had told him until after her death some thirty years later.[‡]

---

[*] Conservative support rose from 25 per cent in December 1981 to 34 per cent in April 1982. By the close of the war in June 1982, it had reached 48 per cent.

[†] For example, economic growth in the first quarter of 1983 reached 1.8 per cent, the highest rate since the Conservative election victory of 1979.

[‡] Interestingly, however, Thatcher does not mention Coles in her autobiography.

THE NO. 10 PRIVATE OFFICE AFTER THE FALKLANDS WAR

In the aftermath of the Falklands conflict, there was an important change in Thatcher's private office as her principal private secretary, Clive Whitmore, left to become Permanent Secretary at the Ministry of Defence. His replacement was Robin Butler. Having joined the civil service in 1961, Butler was a seasoned private office member and had worked at No. 10 as private secretary to both Heath and Wilson. He served in the private office of three different Prime Ministers, and he would go on to serve under three more in his decade as Cabinet Secretary. During his career in Whitehall, he had also been a founder member of the Central Policy Review Staff (CPRS). This gilded résumé led to him being widely regarded by many who knew and worked with him as an outstanding mandarin.[51]* Thatcher herself had previously come across Butler when he, as a relatively junior member of the CPRS, had briefed the Cabinet in 1971.[52] When Butler started working at No. 10, he found his new boss to be 'terrifying and exhausting at the same time. Very professional and very loyal. You had to gain her confidence.'[53] Under Butler's leadership, from 1982 to 1985, the No. 10 operation continued to be effective and efficient. But it was hard work for Butler. Indeed, having seen three Prime Ministers at work close-up, Butler's view was that the workload on officials was heaviest, by far, under Thatcher, whereas it was at its lightest under Wilson.

Almost thirty years on from joining Thatcher's private office, he recalled the intense pressures of the work: 'Particularly when working on speeches, she was indifferent to sleep. I always ensured

---

* Unusually for a civil servant, Butler has been the subject of biography, by Michael Jago. Tony Blair described him as 'famous in his own right and immensely experienced'.

I went home – whatever the time – but when I got back at 8 a.m., she always seemed fine and was ready to go again.'[54]

Butler enjoyed his sleep, but he rarely got enough while he was working for Thatcher, and this was never more the case than on the night of Thursday 11 October. The members of most private offices usually enjoy the week when the governing party hold their annual gathering. It is typically the one time of year when the work of the private office is at a low level. The work and speeches are handled almost exclusively by special advisers, and ministers do not come into the office to work. Private offices may be involved in the process of managing parallel departmental policy announcements to mirror those announced by the party machine at conference. They will often also be involved in the process of fact-checking ministerial political speeches to ensure they are accurate and consistent with government policy. But otherwise, party conferences can often be a time for private offices to relax and almost to put their feet up. Not so, however, for the No. 10 principal private secretary. Traditionally, the leading civil servant in Downing Street would usually accompany the Prime Minister to their party conference to ensure the business of government continued and to provide a civil service link as needed. Butler recalled he had endured a very busy party conference the previous year, in October 1983, when he accompanied Thatcher and got dragged into the aftermath of the resignation of Cecil Parkinson (following the revelation of Parkinson's affair with his former secretary, Sara Keays, and who was, by then, pregnant with his child).[55] Butler knew he could not relax, even at conference time. The Parkinson affair was a good example of the 'left-field' events that tended to occur during such conference weeks.[56]

The following year, Butler once again accompanied the Prime Minister to the Conservative Party conference. And it was in his role as principal private secretary that he was, unwittingly, to save Thatcher's life. Butler recalled that he would always check the leader's speech for any announcements of implications of which the government would need to be aware. But, as he well knew, Thatcher tended to work very late on her speeches. The conference of 1984 was no exception:

> Mrs Thatcher used to work long into the night to complete her party conference speech and on this particular occasion she finished quite early by 2.30 in the morning, and I had a document that No. 10 wanted a decision on by breakfast the next morning, so I said to her would she take this and look at it overnight and let me know what she thought in the morning. By this time all the speechwriters had left the room and it was just she and I in the sitting room of the Grand Hotel. She asked if I didn't mind if she dealt with it that night as she wanted to concentrate on her speech.[57]

The document in question that she stayed up to read was hardly of earth-shattering significance, but Michael Heseltine wanted a response as soon as possible to his latest plans for the future of the Liverpool Garden Festival, for which Heseltine, as Environment Secretary and a minister who was greatly committed to the city, was responsible.[58]*

Butler sat waiting while Thatcher read the note. At that moment a bomb, planted months earlier by the IRA, went off.[59] Thatcher's decision to read the Heseltine note given to her by Butler, rather than go to the bathroom where the bomb was planted, undoubtedly

---

* Michael Heseltine has always taken a close interest in Liverpool and the problems that had led to the Toxteth riots of 1981. He had previously presented a report (entitled *It Took a Riot*) to Thatcher.

saved her life. Speaking a quarter of a century after the events in Brighton, Butler commented:

> I had heard several bombs in my time at No. 10 … so I knew at once what it was and thought: here I am, alone with the Prime Minister and someone is trying to blow her up, so you'd better do something sensible. I said to her, 'I think you ought to come away from the window in case there's another bomb' … She said, 'I must see if Denis is alright' … What I should have done is said, 'Stand back, Prime Minister. Let me go through; I'm more dispensable than you are,' but not wanting to stand between a lady and her bedroom, I let her go in.[60]

The next morning, when the extent of the bomb damage and the number of people killed and injured became clear, Butler tried, unsuccessfully, to persuade Thatcher to return as soon as possible on the Friday morning to London, saying it was 'mad' for her to stay in Brighton. Thatcher would have none of it:

> Mrs Thatcher appeared at 8 a.m. and I said to her it was much worse than we thought, and I told her about the casualties, and she said, 'Well the conference is due to start at 9.30 a.m. and it must start on time.' I said to her, 'You cannot be serious. This terrible thing has happened and some of your closest colleagues have been killed and badly injured. You are not going to go on with the party conference as if nothing has happened, are you?' She said, 'This is our opportunity to show that terrorism can't defeat democracy.' And, of course, she was right.[61]

Thatcher insisted, against Butler's advice, on staying in Brighton and delivering her conference speech – to great acclaim – later that morning. The way in which the Prime Minister responded and Butler's instincts illustrate well their inevitable differences in perspective and approach. Thatcher – as Prime Minister – was firmly focused on conveying to the country the political message that she and her government would stand firm, whatever the cost, in the face of the attack and that terrorism would never succeed. Butler was concerned for her safety and the ways in which the government machine could protect her best and then respond. His view was that such action should best take place back at No. 10.

When John Coles, Thatcher's private secretary for foreign affairs, left No. 10 in 1984, it was down to Butler to find a replacement. He recommended that Thatcher should appoint Charles Powell. It was to be a significant appointment. Thatcher hardly knew Powell at this time, although she had previously chosen Coles in preference to him when Coles had been appointed in 1981. Now, almost three years later, Thatcher was still sceptical of Powell but eventually accepted Butler's advice that he was the best candidate for the job.[62] However, following Powell's interview with Thatcher in 1984, she commented to Butler that 'if I appoint him, he will have taken us all over in six months', a remark which, in Butler's words, 'turned out to be prophetic'.[63] That Powell stayed for over seven years was highly unusual. It was the second longest continuous service of any private secretary to the Prime Minister since 1945.[*] He formed one of the most lasting and powerful relationships between a Prime Minister and a private secretary in the modern era. Powell self-deprecatingly described his role as 'a useful piece of furniture' on which Thatcher

---

[*] Philip de Zulueta served as private secretary (foreign affairs) to Eden, Macmillan and Douglas-Home for almost nine years (1955–64). John Colville served Churchill for seven years (but in three separate postings in 1940–41, 1943–45 and 1951–55). Tim Bligh served Prime Ministers Macmillan and Douglas-Home for five years (1959–64). And Robert Armstrong served Heath and Wilson for five years (1970–75).

could rely but also admitted that, in terms of his professional relationship with the Prime Minister, he probably 'got too drawn into it'.[64] For someone who had never been a private secretary before,* Powell established a formidable reputation.

A year later, Butler left No. 10 to rejoin the Treasury and Nigel Wicks,† another Treasury official, replaced him. Wicks joined a team in which Powell was, by then, well established and, with Butler gone, the power structure in the No. 10 private office began to shift. By the end of 1985, that shift was to exhibit itself, in dramatic fashion, during the Westland affair.

PRIVATE OFFICE AND THE WESTLAND AFFAIR

If the Falklands War had shown private office at its best, the Westland affair showed it at its worst. Thatcher's fight with her Defence Secretary, Michael Heseltine, encapsulated the battle for power at the heart of government. Over the whole post-war period, there have been few events that can match the Westland affair in terms of the demands it put on the private offices and their degree of public exposure. Private secretaries, and other officials, became central to the critical decisions. The battle between Thatcher and Heseltine often appeared to be being fought on their behalf by their respective private secretaries. Over a period stretching from mid-December 1985 to mid-January 1986, the front pages of Britain's newspapers

---

* Of the twenty principal private secretaries who served in No. 10 between 1964 and the present day, all but three had had previous experience in private office, so Powell's experience was unusual but not unique.

† Nigel Wicks (1940–); private secretary to the Prime Minister (Harold Wilson and James Callaghan) 1975–78; principal private secretary to the Prime Minister 1985–88.

were dominated by the fate of the country's only helicopter manu-facturing company.[*]

What exactly was the background to the Westland affair and why did it matter so much to Thatcher and Heseltine? What was Heseltine's management style and how did he use his private office to help shape and deliver his policies? Why did private offices become proxies in arguing their ministers' cases and how, in contrast to the way they performed during the Falklands War, did their roles in this crisis become a hindrance to smooth and effective government? The unseen junction box of government, on this occasion, failed to make the right connections.

While many historians have written about the Westland affair, few have looked at the role played by the private offices. Richard Vinen, for example, focuses more on the economic arguments as opposed to the personalities.[65] Others mention Westland, but only in passing. Patrick Dunleavy, for example, considers the activities of No. 10 and the MoD but does not analyse the role of the private offices.[66] Similarly, few of the memoirs from the period focus on the extraordinary battle between Thatcher and Heseltine and, while both of them devote considerable space to Westland in their auto-biographies, neither comment on the roles of their private offices.[67] The one significant exception is Charles Moore, who chronicles in detail the roles played by the main private secretaries and other Whitehall officials.[68] Hugo Young (writing only three years after Westland) also emphasises the contributions of Powell and Ing-ham.[69] The Westland affair cannot be fully understood without an understanding of the workings of the private office, with the private

---

[*] For example, on every day except New Year's Eve, from 14 December 1985 until 10 January 1986, the day after Heseltine's resignation, *The Times* carried a front-page news story about Westland.

secretaries acting effectively as 'seconds' to their ministers in the political duel being fought. The account provided here is based on the testimonies of many of the key officials involved at the time. Other histories of the period have not had that level of access. That said, there is a risk, as highlighted by Vinen in a recent article, that Moore's analysis relying on civil servants' testimonies may give an exaggerated account of their contributions.[70]

The context of the crisis was as follows. In spring 1985, Westland Helicopters was running dangerously short of orders. It was becoming clear that, if the company was unable to generate new business including from government, it might be necessary to seek a partnership with either Sikorsky (an American company) or a European consortium. Moore recalled how sharply the battle lines were drawn as 'Heseltine instinctively preferred European projects and Mrs Thatcher instinctively favoured American ones'.[71] While, superficially at least, the debate was about the relative merits of the two alternative futures for Westland, in practice it was about the power struggle between Thatcher and Heseltine and whether the government's trade outlook should be predominantly US-facing and more laissez-faire or Eurocentric with a greater emphasis on interventionism. The private offices would be central to the task of making those arguments.

Heseltine was a key Conservative politician of the 1980s. A self-made millionaire and ardent pro-European, he had (allegedly) sketched out, while at Oxford, his path to power that would culminate in his becoming Prime Minister.[72] He had been a junior minister in the Heath government and a member of Cabinet in 1979 as Secretary of State for the Environment. He took an immense interest in the workings of the civil service and refused to leave the running of a department to his Permanent Secretary and officials.

The literature on Heseltine explains how and why he brought this business approach to managing departments.[73] He introduced reporting systems, focusing on how departments were delivering and how they could best be held to account.[74]* He was a 'micro-manager' and looked to his private office to be his eyes and ears in his departments and beyond.[75]

Like Thatcher, Heseltine was generally liked and admired by his close civil servants. He took a great interest in appointments to his private office and how his private secretaries operated. In his autobiography, he stressed the importance he attached to getting the right recruits.† Commenting on his early experience, he said, 'Ensuring an efficient private office is one of the most important steps for a new minister to take.'[76] When he subsequently entered Cabinet, Heseltine used the frustration he had experienced as a junior minister to demand a more senior civil servant as his private secretary than he was entitled to under civil service rules. In addition, in 1979, he said that he 'sought and received an assurance that whoever became my private secretary would remain ... in that role until I left the Department.'[77] He chose David Edmonds as his new principal private secretary in the Department of Environment. Edmonds, Heseltine commented, was

a rising departmental star with the touch of steel that makes the best sort of private secretary, and he proved an excellent choice. Indeed, in January 1983, when the Prime Minister asked me to go to the Ministry of Defence, I suggested to David that he come with me. He explained his reason for refusing ... because the

---

* At the Departments of Environment and Defence, Heseltine introduced the 'management information system for ministers', so that he could see exactly how much each element of the department's work cost.
† By contrast, as has been noted, Thatcher initially seemed to pay little attention to the staffing of her private offices.

Ministry of Defence was a department new to us both, neither of us would know when I was being carved up by the system. I instantly saw his point.[78]

Heseltine's analysis is perceptive. He wanted his private secretaries to add value to his work, to be loyal and challenging and not merely a glorified ministerial postbox. Heseltine always attached particular importance to getting the right principal private secretary and then relying on that official to lead the private office.[79]

Heseltine benefited from Edmonds's decision. In January 1983, on joining the MoD, he inherited, from his predecessor, 'a first-class private secretary in the tousle-haired Richard Mottram, already reputed to be heading for the Permanent Secretary's seat'.[80] Mottram had only been in the post for some six months but was well versed in defence matters. In short, he knew the MoD inside out. Mottram recalled that Heseltine said to him on his first day: 'Nothing personal, but I never accept the private secretaries in post when I go to a new department. I always want to choose my own. So, I won't be choosing you.'[81] When Edmonds decided not to leave the environment department, Mottram remembered, 'Hezza said to me, "OK, I'll try you."'[82] Heseltine made only one stipulation to Mottram, namely that, if he accepted the job, Heseltine expected Mottram to remain as his principal private secretary for as long as he remained Secretary of State. Mottram readily agreed. It was a decision neither man would regret. Mottram was to become the key player for Heseltine just as Charles Powell was for the Prime Minister.

Heseltine did not get on well with Thatcher, even though on many political issues – such as their staunch anti-Soviet policy, their belief in the value of the nuclear deterrent and their support for the deployment of United States cruise missiles on UK soil – they agreed.

He was irritated at her treatment of some of his political friends, such as Sir Geoffrey Howe, who she was prone to bully in public.[83] Westland was the catalyst that hastened their falling out, and in the most dramatic way possible.

The Department of Trade and Industry (DTI), headed by Leon Brittan, should have taken the lead in dealing with Heseltine and the MoD, but Charles Powell thought that the DTI principal private secretary, John Mogg,* was insufficiently effective in countering the MoD's arguments.[84] Powell thus 'seized the subject' and became the lead private secretary in No. 10.[85] He dealt with all aspects of Westland, even though there might have been a strong case for the matter to have been handled by the principal private secretary (Wicks), given the political significance and the cross-cutting nature of the subject matter, or by the private secretary responsible for economic affairs (David Norgrove). Nevertheless, it was Powell who took the lead.[86]†

Mottram recalled that Westland 'first came on the radar in the summer of 1985'.[87] Similarly, Powell recalled how the matter first came to his attention later that same summer. He remembered that, about a year previously, Thatcher had lost an argument with Heseltine on government support for UK shipyards facing closures.[88] Powell's recollection was that 'Thatcher was absolutely determined not to lose another argument with Heseltine over industrial strategy'.[89] Battle lines were therefore drawn.

Powell and Mottram (by their own admission in separate interviews) both readily acknowledged how they amplified their respective ministers' voices and differences.[90] However, throughout the proceedings, Mottram recalled that he and Powell personally

---

* John Mogg (1943–); principal private secretary to the Secretary of State for Trade and Industry 1985–86; created Lord Mogg 2008.

† Charles Moore explains how some in the No. 10 private office saw this as 'empire-building' on Powell's part. Moore cites the views of David Willetts, who was then a member of the No. 10 Policy Unit.

continued to get on well.[91] Mottram's view was that, pre-Westland, No. 10 had a good opinion of the way in which the MoD and its private office worked: 'They thought Heseltine was good, the private office was good and the department was competent.'[92] The relationship with the DTI and its private office was not so harmonious.[93]*

In the run-up to Christmas in 1985, Mottram was concerned that the issue was proving increasingly divisive which, in turn, was causing the relationship between the Prime Minister and her Defence Secretary to deteriorate rapidly. He also believed that their respective private offices, which should have provided the means for cooling off such disputes, were merely serving to inflame matters. Mottram therefore took it upon himself to contact Nigel Wicks, thereby bypassing Powell. He recalled telling Wicks that he feared the situation was 'getting completely out of control [and I said] we need to sort it out and handle it in a normal sort of way. Give Hezza a bit of room. But Nigel [Wicks] made a mistake. He let Charles [Powell] continue. He should have reined Charles in.'[94] Mottram added, 'Mogg, Powell and I were fighting proxy battles on behalf of our ministers, as opposed to saying: "This is a government, and we are civil servants." We should have smoothed it out.'[95] Moore succinctly analyses the dilemma faced by Wicks when contrasted with Powell, in observing that, 'whereas Charles Powell was the most powerful example of the able private secretary who becomes a player in political struggles, Wicks stood at the other end of the spectrum. He behaved more correctly than Powell.'[96] However, the fact that Wicks, as Powell's manager, failed to tackle the issue was a major contributory factor to the way in which the Westland problem

---

* In my interview with him, Mottram described Mogg as 'pompous and a pain in the arse'. Powell, too, recalled that he got on poorly with Mogg.

developed. It was part of his job at least to attempt to reduce the tension and yet he failed to do so.

Early in 1986, things came to a climax.[97] Westland shareholders were due to consider the relative merits of the two bids on 13 January. During a rapid exchange of letters over the festive season, Heseltine prompted a letter to be sent to him on 3 January by David Horne of Lloyds Bank, the advisers on the European bid.[98]* Heseltine wrote back to Horne to explain why the American bid would not work. No. 10 did not see the letter in draft, and it was subsequently leaked, by the MoD, to *The Times*.[99] A document as significant as this should normally have been subject to collective agreement, brokered via the private office network. That meant that a draft would have been circulated at private office level and comments sought from all relevant ministers, including, if necessary, government lawyers. Yet Heseltine instructed his officials not to consult No. 10.[100] That the letter was not cleared in draft by Powell (on behalf of Thatcher) underlines just how bad relations had become.

By this time, at the start of the new year, Powell was determined that Thatcher would win the battle with Heseltine and so took the lead in handling relations with the MoD. According to Moore:

> His next move however, came directly at the behest of Mrs Thatcher, who had become aware that Heseltine's recent letter to David Horne contained a factual mistake [concerning the number of European companies which had said they would rule out participating in a European bid for Westland if it were linked to the US firm Sikorsky].[101]

---

* Mottram recalled that Christmas Day 1985 was the only day in this period on which Heseltine did not contact him.

During the weekend of Saturday 4 January and Sunday 5 January, Powell visited Thatcher at Chequers where the plan to involve the government's legal officers was hatched between the Prime Minister and her private secretary. In view of what was to happen that week, it is not credible that the Prime Minister did not know about the plans for leaking the key document to the media. As Moore details:

> Revenge was about to be executed. As Powell put it, 'Heseltine tried to deploy the Law Officers and got it right back between the eyes.' Mrs Thatcher was now directly involved in a potentially dangerous game of retaliation. On 4 January 1986, Powell reported to Mrs Thatcher that he had got Brittan to speak to the Solicitor General [Patrick Mayhew], who had not previously seen Heseltine's letter to David Horne. Having now read it Patrick Mayhew had concluded that – in a phrase that was to become famous – 'it contained a material inaccuracy'.[102]

Significantly, Powell added, in a note to Thatcher, that Mayhew's letter, when it arrived, should also be given to the press since Heseltine had done the same with his earlier letter to Horne.[103]

The leak of the legal advice from Mayhew to the Press Association on Monday 6 January 1986 was undoubtedly the most significant event in the Westland saga. Over a third of a century on, the actual nature of the dispute seems arcane, namely whether Heseltine's letter contained what were described by the Solicitor General as 'material inaccuracies'. Moore is right to judge the so-called inaccuracy 'hardly an earth-shattering point'.[104] Both Powell and Ingham thought the letter's content needed to be in the public domain as soon as possible but that No. 10 should not be the source. The recipient for the leak was to be the Press Association's political editor Chris Moncrieff.* Mogg, meanwhile, consulted Powell after being told to do so by Brittan, whose own chief press officer, Colette Bowe,† consulted Ingham almost simultaneously. Thereafter, the two accounts differ. Mogg claimed that 'Powell told him that the letter must be got in the public domain'.[105] By contrast, Powell recalled that all he said, when asked by Mogg whether the letter would leak, was along the lines of 'goodness knows but everything else seems to'.[106]

Ingham later wrote that his 'eyebrows shot up' when he was told by Bowe that she had permission to leak the Solicitor General's letter, a somewhat disingenuous statement given that he admitted to having discussed the issue with Powell over the weekend. He claimed subsequently that the DTI wanted No. 10 to do the leaking for which he would then be personally responsible. He wrote: 'I refused to do so point blank. I had no authority to disclose the Solicitor General's letter. I told Colette Bowe that I had to keep the Prime Minister above that sort of thing'.[107] However, shortly after 2 p.m. on that Monday, Bowe read out to Moncrieff selected sections of Mayhew's letter but only those critical of Heseltine. Even Moncrieff described this event and the nature of the leak as a 'major act of deception'.[108]

Did Thatcher know what was happening? She has always denied that she knew of the proposal to leak the Solicitor General's advice and that the discussions over the weekend of 4–5 January were only between Powell, Ingham and the DTI. This seems highly unlikely, if not impossible. Powell had been with her at Chequers and had told her that he thought the Solicitor General's concern should be in the public domain. Ken Clarke, who had recently joined her Cabinet

---

* Chris Moncrieff (1931–2019); political editor of the Press Association 1980–94.
† Colette Bowe (1946–); DTI chief press officer 1984–87.

as Paymaster General, believed that 'it was perfectly obvious to me and other insiders that Margaret had ordered Leon [Brittan] to instruct one of his officials to leak Patrick's advice to the press'.[109] In her autobiography, Thatcher said, 'I was not consulted,' although she added, 'I would have liked the fact that Michael Heseltine's letter was thought by Patrick Mayhew to contain material inaccuracies needing correction to become public knowledge as soon as possible.'[110] It is, of course, possible that Thatcher was drawing a very careful distinction between 'knowing that something was about to happen' and specifically 'being consulted' on how it would happen.

Whatever the truth about what precisely Thatcher knew and when, it is absolutely certain that a note about the issue was circulated in No. 10, including to her, sometime between Monday 6 and Wednesday 8 January.[111] Knowledge of its existence was confined to a small group of officials and all copies were subsequently retrieved and destroyed on 15 January 1986.[112] A source who was privy to its contents, however, has confirmed that it demonstrated the Prime Minister's full knowledge and approval of the leak.[113] In itself, this shows why Thatcher admitted to her close colleagues that she might have to resign over Westland.

The specific point on which Heseltine subsequently resigned on 9 January was the insistence of the Prime Minister that all Cabinet ministers must clear any statements about Westland with the Cabinet Office, effectively a strategy to muzzle Heseltine. He stormed out of the meeting, saying that he would be making a full statement later that day. He returned to his private office where Mottram was surprised to see him back so quickly. Mottram recalls that day in detail:

I had said to Hezza before the key Cabinet meeting, 'Whatever they ask, agree to it. We can manage it.' I knew they would come up with some bloody stupid idea. Why not just accept it and we could manage all that? He then just sort of smiled at me. He never said he was going to resign. He went to Cabinet and then came back early. I said, 'Why are you back so early?' He said, 'I have resigned.' I think he probably had been thinking about this over the Christmas holidays. What then happened was interesting. He said he was going to make a resignation statement in the ministry if the Permanent Secretary [Clive Whitmore] was happy. I contacted Whitmore, who said he was content ... The resignation statement was well drafted and long. The idea got around that it was premeditated. That is completely untrue.[114]

The idea that Heseltine had planned the whole process and wrote the speech in advance seems unlikely. It would not have been clear to him exactly how the first Cabinet meeting of the year would turn out and whether he would be forced to resign and on what particular point. Mottram's explanation that the resignation statement was written that afternoon seems far more plausible. Mottram went on to explain the process for the drafting of the statement:

We sat down and wrote it from scratch. He would write the stuff and give it to me. I would then dictate it to a secretary and correct it, as necessary, and then give him the corrected script to look at. So, we set out to write this bloody speech. It was not written in advance. And then somebody told somebody I had co-written the speech. Rather, I had co-edited his speech. The speech included criticism of Robert Armstrong. Unbeknownst to me, we were also passing the text to Armstrong. As I dictated it, the private office was also passing the text to the Permanent Secretary,

Clive Whitmore. So, Clive would also look at it and if he had any comments [he] would feed them back. However, Clive was also passing the text to Robert Armstrong in Cabinet Office. So, I was black spotted by Mrs Thatcher and by Armstrong.[115]

That incident may also therefore explain why Whitmore did not succeed Armstrong as Cabinet Secretary, given it was in Armstrong's power to recommend potential candidates to the Prime Minister and he confirmed that he did suggest Whitmore, among others, as a potential candidate to Thatcher.[116] Armstrong later commented, 'I suspect that Whitmore's closeness to Michael Heseltine may have worked against him. I have no evidence for that, but I think that he may have been tarred with the Heseltine brush.'[117]

So, if Thatcher knew more about the leak than she admitted – and it is certain that she did – that helps explain the fears she expressed on Monday 27 January, just prior to the crucial debate in the House of Commons. In the event, the Labour leader, Neil Kinnock, made a weak speech which was, later in the debate, overshadowed by a far more powerful critique of Thatcher's government's actions by David Owen, the leader of the Social Democratic Party. Owen later wrote: 'It was inconceivable to me that people of the undoubted calibre of her Press Secretary, Bernard Ingham, or her Private Secretary from the Foreign Office, Charles Powell, who was handling Westland, would authorize any action without knowing her mind or without telling her afterwards what had been done.'[118]

Robin Butler concluded that Thatcher had been 'let down badly by her private office in No. 10 over Westland', a powerful and telling observation from someone who, previously, had been at the heart of her private office, albeit not during the actual Westland events.[119]

Even Powell later commented that Thatcher's 'hands were not entirely clean', but he did not elaborate on this.[120] So, while Butler appears to be criticising Powell (and also perhaps Wicks for failing to rein Powell in), Powell is, at least in part, blaming the actions of the Prime Minister herself for her determination to win the battle against Heseltine, at any cost.

The way in which the various private offices operated during the Westland affair left a stain on the Thatcher premiership. After Westland, Thatcher became even more dependent on the Powell–Ingham axis. According to Hugo Young, 'It was after Westland that her staff, and especially Ingham and Powell, became most indissolubly associated with her, almost as if they were her praetorian guard. They became linked, as it seemed, for ever in a society for mutual protection.'[121] The private offices of No. 10, the MoD and the DTI, which should have been the mechanism for finding a solution to the different ministerial positions, had merely served to inflame the situation. In the subsequent investigation by Robert Armstrong into the leak of the Solicitor General's advice, he effectively exonerated Powell and Ingham. Armstrong refused to let either of them appear before the House of Commons Defence Select Committee, preferring to submit himself to their examination instead. In response to their questioning, he expressed regret for the events but defended the actions of both officials.[122] When the committee reported at the end of July, the intensity of the Westland crisis had died down and there appeared to be little appetite for reviving the issue.[123] The report was excoriating in the extreme:

The disclosure of the Solicitor General's letter without his permission was an improper act. Whatever authority the five officials involved [Powell and Ingham, plus three from the DTI] may have thought they had – whether explicit in the case of the officials at the DTI, implicit in the case of the officials at No. 10 – they were wrong to connive at its disclosure. Yet we understand from Sir Robert Armstrong's evidence that no disciplinary action is to be taken against any of the officials involved. We find this extraordinary.[124]

The day after the report's publication, *The Times* commented that the report had strongly censured Powell and Ingham and, to a lesser extent, Mogg and Bowe. However, in its leading article, it singled out specifically Ingham, rather than Powell, for criticism, saying that officials at No. 10

took too much upon themselves, as they had evidently become accustomed to doing. Much of Mr Ingham's conduct in this matter as in others would be unremarkable if, like Mr Joe Haines in the government of Harold Wilson, he was a political appointee, claiming none of the neutrality that goes with the Civil Service. What distinguished Mr Ingham is a loyalty to the Prime Minister and a bull-dog enthusiasm for politicking on her behalf, which goes well beyond what can be tolerated in a government official. It may also be a style which is no longer in the Prime Minister's political interests.[125]

Heseltine and Mottram came away relatively unscathed from the Defence Committee's report. However, many years later, Richard Mottram rightly described the Westland affair as 'one of the biggest scandals in the history of private office'.[126]

CHARLES POWELL, BERNARD INGHAM AND THE NO. 10 PRIVATE OFFICE

The Westland affair provided the most significant insight into how far the operation of Thatcher's private office had begun to be controlled by the combination of Powell and Ingham. While successive principal private secretaries were all nominally in charge at No. 10, from 1986 onwards, it was Powell who became the most dominant policy figure, while Ingham managed the message and the media. Increasingly, they formed what some described as a *cabinet* system (akin to the Continental system), albeit with only two members.[127] Indeed, Ingham spent eleven years as Thatcher's press secretary, longer than any other senior No. 10 official. Who, precisely, were Powell and Ingham? How and why were they able to form such a formidable team? This section analyses the wider problems caused by their dominance of No. 10, as well as attempts to tackle the issue. It describes Ingham's and Powell's backgrounds, the nature of their partnership and the criticisms that have made against them, and presents an analysis of why Whitehall was unable to restrain the accretion of their power behind Thatcher's throne.

Nearly all the literature about Thatcher and No. 10 in the 1980s alludes to the disproportionate influence of Ingham and Powell. Thatcher, in her autobiography, was generous in praise of both men, describing Ingham as 'a man of total integrity [who] never let me down' and Powell as, 'in all respects, simply outstanding'.[128] Other commentators have been far more critical. Ingham and Powell's joint dominance of No. 10 is a theme running through the second and third volumes of Charles Moore's biography of Thatcher, as well as John Campbell's biography.[129] Dennis Kavanagh and Anthony Seldon, Peter Hennessy and David Richards all underline Thatcher's excessive reliance on them and the problems that this caused for her principal private secretaries and Cabinet Secretaries to whom they, nominally, reported.[130] Of Ingham, Hugo Young commented that he 'was seen at home and abroad to know her mind, speak for her, even on occasion exceed her in the zeal of his commitment to the cause'.[131] Of Powell, he said, 'No politician enjoyed such status. Some civil servants did. [Powell and Ingham] were the replacement for what previous leaders might have called a kitchen cabinet'.[132] Sir Percy Cradock, who understood better than most commentators the extent of their influence over Thatcher, observed that 'ministers and Members of Parliament came to resent their influence'.[133] Michael Jago explains the severe difficulties that the 'Powell issue' caused Robin Butler when he became Cabinet Secretary, which eventually led him to threaten resignation.[134]

What precisely was the Powell issue? In short, it was that Powell, through a combination of hard work and sheer intellectual brilliance, had forged such a strong and sympathetic relationship with Thatcher that she sought his views and advice not merely on foreign affairs but over a far wider range of political issues unconnected with his official job description. This frequently led to his opinions taking precedence over those of other senior advisers in No. 10 and the Cabinet Office and threatened to sideline the guidance offered by the Foreign Secretary and Foreign and Commonwealth Office (FCO) officials. Lord Armstrong, Lord Butler and Lord Turnbull all attested to how difficult Powell was to manage, in that he had an independent line to Thatcher and she would not hear any criticism of him.[135] In addition, Powell made clear that he had no intention of leaving No. 10, unless instructed to do so, and that Thatcher was adamant that she would not allow him to depart. He formed a strong alliance with Ingham – an 'axis' of power – such that his all-powerful position at No. 10 was, effectively, unassailable.

Ingham was appointed as Thatcher's chief press secretary on 1 November 1979, a post he would continue to hold until the day she left office. Thatcher liked his bluff northern approach and directness. He, in turn, felt able to speak openly and honestly to her in a way many of his No. 10 colleagues could not. He instituted a system of giving her a brief daily summary of the media news and reporting, which she read.[136] While never a member of private office, and indeed he saw much less of Thatcher than did any of the private secretaries, he worked closely with them all, especially Powell, and Thatcher trusted him in a way she did few other officials.[137] As a result, she followed his media advice and he achieved considerably more influence than many of the No. 10 private secretaries, including, at times, the principal private secretary.

Powell, though, was the dominant figure. In Hugo Young's opinion, Powell became 'intellectually and half-emotionally too ... the son she never had'.[138] However, Powell's critics argued that he had overstepped the mark between being an impartial and loyal civil servant and being a partial and, at times, political advocate for the Prime Minister.[139] He was respected and feared in equal part and he became indispensable to Thatcher, certainly by the end of her time as Prime Minister. Some even referred to him as the 'Deputy Prime Minister'.[140]

Powell's background was as a Foreign Office diplomat.[141]* Some twenty years after leaving No. 10, he recalled that the workloads for private office were enormous and the long hours 'absurd'.[142] He would be at No. 10 every day before 7 a.m. and rarely left before 9.30 p.m.

---

* Powell joined the Foreign Office in 1963 and followed a traditional route up through that department, including via a range of overseas postings.

There was often weekend work at Chequers, where Thatcher liked to hold informal seminars on issues such as defence and foreign affairs.[143*]

Powell believed that, with some exceptions, Thatcher's ministers were too deferential to her and that he therefore became the conduit of their views. In the case of Geoffrey Howe, Powell said, 'It was a bit like being a marriage counsellor.'[144] He told Howe that he should aim to get across to Thatcher key points within the first two sentences or they would be lost and she would not listen any longer. Howe was unable to do this and, as a result, became 'a disaster in terms of personal relations with Mrs Thatcher'.[145] At times, Powell was far more influential than Howe, whose views he often challenged privately, including on one occasion by not even showing the Prime Minister documents sent to her by Howe.[146†]

One of Powell's greatest assets as a private secretary was anticipating the requirements of his minister perfectly, a pre-requisite of all successful holders of the post but one which he possessed in abundance. He also had a gift for elegant, and occasionally colourful, phraseology, which was not one of Thatcher's skills. Another seasoned diplomat, Sherard Cowper-Coles, who spent over thirty years in the Foreign Office including serving Robin Cook as his principal private secretary, knew and observed Powell closely:

> Powell's ruthless efficiency, his golden pen, his intellectual rigour, his visceral scepticism towards Europe ... all played into his boss's view of the world. But what he really did for Mrs Thatcher was to give her instincts on foreign policy the intellectual respectability

---

* It was one of these seminars that achieved notoriety in the summer of 1990, when it contents were leaked to the media.
† In her memoir, Caroline Slocock explains that Powell held back papers from Howe about apartheid policy 'on the grounds of tact'.

William Hewer was Samuel Pepys's loyal clerk – and perhaps the first ministerial private secretary. He accompanied Pepys on his travels, supporting him on much official and personal business. He was so well trusted that he also acted as the executor of Pepys's will.

Source: Wikimedia Commons

Henry Bilson-Legge (*left*) was private secretary to Robert Walpole (*right*), who is generally regarded as the first Prime Minister of Great Britain. These were the days when private secretaries were also party political animals, and Bilson-Legge went on to become Chancellor of the Exchequer. This painting is currently displayed in the Cabinet Office. Source: Wikimedia Commons

Montagu 'Monty' Corry, later Baron Rowton, was Benjamin Disraeli's faithful private secretary for over fifteen years. Reflecting on their exceptionally close relationship, Disraeli said, 'The relations between a minister and his secretary are, or at least should be, among the finest that can subsist between two individuals.' Source: Wikimedia Commons

Horace Wilson was Neville Chamberlain's 'chief of staff' in all but name. Wilson exercised extraordinary influence over the Prime Minister, even holding one direct meeting with Adolf Hitler on behalf of Chamberlain. On becoming Prime Minister, Winston Churchill wanted Wilson banished to Greenland. © Keystone / Hulton Archive / Getty Images

Throughout the Second World War, the members of Churchill's No. 10 private office proved vital to the nation's success. John 'Jock' Colville (*far left*) was Churchill's favourite private secretary and later helped keep the government running when the Prime Minister had a stroke in 1953. Edith Watson (*centre, with hat*) worked in No. 10 for over twenty years and served six Prime Ministers, being the only woman to hold the title of private secretary until Caroline Slocock was appointed in 1989.

John Wyndham, later Baron Egremont, had worked with Harold Macmillan in Algeria during the Second World War. When Macmillan was elected as Prime Minister in 1957, he asked Wyndham to 'rejoin the old firm'. Wyndham was touched by the personal approach from Macmillan and agreed to return, unpaid, to the private office in No. 10.
© National Portrait Gallery, London

Tim Bligh was an all-purpose factotum and, for five years, principal private secretary to Macmillan and Alec Douglas-Home. But he crossed the line of political impartiality to which all civil servants must adhere, becoming less a robust defender of the government and more a politicised personal cheerleader for the Prime Minister. © TopFoto

Principal private secretary Derek Mitchell was installed in No. 10 to help manage the transition of power from a Conservative to a Labour administration in 1964, but instead, he found himself having to try to manage Harold Wilson's often-fractious entourage, headed by the controversial Marcia Williams.
© Avalon.Red

Marcia Williams, later
Baroness Falkender, was
Wilson's personal and
political secretary. She was
determined and all-powerful,
but she clashed badly with
some of the civil servants
in the private office.

© Trinity Mirror / Mirrorpix /
Alamy Stock Photo

Wilson's press secretary Joe Haines (*right*) was recruited from outside the civil service. He brought clarity through the smoke but never got on well with Marcia Williams. © NLA / reportdigital.co.uk

Robert Armstrong served Edward Heath as principal private secretary for all but the first seventeen days of his premiership, and he personally negotiated with European leaders on Heath's behalf. He was held in such high regard that Wilson retained his services after the February 1974 general election. He was later appointed Cabinet Secretary to Margaret Thatcher.
© Photoshot / TopFoto

Robin Butler was at the heart of government for some thirty years. He served five Prime Ministers from Harold Wilson to Tony Blair – three in the No. 10 private office and two as Cabinet Secretary. © PA Photos / TopFoto

A working-class grammar schoolboy from Dagenham, Kenneth Stowe had served in neither private office nor the Treasury before Wilson offered him the position of principal private secretary. The more Stowe argued that he was not the man for the job, the more Wilson wanted him. He went on to serve as principal private secretary to three Prime Ministers.
© The Times / News Licensing

ABOVE LEFT A safe pair of hands, David Omand headed the Ministry of Defence private office during the Falklands War. © Photoshot / TopFoto

ABOVE RIGHT Charles Powell (*centre, holding umbrella*) was a brilliant operator and an utterly loyal aide to Thatcher over seven years at No. 10. But he arguably strayed over the political boundary too often, not least during the Westland affair. Pictured here keeping an eye out, and an umbrella up, behind Mrs Thatcher and Mr Gorbachev.
© Trinity Mirror / Mirrorpix / Alamy Stock Photo

LEFT Richard Mottram was Michael Heseltine's right-hand man at the Ministry of Defence during the Westland affair, which inflamed a power struggle between Heseltine and Thatcher, ultimately resulting in the former's resignation. © UPP / TopFoto

ABOVE His mistress's voice: Bernard Ingham served as Thatcher's spokesperson for eleven years and resigned the day she left No. 10. © Shutterstock.com

LEFT Pictured here taking an unusual route to work during a train strike in the 1980s, Alex Allan – windsurfer, Grateful Dead fan and civil servant – served for five years as principal private secretary at No. 10. He was universally liked and managed the 1997 John Major–Tony Blair transition smoothly.

© Ken Towner / *Evening Standard*

ABOVE New Labour in action: chief of staff Jonathan Powell (*right*) and chief press secretary Alastair Campbell (*third left*) accompanying Tony Blair and George W. Bush at Camp David.

© Nick Danziger / nbpictures.com

LEFT Jeremy Heywood (*right*) was described by Norman Lamont (*left*) in his autobiography as 'the greatest Private Secretary ever'. He served four Prime Ministers – two as principal private secretary and two as Cabinet Secretary. Seen here in Lamont's Treasury office.

Courtesy of Suzanne Heywood

The intimacy of power: David Cameron walking down Whitehall in 2010 with Cabinet Secretary Gus O'Donnell (*centre*) and No. 10 Permanent Secretary Jeremy Heywood (*right*). Both O'Donnell and Heywood had advised Tony Blair and Gordon Brown in the previous decade.
© Steve Back

Dominic Cummings tried to shake up the centre of government before he was sacked – but he thought highly of many private secretaries: 'Trust private office – they're the only reliable thing between you and disaster.'
© Avalon / TopFoto

Martin Reynolds, aka 'Party Marty' (*left*), was in charge of the No. 10 private office throughout much of Boris Johnson's premiership. He was responsible for maintaining standards and the integrity of the Prime Minister's office, but he turned a blind eye to 'Partygate'.
© David Cliff / NurPhoto / Alamy Stock Photo

and bureaucratic coherence they needed. Charles knew exactly when to amplify, and when to absorb, the messages that the Prime Minister diligently inscribed each night on the papers put in a box which she almost always finished.[147]

Cowper-Coles underlined Butler's view that Powell 'set out to cross the line and become a separate source of [foreign policy] advice'.[148] Powell's growing influence threatened to overshadow Thatcher's relationship with Geoffrey Howe, whom Powell felt sufficiently emboldened to mock privately on one occasion.[149]* The role of any private secretary is, first and foremost, to ensure the efficient management of ministerial business. It is not to challenge systematically the advice going to the Prime Minister even though, at times, a good private secretary should be able to offer alternative views. Powell performed the task far more overtly and, as a result, became a far more independent policy adviser than any No. 10 foreign affairs private secretary before or since.

The Ingham–Powell axis, and the level of influence that it enabled those two officials to bring to bear, should have been tackled sooner than it was. As noted above, during the Westland affair, Mottram went directly to Powell's manager to appeal for his intervention. It is not clear why the No. 10 principal private secretary, Nigel Wicks, chose not to seek to assert greater control over Powell. One possible explanation is that Wicks believed that such an approach was likely to be resisted by Thatcher and therefore was simply not worthwhile. If so, his inaction had far-reaching consequences.

Wicks, with a background in international finance, was far less

---

* According to Charles Moore, in the autumn of 1986, following Thatcher's Reykjavik summit with Reagan, Powell felt bold enough – in a private minute to Thatcher on 21 October 1986 – to describe Howe as 'the plump chap with glasses who used to work across the road and whom we haven't seen for a long while!'

of a political animal than Powell. Although Wicks had served previously in No. 10 during Callaghan's premiership and was very experienced, Thatcher was already over-reliant on Powell, who some found a difficult official to manage.[150] As has been established elsewhere, Powell took full advantage of that opportunity.[151] Wicks admitted to Charles Moore that he himself 'adhered strictly, perhaps too strictly, to the doctrine that private office should not do "interministerial diplomacy".[152] In fact, no Prime Minister's private office can ignore such diplomacy entirely as Wicks claimed. That explains also why Thatcher far preferred Powell's approach.

The growing criticisms of Powell's behaviour, post-Westland, centred on two main points. The first, and the more serious, was that he had become politicised in his role at No. 10, contrary to the civil service ethos of impartiality, which was therefore undermining his position. Powell was increasingly thought to be, at best, an over-zealous gatekeeper to the Prime Minister and, at worst, no longer an unbiased civil servant. Butler certainly believed this, by the time of Westland.[153] The second view was that Powell had already served long enough in No. 10 and ought to be replaced. This was the view of Armstrong, while he was Cabinet Secretary, and it was even more strongly felt by Butler on his succeeding Armstrong in 1987.[154] The Foreign Office felt that Powell was not serving its interests well because, by his own admission, 'he saw his loyalty as being to the Prime Minister; he was adamant: he was not the FCO's man in No. 10'.[155] This ran counter to the usual presumption that the No. 10 foreign affairs private secretary would demonstrate greater loyalty to the Foreign Office by ensuring that its advice at least got a good hearing in No. 10 and certainly that they would not challenge systematically the department and its views. Powell, by now, had no love for his former department, which was not offering him any inducement to leave No. 10, such as, for example, an attractive ambassadorship. However, while the Powell problem was simple to state, it was not so simple to tackle. With Powell apparently unwilling to consider giving up his role and with Thatcher unlikely, in any case, to countenance his departure, the position appeared to have reached an impasse. The only two people who could do anything were either his immediate manager, the No. 10 principal private secretary, or the Cabinet Secretary himself.

The worry among the senior officials in the Cabinet Office and No. 10 was that, by having so much influence and power,[156] Powell and Ingham were, in effect, creating what could best be described as a 'cabinet à deux'. A cabinet is the method of managing a private office with a wider group of advisers, including political appointees as well as impartial civil servants. It is prevalent in Continental European governments, including in France and Germany, as well as in the European Commission. However, such a system is anathema to the British method of governing, as it blurs the distinction between independent civil service advice to the government of the day and the input of political advice (although arguably some private secretaries in the 1950s and early 1960s, such as Philip de Zulueta and Tim Bligh, acted in this way). As such, it cuts across one of the fundamental tenets of Northcote–Trevelyan which forms the basis of a non-political civil service. In the British system, political advice is usually submitted via special advisers or directly from party sources. That function is not, and never has been, a part of private office. The cabinet-type system which developed at this point in No. 10 comprised Powell, based in the private office, as the main source of advice to Thatcher, especially on foreign affairs, together with Ingham, based in the press office, who was in control of relations with the media.

Westland had served to underline, in very stark terms, Powell's growing influence and power. Nigel Lawson, who as Chancellor had observed the Westland stand-off, reflected:

> The longer-term effects of the Westland affair, however, were wholly adverse. The lesson Margaret took from it was that her colleagues were troublesome and her courtiers were loyal. From then on, she began to distance herself even from those Cabinet colleagues who had been closest to her – certainly those who had minds of their own – and to retreat to the Number 10 bunker, where the leading figures were Charles Powell and Bernard Ingham.[157]

When asked about the suggestion that he and Ingham had effectively became a French-style *cabinet*, Powell said:

> I think, fundamentally, it is accurate, although it is an exaggerated description. It arose from many things. Partly the isolation of being a woman … [Thatcher] had to be on her guard against the men who would plot and cabal against her … The people she felt she could rely on were those in No. 10 who had no political agenda and whose job there was to get things done … Very few Prime Ministers, before or since, have had such a sharp agenda … There had to be a vanguard if ever anything was going to get done. If you left it to Whitehall, nothing would get done. It would all get bogged down … So, to get it done, No. 10 had to be clear what she wanted and what she expected.[158]

Between them, Powell and Ingham became the No. 10 team who, in Powell's own view, 'got things done'.[159]

In 1987, Powell went further and advised the Conservative Party on the wording of their election manifesto by assisting in the drafting of the sections on defence and foreign affairs. Whereas it might have been appropriate for a private secretary to check the facts in a political document, it was not and is still not legitimate for a serving civil servant to write sections of a party manifesto, particularly when it was on the spurious justification that 'policy was "too important to leave in the hands of [Conservative Party] Central Office hacks"'.[160]

By the start of her third term, Thatcher had become even more dependent on Powell's foreign policy advice and Ingham's communications guidance. Powell was becoming defensive and personally keen to protect her and even admitted that 'an emotional relationship had developed'.[161] Their relationship certainly went beyond the usual boundaries of that of a politician and their adviser. Powell was concerned for Thatcher's political position but also her personal well-being. In particular, he found the attacks on Thatcher from the media and elsewhere hard to take. Following her third election victory, he wrote her a personal note:

I hope that you will not put yourself through it again. The level of personal abuse thrown at you during the campaign was unbelievable and must take some toll, however stoic you are outwardly. There comes a point when your reputation and standing as a historic figure are more important to your party, to your cause and to the country than even you yourself can be, and it's not right that you should be subjected to a further round like this time. I fear that, because the left know that they cannot defeat you on substance, they will only redouble this abuse over the next few years. In two or three years' time you will have completed the most sweeping change this country has seen in decades and your place in history will be rivalled in this century only by Churchill. That's the time to contribute in some other area!'[162]

Powell himself acknowledged the unusual nature and tone of his letter. Retrospectively, he said that he had forgotten that he had sent it and he accepted that it was 'a strange letter for a civil servant to write, I would concede, but a deeply felt one. I think it is a letter a friend would send.'[163]

Andrew Turnbull was Powell's manager for his final three years at No. 10, and he described how Powell worked – day and night: 'Powell had a different view of his role compared to his predecessors. He saw himself as a foreign affairs adviser, as well as a foreign affairs private secretary. [Thatcher] was becoming more detached from the FCO view and Powell encouraged this.'[164] (By her third term, Thatcher thought that the FCO was far too pro-European, although there does not appear to have been any specific event that changed her thinking.) Turnbull's view is perceptive. By increasing the advisory function of his job, specifically by often challenging the Foreign Office's advice and knowing that the Prime Minister instinctively favoured his views, Powell was undermining the authority of the Foreign Secretary, Howe, in whom she already had such little faith. As her most trusted source of advice on foreign affairs, Powell's influence was inevitably strengthened. Robert Armstrong observed that Powell did not act as many private secretaries did: 'Instead of trying to ease the passing of the views of the Prime Minister on to departments, he would report the Prime Minister's view with knobs on. He egged the Prime Minister on.'[165]

Ministers and senior officials, including successive Cabinet Secretaries, were concerned about their restricted levels of access and influence. In terms of foreign affairs, the Foreign Office and the Foreign Secretary were certainly being sidelined. The solution to the Powell problem would normally have been to carry out what the civil service called a 'managed move' to a post elsewhere within the Foreign Office empire. The first move to replace Powell took place in 1987, once he had served what was generally seen to be the 'standard' term of around three years for a No. 10 private secretary. Armstrong, who was due to retire as Cabinet Secretary on, or soon after, his sixtieth birthday in March that year, said that he 'got agreement to a move, including from both the Prime Minister and Powell. Powell agreed to go. [Thatcher] then changed her mind and said she could not put up with both me and Powell leaving.'[166]

Peter Hennessy relates a second attempt the following year, after Armstrong had retired:

> Butler and the Head of the Diplomatic Service, Sir Patrick Wright, called on Mrs Thatcher and urged her that Powell's secondment from the Foreign Office had been longer than the standard two to three years. It was not in her interests, Powell's or that of the public service generally, for such a figure so personally identified with her to stay on … The Prime Minister would have none of it. She needed Powell. No one understood her thinking as he did. Nobody but him could write the kind of speeches she required.[167]

This deeply frustrated Butler in particular. According to Charles Moore, Butler felt that his authority as Cabinet Secretary would be called into question if he could not remove Powell.[168]

Powell was, by now, acting more like Thatcher's Foreign Secretary.[169] She was becoming almost totally reliant on him. Thatcher had pleaded with Butler to keep him, 'not because he was "political", but because he was so "exceptionally competent". He was brilliant both at writing speeches and at advice – ("She indicated that on many occasions she was dissatisfied with the advice from the FCO") – and he gave "wonderful service".[170] Extraordinarily, according to Moore, Thatcher even threatened to resign if she could not keep Powell.[171] Powell's recollections are somewhat at odds with this. His view was simply that, by then, he occupied 'by far the best and most influential job I would ever get in the public sector'.[172] He saw no reason why he should leave No. 10 while the Prime Minister wanted him to stay, even if the Cabinet Secretary wanted him to go. In retaining him, even though he was by then one of the longest-serving No. 10 private secretaries, Thatcher was only doing what other Prime Ministers before and since had, on occasion, done.

Finally, Turnbull also tried, unsuccessfully, to remove Powell.[173] Whenever the issue was raised, Powell simply refused to move from No. 10, safe in the knowledge that Thatcher would always back him. He was apparently offered what he saw as second-tier ambassador-ships (including to Madrid) but nothing at a sufficiently high level in the diplomatic service to induce or persuade him to leave.[174]*

THE BRUGES SPEECH

If there was one event amid many which, for his critics, epitomised how Powell had exceeded his brief as private secretary for foreign affairs to Thatcher, it was his contribution to the Bruges speech of 20 September 1988. This was the occasion that Thatcher delivered

---

* The Conservative MP Alan Clark suggested that Powell was short of money but that he had told Clark that he would only have left No. 10 if a 'real cracker' of an ambassadorship, such as Washington or Paris, were offered.

a speech which became synonymous with her growing antipathy towards the European Community (EC). It was an indication of how out of step she had become with her more pro-EC Cabinet members and also of the continuing influence of Powell and Ingham. This speech marked the end of any further UK alignment with Europe during Thatcher's premiership and, in particular, drew a firm line in the sand against further European harmonisation or integration.[175*] It represented further evidence, if any were needed, of Powell's dominance over the government's foreign policy-making.[176] Rarely in UK political history has a single speech been so powerful in policy terms that its location became the title of a think tank devoted to free market thinking. The Bruges speech did that.[†] The speech was delivered by Margaret Thatcher, but Charles Powell was the speech's architect.

Ironically, Powell had initially tried to prevent the speech ever taking place. He had tried to persuade Thatcher, against Foreign Office advice, that she should not accept an invitation from the College of Europe based in Bruges, to make a speech about Europe on the grounds that 'she would only come to regret it'.[177] He saw two possible outcomes: either a conciliatory speech which might appear to be a softening of her increasingly hard line towards Europe; or a robust speech which would promote greater hostility to her within the European Commission and further isolate her from those in her party and government who were Europhiles, not least her Foreign Secretary, Geoffrey Howe.

Despite Powell's early strictures, the invitation to speak was eventually accepted and the Foreign Office produced a first draft

---

*   Both Charles Moore and Hugo Young describe the lengths to which the Foreign Office went to rein back Powell's original draft.
†   The Bruges Group is a right-wing free market think tank.

for No. 10 to consider. Powell thought the first draft was unacceptable in that he thought it was not sufficiently robust in setting out Thatcher's views on the future development of Europe.[178] In particular, Powell thought it important that Thatcher should sketch out a vision to contrast with the views of the then president of the European Commission, Jacques Delors,* who was emerging as a strong proponent of an ever-closer European Union and who, as a French socialist, had little in common ideologically with Thatcher. Powell set about producing a new draft version with two aims: 'to rebuff Delors's declaration that, within ten years, 80 per cent of European social and economic legislation would be made in Europe; and to set a new course for Europe based essentially on [Thatcher's] principles.'[179]

The speech went through many iterations between Powell and the Foreign Office. And Powell, for his part, ensured the Foreign Office was updated on Thatcher's thinking at all times. They could therefore anticipate what was coming. In his words, 'I was meticulous in keeping the FCO informed. They knew.'[180] Indeed, John Kerr[†] – the lead FCO official – effectively acknowledged this when commenting on Powell's final draft of the speech to the Foreign Secretary's private office. He said:

> The [latest version of the Bruges speech circulated by Powell] buys some 80 per cent of the suggestions set out in our 7 September version which was strongly supported by the Chancellor ... In the attached draft we are effectively trying to secure another 10

---

* Jacques Delors (1925–2023); French politician; president of the European Commission 1985–95.
† John Kerr (1942–); FCO civil servant and diplomat; seconded to the Treasury as principal private secretary to the Chancellor of the Exchequer (Nigel Lawson) 1981–84; assistant under-secretary FCO 1987–90; UK ambassador to the EU 1990–95; ambassador to the USA 1995–97; Permanent Secretary to the FCO 1997–2002; created Lord Kerr 2004.

per cent. The remaining 10 per cent don't really matter (and concern areas where No. 10 are probably incorrigible). It thus looks as if our damage limitation is heading for success. While it isn't going to pick up many tricks across the channel, I don't think that the Bruges speech is now likely to cause trouble with community partners.[181]

Kerr spoke too soon. While he had negotiated a text with Powell which he felt was broadly acceptable to the Foreign Office, the delivery of the speech and the briefing of its key messages by Ingham served to underline the scale of the rift that had developed between Thatcher's view of Europe and that of her Foreign Secretary, Geoffrey Howe, and his department. Powell later recalled that the speech backfired for two reasons: 'First, she hated the location of the speech [a long and badly lit room] and that, as a result, it was delivered as somewhat "in your face" – even by her standards. And second, rarely for him, Bernard Ingham briefed it poorly [to the British media].'[182] Speaking to Thatcher's biographer, Charles Moore, Powell explained that he felt 'Bernard's analysis mis-sold it to the British press as "Smash Brussels". It wasn't a great bovver-boy attack.'[183] But by then, the damage had been done and its reception in Brussels, not least by Delors and his office, served to underline just how poor the relations between Thatcher and the EU leaders had become. Delors apparently even blamed Powell more than Thatcher for the worsening relationship between himself and the British Prime Minister.[184]

From the time of Bruges onwards, Powell began, increasingly, to cross the line in terms of politicising the post. By now, he, and not the principal private secretary, was advising Thatcher across almost the full range of issues, including even on who she might promote and sack in her next Cabinet reshuffle – an extraordinary role for a private secretary.[185] He, and not the Foreign Secretary, was advising her (without recourse to the Foreign Office) on many European issues. For example, he managed the infamous seminar at Chequers early in 1990 on Germany, where Thatcher and a group of historians considered whether Germany still posed a threat to Europe and the United Kingdom. In his briefing for that seminar, he proposed a question on 'have the Germans changed in the last forty years ... Or are we really dealing with the same old Huns?'[186] As Thatcher approached the end of her term at No. 10, Ingham and Powell continued to support her in both their official capacities and, increasingly, personal roles. The 'bunker mentality' became more pronounced and eventually contributed to her fall.

PRIVATE OFFICE AND THE DOWNFALL OF THATCHER

Following Thatcher's tenth anniversary as Prime Minister, some commentators began to ponder when she might step down. Her husband Denis certainly encouraged her to do so, and even Powell had suggested she might consider a different role.[187] By now, some of her Cabinet colleagues, including Geoffrey Howe and Nigel Lawson, were privately beginning to consider if and how there might be a change of Conservative leader, including the possibility of a joint 'plot' to oust her.[188] Michael Heseltine, biding his time on the back benches, was another obvious contender. The one person who seemed to be in no hurry to move was Thatcher herself. Yet there had already been signs that her time in office might be limited.

In the autumn of 1989, just over one year after the Bruges speech, Thatcher had faced the first formal challenge to her leadership from the Conservative backbencher Sir Anthony Meyer.* Meyer stood no realistic chance of ousting the Prime Minister, but when it emerged that sixty Conservative MPs had declined to back Thatcher, a post-mortem was conducted in order to assess the reasons for their opposition and how the Prime Minister could regain their confidence. Powell and Ingham came in for particular criticism and the whips discussed what could be done to curb their influence and make Thatcher more accessible to the views of others from within the party. George Younger,† who co-ordinated the Prime Minister's campaign against Meyer, concluded:

If colleagues feel they are not being consulted and their relationship [with the Prime Minister] is weak it gets out and adds to their unhappiness ... Whether that relationship can ever be as good as it should be so long as Bernard [Ingham] and Charles [Powell] remain at No. 10, but they have got to be lived with.[189]

Mark Lennox-Boyd, a Conservative whip, reported that Robin Butler was 'going to speak to her about Charles', while Ian Gow, one of her closest confidants, said, ominously, that 'she will feel lost without Charles'.[190]

Pressure on the Prime Minister continued to mount throughout 1990, culminating in the resignation, on 1 November, of the Foreign Secretary, Geoffrey Howe. Howe's speech to a packed House of Commons two weeks later, in which he delivered a devastating critique of Thatcher's leadership, became the trigger for Michael

---

* Sir Anthony Meyer (1920–2004). Meyer stood against Thatcher in autumn 1989 and she beat him by 314 to thirty-three votes, on 5 December, with twenty-seven spoilt votes or abstentions, in what became known as the 'stalking horse' challenge.
† George Younger (1931–2003); Conservative MP; Secretary of State for Scotland 1979–86; Secretary of State for Defence 1986–89.

Heseltine to challenge her for the leadership of the party.[191] In the subsequent leadership election, Thatcher's and Heseltine's supporters lobbied hard to build support for their respective candidates. Thatcher's campaign manager was Peter Morrison.* A strange choice in many ways, Morrison was widely perceived as lazy and was certainly a heavy drinker. Powell commented that 'she had a drunkard as a campaign manager'.[192] That undoubtedly hampered her chances. What followed, though, again showed how Powell was crossing the line between what an impartial civil servant should do and what a party political adviser might do.

The result of the first ballot was due to be announced on Tuesday 20 November while Thatcher was in Paris attending a European summit meeting. Ingham and Powell were both with her at the British embassy. Powell was determined to know the result as soon as possible and ensured that he had an 'independent source' to communicate the outcome to him right away.[193] This was, in itself, a highly unusual approach for a civil servant to take, but it meant he got the news first. Thatcher was four votes short of the 15 per cent majority needed to win outright. Before this devastating result came through formally, Powell was able to give Thatcher the 'thumbs down' before anybody else could tell her.[194]

Back at No. 10, the rest of the private office was preparing for the contingency of a change of Prime Minister. Turnbull, as principal private secretary, knew that he would be in charge of a transition and so had begun to prepare himself. He recalled:

Following the stalking horse challenge of the previous year and the likelihood of a further challenge in 1990, I read all the Cabinet

---

* Sir Peter Morrison (1944–95); MP for Chester 1974–92; parliamentary private secretary to the Prime Minister 1990.

Office guidance and the Privy Council stuff on the resignation of a Prime Minister. Prime Ministers do not just resign and walk out like Heseltine did over Westland. Mrs Thatcher had said to me that she would tender her resignation to the Queen once the party had completed its process.[195]

Turnbull thought through all potential scenarios and outcomes and how the private office would respond. He confirmed that Morrison had assured Thatcher before she left for Paris that she could count on receiving 238 votes and that would easily be enough to win the contest in the first round. 'The trouble was that some 15 per cent of those were lying and the final figure was only 204,' said Turnbull.[196] Under the rules, a second ballot was therefore required.

The events of the subsequent days after Thatcher returned to Downing Street on Wednesday 21 November have been well documented.[197] Thatcher was initially keen to continue to fight to the second ballot and so agreed to meet with all her Cabinet ministers and a select number of officials, junior ministers and backbench MPs. Caroline Slocock, who had joined the No. 10 private office in 1989 as private secretary for home affairs (and who was the first ever female private secretary in No. 10), has chronicled the people who turned up.[198] Turnbull attended nearly every meeting with Thatcher's Cabinet colleagues, given that the future of the Prime Minister was being addressed and not just that of the leadership of the Conservative Party. In his words:

[Later that evening,] she called them all in and some eighteen out of twenty-two said something along the lines of 'I'll vote for you, but you are going to lose.' I sat in on every one of these bilateral meetings [with members of the Cabinet] and recorded all of them. I, or Paul Gray [private secretary for economic affairs], sat in on every other ministerial bilateral. There was complete trust in the officials supporting her.[199]

Powell did not attend Thatcher's formal discussions with Cabinet ministers. However, he did lobby Douglas Hurd and encouraged him to sign the Prime Minister's nomination papers for the second ballot.[200] This was another example of how Powell veered into political territory and well beyond his official responsibilities. According to Kenneth Baker, 'Douglas Hurd, who was with Margaret in Paris, became annoyed when Charles Powell, Margaret's civil service Private Secretary, urged him to sign Margaret's second ballot nomination form. As Foreign Secretary, Douglas rightly thought it was improper for a civil servant to act in this way.'[201]*

Faced with this haemorrhaging of support, Thatcher decided to withdraw from the leadership contest. On Thursday 22 November, she announced her resignation as Prime Minister, although she would remain in office until the result of the second ballot. Over the next six days, the private office began the task of preparing for the new Prime Minister. While Turnbull led on the overall planning, Powell helped to ensure that the final aspects of the transition were completed. He prepared draft replies to the many letters received from foreign political leaders and heads of state. By this time, he had decided that he would not be able to return to the civil service on leaving No. 10.[202] In practice, there was probably nowhere in the Foreign Office, or any posting elsewhere in the civil service for that matter, that he would have accepted.

On Tuesday 27 November, it was announced that John Major

---

* Interestingly, Hurd does not relate this event in his memoirs.

had won the contest to succeed Thatcher as Prime Minister, and the transition took place on Wednesday 28 November. Thatcher went to see the Queen in the morning, accompanied in the car to Buckingham Palace by Turnbull. She then left the palace separately. Turnbull, the principal private secretary, remained and, once Major had kissed hands, returned to No. 10 Downing Street in the Prime Minister's car with him, just as Ken Stowe had done with Thatcher eleven years previously.

HUBRIS AND THE FALL OF MARGARET THATCHER

As was the case with so many areas of British public life, government and administration, Margaret Thatcher's long tenure in No. 10 had a significant impact on the ways in which her private office operated during that eleven-year period. There was considerable continuity in terms of the type of people who were appointed to the private office. They remained, typically, male, privately educated, Oxbridge educated and predominantly from major departments such as the Treasury and the Foreign Office. However, there were significant and far-reaching changes to the way in which the private office worked and the Prime Minister's expectations of it, as well as her relationship with individual members of her immediate team of civil servants.

Thatcher inspired great loyalty from those people who worked in her private office, in some contrast to her scepticism about the civil service in general. She was demanding and staff worked exceptionally hard. Many of her most trusted officials stayed in No. 10 far longer than was usual for such postings. Similar changes in the nature and influence of the private office took place in other departments but to a lesser extent than at No. 10.

In general, the civil service absorbed such changes in style and emphasis and some of the changes would be accepted and built on under future Prime Ministers.* The system was capable of enduring and responding to the intense pressure of events, such as during the Falklands War. However, the system came closest to breaking point in cases such as the Westland affair and the build-up to the Bruges speech, where the No. 10 private office clashed with private offices in other government departments. On such occasions, Thatcher exercised her dominance over Cabinet colleagues, and individuals in her private office who had developed a close relationship with her used their position to press the system to pursue particular issues. This risked undermining the established conventions and the role of the private office as enablers rather than direct participants in policy-making and the business of government and politics.

In this context, the dominant figure was undoubtedly Charles Powell, who was one of the most notable private secretaries to work at No. 10 in the post-war years. In terms of his intellect, his capacity for hard work, his reputation across Whitehall and the way in which he defended and represented the Prime Minister, he was remarkable. While nominally the private secretary for foreign affairs, he effectively usurped the role of Foreign Secretary and the advice of the Foreign Office.

How did he become so influential and why was nothing done about it? His workload and output were enormous and, certainly by the end, he had also become indispensable to the Prime Minister. As one diplomat from that time said, it was almost impossible 'to establish where Mrs Thatcher ended and Charles Powell began'.[203] Powell himself admitted that he believed he had something of a sixth sense

---

* For example, the growth in number, powers and influence of special advisers which would continue under both John Major and Tony Blair.

of Thatcher's feelings and so was able to say to Whitehall colleagues: 'I am confident that the Prime Minister would wish that...'[204] He could be sure that he knew her mind, an invaluable skill to be able to deploy as a private secretary, and one of which he often took full advantage. He did not always share his thoughts and he did not always seek to promote compromise. Thatcher repaid Powell handsomely in that, on at least three occasions when the Cabinet Secretary or her principal private secretary sought to remove him, she blocked his departure from No. 10. He had become her essential aide.

Personalities have always mattered in private office and most Prime Ministers become reliant on their trusted advisers. However, Thatcher's reliance on both Powell and Bernard Ingham was altogether in a different league. In her later years of office, they effectively became her personal *cabinet*. Jointly, they undermined traditional Cabinet government and were seen as confrontational with other parts of Whitehall. Nigel Lawson was perceptive in his recollection:

> When I complained about [Ingham's] activities, [Thatcher] roundly denied that he could possibly have been guilty of what I was alleging, even though it was well known to the press that that was exactly what he had been doing. Other Ministers met precisely the same response. Charles Powell ... was as polished as Ingham was blunt. He wrote the best and wittiest notes of meetings of anyone in Whitehall ... However, he never saw it as his role to question her prejudices, merely to refine the language in which they were expressed. And like Ingham, he stayed at Number 10 far too long.[205]

Yet the most damning criticism of Powell is that he politicised his civil service role. This is something that even he has partially accepted.[206] The evidence against him is strong. During Westland, he went beyond what would normally be expected of a private secretary and helped to undermine a member of the Cabinet. In 1987, he wrote parts of the Conservative Party manifesto. He was complicit in sidelining the Foreign Secretary. And finally, at the time of Heseltine's leadership challenge in 1990, he assisted in Thatcher's re-election effort by trying to generate political support for her. Such actions were unacceptable for a civil servant. The 1996 Civil Service Code now makes this explicit.

Cabinet Secretaries and the No. 10 principal private secretaries were concerned by Powell and his influence, but they appeared powerless to do anything about it. This fact reveals much about the limitations of traditional methods used by the civil service to curb the power of specific individuals in private office. If private secretaries become more akin to political advisers, there is always the risk of politicisation. Powell, though, took his loyalty to Thatcher to an altogether different level. By the end of her premiership, she was almost totally reliant on him.[207]*

As a result of the regard in which Margaret Thatcher held Powell, he became virtually unassailable. He also made enemies and, as one of his former colleagues put it, 'Did Powell overstep the mark? Yes. Did he ever try to build bridges with the FCO as opposed to kick the bridge away? No. He never tried to be conciliatory. She stuck to her guns, and he provided her with the ammunition to do it. He was high-risk stuff.'[208]

Both Charles Powell and Bernard Ingham remained ferociously loyal to Margaret Thatcher until her departure from No. 10. When John Major replaced her as Prime Minister in November 1990, it was obvious that he would usher in a new style of politics, including a new approach to the way in which he would use his private office.

---

* On leaving No. 10, Thatcher even had to contact Powell when her hot water system broke down and she had no idea how to find a plumber. He ended up having to fix the system himself.

8

BACK TO BASICS? PRIVATE OFFICE 1990–97

The transition from Margaret Thatcher to John Major marked a clear break. Major's style and outlook on politics were very different from Thatcher's, as was his approach to the civil service and private office. From his first days in Downing Street, it was evident that his premiership would represent a new style of politics. That was certainly his intention. There was a far greater openness, the style of government was less dogmatic and debate was welcomed. There was a sense that Major would be more willing to listen than his predecessor and that his premiership would be far more collegiate. He said, 'I wanted to … refresh the whole conduct of government. Nowhere was this more apparent than in Cabinet … I chose consensus in policy-making, if not always in policy.'[1] Ken Clarke wrote that 'the atmosphere was utterly transformed. John was obviously prepared to engage at considerable length in efforts to produce truly consensus conclusions on most major issues … We all found the new style of Cabinet debate enjoyable and stimulating.'[2] Michael Heseltine, who returned to the Cabinet as Environment Secretary, reflected that, 'in contrast to the Thatcher years, everyone was allowed their say. Arguments were countered by reason and not interrupted or shouted down.'[3]

This chapter analyses the changes to the style and operation of the private office during the Major years and how these resulted in a more collective system for the conduct of government business. It ends with a comparison of Thatcher's and Major's use of private office. It argues that it was the private office and key officials who helped to hold the centre of government together in the face of severe economic and political difficulties. It also shows how Major brought Heseltine even further into the centre of the government as Deputy Prime Minister in an attempt to improve cross-government planning, including via the network of private offices, but that it soon became apparent that electoral defeat was looming.

Bernard Ingham retired as press secretary on the day that Thatcher left Downing Street and was replaced by Gus O'Donnell,* who moved to No. 10 to perform the same role he had held with Major at the Treasury. And within six months, Charles Powell too left, to be replaced by Stephen Wall† from the Foreign Office. Major, though, was deeply grateful for the support that he got from Powell following the transition, especially when, as a new Prime Minister, he was thrust into the First Gulf War which had started in August of 1990. Some commentators might have thought that Powell would remain loyal only to Thatcher and would want to leave No. 10 as soon as possible. Not a bit of it. In Major's own words, 'I can only say that, as far as Charles was concerned, I worked with him [as my foreign affairs private secretary in that transition period] and I found Charles to be "Rolls-Royce".'[4]

But change in the No. 10 private office was inevitable after the fall of Thatcher. Andrew Turnbull left in April 1992 shortly after

---

* Gus O'Donnell (1952–); chief press secretary to the Chancellor of the Exchequer 1987–90; chief press secretary to the Prime Minister 1990–94; Permanent Secretary to the Treasury 2002–05; Cabinet Secretary 2005–2011; created Lord O'Donnell 2011.

† Stephen Wall (1947–); private secretary to the Foreign Secretary (Geoffrey Howe, John Major and Douglas Hurd) 1988–91; private secretary (foreign affairs) to the Prime Minister 1991–93; ambassador and UK permanent representative to the EU 1995–2000.

Major had, unexpectedly, won the general election of that year.* He returned to the Treasury, becoming Permanent Secretary in 1998 and, four years later, Cabinet Secretary. He admitted that he 'never quite got on as well with John Major, who was more comfortable with people like Gus O'Donnell. Major thought I was a bit too mandarinesque.'[5] Major, having never been to university, was always somewhat ill at ease with the classic Oxbridge-style civil servants into which group he (possibly rather unfairly) put Turnbull.

Turnbull had been expected to be replaced as the No. 10 principal private secretary by Richard Mottram (of Westland notoriety), but Major decided that he would prefer a choice of candidates. According to Major, 'I don't think I was rejecting Richard Mottram at the time. I just thought there should be a competition.'[6] Mottram's candidacy had been lined up by the Cabinet Office with the agreement of the Cabinet Secretary, Robin Butler, although Major had not finally signed off on the decision. When Alex Allan, a highly regarded Treasury official, heard that Turnbull was leaving No. 10, he expressed an interest in the job. Major asked to see Allan, whom he had come across as a Treasury official when he had been Chief Secretary to the Treasury and Chancellor of the Exchequer. The two got on well and Major chose Allan as his principal private secretary.[7] Allan remained with Major for the rest of his time in No. 10 and he was to become the key figure during those five years. He was well liked and had a high reputation built on his time as principal private secretary to the Chancellor of the Exchequer when Nigel Lawson held that post. Lawson had said of him that 'he possessed a quick and logical mind, was hard-working, loyal and straight as a die, and had a better understanding of the politics and parliamentary

---

* The Conservatives won 336 seats compared to Labour's 271, an overall majority of twenty-one.

dimension than most officials, perhaps because his father had been an MP and junior minister in the Macmillan Government'.[8] Major, in his autobiography, was equally glowing in his praise, describing Allan as

intelligent and likeable [but] by no means an identikit civil serv-ant. A fan of the Grateful Dead rock band, he had once wind-surfed down the Thames, and photographs of a younger Alex with shoulder-length hair were to be found in his office. He worked the most unbelievable hours and was universally popular as well as effective.[9]

Major recalled Allan's 'phenomenal work ethic' thus:

Alex was quite extraordinary ... He would be in the office at 6.30 in the morning. He would be the first one in and the last one out. It was quite phenomenal. He had a forensic eye for detail and so much so that his antennae, whether it was spotting a problem ten paces away (which I tried to match but could never come up to Alex's standards) but also his political antennae, were acute. I couldn't tell you what way Alex voted but ... he also had tremen-dous empathy which, in that job, was vital.[10]

Few private office members receive such glowing tributes from their former political masters. So, in choosing Allan, Major selected an official who represented a direct contrast to the Thatcher years and the influence of Powell and Ingham, when too much power ac-crued to too few people at the centre. He wanted someone commit-ted to building the collegiality and teamwork that he hoped would underpin his new style of politics. Allan fitted that bill perfectly, whereas the more cavalier Mottram would undoubtedly have ruf-fled feathers. The relationship between the No. 10 and Treasury private offices also became more harmonious than it had been at the time of the Thatcher versus Lawson disputes. That Allan had worked for Lawson on the Treasury side of that divide in the 1980s undoubtedly helped him see things in a more balanced way when he reached No. 10.

The overall effectiveness of No. 10, in terms of its relations with the rest of Whitehall, was improved considerably by the lack of an alternative power base disrupting the normal flow of information and advice to the Prime Minister. From 1992 to 1997, Allan was to run No. 10 with a combination of hard work, political nous, charm and efficiency. For the first time since the early Thatcher years, the pre-eminent role of the No. 10 principal private secretary was firmly re-established. As one political adviser said of that period, 'You knew who was in charge at No. 10. Alex was in charge.'[11]

While Major clearly had a different political style and outlook from that of Thatcher, he was quickly at ease with his private office and the team he inherited. As he commented:

I knew Margaret Thatcher's private office pretty well. I had been Chief Secretary to the Treasury when I saw a lot of her because she was very concerned about public spending. I was then For-eign Secretary and saw a great deal of her because we were forever discussing Europe and then, as Chancellor, I also saw a lot of her. So, I knew her private office pretty well.[12]

Major was thrust immediately into the management of the First Gulf War and was very reliant in his first few months on Charles Powell, who had served his predecessor so loyally. And, although

Powell was to leave No. 10 and the civil service within six months of Major becoming Prime Minister, he nevertheless impressed his new political master. Hence, Major's description of Powell as a 'Rolls-Royce private secretary'.[13]

Powell was replaced as foreign affairs private secretary by Stephen Wall. Wall continued the tradition of taking a keen interest in the detail of foreign policy-making for the Prime Minister. Once again, arguably, the No. 10 foreign affairs private secretary was crucial in shaping UK foreign policy. Major confirmed that, at times, it was Wall and he who shaped UK foreign and defence policy – and not the relevant departments. For example, and again in the words of John Major:

> I will give you a practical example of a discussion between Stephen Wall and me. It was at the end of the Gulf War, when Saddam Hussein was still bombing the Kurds in the north of Iraq. And I remember a conversation with Stephen Wall in which we wondered what could be done about it – and I can't remember who said what in that conversation – but we came up with the idea of 'safe havens for the Kurds'. I then went to Europe and sold it to [German Chancellor Helmut] Kohl and [French President François] Mitterrand at a European summit. They agreed to back it. The Foreign Office then talked to the Commonwealth who largely backed it. And the Americans, who didn't want to do it because they would have had to provide most of the hardware, were forced into a diplomatic position in which they were effectively forced into accepting it. And that policy came out of a conversation with the private office.[14]

Alex Allan, meanwhile, started to reshape the No. 10 operation which he inherited and which had effectively been operating in pretty much the same way throughout the Thatcher years. He looked at the systems that No. 10 was using, the structure and also the people in No. 10. One thing which Allan introduced during his time at No. 10, albeit with limited success, was a greater sense of urgency on the importance of information technology and the need for private offices specifically, and Whitehall more generally, to be alert to the potential of the internet to improve the workings of government. He was using the internet and mobile data when many civil servants still inhabited the world of hard copies and the postbag. He launched the first ever No. 10 website and persuaded John Major to put out the first prime ministerial statement on the web. Other members of the No. 10 private office were not so technologically aware or inclined. Mark Adams,* who served as private secretary to John Major and, briefly, to Tony Blair, admitted that he never once accessed the internet when he worked at No. 10. There were a number of reasons why Allan's focus on promoting the greater use of technology was only partially successful. First, it was he personally who was driving the initiative and he simply did not have the time to lead a major change programme of such magnitude. Second, there was only limited support from the Cabinet Office and the centre of the civil service for the work. Third, departmental IT systems and hardware were often incompatible and not fit then for that purpose. Finally, many departments and private offices did not take the work seriously and so continued to rely on paper-based systems to manage their work. Allan was way ahead of his time and, nowadays, all private office business is transacted electronically, albeit with paper copies when needed. On leaving No. 10 in

---

* Mark Adams; civil servant; private secretary to the Prime Minister 1992–97. He is currently serving a prison sentence after being convicted twice of rape.

1997 (and following a spell as Britain's high commissioner to Australia), Allan was to become the government's first ever 'e-Envoy', responsible for promoting the wider use and application of modern technologies across government.* And, while Allan kept broadly the same structure as operated during the Thatcher years, he did make the first concerted efforts to recruit women into the senior echelons of No. 10.†

In April 1992, Major had been returned again as Prime Minister following a general election that some commentators felt the Conservatives could lose to the Labour Party, led by Neil Kinnock.‡ While he might have expected his new government – with a small but working majority of twenty-one seats – to have something of a political honeymoon, that proved wide of the mark. The economic crisis during the summer of 1992 and the growing tensions between No. 10 and No. 11 were once again played out between the respective private offices. The Treasury private office – and, specifically, one key private secretary – was to play a key role in 1992.

THE TREASURY PRIVATE OFFICE, JEREMY HEYWOOD AND BLACK WEDNESDAY

Soon after Major had become Prime Minister, economic pressures grew, culminating in the 1992 sterling crisis, also known as Black Wednesday. They stemmed from the decision taken in 1990 by Major, while Chancellor, to enter the European Exchange Rate Mechanism (ERM), a decision which his own Chancellor, Norman

---

* The office of the e-Envoy was established in 1999. Allan was its head for the first year of its existence.

† For example, it was Allan who was responsible for recruiting to the No. 10 private office the following: Mary Francis (later a private secretary to HM the Queen), Moira Wallace (later a Whitehall Permanent Secretary at the Energy Department) and Rachael Reynolds. All served as private secretary to Major.

‡ The election results were as follows: Conservatives 336 seats, Labour 271, Liberal Democrats twenty and others twenty-four.

Lamont, later admitted that he personally would not have taken.[15] By early 1992, the pound and its rate against other European currencies – especially the deutschmark – seemed to be under permanent pressure.

Lamont, who had succeeded Major as Chancellor, had already made a significant decision when, in 1991, he had appointed Jeremy Heywood as his new principal private secretary at the Treasury. Heywood was then an up-and-coming Treasury official who had impressed ministers and senior civil servants alike. He was clearly destined for the top of the civil service, although eyebrows were raised by his relative youth and his closeness to Lamont. Lamont wrote of him:

> Heywood ... had been my Private Secretary when I was Financial Secretary and Chief Secretary [1986–88]. After that he had gone off to a glittering job with the IMF and World Bank ... I knew him to be one of the brightest and the best, and I was keen to have him.[16]

Heywood was then aged only twenty-nine.[*] Over the next quarter of a century, he was to become one of the most prominent civil servants to work at the centre of government, including for much of the time as the principal private secretary to the Prime Minister and, finally, as Cabinet Secretary. His career mirrored those of Robert Armstrong and Robin Butler, two of his predecessors as Cabinet Secretary, in that they both served as private secretary to the Prime Minister and subsequently as principal private secretary,

---

[*] The Treasury traditionally appoints principal private secretaries when they are relatively young. Heywood's successor, Nick Macpherson, was thirty-three and Tom Scholar was twenty-eight. Both Macpherson and Scholar went on to be Permanent Secretary at the Treasury.

a position that Heywood was to hold twice, for Tony Blair and then for Gordon Brown.

Heywood was exceptionally hard-working and had the ability to generate genuinely creative solutions, often to seemingly intractable issues. Ken Clarke (who inherited Heywood as his principal private secretary when Norman Lamont resigned) described him as 'a high-powered and very intelligent workaholic and we got on extremely well in the short time we worked together. And we were still friends when I encountered him nearly twenty years later when he was David Cameron's Cabinet Secretary.'[17] Cameron, who at the time of Black Wednesday was a special adviser at the Treasury, put it more succinctly, saying that 'the principal private secretary to the Chancellor of the Exchequer at that time was none other than Jeremy Heywood, and so I learned at the feet of the master'.[18] These attributes help explain why, later in his career, Heywood became an almost indispensable aide to four different Prime Ministers from both parties.[19*]

Early in 1992, and in the run-up to the Budget, ministers were trying to devise plans to cut taxation so as to be able to appeal to the electorate in the forthcoming general election, yet without a massive increase in public spending. The Treasury was opposed to an across-the-board cut in the standard rate of income tax. According to Major's biographer, Anthony Seldon, 'a compromise emerged late in the day from Jeremy Heywood, Lamont's brilliant Principal Private Secretary, who produced the idea of a new 20p income tax band for the first £2,000 of taxable income, to benefit four million low-paid people'.[20] Such initiatives were typical of Heywood's

---

* Heywood died in November 2018. At a memorial service in June 2019, the four Prime Ministers who he served directly – Tony Blair, Gordon Brown, David Cameron and Theresa May – all paid very warm tributes. These are contained in the biography of Heywood written by his widow, Suzanne.

creativity. As the economic crisis of 1992 approached, his role was to become even more significant.

Lamont had previously worked for Lawson, as Financial Secretary to the Treasury, and had been described as almost akin to a 'senior special adviser' developing policy ideas and providing a useful challenge function to Lawson.[21] As Lamont's private secretary, Heywood knew that he was expected to contribute analysis and ideas in a similar manner, and not merely to be a conduit for others' views.[22] This was not an unprecedented role for a private secretary to play, but Heywood took full advantage of the scope that this offered him. Alex Allan commented that, when he was principal private secretary to Lawson who was then a 'driving force' in the Treasury and 'full of ideas', it was very clear that 'many of the suggestions he received from Lamont had clearly been written by Jeremy'.[23]

By 1992, Lamont, despite having been reappointed by Major as Chancellor of the Exchequer after the election, was increasingly frustrated. He was having renewed doubts about the ERM and the orthodox Treasury lines he was receiving, many of which were very 'pro-European [Community]'.[24] Heywood, for example, had to make clear that Lamont 'had commented – quite emphatically – that he has no intention of joining the narrow [ERM] bands in the foreseeable future', whereas some other European countries, and some Treasury officials, appeared to think such a policy worth considering.[25]

By August 1992, with the pound coming under increasing pressure, Lamont was looking at the full range of options. Heywood became personally convinced that the pound could not, even in the medium term, survive within the ERM. He therefore suggested, in two personal and private notes to Lamont, that he should consider proposing to the Prime Minister and Cabinet colleagues that the UK withdraw unilaterally from the ERM to avoid such an outcome being forced on the government.²⁶ Heywood, perhaps unwisely, decided not to share these notes with anyone in the Treasury other than the Chancellor. In the words of Heywood's biographer, his widow Suzanne:

> Over the preceding weeks Jeremy had written two notes to the Chancellor about this economic trap. Neither of these, he recalled with a twinge of guilt, had he shared with Terry Burns [the Permanent Secretary to the Treasury] even though they'd both argued against the Treasury's official view that, if the pound didn't stay strong within the ERM, inflation would rise, and living standards would fall. Instead, in his first note back in June 1992, Jeremy had suggested that, if the Germans weren't willing to reduce their rates, the best option might be for sterling to devalue, possibly together with the lira … By the time Jeremy had written his second note in August 1992, a summer holiday in Turkey had given him time to harden his opinion. The UK's membership of the ERM was no longer sustainable, he told the Chancellor, unless German rates came down or the dollar strengthened. If neither happened, the UK should pull out [of the ERM].²⁷

Lamont does not appear to have acted on Heywood's note or, if he did, his private advice to the Prime Minister was ignored or overridden.²⁸* Heywood, in writing that proposal, showed just how influential he had by this stage become as principal private secretary

---

* The minute that Heywood wrote to Lamont in the run-up to Black Wednesday does not appear in the National Archives. That said, a number of Treasury internal files and notes are still withheld (from public access) in the National Archives.

in providing, at times, separate and private policy views from the Treasury's official advice. Lamont clearly welcomed this style and, in turn, referred to Heywood as 'the best ever Private Secretary'.[29] Heywood, for his part, was displaying, in a way that few private secretaries do, the ability to act as someone with not only immense organisational and administrative skills but also the policy skills which meant that Lamont was usually willing to accept his advice even if it conflicted with that of the most senior Treasury officials. Yet in not sharing his advice with any other officials, Heywood was stretching the role of the private secretary to its absolute limit. Such confidence and skills in a private secretary are rare. The fact that Heywood managed to do this and maintain enormous respect and admiration from many of his contemporaries says much about his capacity and intellect.

Heywood stayed on as principal private secretary after Lamont was sacked (thereby underlying his loyalty to the post and not to the politician). He became principal private secretary to Ken Clarke, the incoming Chancellor. The pair became good friends. Heywood moved on, soon after the 1993 Budget, but, before he did so, he was paid perhaps the greatest tribute, albeit possibly unwittingly, by Ken Clarke. Clarke commented about a paper that Heywood wrote for him on fiscal policy for Clarke's 1993 Budget speech in the following way:

If I may say so, your re-draft is brilliant. I do not know if:

1. you and I are completely agreed on macro-economic policy;
2. you really seek to set out my views in a clearer way than I usually manage; or
3. you have subtly influenced my views over the last four months

so that they have changed without me realising it and now co-incide with your own.[30]

Yet, however good Heywood and other individual officials were, the fallout from Black Wednesday continued to dominate politics for the next five years and permanently hampered the Conservatives' electoral chances. Many officials in the civil service and, especially in private office, recognised the inevitable. Discreet preparations were by now underway in private office and elsewhere for what would be the first transition in eighteen years.

PRIVATE OFFICE AND THE RUN-UP TO THE 1997 GENERAL ELECTION

The Prime Minister and the Conservative Party never recovered from Black Wednesday.[31]* Yet, despite this being a period of immense political turmoil for Major – including his 'Back Me or Sack Me' resignation from the leadership of the Conservative Party in June 1995 – the private offices of No. 10 and of departments continued to function effectively.[32] There were no major internal clashes between private secretaries on a scale of those that occurred over Westland, although Major suffered serious political setbacks, not least over the European question. There were also unexpected crises, such as that concerning BSE (so-called mad cow disease) and the genuine concern about whether this animal disease could mutate and infect humans.

However, throughout this strained political period, private office postings across Whitehall, and especially at No. 10, were still highly

---

* From October 1992 until May 1997, Labour's lead over the Conservatives never fell below 9 per cent and was, at times, over 30 per cent.

sought after and continued to attract high-quality officials. At No.
10, Alex Allan was the key to this smooth operation. He appointed,
as private secretary for economic affairs, the first two women to
occupy that post, Mary Francis* and then Moira Wallace,† respectively, which finally began to tackle the notion that the No. 10 private office was a male bastion. Francis later became deputy private
secretary to the Queen, while Wallace went on to become Permanent Secretary at the Department for Energy and Climate Change.
This reflected Major's desire for a wider, more diverse, group of
advisers at the centre. At the Treasury, Kenneth Clarke appointed
Nick Macpherson‡ as his principal private secretary in succession to
Heywood. Macpherson later served for over a decade as Permanent
Secretary to the Treasury. At the Foreign Office, Douglas Hurd's
principal private secretary was John Sawers,§ who became private
secretary to Tony Blair and later head of the Secret Intelligence Service (or MI6). While there continued to be a strength and depth
of quality in the private office, civil servants in No. 10 and across
Whitehall, it made little difference to the Conservatives' electoral
prospects, which were in sharp decline.

Following Major's re-election as party leader on 4 July 1995, he
made a number of changes in an attempt to reassert his authority and to restore the fortunes of the government. Specifically, he
sought to improve the co-ordination of government policy and
communications and to prepare for the next general election, due in

---

*   Mary Francis (1948–); private secretary (economic affairs) to the Prime Minister 1992–95; assistant/deputy
    private secretary to the Queen 1996–99.
†   Moira Wallace (1961–); private secretary to the Chancellor of the Exchequer 1987–90; private secretary
    (economic affairs) to the Prime Minister 1995–97; Permanent Secretary Department of Energy and Climate
    Change 2008–12.
‡   Nicholas Macpherson (1958–); principal private secretary to the Chancellor of the Exchequer (Ken Clarke
    and Gordon Brown) 1993–97; Permanent Secretary to the HM Treasury 2005–16.
§   John Sawers (1955–); principal private secretary to the Foreign Secretary 1993–95; private secretary (foreign
    affairs) to the Prime Minister 1999–2001; chief of the Secret Intelligence Service 2009–14.

less than two years. The politician Major chose to lead this task was Michael Heseltine, who was promoted to be the First Secretary of State and Deputy Prime Minister, based at the centre of government in the Cabinet Office.

Heseltine looked to the private offices to ensure the smooth running of the new system.[33]* With his authority and his belief in management reporting systems, Heseltine was the obvious politician to lead this work. To run his new private office, Heseltine brought with him Mark Gibson,† whom he described as his 'focused and unflappable Principal Private Secretary from the DTI'.[34]

Heseltine's remit was broad and far reaching. In his own words, '[Major] said he wanted me to … set up a new co-ordinating committee to draw together the presentation of government policy and move us to an election footing.'[35] The committee's remit inevitably straddled official and party political business, and policing that boundary was not always easy. Gibson recalled that Heseltine was 'punctilious' in ensuring that the distinction between party political work and government activities was properly observed: 'Never once was I asked to do anything remotely party political.'[36] Indeed, the relationship between Heseltine and his private office appears to have been an excellent one, based on mutual respect between him and Gibson. According to Gibson:

[Heseltine] was interested in my views and used the principal private secretary as a sounding board on whether the department was working well. He never minded second opinions from his private office. He liked to be challenged in meetings. He said that

---

* Anthony Seldon described Major's faith in Heseltine to lead this work as the 'Heseltine Gamble'.
† Mark Gibson (1953–); principal private secretary to the president of the Board of Trade and subsequently to the Deputy Prime Minister 1994–97.

if you just want civil servants to agree with him, then he could agree with himself any time of the day.[37]

Heseltine's relationships with his principal private secretaries worked well because he was absolutely clear what he wanted from them as members of his team. First, he always personally selected candidates from among the highest quality officials of a senior grade. Second, he insisted that they stay for the full length of his ministerial posting, wherever that was. And third, his style of management clearly defined who did what and how the political and civil service functions would be separate but mutually supportive of each other.

Heseltine was immediately concerned about the fact that departments seemed too free to announce whatever they wanted and whenever, with little central oversight. He decided that private offices should get authority for all departmental statements or policy launches from the Cabinet Office.[*] The system predated, by some three years, the process subsequently introduced by the New Labour government, and which is still in operation to this day, of the No. 10 'Grid', whereby any government department had to have authority to deliver and announce any item of government activity (see Chapter 9).[†]

Heseltine chaired a new committee responsible for the co-ordination and presentation of government policy (EDCP), which underscored the growing emphasis on communications and the media. The committee met daily at 8.30 a.m. and gained a reputation as the forum in which the government and the party came together to oversee the news agenda. It sent out action points to private offices across Whitehall, instructing them on how they should manage

---

[*] The new IT system to monitor the process was called 'Cab-E-Net'.
[†] The 'Grid' was run by a small team reporting to the chief press secretary in No. 10.

departmental activity. However, it became criticised for bringing the civil service too much into the political arena. EDCP's task was to 'counter the remorseless wave of attacks to which the government was subjected from 1995 onwards by Labour's formidable election machine'.[38] As Hennessy has written, one Cabinet minister described EDCP as 'absurd' but that it was 'part of Michael's settlement with the Prime Minister'.[39] Similarly, the journalist Simon Jenkins suggested that 'the private offices of some Cabinet ministers have become de facto press rooms seeking photo opportunities, press briefings and interviews, hour by hour'.[40] Such comments were revealing about the inability of ministers and their private offices to prevent a decline into the short-termism and bunker mentality that plagued the last years of Major's administration in the face of the political juggernaut being driven at them by New Labour.[41]

On 1 May 1997, Major's government succumbed to a landslide defeat. After watching the early results at his home, Major telephoned Tony Blair to offer his congratulations, before attending his own count and then travelling on to Downing Street for the last time as Prime Minister.

In his words:

When I arrived in the early hours of the morning [of Friday 2 May] I found the flat above the official rooms largely empty; we had already packed and prepared to leave. Only a few people were still in the building. Alex Allan, who had run No. 10 with such spirit and professionalism for most of my time there and was a friend as well as one of the best principal private secretaries any Prime Minister could hope to have, was solicitous with tea and comfort, but we both knew that he already had to begin the task of installing the new government.[42]

Later that morning, Major held a brief meeting with all his staff, who then lined the corridor leading to the front door of No. 10. Many of the staff were in tears as they clapped him out of the building. Major said farewell to Allan and then left to watch cricket at the Oval. Allan returned inside, ready for the next stage of the handover of power to the new Prime Minister.[43] The private office's first transition in eighteen years, from one political party in government to another, was underway.

PRIVATE OFFICE UNDER THATCHER AND MAJOR: A COMPARISON

Superficially, the No. 10 private office to which John Major said farewell on Friday 2 May 1997 bore a resemblance to that which Margaret Thatcher had inherited some eighteen years previously in May 1979. It was similar in size, based in the same set of rooms next to the Cabinet Room where Major worked and the overall No. 10 operation was managed by the principal private secretary. However, over that period of political change, there had been many different private secretaries and varied styles of operation.

Thatcher was very decisive. She was not, by nature, consultative and liked to rely on a small number of advisers. Her private office was the tool which she used to help make decisions, to impose her vision, at times without proper consultation or collective agreement. Conversely, Major was far more collegiate and usually looked for consensus; he often took more time to make decisions. The No. 10 private office had probably been at its most effective in the early 1980s, under the leadership of first Clive Whitmore and then Robin Butler.[44] It oversaw the network of private offices across Whitehall, and, alongside Thatcher's efficient ways of working, issues were addressed, decisions taken and communicated quickly. In her first period of office, Thatcher was also more willing to listen to a wider range of advice than she would be later in her premiership. This approach paid off handsomely during the Falklands conflict, when the No. 10 and MoD private offices shared information and worked together effectively in support of the war effort. Yet, less than four years later, and after her second electoral victory, the Westland crisis and the operation of private office in that period underlined the fragility of the system. No. 10 and the MoD no longer shared information and their private offices failed to co-operate, in spectacular style.

Comparing and contrasting the ways in which private office handled the Falklands War and Westland is instructive. On one level, they were completely dissimilar events. The Falklands War was a major international conflict in which the armed forces of two nations engaged in full-scale military combat. The United Kingdom was reacting to an illegal act by a foreign power, with a direct risk to its citizens of an overseas Crown dependency. Lives were lost on both sides and national prestige was at stake. A small War Cabinet was established; Thatcher, her Defence Secretary and private office workers had a unity of purpose. The issue was how to support the military in a way that would have the most chance of success. Unlike Westland, it did not pit departments against one another and No. 10.

By contrast, the Westland affair was essentially an internal political argument between the Prime Minister and one of her leading ministers, using the fate of a commercial company as a proxy. The nation was not in peril, no lives were at stake and other countries were not directly involved as during the Falklands. Yet during the crisis over Westland, effective collective decision-making (which had operated well during the Falklands) all but broke down. The

overall objective of the government was not clear. The private offices and the leading private secretaries, Charles Powell and Richard
Mottram, acted forcefully on behalf of their respective ministers.
The discipline of private office which should have been the civil
service mechanism, and part of the 'hidden wiring', that would
resolve issues on behalf of their ministers instead became part of
the problem.[45]* The junction box of government was no longer
properly connected. There was a lack of any strategic objective akin
to that of retaking the Falklands. The objective during the Westland affair seemed, at times, simply to do the other side down. The
two key private secretaries became far too involved in the political struggle and no one could or did take control with an overall
government-wide perspective. Westland was not private office's
finest hour. By contrast, in the Falklands, it had been a critical factor
in the successful management of the war. What private office did
help to do in the Westland affair, from No. 10's perspective at least,
was to defeat Heseltine, Mottram and the MoD private office. In
doing so Thatcher, with the support of Powell, neutralised a potential threat to her premiership.

However, with the demise of Thatcher, private office changed.
Under Alex Allan's skilful influence at No. 10 from 1992 to 1997,
and with other operators, such as Jeremy Heywood at the Treasury
from 1991 to 1994, private office returned to being a more collegiate
operation. Both Allan and Heywood were canny political operators,
yet neither ever became politicised. All the Chancellors and Prime
Ministers whom they served would attest to that, although by the
mid-1990s, the style of many of their political masters, especially
Major, was far less strident.

---

* The phrase used by Peter Hennessy to describe the ways in which this part of the United Kingdom's
unwritten constitution operates.

By 1997, pressures on the traditional model of private office were growing and the demands were becoming more complex. The core function of private office, as the junction box between No. 10 and government departments, remained, but stresses and different challenges for private office were emerging. Special advisers were becoming more numerous and more influential. The Policy Unit was an established part of No. 10. New technologies and the growth of the 24-hour news cycle would, in time, mean that private offices would have to develop new methods and more agile ways of working.

Under Major's premiership, there was a distinct swing back to the more traditional model of private office, without the kind of patronage that protected Powell from attempts to neutralise his disproportionate influence over the Prime Minister. Major wanted to do this for political reasons to mark out the distinctiveness of his approach. However, he also undoubtedly believed in the reassertion of the integrity and independence of the civil service. The pendulum which had swung back and forth throughout this period of Conservative rule moved firmly towards the centre and the traditional model of private office. Under Major, the private offices in No. 10 and government departments once again became the junction boxes with proper oversight by the Cabinet Secretary. Conventional practices were re-established. Strong, well-managed private offices across Whitehall became the norm again, yet they were powerless in terms of the government's political difficulties. This was something that some politicians noted. After 1997, there was to be a further concerted effort to rewire the system within a more political climate. The pendulum was to swing again.

9

NEW LABOUR, NEW PRIVATE OFFICE? PRIVATE OFFICE 1997–2010

Tony Blair did not actually start his first Cabinet meeting by saying, 'Call me Tony'. Yet, in the folklore of modern politics, akin to other famous political quotations such as Callaghan's 'Crisis? What crisis?' and Macmillan's 'You've never had it so good', Blair's phrase captured a new style of government.[1] Such informality, as reported by the *New York Times*, 'tossed away centuries of British custom under which ministers always addressed one another by their titles'.[2] The truth of what happened on Thursday 8 May 1997 was slightly more prosaic. The Prime Minister's principal private secretary, Alex Allan, suggested that they might dispense with the use of formal titles just before the new Cabinet was due to meet for the first time, with Blair readily agreeing to continue the practice that had already been in place at shadow Cabinet meetings. Allan informed Blair's chief press secretary, Alastair Campbell, who recognised the potential significance of the change and coined the phrase 'Call me Tony' for use with the media.[3] Campbell had begun an era of unprecedented 'spin' and media management in British politics. Also, a small footnote of history had been written. Familiarity was not the only hallmark of New Labour's early period in government. Another key element was its relative inexperience. No Cabinet member had served previously in that body, and being unencumbered by past practice allowed them to look afresh at the way in which Whitehall operated. For private office, it meant that changes were not long in coming.

Blair and the New Labour years have already produced a large literature. The era has also generated much associated information on both his style and the style of his advisers. Early in his premiership, several works by well-informed journalists and commentators were published, focused on the politics and style of New Labour and, in particular, the well-known tensions between the Blair and Brown camps.[4] In due course, further books and articles appeared, dissecting the media operation under Blair, including the alleged disproportionate influence of his special advisers, including Campbell.[5] More recently, historians have sought to analyse the nature of the Blair government in an increasingly forensic way. Much of this work, without access to published papers of this period, has been informed by in-depth interviews with many of the key participants.[6] There has been an increasing focus on the role of 'delivery', which became a particular theme of Blair and his senior advisers, including private office, after their second election victory in 2001.[7]

There have been several biographies of Blair in addition to his autobiography.[8] Other politicians of the period have produced memoirs, as have some of the key advisers of the period.[9] Campbell also kept a detailed diary, which was subsequently published in four parts. These publications all now form a rich source of primary material on New Labour's preparations for government and its period in power from 1997.[10] Campbell's diaries, in particular, provide valuable insights into how the new government viewed the civil service and how, over time, it came to work effectively with the private office. They also underline the greater complexity of government compared to opposition.

Much of the secondary literature has focused on the nature of Blair's New Labour policy agenda, his style of operation and his emphasis on 'modernisation and reform', particularly with reference to public service delivery, as well as the handling of crises and military interventions.[11] There is a far smaller body of literature on the Brown premiership, but there are several valuable studies on, in particular, the global financial crisis of 2008 and Brown's response, which he also covers in depth in his autobiography.[12]

Political historians, notably Anthony Seldon, have also analysed many of these issues. Yet, in this emerging literature on New Labour, there has been little focus on the private office, as opposed to the role of media management, special advisers and the development of what became known as 'sofa government'.[13] Many of Blair's critics claimed Blair relied too much on that style of operation, whereby decisions were said to have been taken in small, more informal meetings, as opposed to at Cabinet or by official committees – a charge which Blair and his senior aides have always rejected. Powell claimed that there were 'myths propagated about Cabinet government versus "sofa government" and about the supposed lack of parliamentary accountability'.[14] In his evidence to the Iraq Inquiry, Powell said:

I don't think it matters whether a meeting takes place in the Cabinet room, where John Major used to hold meetings, or in the sitting room, where Mrs Thatcher or Tony Blair used to hold their meetings. I think the key thing is that you have the right people there, the people who need to be involved in a decision, that they are properly informed, have the proper material before them, in written or in oral form.[15]

Campbell was characteristically blunter in his analysis, arguing that 'any Prime Minister is likely to be more effective if surrounded by the people and systems he or she feels best make the use of the centre's time and thinking. The choice of soft or hard chair frankly makes not a blind bit of difference.'[16] The one sustained piece of analysis on 'sofa government' by Jon Davis and John Rentoul concludes that 'the idea that the core business of government was carried out through uninformed, unstructured chats on Downing Street sofas ... was not supported [by the evidence] ... and Blair's critics have never sustained the allegation.'[17]

Yet the Blair style of operation, built as it was on his close-knit team of trusted political advisers, marked a change from the traditional private office which was the hallmark of Whitehall in the 1950s – half a century previously. The Blair government marked a further shift away from the monopoly power of civil servants advising ministers to one where power and influence were increasingly diffused and in the hands of a limited number of close advisers and others within his coterie. Blair himself had little understanding of the ways of Whitehall and little interest in questions about the machinery and structure of government departments. Blair certainly had limited knowledge of the workings of private office. His first three Cabinet Secretaries (Robin Butler, Richard Wilson and Andrew Turnbull) often found his approach to decision-making unusual, as he did not tend to follow the well-established conventions, which had the effect of confusing or frustrating the system. His chief of staff, Jonathan Powell, said, 'Blair hadn't thought about [private office] at all. I don't think he even realised he was going to have a private office.'[18] That was an astonishing admission.

This chapter examines three central questions. First, why was New Labour ill-prepared or unwilling to utilise the Whitehall machine in order to govern more effectively? Was too much attention paid to policy and communication issues, with insufficient effort devoted to discovering the best ways to utilise the machinery of government, including the private office, to help deliver the new government's objectives? Second, how did the private office system function under Blair and, in particular, how did it operate at times of crisis? Did private office and Blair's advisers pay insufficient attention to how best to help develop a coherent strategy for New Labour in office? Even Blair himself admitted that, on reflection, he should have focused far more on some of these organisational matters during his first term, particularly with regard to how he could have used his private office to better effect.[19] This chapter considers how the private office responded when the government came under pressure and found itself facing a series of crises from 2000 to 2003. It also examines the attempt during Blair's second term to merge the private office with the Policy Unit, which was unsuccessful. Third, what changes occurred under Brown's three-year premiership and what role did the private office play in the run-up to the 2010 general election and the subsequent transition to the coalition government? This chapter also considers the legacy of the private office under New Labour, including whether its innovations stood the test of time and what legacy, if any, it left for future governments.

THE PRELUDE TO POWER, 1994–97

Tony Blair was elected as leader of the Labour Party on 21 July 1994. From that point onwards, New Labour's consistent lead over the Conservatives in the polls suggested a strong probability that his party would win the general election, which had to take place by

May 1997.[20]* Readiness for government would become increasingly pressing for Blair and New Labour in opposition, but the fact was that he took power over his party, and then his country, with no working knowledge or personal experience of the Whitehall machinery. Unlike in 1964, when Wilson wanted to shake up Whitehall by tackling the excessive influence of the Treasury and by importing expertise or, in 1970, when Heath sought to introduce modern management methods, Blair arrived at No. 10 with no plans for operating the system, let alone reforming it. He was more like Thatcher, who took little interest in how the system worked, despite having served as a Cabinet minister. Blair has made no secret of his ignorance and has described how he and his colleagues 'were going to come to power as utter novices'.[21] Other commentators have underlined Blair's lack of understanding of Whitehall but with seemingly no desire on his part to learn about it.[22] Blair himself later reflected that 'everything is new, including your private office. If you come direct into power from opposition (and unless you have been in government before), you are very ill-informed about how government works and how to use the government machine'.[23] In fact, he was the most inexperienced Prime Minister since the Second World War, and the first since Ramsay MacDonald, in 1924, to enter Downing Street with no ministerial experience at all.

Ministerial experience of Prime Ministers 1945–2010

Prime Minister	Period in office	Ministerial experience before joining Cabinet	Years served in Cabinet before first becoming PM
Attlee	1945–51	2	5
Churchill	1951–55	3	18

---

* In the three years leading up to the 1997 general election, Labour led the Conservatives in the polls by between eighteen and thirty-one percentage points.

Eden	1955–57	4	13
Macmillan	1957–63	5	6
Douglas-Home	1963–64	4	8
Wilson	1964–70	2	4
Heath	1970–74	8	5
Wilson	1974–76	2	4
Callaghan	1976–79	4	8
Thatcher	1979–90	3	4
Major	1990–97	4	3
Blair	1997–2007	0	0
Brown	2007–10	0	10

Despite Blair's lack of understanding of the role of Prime Minister, it does appear that he felt he could learn the job through doing it, rather than by taking advice beforehand from those who had experience of the role. For example, in June 1996, the Cabinet Secretary, Robin Butler, invited Blair and his wife Cherie for an informal supper to get to know each other and to discuss the tasks of the Prime Minister. Alastair Campbell commented then that he did not think that either Blair or Cherie 'had really got the measure of the scale of change that was coming if we won'.[24] (It is not clear from Campbell's diaries whether he even knew which aspects would be most difficult to handle.) Blair did not discuss with Campbell or Jonathan Powell (his chief of staff) the meeting in advance and does not appear to have used the outcome to prepare himself better. Richard Wilson, who would become Blair's Cabinet Secretary in 1998, recalled in 2020 how the new Labour leader was strikingly ambivalent about furthering his knowledge in this area:

When he became Leader of the Opposition, he had absolutely no idea how government worked, including the role of private office, or what language to use and what the protocols were. [Jonathan] Powell very gently educated him in how to behave in opposition.

Blair ... had no idea how a private office worked and what it was for, or what anyone previously had done. Nor did he have any interest in learning ... He simply wanted to 'modernise' the system at No. 10 and for things to work better around him. He didn't want to learn how to be Prime Minister.[25]

Blair's reluctance to involve himself too deeply in this area, and even his caution about what language to use, may have betrayed a concern that to do so might have given the impression that he regarded victory as inevitable. The scars of the 1992 campaign (when opinion polls had shown Labour maintaining a consistent, if narrow, lead right up until polling day) were still sufficiently raw for Blair privately to describe Robin Butler's briefing for the media during the 1997 election campaign, on how the civil service would handle a transition to a Labour government after eighteen years of Conservative rule, as demonstrating a degree of 'political naivete that [was] breathtaking'.[26] Nonetheless, this determination not to appear complacent did not prevent Labour from making preparations for the likelihood of assuming power once more. The responsibility for such planning, as will be seen, was devolved to key advisers, but it was undermined by a lack of consistent support from the party's senior leadership, whose oversight was neither enthusiastic nor sustained.

PEOPLE

On becoming leader of the Labour Party, Blair had nothing that resembled a private office. Few opposition leaders, at any time, would have had such an organisation. His most loyal aide Anji Hunter, together with a small team, supported him in Parliament. Blair also had a network of allies who formed a tight entourage of political advisers. The central figures in that group were Gordon Brown and Peter Mandelson, whose previously close relationship had been tested when the latter supported Blair rather than Brown for the party leadership.[27] Blair's immediate challenge was to recruit key people to establish a larger and more effective office for him as the new Leader of the Opposition and to manage his media relations.[28] The two individuals who would fill these roles would be critical to his success.

In the summer of 1994, Blair persuaded Alastair Campbell, then working as the political editor of the *Today* newspaper, to become his press secretary to bolster the party's communications strategy and to tackle a national media which had been openly hostile to his immediate predecessors. Campbell had been surprised by the offer and somewhat reluctant to accept it, doubting that he possessed the temperament and diplomacy required for such a role. However, as he recalled, 'Even as I left the office, though I'd raised all the reasons against, I had a feeling I would end up saying yes.'[29]

Campbell took the job and remained in it for nine years. He became crucial to Blair, not just in terms of media management but also by helping to develop the government's wider political strategy and managing cross-departmental relationships. In Blair's opposition office, Campbell was popular and efficient. He knew most of Blair's work colleagues already and had all the necessary top-level media contacts from his past career. Yet he felt that Blair's office was not run firmly enough, and he complained, at one point, that 'there were too many people allowed just to wander in and out of his office, and Anji [Hunter] had to have the authority to stop them.'[30]

To address this need for a more disciplined operation, Blair also wanted to appoint a chief of staff, a role with only some pedigree in the British government system, although it was more of a standard feature of US politics. Having met the FCO diplomat, Jonathan Powell, in the USA while visiting the Clinton administration, Blair was impressed enough to ask him to take the post, when the only other potential candidate turned down the offer. Powell, who was the younger brother of Charles Powell, would become one of the central figures in Blair's team.* He brought with him a wealth of foreign policy experience; having joined the FCO in 1979, he had spent the following sixteen years in a variety of diplomatic postings. In 1992, he had been the nominated British embassy staff member in Washington covering the Democratic Party election campaign and had studied the success of a party machine which was to serve as a key inspiration for New Labour. Blair gave Powell the task of building a professional office that would oversee the next general election campaign.

In addition to these five close members of his inner group (Brown, Mandelson, Campbell, Powell and Hunter), Blair also used a wider network of colleagues, including his old head of legal chambers, Derry Irvine,† who had been a life peer since 1987. Ed Balls,‡ Brown's closest aide, provided economic advice; while David Miliband,§ who had previously worked for the Institute for Public Policy Research, became his head of policy. Sally Morgan¶ handled

---

* The narrow first choice has been Julian Priestley, secretary-general of the Socialist Group in the European Parliament, but he turned down the offer of the job.
† Lord Irvine of Lairg (1940–); Lord Chancellor 1997–2003.
‡ Ed Balls (1967–); special adviser to the Chancellor of the Exchequer 1997–99; chief economic adviser to the Treasury 1999–2004; Economic Secretary to the Treasury 2006–07; Secretary of State for Children, Schools and Families 2007–10.
§ David Miliband (1965–); acting head, then head, of the No. 10 Policy Unit 1997–2001; Minister of State, Department for Education and Skills, 2002–04; Minister of State, Cabinet Office, 2004–05; Minister of State, ODPM, 2005–06; Secretary of State for Defra 2006–07; Foreign Secretary 2007–10.
¶ Baroness Morgan of Huyton (1959–); political secretary to the Prime Minister 1997–2001; Minister of State, Cabinet Office, 2001; director of political and governmental relations, Prime Minister's office, 2001–05.

relations with the Labour Party, and Philip Gould,* the party's poll-ster, was a close adviser on strategy and 'messaging'. Finally, Blair's wife, Cherie Booth,† remained throughout a constant source of support and advice. Between them, these dozen operators in total (no fewer than seven of whom later became Labour ministers, six at Cabinet level) were the team that ran New Labour in opposition. Of the twelve, Powell was the only one with any direct experience of the civil service, and yet there was somehow a belief that the opposi-tion team and processes could be simply lifted into government and operate in a similar way. Peter Mandelson summed up neatly what became Labour's problem soon after they won the general election:

> The real problem was a lack of hard policy preparation before we got into Number 10, and now a lack of structure and rigour in the way we, and Tony, set priorities, reached decisions and took them forward. Just two weeks after the election I wrote Tony a note: 'Government is bigger, more complex, than opposition. We used to rely on speedy, informal ways of working – including daily knowledge of your thinking and demands.' That would no longer work.[31]

The New Labour team came to power without a clearly defined stra-tegic vision. Blair used the phrase 'modernisation and reform' but rarely defined what it actually meant. Similarly, their more narrow political pledges from the election campaign proved remarkably dif-ficult to frame and measure once in government.‡ Blair personally had no plans for civil service reform, and he and Brown had both

---

* Baron Gould of Blackwood (1950–2011); Labour Party polling adviser.
† Cherie Booth KC (1954–); barrister; wife of Tony Blair.
‡ The 'pledge card' produced by the Labour Party for the 1997 general election had five specific policy commitments.

deliberately chosen not to engage with the civil service beforehand but instead let their proxies (mainly in the shape of Powell and Balls) do so on their behalf. Powell and Balls had different approaches to this task, which were not always co-ordinated. So, on day one, the new government was starting from scratch with limited knowledge of the system. The one person who could have helped them in advance, the Cabinet Secretary Robin Butler, had been unable to establish a good working relationship with Blair in opposition or to clarify exactly how Blair intended to use his two key members of staff (Powell and Campbell). Since they would be working most closely with the private office and with the press office, Butler designed a rather clunky mechanism whereby two 'Orders in Council' were passed to allow Powell and Campbell to give instructions to civil servants, if necessary. This made some think that Butler was somehow unsympathetic to Blair and New Labour, which he was not. He merely sought clarity on how the new regime would operate in practice.[32] Butler insisted that this procedural arrangement was necessary to legitimise Powell's and Campbell's powers and to allow them to manage civil servants directly. Powell became a powerful figure in No. 10 and a close confidant of Blair, especially on issues such as Northern Ireland. Campbell's title was the Prime Minister's chief press secretary and official spokesman, but, in practice, this involved much more than that title suggested. He was a key strategist and political adviser who operated across all areas of government. As such, Campbell was personally responsible for introducing many new elements of modern communication structures and strategies within Whitehall departments, which represented a step change from the systems used in the Thatcher/Major era. While Campbell and, to a lesser extent, Powell became figures of media scrutiny and criticism, the model which they designed has, in broad measure, survived.

POLICY AND MACHINERY

While Labour was not necessarily seeking to change the civil service in the ways that Wilson had considered in 1964, it did want to reform the centre of government and, specifically, to do this in the domain of the powers of No. 10 and the authority of the No. 10 private office. Some thinkers on the left tried to provide a stronger strategic framework and a number of books were devoted to this after Blair became Labour Party leader.[33] However, Blair's regular articulation of the need for 'modernisation' was vague and, in the words of John Rentoul, 'was not a coherent ideology like, say, Croslandite revisionism'.[34] Peter Riddell, in a damning phrase, described the Third Way* as having "'over-reached itself by exaggerating its novelty and coherence" and ... [by being] dominated far too much by "grand, but often vague theories"'.[35] It was in this context that Peter Mandelson and Roger Liddle produced a document that was to help shape Labour's policies for power.

The Blair Revolution was published in 1996 and, over some 250 pages, articulated the New Labour policy agenda.[36] Unlike the Fabian pamphlet *The Administrators*, published thirty years previously in the run-up to the 1964 general election, *The Blair Revolution* did not recommend a radical reform of the senior civil service (and it explicitly opposed the establishment of ministerial *cabinets* on the French model instead of private offices), but, in three chapters entitled 'A New Politics', 'A New Party' and 'A New Government', it made a robust case for a more powerful centre of government. It proposed an enhanced role for No. 10, a 'beefed-up Policy Unit' and the Cabinet Office to act more like a Prime Minister's department.[37]

---

* The Third Way was the loose set of ideas of 'Blairism', based on the concept discussed in Anthony Giddens's book *The Third Way*.

It also argued that there was a 'need to make more [independent] specialist advice available to the Prime Minister', with a 'stronger political presence in No. 10'.³⁸ In addition, Mandelson and Liddle proposed the appointment of 'a non-ministerial political manager – a "straight" player – who is trusted by all, especially by the official machine, whose job is to bring together the political and non-political sources of prime ministerial advice and ensure that the Prime Minister's political strategy is kept on track'.³⁹

That effectively was a job description for the role Powell would eventually take in No. 10. By contrast, the authors saw the value of the private offices of Cabinet ministers and their role in providing continuity. They did not propose major changes here and instead emphasised:

> Ministers who are new to their jobs and their departments need to be guided by people who know the ropes, not those who are as inexperienced as they are and, in the case of ministers' private offices, there is great advantage in having individuals who provide continuity, who are trained in the ways and standards of the civil service and, through their contacts in the system, can plug their minister fully into the Whitehall network.⁴⁰

The Blair Revolution outlined a new role for the Cabinet Office, arguing that it 'should be more akin to a Department of the Prime Minister and Cabinet, charged with actively carrying forward the cross-departmental polices agreed by the cabinet'.⁴¹ It argued for a far more proactive Cabinet Office which would be managed by the Cabinet Secretary and focus on cross-departmental policies. However, it did not set out the practical steps by which these aims might be achieved. *The Blair Revolution* was, therefore, more of a sketch, not a fully designed strategy for fundamental reform, and despite this body of initial preparatory ideas, reform of the centre of government did not feature at all in New Labour's 1997 election manifesto.[42] The text could have represented a framework for fundamental changes but, once Labour came into power, there was no practical plan for how the vision of a stronger centre might be brought to fruition. It is not clear, in fact, that many people at the centre of New Labour or the new government had even read the book.

PRACTICALITIES

As chief of staff from 1995 to 1997, Powell was in charge of developing a more professional operation for Blair's opposition office and one that would be ready for the transition to power, but Blair himself took little interest in the work. This was unusual because Blair knew he was inexperienced in this area. In that respect, he was different from Wilson and Heath but closer to Thatcher. Campbell's view was that Blair concentrated on campaigning and 'he didn't think there was much point in addressing structures [in advance] that he would need to assess as he observed them [once in power]'.[43] First, Powell ensured that the administrative work was better managed. As Rentoul writes, 'the Blair team were initially taken aback by Jonathan's Civil Service formality, especially the fact that he took minutes, but he soon impressed with his quiet efficiency'.[44] The attention of Blair, Mandelson and Campbell at this stage was focused on communications and seeking to expose the shortcomings and scandals, as they saw them, of the Major government. Blair and his team were good at that but lacked organisational rigour. That was one of the elements that Powell was able to import with his background in government. He also had a number of interlocutors in the diplomatic world (such as Michael Butler* and David Hannay†) who were happy to provide advice on diplomacy and foreign affairs to the ministerial team of the potential next Prime Minister.[45] Blair later commented that Powell 'had had difficulty settling into the role … finding the change from career diplomat to politico tricky. Once settled in, though, he was brilliant.'[46] Powell had the following three overarching tasks: to run Blair's office of Leader of the Opposition as efficiently as possible; to get potential ministers prepared for the challenge of government; and, in the longer term, to engage with the civil service to make the necessary preparations for the expected Labour victory.[47]

Hardly any of Labour's putative ministers had ministerial experience or knew what a private office was for. Powell, therefore, devised a programme of seminars for potential ministers, which took place in the two years before the election and 'from this group came the idea of training shadow ministers', including in how to use their private offices.[48] While a good idea, in practice these seminars were ineffective because Blair and Brown did not attend and neither did potential ministers whom Powell thought needed training most.[49] In addition to these seminars, the Fabian Society arranged a series of meetings between Labour frontbench spokespeople and former civil servants on the workings of government. Again, this process (chaired by the historian Peter Hennessy) was designed to prepare New Labour on best use of the civil service, especially private office and the role of their own advisers. The subsequent pamphlet produced by the Fabian Society summarised the meetings that had

---

* Sir Michael Butler (1927–2013); retired Foreign Office diplomat.
† Lord (David) Hannay of Chiswick (1935–); retired Foreign Office diplomat.

been held and included practical guidance on how ministers should engage with their private offices and civil servants.[50] That pamphlet, like *The Blair Revolution*, argued the case for a stronger centre of government, based mainly in the Cabinet Office. In contrast, it was a far shorter document and presented more as an introductory guidebook for potential ministers. It did not get wide coverage and was not promoted via the media, in part because some of the ex-civil servants involved specifically did not want any publicity.[51] It stated that 'there was a general agreement amongst the former civil servants and political advisers [who had attended the Fabian meetings] that the Centre, the system which supported the Prime Minister and No. 10 needed to be strengthened'.[52]

The Fabians also recommended a more regular series of six-monthly meetings with ministers to review 'how well the Government was adhering to its strategy'.[53] This was something Blair finally did establish, and with enthusiasm, when he created the Prime Minister's Delivery Unit (PMDU) at the start of his second term. The unit, led by Sir Michael Barber, a former expert adviser at the Department for Education and Employment (DfEE) from 1997 to 2001, instituted periodic 'stock takes' with the key ministers responsible for delivery of the government's priorities and targets.[54]

It is clear that New Labour had undergone some preparation for government, even though Blair had not been deeply involved in the work. Blair had an experienced chief of staff, who had built an efficient opposition leader's office, alongside a powerful press secretary, policy advisers and a programme of seminars on how to work in Whitehall. Yet the whole area was not a priority for the Labour leader and the detailed workings of Whitehall and private office did not interest him, as testified to by his first two Cabinet Secretaries, Butler and Wilson.[55] The fact that neither Blair nor Brown attended the seminars on preparation for power was testament to how seriously they took this matter. Despite the Mandelson/Liddle recommendations and the ideas advanced in the Fabian seminars, there was no blueprint of what to do with the 'centre'.

PREPARATIONS FOR THE TRANSITION

In January 1996, Major wrote to Blair to inform him that, with sixteen months to go until the next general election and in accordance with Douglas-Home rules, pre-election contacts with the opposition party could commence.[56*] Accordingly, the Cabinet Secretary, Robin Butler, held meetings with Jonathan Powell, who, in turn, began to liaise with Alex Allan, Major's principal private secretary. These discussions included the question of how No. 10 would operate under a New Labour government, including Powell's new role as chief of staff.[57]

Only five of Blair's ministers had any previous experience at all of office (although Clare Short, who was to become International Development Secretary, had previously been a civil servant and served as a private secretary to a junior Home Office minister from 1974 to 1975).[†] Powell was the only one with any real understanding of the processes of government and was in charge of the transition preparations, although, as he admitted, his background had not been in the mainstream civil service but as a diplomat:

---

*   Prior to 1993, such contacts between the main opposition party and the civil service could take place only during the last six months of a parliament.

†   Five ministers appointed in 1997 had served as ministers before 1979. Three had been junior ministers (Margaret Beckett, Jack Cunningham and Gavin Strang) and so would have had experience of small private offices. In addition, Ann Taylor had been an assistant government whip. John Morris had been Secretary of State for Wales from 1974 to 1979 and, under Blair, served as Attorney General (but not in the Cabinet) from 1997 to 1999.

I was a fairly unusual civil servant. I had never, for example, worked in private office and had spent a lot of my time abroad and on negotiations. I did not, therefore, have that wide knowledge of the civil service which others had but, by comparison [to everyone else in Blair's team] (whose backgrounds tended to be in politics, journalism or academia), I was a real expert.[58]

In the run-up to the election, and for at least six months, Powell 'had been meeting secretly with Alex Allan … and Robin Butler … to agree what would happen if New Labour won the election'.[59] Powell wrote that these visits had even included 'a private tour of Numbers 10, 11 and 12 for me early one evening when John Major and Ken Clarke, the inhabitant of No. 11, were both away'.[60] Allan recalled that he and Powell worked well together and, by the time the election campaign was underway, they had planned all the logistics and details of the transition day itself, including which members of Blair's team were expected to be based at No. 10 and how they would relate to the existing private office and other staff.[61] Allan was prepared, for example, for a large increase in the number of special advisers to be appointed in No. 10 (all of whom would need desks) when compared to the previous regime.

Powell had also worked closely with David Miliband (the party's head of policy) on the manifesto and policy priorities. Together they had produced a 'first 100 days plan' (as Clinton had done in 1992), and yet Powell was frustrated by Blair's continued lack of interest in engaging with this process.[62] For example, the list of who might be Cabinet members, which Powell and Miliband passed to Butler shortly in advance of the election, remained provisional. When Powell gave the documents to Robin Butler, a few days before 1 May, he had to caveat them with the fact that Blair had still not fully approved them. 'Tony wouldn't engage in the planning for government', thinking it might appear that he was already 'measuring the curtains in Downing Street'.[63] Blair only really turned to this aspect on the afternoon of 1 May at his constituency home in Sedgefield, by which time even he finally acknowledged that Labour was going to win and to win well.[64]

One of the most critical issues which arose was about the relationship between Powell and Allan and their division of responsibilities. Powell made it clear to Butler that his position as chief of staff, akin to that post in the White House, would be senior to all the civil servants in the No. 10 private office. As Powell explained, 'The reason I created the job of chief of staff was that, unless there was someone to pull everything together, the only other person who could do that and resolve disputes within No. 10 was the Prime Minister himself.'[65] The new post of chief of staff had obvious implications for the role of principal private secretary at No. 10. Having spent almost five years in this role at No. 10, Allan 'assumed that Jonathan Powell would fulfil the role that I had had with John Major. I was not therefore convinced of the need for the principal private secretary post as well.'[66] By contrast, Butler was adamant that Powell could not become principal private secretary as well as chief of staff and that there had to be two separate posts:

> From the beginning of 1996 [when talks began], I was preoccupied that Jonathan Powell should not become principal private secretary. At Easter 1996, I invited Tony and Cherie Blair for supper, where we talked about what he would do if he became Prime Minister … I made it clear that I was happy for Jonathan Powell to become chief of staff, but not principal private secretary.[67]

A few days before polling day in 1997, and with the issue still unresolved, Butler met Blair at his Islington home. The issue of whether Powell should become principal private secretary, as well as chief of staff, was again discussed. Blair, though, did not really engage with the issue and, without experience of government, did not realise the wider implications of such a decision.[68] Butler reiterated his opposition, not least because there were some tasks (including liaison with Buckingham Palace, honours, intelligence questions and a range of issues connected to sensitive appointments) which he believed were inappropriate for a political appointee to carry out, however well he understood the civil service.[69] Butler also pointed out, in practical terms, that Blair would inherit a well-respected principal private secretary in the shape of Alex Allan. According to Michael Jago, 'Butler's distinct impression was that Blair had focused solely on the campaign, rather than on what was involved in being Prime Minister'.[70] It is extraordinary that this issue was not addressed fully until the last few days of the election campaign. This is further evidence that Blair chose not to address some of these critical operational questions until he was forced to do so, and often at the last minute. Powell, for his part and not unreasonably, argued that he never actually wanted to be principal private secretary and that if that had been his career aim, he would have remained in the civil service.[71]

Butler's eventual solution to the chief of staff issue had two elements. Powell and Allan would initially operate in parallel in No. 10 (and, in practice, they chose to work from the same office). In addition, as noted, Butler had also introduced the two Orders in Council to allow Powell and Campbell to give orders to civil servants. This decision, while seen by Powell and Campbell as 'over the top' and something which Butler himself later acknowledged was unnecessary, did put the issue to bed and ensured clear propriety for Powell's and Campbell's new roles in government.[72] Butler had insisted on the orders as a point of principle, as he had the division between the chief of staff and the principal private secretary role, to defend the propriety of the civil service and draw the line between it and political advisers.

In practice, the arrangement succeeded because Powell and Allan developed an excellent working relationship which contributed to the overall success of the transition. Butler's worries proved to be exaggerated and the 'insurance policy' of the Orders in Council was, in practice, unnecessary. On the day Blair became Prime Minister, Campbell wrote that 'Alex Allan seemed a really nice bloke'.[73] Powell described him as 'incredibly helpful during the transition', and Blair said, 'He was extremely important ... and extremely professional.'[74] Allan's wider skills as well as those of the private office were soon to be tested further. He himself was due to leave No. 10 in three months' time, so the challenge thereafter would be for the rest of the private office to assimilate to the new regime. With Allan gone, Powell became the dominant figure in No. 10, a realignment which some private office members found less than straightforward.

PRIVATE OFFICE UNDER NEW LABOUR: THE TRANSITION IN NO. 10

On Friday 2 May 1997, Tony Blair entered Downing Street as Prime Minister of the first Labour government for eighteen years, swept to power on the back of his party's landslide election victory. At No. 10, Allan welcomed the new Prime Minister and Powell. The private office consisted of Allan and four other private secretaries, none of whom Powell had met – John Holmes (foreign affairs), Moira Wallace (economic affairs), Mark Adams (parliamentary affairs) and Angus Lapsley (home affairs). Powell was joined at No. 10 by Alastair Campbell, who immediately became chief press officer.[*] Anji Hunter also came to No. 10, although Allan was only told about this on the Friday after the election, having previously been assured that she would not be working there. Her post was originally titled 'special assistant to the Prime Minister' in 1997 but was later renamed as 'director of government relations'. She continued to play an informal role for Blair outside of the private office, focusing on planning events and personal support to him. David Miliband became the acting head of the No. 10 Policy Unit and a large team of special advisers (twenty-eight, compared to just six under Major) joined soon afterwards to work within the unit.

Allan fitted in very well and quickly with the New Labour team, who found him friendly, flexible and creative.[75] They trusted him from the start – and he was immediately engaged with the task of appointing the new Cabinet. He was struck by how willing the New Labour team were to take his advice on appointments, thinking that they might, in some way, have resented his advice given that he had worked for Major for five years. Allan was also impressed by the approach of Campbell, whom he described as 'incredibly effective and professional. He was just very good at his job. He knew Blair's mind and he knew when and how to push back at Blair. I got on well with him.'[76] Not everything about the transition, though, was smooth. Others in the private office were more 'shell-shocked', according to Powell.[77] Moira Wallace found the transition difficult in terms of dealing with the Treasury and handling the Blair–Brown relationship. Some New Labour appointees did not fully trust Mark Adams on account of his close association with Major and because

---

[*] Campbell replaced Jonathan Haslam, Major's civil servant appointee in that post. (Haslam moved to be director of communications to David Blunkett, the Secretary of State for Education and Employment.)

he made clear his admiration for the previous administration.[78]* He also tended to push Labour to do things in the ways in which they had been done under Major, which did not appeal to Powell or Campbell.[79] Of Adams, Campbell wrote, early on, that

> the one I was keeping a close eye on was Mark Adams ... He was cocky without the obvious talent to justify it ... and when he was giving it large about how we should prepare for PMQs, I couldn't help pointing out that Major's PMQs was one of his biggest weaknesses.[80]

There were significant teething problems involved in establishing Blair's private office as an instrument for providing momentum for New Labour's policy agenda. This was not the result of a lack of enthusiasm on the part of civil servants, many of whom were eagerly anticipating the challenges presented by a new administration, but owed more to a lack of understanding about the extent to which implementing those pledges would be driven by the centre of government. Butler, Allan and their teams had prepared copious briefing files on the manifesto and on early decisions needed for Blair, much of which remained unread.[81]† The new relationships with, for example, Campbell, Mandelson and Powell worked well. However, the private office had no concept of how strained relations between Blair and Brown would become or how much more difficult the atmosphere in No. 10, including its relationship with No. 11, would be.[82] When Allan left No. 10 for his new post, he reflected on his short period as principal private secretary:

---

* He was later responsible for leaking to the *Mail on Sunday* details of some Cabinet meetings which he had observed.

† These briefing files were released following a freedom of information request.

It became quite clear early on that No. 10 was not geared up to driving forward the New Labour agenda in the ways that they had hoped. John Major had been a far more passive Prime Minister. He cared deeply about a few things but was not trying to drive the whole agenda across government. The machinery was simply not set up to support Blair in driving the whole of his agenda forward at once. This, and the Cabinet Office's failings, led eventually to the setting up of the Prime Minister's Delivery Unit, which helped to make the second term [of the Labour government] more of a success.[83]

This is the most telling analysis of the failure of the civil service in early 1997 to prepare itself for the New Labour style of operation and the shortcomings – specifically of the private office. Despite Allan's efficient management of the handover and the fact that he gained the immediate trust of key New Labour officials, the operation that he oversaw was essentially the same one he had managed for John Major but with a different Prime Minister. Allan's analysis tallies with Blair's reflection that, with the benefit of hindsight, much of his first term was a missed opportunity to begin his reform agenda sooner. The No. 10 private office collectively must take part of the blame for that failing.

THE TRANSITION AT THE TREASURY

Like Blair, Gordon Brown was also superstitious about any presumption of a Labour victory and so he too had done little to prepare for transition.[84] His contacts with the civil service had been even less than Blair's and his first experience in the Treasury building came on the day that New Labour took power. However, on his behalf, his economic adviser Ed Balls had been working behind the scenes for over a year and had put in place detailed transition plans with Treasury officials. Balls's interlocutor had been mainly the Treasury Permanent Secretary, Terry Burns. They held meetings weekly for a year and had covered most issues, apart from the detail of policy. Balls also regularly met Nick Macpherson, the principal private secretary who was expected to see the transition through. When Burns tried to replace Macpherson, before the 1997 general election, Balls and Brown ensured that he remained in post. A new inexperienced principal private secretary (whom they would have had no say in appointing) would have been a risk.[85]

It was assumed, certainly by the Treasury team, that more formal meetings between Brown and Burns would happen in advance of the general election, but, despite a year of planning, only one brief twenty-minute meeting took place in Brown's House of Commons office. The only decision taken was on the font and the size of typeface that the Treasury would use for the new Chancellor on account of his poor eyesight. Balls's meetings therefore assumed far more significance. They also reflected a slight mistrust of his future Permanent Secretary by Brown, who was wary of the fact that Burns had originally been recruited as a political appointee to the Treasury by the Conservatives in 1981.[86] The pair never developed a strong working relationship and, as a result, the role of the private office and Macpherson's management of the transition became even more important. Brown had a different pattern of working from the informal style of his predecessor. For example, Macpherson found Brown wary of making quick decisions and so he rarely committed his views in writing. Brown was far less keen on large meetings than

Ken Clarke and his red boxes would often come back either seemingly untouched or with papers removed for him to think about. Macpherson ultimately developed a good working relationship with Balls and earned Brown's trust to such an extent that, in 2005, he was appointed the Treasury's Permanent Secretary.[87]

The roles of the No. 10 and Treasury private offices were immediately tested on the first weekend that New Labour was in power. On the day of the election, Balls gave Burns a note with the details of the policy proposals that Brown would wish to introduce, thus giving the Treasury private office and officials twenty-four hours to check the key points were covered in the introductory briefing.[88] The Treasury had assumed this was the full list, but one major policy change was omitted. On Friday 2 May, and having been formally welcomed by Burns and Macpherson, Brown and Balls dropped their bombshell that the new government intended to make the Bank of England independent.[89]

The Treasury rapidly assembled a team to work on the plans over that bank holiday weekend. It was led by Tom Scholar,* a brilliant young official who later succeeded Macpherson as the department's Permanent Secretary (and later still was sacked on day one of the Truss administration in 2022). Brown and Balls set off to discuss the issue with Blair. They met on the Saturday morning in his Islington house. According to Balls, 'the place was a bustle of activity and we sat down with Tony and the No. 10 [private secretary] responsible for economic policy, Moira Wallace'.[90] When Blair said to Wallace that Brown was going to make the Bank of England independent,

---

* Tom Scholar (1968–); civil servant; principal private secretary to the Chancellor of the Exchequer 1997–2001; chief of staff and principal private secretary to the Prime Minister 2007–08; Permanent Secretary to the HM Treasury 2016–22.

'Moira was clearly gobsmacked by this decision, and the nature of the decision-making process'.[91] Another commentator said that Wallace, who was 'unschooled in New Labour's ways of transacting major decisions, asked the Prime Minister: "Would you like a detailed strategy paper?"'[92] Blair just shrugged and said that if Gordon was content, then he too was.

According to Brown:

With [Blair] was his new private secretary, Moira Wallace, a Treasury civil servant who had moved seamlessly from serving a Conservative government to working for a Labour one. Moira, who was as intelligent as she was forceful, had a very different view from mine – and I think Tony's – on how the issue should be handled. She advised him that we ought to wait until we had run the gamut of a whole series of formalities [but] at our Saturday meeting Tony concluded our discussion with one word: 'Fine'.[93]

Brown had witnessed, at first hand, how the private office workers, including Wallace, were changing their allegiance (literally overnight) from Major to Blair, as would have happened in all Whitehall private offices that weekend. Brown did admit that 'we broke with all the conventions' and that while 'Robin Butler, Terry Burns and Moira Wallace were justified in their reservations', as the new Chancellor, he wanted to move quickly and decisively.[94] Yet the exchanges with Wallace left a difficult legacy in that Brown did not trust Blair's private secretary for economic affairs to join their bilaterals and so these meetings would often go unrecorded. For a private secretary not to be able to attend official meetings undermines the role of the private office and prevents the proper conduct of government business. The issue was finally resolved in the autumn of that year when Wallace left No. 10 to head the new Social Exclusion Unit.

CHANGES IN THE NO. 10 PRIVATE OFFICE

As the Prime Minister and his team of advisers grew in confidence in their first months in office, they concluded that a stronger private office was required. Moira Wallace's departure was not therefore the only one. As Alex Allan was about to leave No. 10 after serving five years as principal private secretary, Alastair Campbell recorded that '[Blair] said we needed a shakeup of private office. Alex [Allan] was great but he had allowed them all to get a bit cocky.'[95] Three changes were to happen over the summer and early autumn which would affect the structure and improve the effectiveness of No. 10. First, John Holmes replaced Allan as principal private secretary. Holmes had been private secretary for foreign affairs since 1995 and provided the New Labour government, which he had impressed, with much-needed expertise on Northern Ireland and on foreign policy. He took on both the principal private secretaryship together with the foreign affairs portfolio. Robin Butler was content with this arrangement because it meant that the role remained within the mainstream civil service and there was no further pressure for Powell to assume the role as well as that of chief of staff. Second, Mark Adams left and was replaced by Rob Reid from the Department for Education and Employment where he had impressed ministers with his work on Labour's Education White Paper. Finally, and most significant of all in terms of who was chosen, was Moira Wallace's replacement as private secretary for economic affairs. It was not straightforward to identify a suitable candidate from the Treasury who would satisfy both Blair and Brown. A number of names were considered, including Martin Donnelly,* Brown's preferred choice. Eventually, Jonathan Powell contacted Jeremy Heywood in the Treasury and said that Blair wanted a private secretary who would be more of a 'domestic policy supremo' alongside Holmes, the foreign affairs private secretary (and principal private secretary).[96] After being interviewed by Blair and Lord Irvine, Heywood got the job. However, and as part of the terms of the appointment, he insisted that, unlike Wallace, he must be allowed to attend every official bilateral between Blair and Brown, something which Brown agreed to on condition that Ed Balls could also attend on his side. In addition, Heywood proposed that he should sit with Powell and Holmes in the immediate outer office next to the Cabinet Room. He also wanted to be considered for promotion to the position of principal private secretary were Holmes to leave No. 10. As Powell recalled:

> Jeremy [Heywood] joined me and John [Holmes] and insisted on sharing our room ... We were initially rather taken aback by this young whippersnapper coming in and saying that this was what he wanted to do, but it was absolutely the right thing. Jeremy made himself an integral part of the operation and worked closely with [David] Miliband and later [Andrew] Adonis [in the Policy Unit] to ensure that the policy-making function worked far more effectively.[97]

---

* Martin Donnelly (1958–); civil servant; private secretary to the Financial Secretary to the Treasury 1982–83; private secretary to the Secretary of State for Northern Ireland 1988; Permanent Secretary Department for Business Innovation and Skills 2010–16; Permanent Secretary Department for International Trade 2016–17.

Blair also viewed the appointment of Heywood as critical. It gave him two people in his immediate private office on whom he could fully rely to oversee domestic and foreign policy work and, while not politicising the civil service, would ensure greater emphasis on the political direction in which he wished to travel:

> With Jeremy's appointment, it was the first time, in terms of domestic policy, when I felt I had someone I could depend on who was very much part of the team. He also obviously had the extremely valuable 'small p' political skills. John Holmes had also become very important. He was the first person from the private office that I came to depend on in terms of policy because, obviously, my knowledge of foreign policy was initially fairly limited.[98]

These changes were significant collectively. They meant that, by the end of 1997, the private office was beginning to work as Blair wished and the emerging strains between Blair and Brown (especially concerning the possibility that the UK might give up the pound in favour of the euro) were being better managed at the official level. Butler retired as Cabinet Secretary at the end of 1997, to be replaced by Richard Wilson, and early tensions across the Whitehall communications network, caused by Campbell's appointment, had been ironed out when a number of heads of information retired. There was also a recognition within much of the civil service that, at the transition, there may have been too much of an assumption that it would be 'business as usual', whereas Blair and many of his No. 10 special advisers wanted a more interventionist and political centre (without seeking to politicise the civil service) and one that was more directive across Whitehall. As Alex Allan had observed, the private office had been slow to appreciate this in the immediate aftermath of the election.

In Powell's view, once the personnel changes had been properly bedded in, this period represented one of the two times in which the private office was at its most effective under Blair.[99]* There was clear political direction from the Prime Minister (supported by Powell and Campbell), with a strong principal private secretary in place in Holmes (who, in 1999, was indeed replaced by Heywood on promotion). There was a team of private secretaries who had good political intelligence and worked well together and with the Policy Unit led by David Miliband, and the power and influence of the private office was widely respected across Whitehall. Yet despite the harmonious and disciplined operation of his private office, Blair's frustrations with Whitehall began to grow over what he regarded as the slow progress being made on implementing the concepts of 'modernisation' and 'delivery' across their departments.

Such frustrations led to the revival of the proposal for a Prime Minister's department which had been mentioned in *The Blair Revolution*. As early as 1999, Blair, Powell and Heywood considered the idea of some type of reconfiguration of the centre of government. Powell believed that the Cabinet Office was too weak and that the Prime Minister should have 'a larger office with a proper staff and budget, capable of taking on departments in argument'.[100] However, there was no clarity on precisely what type of changes were required and, in any case, the Cabinet Secretary, Richard Wilson, who would have been responsible for making the changes was so opposed to them that he threatened resignation.[101] No progress was made, but the centralisation of power at No. 10 continued.

---

* According to Powell, the other time was in 2007 in advance of the transition to Brown.

PRIVATE OFFICE IN TIMES OF CRISIS:
THE FUEL CRISIS, FOOT-AND-MOUTH, 9/11 AND IRAQ

Before Blair could make any changes to the operation of the centre of government, he was tested by some major crises, none of which could have been predicted. This section of the chapter looks at the challenges posed by those crises, including how Blair and No. 10 responded. First, in September 2000, an industrial dispute about fuel halted petrol supplies to filling stations. Then, for much of the first half of 2001, Britain's agricultural and rural economy was devastated by the foot-and-mouth epidemic. Third, the attacks on the Twin Towers in New York on 11 September 2001 took place and, finally, in 2003, Britain went to war in Iraq. Blair, his ministerial colleagues, his key advisers and his private office were involved in the response to each of these. All of these crises convinced him that the crisis management systems of government were not fit for purpose. As a result, he tended to rely increasingly on Powell, Heywood and the private office.

The fuel crisis came virtually out of nothing and, initially, No. 10 seemed unable to do anything in response that had any effect on the worsening situation. In Jonathan Powell's recollection, 'I pulled every lever available and none of them seemed connected to anything.'[102] Blair himself also described the official machine as 'curiously paralysed'.[103] Within days, fuel supplies in the country were running low and Blair's frustration about the inability of Whitehall to manage the system led him to take a leading role, working through Powell, Heywood, Campbell and others. Blair was concerned by the inability of the traditional Whitehall mechanisms to have any effect on the growing crisis. Campbell recalled that he could 'sense [Blair's] irritation every time David Omand [the Home Office Permanent Secretary] tried to convey the idea that everything that could be done was being done'.[104] In the end, No. 10 simply took over. As Powell put it, 'We got the operational heads of all the major oil companies and the police representatives to come into the Cabinet Office ... Jeremy Heywood and I moved in there with them, and we kept them working night and day to try to get fuel out of the depots.'[105] It was the first of many occasions when Blair found it more effective to work through his No. 10 team to manage a crisis directly rather than to rely on the wider civil service. Within four or five days, the fuel crisis was coming to an end. The next major crisis was to last far longer and prove far more costly.

Foot-and-mouth disease had last occurred on mainland Britain in the epidemic of 1967–68 and, since then, was generally thought to have been eradicated from the developed world.* When the disease unexpectedly appeared at an abattoir in Essex in February 2001, there were no plans in place for dealing with such a major epidemic, but, in any case, the Ministry of Agriculture, Fisheries and Food (MAFF) assured the No. 10 private office that all was under control. Blair was on a visit to the USA and his private secretary for domestic affairs, David North, cut short a holiday to return to No. 10 to deal with the response to the outbreak.[106] On 23 February, North was once again assured by MAFF's private office that there was no cause for immediate concern but that, to prevent the spread of the disease, it would be necessary to ban all animal movements throughout the United Kingdom. The Minister for Agriculture, Nick Brown, spoke to the Prime Minister in Washington to get his agreement and to confirm that such a ban was necessary for disease control.[107] By the time Blair returned to the UK, he began to focus increasingly on the disease, including on MAFF's capacity to manage the situation.

---

* There had been a very minor outbreak on the Isle of Wight in 1981.

Blair was unconvinced that MAFF could handle the disease, as were Powell, Heywood and North in his private office.

As the disease worsened, No. 10 again effectively took control of the government's overall management of the situation, with Blair convening and usually chairing the cross-government crisis management system, known as COBRA, which Nick Brown chose not to attend.[108] Instructions to departments and ministers were sent directly from Heywood, on Blair's authority, to ministers across government. These allocated specific tasks to tackle the disease and deal with its wider effects across the economy.[109] Brown became so frustrated by No. 10 taking charge that he said to Brian Bender, his Permanent Secretary at MAFF, 'Who is in charge of this department: me, you or Jeremy Heywood?'[110] In spite of Brown's frustrations, Heywood and North, on behalf of Blair, instructed other departments in MAFF's policy area, because it had been seen to be ineffective. Again, this state of affairs served only to strengthen Blair's belief that the traditional methods of Cabinet government and departmental management were severely lacking. In his memoirs, he reflected that 'sometimes the machinery [for crisis management] is non-existent or inadequate and that you have to think first. Otherwise, the activity is useless or, even worse, counterproductive.'[111] As such, Blair would tend to turn to his chief of staff and to his principal private secretary.

The foot-and-mouth epidemic led to a delay in Blair calling the 2001 general election, which eventually took place on 7 June of that year. Labour was returned with an overall majority of 167. Only three months after the general election, 9/11 occurred. Partly as a result of the previous two crises, but also because it was an international crisis, the response was more effectively co-ordinated. Foreign and defence policy, planning and response has historically been managed by the defence and overseas secretariat of the Cabinet Office according to agreed and tested protocols which did not exist for handling domestic crises. Blair himself paid tribute to this element of the system:

> Back in Downing Street and during the first of several emergency sessions with ministers and officials, we ran through the measures we had to take … Every part of Whitehall was buzzing and alive with activity. At such moments the machine is at its best, covering all bases, setting an agenda for the decision-making, joining up the disparate parts in some sort of semi-automatic cohesion. It was impressive. I was glad of the steady hand of Richard Wilson and his senior Civil Service colleagues.[112]

The contrast with Blair's experience of the management of earlier domestic crises is palpable. Accordingly, the private office post-9/11 played a much more traditional role and was far less interventionist than during the foot-and-mouth crisis.

However, eighteen months later, during the Iraq War, Blair and No. 10 were at the centre of the biggest crisis of his whole premiership. It led to enormous scrutiny of the processes of government and, specifically, the way in which Blair took decisions and how, during the conflict, he used his close advisers at No. 10, including the private office. The history of the Iraq War, its origins and management, have been told elsewhere in immense detail, particularly in the 2016 report of the inquiry chaired by Sir John Chilcot.[113] Notably, however, much of the narrative used by Chilcot to describe events in No. 10 at the time of the war was taken from Campbell's diaries.[114] One of the surprises in the Chilcot report was that Campbell's diaries often proved to be 'a better record of the workings of government than the official minutes'.[115] Jon Davis and John Rentoul point out that 'on several occasions, Chilcot gives a brief account of the official record of Cabinet meetings, followed by a fuller account of who said what taken from Campbell's diary'.[116]

In his report, Chilcot levelled specific criticism at Blair and his private office, including concerning the lack of due process in recording meetings and decisions made: 'The way in which the policy on Iraq was developed and decisions were taken and implemented within the UK Government had been at the heart of the Inquiry's work'.[117] Chilcot also noted that most decisions on Iraq before the conflict were taken by different meetings of ministers and officials and that while 'some of those meetings were minuted; some were not'.[118] That was a reasonable criticism of the private office processes at the time, assuming as it did that a private secretary was present in all meetings. The key officials in No. 10 at the time were Powell and Heywood, together with Matthew Rycroft,* the private secretary for foreign affairs. Rycroft attended many of the meetings and at one point was asked by the inquiry: 'Why didn't No. 10 officials minute more of the Prime Minister's internal meetings and indeed phone calls with Cabinet colleagues on these subjects?'[119] Rycroft's reply was that 'my job going into No. 10 and throughout my time in No. 10 ... was to minute in some way or other everything that was related to policy, British policy, on the issues that I was responsible for within No. 10'.[120] The evidence shows that much of the Iraq discussion was not minuted and therefore that a private secretary was probably not even present in some of the key meetings or listening

---

* Matthew Rycroft (1968–); civil servant; private secretary to the Prime Minister 2002–04; Permanent Secretary DfID 2018–20; Permanent Secretary Home Office since 2020.

in to the phone calls which took place at the critical moments prior to agreement of the invasion strategy. According to the questioning of Rycroft, there were 'over thirty phone calls with Jack Straw [the Foreign Secretary] in the period in question [July 2002], only one of which was minuted'.[121] Therefore, in this period of the development of policy on Iraq, one of the most fundamental roles of the private office (that of recording notes of meetings and phone calls by the relevant private secretary) was not taking place in any systematic way. So, while Rycroft recorded the meetings he had attended, there were many which he did not attend and which were therefore not recorded. The central junction box function provided by the private office failed on this occasion because it simply did not have the basic core material to share with the key players. Jonathan Powell, in his evidence to the Iraq Inquiry, said that 'the key thing is that ... decisions are taken, then recorded and then distributed to government to be followed up'.[122] It seems that some of the key decisions were taken orally and not recorded. For example, the critical note from Blair to George W. Bush in which he said 'I will be with you whatever' was the subject of much debate between Blair, Powell and David Manning (Blair's foreign policy adviser at No. 10), concerning specifically whether the word 'whatever' should be included. None of this debate was recorded because there does not appear to have been a private secretary present.[123] The records kept by the private office are essential in providing clarity about what actions should be taken, particularly with regard to serious events and those concerning security. The somewhat perfunctory nature of recording only some decisions was criticised in both the Chilcot report and the Butler Review of Intelligence on Weapons of Mass Destruction, published in 2004.[124]

PRIVATE OFFICE AND 'DELIVERY'

By this time, on the domestic front, and following Labour's second general election victory in June 2001, Blair had already decided to enhance the powers of the centre of government to oversee government strategy and policies. He wished to address the shortcomings exposed by the fuel and foot-and-mouth crises by undertaking a reorganisation of the centre as well as by restructuring government departments. MAFF was abolished and replaced by a new department, the Department for Environment, Food and Rural Affairs (DEFRA), and, more significantly, the powers of Blair's central machine were enhanced. The Prime Minister's Delivery Unit (PMDU) was established to oversee the achievement of key government targets and to challenge departments on their strategies and planning.[125] It represented a further accretion of power to the centre of government.[126*] The PMDU was generally recognised as a successful initiative, with Brown and the Treasury supportive of its approach. Michael Barber worked well with Gus O'Donnell, the Permanent Secretary and 'a strong supporter of our relationship with the Treasury'.[127] Barber underlined the significance of this, emphasising that 'with the Treasury as an ally, we seemed to speak not just for the Prime Minister, but also for the Chancellor'.[128]

Blair also made changes to his private office. Largely on the advice of Heywood and Andrew Adonis, the new head of the Policy Unit, Blair decided to merge the private office with the Policy Unit to form a larger Policy Directorate. The idea was to join the work of the two units and, for each key policy area, to have one official

---

* A separate office for public service reform was also created but was unsuccessful and so was soon wound up.

responsible for managing policy development work (previously managed by the Policy Unit) and all the associated administrative tasks (previously handled by the private office). Heywood believed the outcome would be more efficient and would streamline the overall policy process and 'give a single No. 10 voice on policy'.[129] He hoped that Blair would use the merger to reduce the total number of staff in the new Policy Directorate, but he failed to do so. It became, even in Heywood's view, 'too big to support the Prime Minister', with 'too many people claiming to speak on behalf of the Prime Minister'.[130] It blurred the relationships between the private office, entirely staffed by civil servants, and the Policy Unit, which was predominantly staffed by special advisers. There was a feeling among some civil servants, including the Cabinet Secretary, that the new arrangement risked greater politicisation of some members of the newly merged unit. When both Powell and Heywood realised that the new arrangements were not working well, the experiment was ended and a separate Policy Unit was reinstated.[131] What the episode did underline was that there remained a distinct part for the private office to play in its traditional independent role of co-ordinating material and advice for the Prime Minister, controlling access to the Prime Minister, summarising issues, advising on policy matters when appropriate and recording decisions promptly and accurately.

On the domestic front, Heywood was by now powerful in his own right. Michael Barber, in addressing ways in which the Home Office might tackle street crime, commented that he took the advice of Heywood 'who had almost acted on behalf of the Prime Minister on foot and mouth the year before' and who now urged Barber to press the Home Office senior officials for 'greater rigour and more urgency, and rejecting any excuses or backsliding'.[132] Heywood could act in this way because he had the full backing and authority of the Prime Minister. Blair, in turn, described Barber as 'strategic and transformative'.[133]

By 2003, Heywood had been at No. 10 for almost six years and was, by this time, probably the most influential No. 10 private secretary since Charles Powell, although he was never accused of politicisation. Heywood was restless and seeking a new challenge. Blair wanted him to stay and refused to countenance a move from No. 10. He would not even discuss a possible leaving date despite Heywood's requests.[134] In the end, Heywood took the initiative himself and left the civil service to join the investment bank Morgan Stanley. He was replaced by Ivan Rogers,[*] another senior Treasury official. This was at a sensitive time for the Blair–Brown relationship since, by now, Brown was pressing Blair hard to leave No. 10 and set a date for handing over as Prime Minister. Whereas Heywood had managed to forge a good relationship with Treasury officials, usually by working through Ed Balls, Rogers found it harder to maintain effective links with his former department at a time when Brown's frustration with not getting the top job was mounting.[135] Powell's view was that Rogers 'brought different skills to No. 10. He was brilliant and was slightly sceptical with a cynical eye. At the same time, he worked tremendously hard, but he had terrible relationships with the Treasury. Whereas Jeremy could deal with the Treasury, Ivan found it harder to engage with Brown and his team, which was largely their fault.'[136] This was both a tribute to Heywood but also ominous for No. 10 in that the private office knew that, at some stage, there would be a Blair-to-Brown transition. Brown was

---

[*]   Ivan Rogers (1960–); Treasury official; principal private secretary to the Prime Minister 2003–06; UK permanent representative to the European Union 2013–17.

hardly on speaking terms with Powell and so was certain to dispense with his services once he reached No. 10.[137] If the principal private secretary was similarly not in tune with Brown's department, the prospects for a smooth and effective transition were much lower. Following the 2005 general election, which Labour had won but with a much-reduced majority, the pressure for a change of Prime Minister and Brown's demand for the job grew inexorably.[*]

In 2006, when Rogers also left No. 10 for the private sector, Gus O'Donnell (by now Cabinet Secretary) selected as his successor one of his younger protégées at the Treasury, Olly Robbins.[†] Robbins was then aged only thirty-one, making him the youngest ever post-war principal private secretary to the Prime Minister. His most important task was to ensure a smooth transition at No. 10 when it came. According to Jonathan Powell, 'Olly [Robbins] was so young but brilliant at getting on with the staff … He made the system work well for Tony and then managed the transition to Gordon Brown.'[138]

GORDON BROWN AND THE 2007 TRANSITION

Brown had always wanted to be Prime Minister and, during his decade as Chancellor, had positioned himself to succeed Blair. He had a clear policy agenda, yet he paid far less attention to the type of office he wanted to establish on becoming Prime Minister to support him in that role, such as who would be his key advisers or what he would want them to do when he got the job. Specifically, he did not consider what to do about the No. 10 office that he would

---

* The 2005 general election results were: Labour 355 seats, Conservatives 198 and the Liberal Democrats sixty-two; an overall majority of sixty-six compared to 167 in 2001.

† Oliver 'Olly' Robbins (1975–); principal private secretary to the Prime Minister (Tony Blair and Gordon Brown) 2006–07; Permanent Secretary Department for Exiting the EU 2016–17; UK chief Brexit negotiator 2017–19.

inherit. By 2007, he had a decade of ministerial experience and knew how the private office worked but, perhaps significantly, only in the Treasury context. The Treasury is unlike many other departments and certainly different from No. 10. As Chancellor, Brown could be far more measured and take more time over what he did (based around the annual financial cycle), but, once Prime Minister, he had to be reactive and nimble in response to events. According to James Bowler, who served as Brown's principal private secretary when he was Chancellor of the Exchequer and Prime Minister, 'Brown particularly liked to make policy [at the Treasury] through his speeches. He would spend hours working up, for example, a Budget speech and that would determine what his [future] policies were going to be.'[139] As Prime Minister, he simply did not have the time or space to do that. In addition, there was a large turnover of staff after Blair left No. 10 and not just of the special advisers such as Powell. Several civil servants took the opportunity of the change to move elsewhere and so there was a lack of in-depth No. 10 experience among the staff at the start of the Brown premiership.

For some inside No. 10, it felt more as if there had been a change of party of government and not just a change of leader from the same political party.[140] Brown recalled that he had 'wanted many of Tony Blair's people to stay in the private office in 2007 but many of them left so there was quite a large changeover of people but not of my seeking. I therefore brought in a lot of new people from the Treasury.'[141] Brown also wanted to entice Ed Balls back to work for him in a central role. As Balls recalled, 'Gordon's main preoccupation was his own Number 10 operation, and the need for a strong unit of people around him. He asked me if I would consider a joint role as Treasury Chief Secretary and lead minister in the Cabinet Office. I thought that was a doubly bad idea.'[142]

In his memoirs, Brown contrasted the nature of transition in the UK with that in the USA:

> When an administration changes hands in the United States, up to 5,000 staff come and go; in the United Kingdom, new appointees – political advisers as well as ministers – number at most around 200. In fact, as I moved in and Tony moved out, only forty or so new people would come into No. 10.[143]

In the No. 10 team, which totalled less than 200 people, this was approaching a turnover of some 25 per cent of total staff numbers. Although Brown was clear that he wanted to move away from what he saw as the informality of the Blair years, as with many previous Prime Ministers, he was less sure about what he wanted instead. He was 'determined to send out a clear message as to what kind of prime minister I would be'.[144] Hence, he decided he would 'immediately rescind the ten-year-old Order in Council that had given Tony's political advisers the power to give civil servants instructions, restoring the constitutional practice that only elected ministers were allowed to'.[145] In fact, that was little more than a gesture rather than something that made any practical difference. Campbell had left No. 10 four years previously and Powell had never needed the Order in Council to operate effectively, as even Butler himself later admitted.

Powell's departure, though, left a large void. This was filled by Tom Scholar (Brown's former principal private secretary at the Treasury), who took over as his chief of staff. Anthony Seldon and Guy Lodge quote an adviser who said it had been 'axiomatic that Tom would become chief of staff in charge of No. 10 when Gordon became Prime Minister. Gordon loved him. Tom was unstuffy, popular and extraordinarily able.'[146] In early autumn, Scholar also took on the task of principal private secretary from Olly Robbins, who transferred to the Cabinet Office. However, from the start, Scholar's role was unclear and he did not have the same authority as Powell had had under Blair, although formally they both had the same title.[147] Scholar was a civil servant whereas Powell had been a special adviser, so Scholar lacked Powell's authority to knock political heads together and impose a solution.[148] Scholar was the only civil servant ever to combine the roles of chief of staff and principal private secretary (the risk of which had so concerned Robin Butler in 1997). Scholar 'was much more comfortable as a principal private secretary than as a political enforcer. He had neither the interest in nor the mandate for the latter role.'[149] Ideally, Brown had wanted his close political friends around him at No. 10, but Balls had turned down the opportunity to run the Cabinet Office and other political advisers had also become ministers.[150*]

In the autumn of 2007, Brown had chosen not to call an early general election. Instead, political, economic and European problems were mounting and No. 10 was increasingly seen as 'dysfunctional'.[151] Brown was relying on fewer and fewer people for advice, including his former special adviser Shriti Vadera,[†] whose abrasive style did little to build wider trust in Brown's central team. Scholar unsuccessfully tried to bring order, by instigating a daily meeting at 8.30 a.m., which the political advisers and private office civil servants would attend with Brown in order to agree key tasks, but the Prime Minister often did not turn up.[152] In frustration, Scholar sought to

---

[*]   Ed Balls, Ed Miliband and Douglas Alexander all became Cabinet ministers under Brown and so were not able to serve Brown in No. 10.

[†]   Shriti Vadera (1962–); member of Council of Economic Advisers 1999–2007; created Baroness Vadera 2007; parliamentary under-secretary of state DfID 2007–08; parliamentary under-secretary of state BIS 2008–09.

leave No. 10 and began to consider a return to the Treasury at the end of the year. Brown, in turn, did what many Prime Ministers of the past twenty years had done. He turned to Jeremy Heywood for help.

Heywood had recently been persuaded by the Cabinet Secretary, Gus O'Donnell, to take up a new post in the Cabinet Office as head of economic and domestic affairs, a kind of 'domestic supremo' across all home affairs. He does not appear to have been keen to return to his old job at No. 10 as principal private secretary and, over Christmas of 2007, the issue was compounded by Brown's appointment of the little-known Stephen Carter* as chief of staff. Carter had never met Brown before and lacked the necessary party political contacts to enable him to fulfil the role the Prime Minister intended him to perform. As a result, Carter remained in the post for less than ten months before being appointed as a government minister in the House of Lords. In his place, Heywood was promoted to the newly created position of Permanent Secretary at No. 10, the first time in history that No. 10 had been headed by such a senior civil servant. James Bowler also joined No. 10 as principal private secretary. Brown's ministerial team was further strengthened by the return of Peter Mandelson to the Cabinet as Business Secretary, so there was now a strong private office in support of the Prime Minister. It would be needed over the next two years to manage the fallout from the global economic crisis. The decision not to replace Carter on his departure and to create a new and more senior post for Heywood was a recognition that, less than one year into Brown's premiership, the organisation at the centre of government had been seriously flawed. Heywood, supported by Bowler, was able to bring

---

* Stephen Carter (1964–); chief of staff and principal adviser to the Prime Minister 2007–08; created Baron Carter 2008; parliamentary under-secretary of state BIS/DCMS 2008–09.

some sense of order, a far greater discipline and co-ordination to the work of the centre, coupled with the great respect in which he was held across Whitehall.

The difficulties which Brown had in establishing his private office were a result of insufficient planning. Unlike in 1996–97, when Balls had acted as his advance emissary to the Treasury, nobody had performed that role a decade later when Brown knew that a number of key figures at No. 10 (notably Powell) would be leaving on his first day as Prime Minister. It was only once Heywood and Bowler were in place that the private office operation began to function better. Brown also moved the private office operation from No. 10 to No. 12 Downing Street (traditionally the location of the Chief Whip's office). He sat in an open-plan style, with his private office and his close advisers in a horseshoe shape around him. However, that configuration was soon abandoned. Although on the one hand it meant that Brown had his main lieutenants – such as James Bowler (his principal private secretary) and key special advisers – always close at hand, it also meant that Brown could emerge from his office and give them the most menial tasks to do, simply because they were the first people he came to.[153] In Brown's opinion:

> The political advisers and the civil servants generally did work well together, and I don't see how you can diminish the role of political advisers or the private office in future. When you have political advisers and your private office working well together with a common interest, that's the secret to success.[154]

With hindsight, that was too rosy an assessment of the way No. 10 was working at the time and, in any case, by then the country and Brown were plunged into the global economic crisis.

THE 2007 FINANCIAL CRISIS AND PRIVATE OFFICE

From September 2007, when the Newcastle-based bank Northern Rock got into difficulties, until the end of Brown's premiership, the financial crisis and its implications dominated the life of his administration. The details of the crisis have been analysed in great depth elsewhere.[155] This final section of the chapter considers how the private offices of No. 10 and in particular that of the Chancellor, Alistair Darling, handled the most spectacular moment of the crisis, namely the collapse of the Royal Bank of Scotland (RBS).

The Treasury and the Bank of England had responded to the 2007 Northern Rock collapse by stepping in and, eventually in February 2008, Brown and Darling announced that the bank would be nationalised.[156] Darling recalled that the collapse of Northern Rock had 'been a well-disguised blessing' for the Treasury: 'All the people who had been there in 2007 were still there in 2008 and corporate memory was a big thing.'[157] So, in the autumn of that year when RBS appeared to be overextending itself and was eventually to run out of money, Darling was able to turn to his Permanent Secretary, Nick Macpherson, and ask him to prepare the Treasury for a further run on a bank, based on the Northern Rock experience. As Darling recalled, 'The crisis wasn't out of the blue, although the sheer scale of it was a surprise.'[158] Events came to a climax on Tuesday 7 October, when Darling was in Luxembourg for an EU finance ministers' meeting. He was accompanied by a private secretary and his special adviser, Geoffrey Spence, who was 'no orthodox special adviser, he was a specialist, with years of banking knowledge'.[159] Darling flew early to Luxembourg and was in the meeting when Spence signalled to him, waving from the doorway, that something was wrong. The RBS share price was collapsing. An hour later, his private secretary asked him to take a call from the RBS chairman, Tom McKillop. Darling recounted, 'He sounded shell-shocked. I asked him how long the bank could keep going. His answer was chilling: "A couple of hours, maybe" … I rang Nick Macpherson and told him his hour had come.'[160]

Darling flew back to London and that night his private office, his special advisers and his Treasury team worked non-stop to put together the rescue package which the banks had to accept. Darling recalled that evening that 'the atmosphere in the Treasury was calm. Everyone knew what they had to do … An announcement had to be made at 7 a.m. the following morning.'[161] Darling managed the overall process and kept the Prime Minister updated at all times. 'This was probably the best period of our time working together while I was Chancellor. We were of the same mind and in complete agreement.'[162] At 1 a.m. on Wednesday 8 October, Darling insisted on going to bed for four hours: 'I said to my private office, whatever happened I needed sleep. If I had to do media interviews the next day, I couldn't look like I had been up all night.'[163] His private secretary, Dan Rosenfield (who some years later was to return to No. 10 as chief of staff to Boris Johnson), worked through the night with the Treasury officials to deliver the deal, just as had happened thirty-two years previously when the Treasury team had worked to put the IMF loan package together for Denis Healey. Darling was up at 5 a.m. and met Brown, Heywood and others from No. 10. Apart from a last-minute quibble about how to describe the £50 billion bail-out (which was eventually described as two tranches of £25 billion each), the deal was finalised and RBS was effectively nationalised with funding from the Bank of England, all underwritten by the government. Following Brown's agreement, the deal was signed off at 5.28 a.m., ready for the market announcement at 7 a.m.

The management of this critical part of the crisis worked relatively smoothly because every player knew their role. As Darling recalled, 'The special advisers never got in the way of the private office. They worked as a team, recognised that they all had a part to contribute, and they got on well with the civil servants managing the detail. They understood each other's roles.'[164] Of his private office, more generally, Darling was to comment that 'the relationship between a minister and his private secretaries is critical: I was never let down.'[165] Of his No. 10 team, Brown was also complimentary, saying:

> Heywood was the key person I was working with during the financial crisis, along with James Bowler. We made a practice of bringing people from the Treasury into No. 10. Heywood was very interested in ideas and very good. [Heywood], Shriti [Vadera] and others were also later to work very closely with the Treasury on recapitalisation of the banks.[166]

PRIVATE OFFICE UNDER NEW LABOUR: AN ASSESSMENT

New Labour was, undoubtedly, transformational in many ways. Across a wide range of policy areas – from independence for the Bank of England, through to the introduction of the national minimum wage and other economic measures, as well as in fields such as devolution and delivering the Northern Ireland Good Friday Agreement – the new government made impressive progress. However, in terms of civil service reform and the use of the private office, little changed, particularly in New Labour's first term. The success of New Labour in the three years before it achieved power had been in communications and its campaigning strengths in comparison to the lacklustre Major government, and not in terms of a vision for better governance. The idea that Blair might concentrate on the workings of his future office may well have been anathema to him. That was what Powell was there for and Blair felt he had delegated the task (just as Brown had delegated the task to Balls). Powell established a better operation, yet it was still mainly focused on campaigning and not on the challenges of government. Reflecting on this omission two decades after becoming Prime Minister, Blair himself acknowledged he should have done much more early on to build what he described as greater 'central capacity' at No. 10.[167] He was full of praise for the private office and the people who worked for him but believed he should have focused more on innovation at No. 10, the better use of technology and greater interchange of staff between the public and private sectors.[168] Moreover, in giving advice to African Presidents, from the 2020 vantage point of his Institute for Global Change, Blair even urged future leaders to 'invest in an efficient private office', because, 'the private office makes sure the President's time is used efficiently (diary management); manages the flow of quality information when they need it; and ensures that decisions are acted upon in a timely manner'.[169]

Blair and other senior figures could have met experts on government and governance, on the constitution and the role of the Prime Minister in office. He could have developed a plan to discuss how to reform the centre of government based on the Mandelson/Liddle proposals. Equally, he could have planned how he might use his private office better to track delivery in the early stages of the new government and so hold departments to account via regular stock-takes, as proposed by the Fabians. That he chose not to do so undoubtedly hampered the speed at which the new government was able to get to grips with its new responsibilities.

Once in No. 10, changes were made to the operation of the private office, but they took time to bed in. Alex Allan's recognition that, with hindsight, the private office was not up to scratch explains some of the frustrations felt by Blair and his close advisers. The assumption that the private office should simply continue to do and act for Blair in the way it had done for Major was fundamentally flawed. In Powell's judgement, the office only came to work better when Heywood managed domestic policy and Holmes led on foreign policy, yet there were still failures around what Blair called 'delivery'. That issue was not resolved, in Blair's eyes at least, until 2001 with the establishment of the Prime Minister's Delivery Unit led by Michael Barber. At the same time, the creation of the Policy Directorate run by Heywood with Andrew Adonis as his deputy was not deemed a success. It failed to add value and gave the impression that some civil servants might be dragged into more political areas than they would wish to be. Within four years, the experiment had been quietly dumped and the private office in its previous configuration was reinstituted. By way of contrast, the Treasury private office did change in 1997 to respond to Brown's ways of working and that of his advisers. Nick Macpherson and Ed Balls formed a good working relationship and the Treasury functioned effectively in the first decade of New Labour. The problems faced were not within the civil service but rather stemmed from the political difficulties between the Prime Minister and his Chancellor. The poor relationship between the private offices of Blair and Brown was eventually tempered by the fact that the two private offices established a better 'modus vivendi', brokered by Heywood on behalf of Blair, and Balls on behalf of Brown.

10

AN INSTITUTION IN DECLINE: PRIVATE OFFICE 2010–22

The general election of 2010 had to be called by May of that year and so the Prime Minister had little room for manoeuvre as to the choice of date. Accordingly, the election was held concurrently with the local elections on Thursday 6 May. Gordon Brown's government remained unpopular, and the nation was still recovering from the world economic crisis. Many people and businesses had been seriously damaged by the events of 2008–09 and, additionally, the MPs' expenses scandal had undoubtedly damaged the standing of all Members of Parliament as well as that of the Brown government. More generally, there was, in some quarters, a view that the government had 'run out of steam' and that, after thirteen years of Labour rule, it was perhaps time for a change. David Cameron's Conservative campaign slogan badged 2010 as the 'Year for Change', in a deliberate echo of Barack Obama's USA presidential slogan 'Time for Change' two years previously.[1] As the election approached, private offices across Whitehall prepared for all possible outcomes, as is one of their main pre-election tasks. The possibility that the Labour Party could lose – as the opinion polls suggested – was far higher in 2010 than had been the case in the three previous elections.[2*] In addition, the Liberal Democrats again promised to perform strongly and the added uncertainties of the Scottish and Welsh dimensions meant there was a far wider range of possible electoral outcomes to plan for than there had been at the 2001 and 2005 general elections.

Unlike in 1974 – the last time there had been a hung parliament – Whitehall and private offices were far better prepared for how they might handle an uncertain electoral outcome, including a possible coalition government. The Cabinet Secretary Gus O'Donnell had already produced a draft of a new document – the Cabinet Manual – in order to help guide ministers and the civil service on the 'laws, conventions and rules on the operation of government'.[3] The document had first been commissioned in 2009 by Brown but was not published until early in Cameron's premiership. O'Donnell and his Cabinet Office team had put considerable work into this, including studying international comparators in New Zealand and elsewhere. The Cabinet Manual represented the nearest thing there was to a written constitution on these matters. Its sections on the processes for handling changes of government after a general election were crucial in the subsequent negotiations after the May 2010 election. Over the next ten years, there were to be three further general elections and four changes of Prime Minister. The constitutional aspects of the Prime Minister and ministers were to be tested considerably during this period, and the role of the private office was also to be stretched during the next decade, and not always to best effect.

In 2010, three key players at the centre of government were in charge of the overall preparations for the range of outcomes: O'Donnell, who focused on handling the possible ramifications of a hung

---

* The monthly 'poll of polls' for the year prior to the general election showed a Conservative lead over Labour of between 7 per cent and 18 per cent.

parliament; Jeremy Heywood, by now installed in a newly created post as Permanent Secretary in No. 10; and James Bowler, the principal private secretary. Heywood and Bowler did most of the detailed private office preparations for handling a change of Prime Minister. The eventual result was a hung parliament and, after five days of negotiations, agreement was eventually reached on the terms of a full coalition between the Conservatives and the Liberal Democrats. The Liberal Democrats, led by Nick Clegg, were rewarded with five Cabinet seats, compared to the Conservatives' eighteen. Inevitably, some Conservative politicians were disappointed at not being made Cabinet ministers and others were placed into portfolios they had not previously shadowed. As often happens, private offices had to welcome ministers they had not expected and, in the case of those departments now headed by Liberal Democrat ministers, had to deal with a political party last in government in the 1930s.

The new Prime Minister, David Cameron, was later to reflect that the way in which he was then supported by the No. 10 private office was 'an incredible performance. They were working for Brown one moment and then they were working for me without missing a heartbeat.'[4] He was, in particular, impressed by the professionalism of Bowler, his principal private secretary, who Cameron simply described as 'excellent, and working well alongside Heywood and the team', including his incoming chief of staff and special advisers.[5]

In his autobiography, Cameron said:

The 'one team' spirit also applied to the No. 10 operation, where I wanted the political appointees and the civil servants to work together. And I wanted that open, trusting, collegiate atmosphere to flow through the coalition too. That meant, rather controversially, that our [special advisers] would work side by side, sharing offices. Sometimes people would walk into a room and find it difficult to tell who was the Tory, who was the Lib Dem and who was the civil servant.[6]

While Cameron, like Blair, had never held ministerial office before, he brought to No. 10 much experience from his time as a special adviser in the Major years. In his words: 'When I was in Norman Lamont's office as a special adviser in the Treasury, the private secretary then was none other than Jeremy Heywood, and so I learned at the feet of the master.'[7] A fine tribute indeed. By 2010, Heywood had been made the Permanent Secretary to No. 10 and, even when he succeeded O'Donnell as Cabinet Secretary in 2012, still maintained a close interest in the day-to-day operation of the Prime Minister's office.

Cameron was determined to work closely and co-operatively with his Chancellor, George Osborne, and, in a way that No. 10 and No. 11 had not really done before, they quickly began to shape their economic plans jointly. As part of that process, Cameron also wanted the private offices and the special advisers of No. 10 and No. 11 to work better together. Having witnessed the Blair–Brown disputes, he was determined that such tensions should not happen during his premiership:

> Like all organisations, hierarchical courts build up and around Prime Ministers and Chancellors. Those courts then thrive on animosity and conflict in that the way the people perceive they are serving their masters is to tell them all the terrible things that the next-door court is trying to do. No. 10 never really fully came to terms with the fact that this was not the way it was going to be with us. And so, the Chancellor would always come to my

morning and afternoon meetings and things would be decided jointly.[8]

Cameron took the wise decision not to make any immediate changes to the machinery of government. Departmental structures stayed as they had been before the election under Labour, in contrast to 1997 when Tony Blair had brought in some major changes on day one in office. Such organisational changes inevitably tend to distract the machine from the political priorities of the day.

Cameron immediately appointed his new political advisers to work with the unchanged No. 10 private office. Two key people were Ed Llewellyn,* who became his chief of staff, and Kate Fall, who became deputy chief of staff. Llewellyn, a contemporary of Cameron from Eton, was a former European diplomat and had worked with Cameron for five years. He was to remain as chief of staff throughout the Cameron premiership, and his style of operation was similar to that of Jonathan Powell, who had worked under Blair, although Llewellyn was more of a personal support to Cameron and specialised in foreign policy, not domestic issues. Notably, Powell led as Blair's key negotiator in the Northern Ireland peace talks while Llewellyn had a strong focus on Europe. Significantly, as chiefs of staff, neither of them attempted to tackle the wider domestic/economic agenda on which the private office workers tended to lead. This was in contrast to the way in which many US presidential chiefs of staff, such as James Baker, tended to operate, often covering a far wider canvas of policy issues.[9]

Cameron was determined to have a close-knit team that agreed

---

* Ed Llewellyn (1965–); chief of staff to the Leader of the Opposition 2005–2010; chief of staff to the Prime Minister (David Cameron) 2010–2016; created Baron Llewellyn of Steep 2016; UK ambassador to France 2016–2021; UK ambassador to Italy 2022–.

all issues across the private office and special adviser axis, with the aim of avoiding a potential divide between those two groups. In the words of Kate Fall: 'We made it a rule that David did nothing without me, Ed and the principal private secretary agreeing to it.'[10] This way of managing the No. 10 business was, under later Prime Ministers, to fall apart. The tight collaboration between the civil servants in private office and the special advisers was mirrored by the close co-operation between the No. 10 and No. 11 teams, in sharp contrast to the relationship between previous Prime Ministers and Chancellors. Cameron also appointed Andy Coulson* as his director of communications. Although Coulson, as a former tabloid political journalist and an able operator, had a lot of relevant skills to bring to the role, as did Alastair Campbell in 1997, the appointment did not work out. Coulson was soon to be accused of illegal phone hacking in his past life when he worked for the *News of the World* and, eventually, in January 2011 he had to resign.

Notwithstanding all the policy differences and the challenges of making the coalition work, the way in which No. 10 operated in the first years of the Cameron government was, in part at least, a tribute to the private office team and Bowler's initial leadership of that institution after the 2010 election.

Looking back on the role he played, Bowler commented:

One of my absolute proudest things in my entire career is that I – as principal private secretary to Gordon Brown – ran a private office for him that was incredibly impressive, supportive and good at delivering the government's agenda of the day. It is with immense pride that that exact same private office was in-situ one

---

* Andy Coulson (1968–); editor of the *News of the World* 2003–07; communications director, 10 Downing Street, 2010–11.

year after David Cameron's anniversary. Each individual member of the private office was still in place. That is an example of the civil service working superbly – that the same private office completely and utterly served two Prime Ministers of different parties, and with the added challenge of coalition. And huge kudos also to Cameron, who could have been suspicious of us but wasn't.[11]

However, if there was one area where tensions remained, it was around the nature of decision-making in the coalition and the ways in which the junior party (i.e. Nick Clegg's Liberal Democrats) might best be supported. Initially, Clegg had a relatively traditional-sized private office for a Cabinet minister (with a limited number of special advisers). At No. 10, the Policy Unit formed immediately after the coalition was a hybrid of Conservative and Liberal Democrat advisers. In practice, Cameron and others felt that simply did not work. Heywood was, at first, sceptical about the need for further resources to support the Liberal Democrats and feared the build-up of a power base other than at No. 10.[12] However, despite Heywood's initial strictures about the risk of creating a separate power base working for Clegg, it was soon agreed that the Deputy Prime Minister should have a bigger private office. As Suzanne Heywood noted, 'despite [Clegg's] huge brief the office supporting the Deputy Prime Minister was smaller than those of most secretaries of state – an unintentional oversight that reflected the Civil Service's lack of experience supporting a coalition government.'[13] As a result, Clegg was given a senior adviser to mirror Heywood's role supporting Cameron. The Liberal Democrats were also given more special advisers. With hindsight, Cameron agreed that was a good idea and probably should have been sorted out on day one, not after almost two years of coalition government.[14]

The independent research body the Institute for Government reviewed the working of the coalition in 2012, two years on from the general election. It commented:

> For the Coalition to operate effectively, each party must be provided with adequate resources to contribute to ongoing policy development. At the centre, this has led to the strengthening of the deputy prime minister's office. The initial vision was that there would be a single unified centre serving both prime minister and deputy prime minister, but, a senior official reflected, 'in practice it emerged that that wasn't working very well, and the Liberal Democrats were under-supported'. The deputy prime minister's office was expanded in late 2010, following Institute for Government recommendations.[15]

With hindsight, what was most impressive was just how smooth was the functioning of the coalition and the ways in which the civil service supported the process. Given that there had not been a coalition government in the United Kingdom since 1945, and that that one had been operating in the extraordinary circumstances of managing a world war, the fact that there were, relatively, so few tensions between private offices from 2010–2015 was a tribute to the workings of the Cameron administration.

THE EXTENDED MINISTERIAL OFFICES EXPERIMENT

While many Cabinet ministers in the coalition were broadly content with their officials and private offices, the one department where there were significant tensions reported, early on, was the

Department for Education. Michael Gove* had been appointed Secretary of State and was already looking to embark on a major programme of educational reform. Soon after taking up post, Gove had complained about the quality of some of the work produced by the department. In particular, he thought that the quality of departmental correspondence was poor. In early 2011, Gove appointed Dominic Cummings as his special adviser. Gove had wanted to do this at the start of the coalition, but Cummings's appointment had been, with hindsight wisely, blocked by Coulson, then head of communications at No. 10. Cummings was a combative special adviser and wanted to support Gove in shaking up the department and education policy more widely. He deliberately set out to antagonise the education establishment by referring to it as 'the blob'.[16] But, in terms of private office, Cummings and Gove were attracted to a far more political structure, more akin to the Continental *cabinet* model.

Francis Maude, the Cabinet Office minister responsible for the civil service, was equally attracted to this approach and thus well placed to support it. He took a radical approach to reform of the system and his vision was first set out in the 'Civil Service Reform Plan', published in June 2012.[17] But this initial document did not even mention reform of private office. The next year, in a 'one year on' progress report on implementation of the plan, the concept was first floated, although somewhat as an afterthought rather than as a central proposal for reform.[18] The concept of partially replacing the traditional private office by the establishment of what were called 'extended ministerial offices' (EMOs) was explained as follows:

---

* Michael Gove (1967–); Conservative MP since 2005; various Cabinet posts under Prime Ministers David Cameron, Theresa May, Boris Johnson and Rishi Sunak.

The Extended Ministerial Office could comprise existing civil servants fulfilling the traditional private office role, with special advisors and external appointees. Members of the office would be personally appointed by the Minister and be directly accountable to them. Civil servant appointments would be made in accordance with the requirements of the Civil Service Commission's recruitment principles. The office could comprise a number of functions including support for policy formulation, implementation, media handling and responding to correspondence, as well as the traditional private office function.[19]

The introduction of personal ministerial appointees working alongside traditional civil servants would have represented a sharp change from the Northcote–Trevelyan model of appointments all being made on the principles of merit, and, in practice, the plans for EMOs had not been sufficiently thought through. There was only limited support for the idea, and it came too late in the parliament to be widely adopted. In the end, only five EMOs were established. This short-lived initiative was a further attempt to establish what would have been more akin to a '*cabinet*' system for all ministerial support, based on the European model.[20] There was some qualified support for the process, including from the non-partisan Institute for Government which recognised the value of some private offices having greater access to expert advisers, although it also acknowledged the risk that ministers could become more detached from their departments if they relied too much on only their political appointees for advice.[21] Finally, the five EMOs were quietly abolished by Theresa May's government in July 2016.[22] One former Conservative minister (David Willetts) had already gone so far as to describe them as 'bonkers' because 'EMOs would create "a second structure of mini experts within your own private office" and as such isolate ministers from their departments'.[23]

Meanwhile, at No. 10, James Bowler had returned to the Treasury and been replaced by Chris Martin (another Cabinet Office/ Treasury man) as principal private secretary. Jeremy Heywood was promoted to become Cabinet Secretary, and the post of Permanent Secretary to No. 10 was abolished (at least for the time being). Martin, therefore, became the No. 10 principal private secretary more in the traditional historic mould for that position. Alongside Ed Llewellyn – the chief of staff – Martin was the most senior official in No. 10 and was well liked and respected by the Prime Minister downwards. Kate Fall explained how Martin liked (somewhat bizarrely) to call No. 10 'the House' and the machine of government 'the system', and how he was able to get 'the House' and 'the system' better able to serve the government of the day.[24] Cameron himself was impressed by Martin, describing him as follows:

> Chris [Martin] was outstanding. A Heywood-like persona in that he had that combination of a capacity for hard work, a huge range of knowledge across the piece, good with people and he didn't mind talking through the politics of an issue. You felt he was working flat out for you all the time. He simply had the full range of capabilities.[25]

At the 2015 general election, the Conservatives won an overall majority, and thus could bring to an end their coalition with the Liberal Democrats.[*] The SNP, rebounding from the defeat of their

---

[*] In the 2015 general election, the Conservatives won 330 seats, Labour 232, the SNP fifty-six, the Liberal Democrats eight and others twenty-four. A Conservative overall majority of ten seats.

independence campaign in the Scottish referendum the year previously, won fifty-six out of the fifty-nine seats in Scotland. However, no sooner was Cameron returned as Prime Minister than the focus of all his government's work shifted to the forthcoming referendum on Britain's membership of the European Union, which had been promised in the Conservatives' manifesto.

At this critical time – when the pressures on the No. 10 private office were growing – it lost its principal private secretary. Martin died of cancer, in November 2015, aged only forty-two. He was replaced as No. 10 principal private secretary by Simon Case, who had deputised for Martin when he was ill. Case, though, was far less experienced than Martin and, with Heywood now installed as Cabinet Secretary and less able to spend time in No. 10, the pressures on the government began to mount as the referendum approached. The balance between the power and influence of the permanent civil servants in No. 10 shifted towards the No. 10 special advisers. Anthony Seldon, that seasoned observer of all Prime Ministers over the past quarter-century, argued that the 'increasing efficiency and effectiveness' of the Cameron operation in the second part of his premiership was something 'for which Cameron's three principal lieutenants – Ed Llewellyn, Kate Fall and Craig Oliver [Director of Communications] – must take credit'.[26] Llewellyn, Fall and Oliver were all special advisers and so this represented a further reduction in the influence of the civil servants in the No. 10 private office (as previously exhibited by permanent civil servants such as Bowler, Heywood and Martin) and an increase in the influence of the special advisers. That was a trend that was going to have profound and damaging consequences when it continued and deepened under Boris Johnson's premiership, over three years later.

PRIVATE OFFICE AND THE AFTERMATH OF THE BREXIT REFERENDUM

On 23 June 2016, Britain voted to leave the European Union after over forty-three years of membership. Cameron, who had promised a referendum and then led the remain campaign, resigned the morning after the vote. He was replaced as Prime Minister by the Home Secretary, Theresa May, who, in her words, promised to 'get Brexit done'. She became Prime Minister on 13 July 2016. Despite her long tenure at the Home Office, traditionally a very difficult ministerial portfolio, she did not demonstrate any great knowledge of the workings of No. 10 or the premiership. In addition, and in something of an echo of Brown's premiership, she made it clear that she was not going to maintain any of Cameron's political staff. Llewellyn, Fall and Oliver left immediately and so May had to start from scratch. She had many challenges, as her biographer, Anthony Seldon, made clear:

> She understood little about government, including the power and limitations for her office, how to make Cabinet government and the civil service work for her, and how to advocate and persuade. These skills were not optional extras for the task in hand. Her six years at the Home Office were not a good preparation for her, especially because she imported wholesale her same inward-looking philosophy into Downing Street.[27]

Seldon is too hard on May who, undoubtedly, had learned much about the workings of government as seen from her Home Office vantage point. However, the swift removal of her predecessor's close advisers – as Brown had also found previously to his cost – had a profound and unexpected effect. On her arrival in Downing Street, amid the major constitutional crisis of Brexit, May might have benefited from the continuity that her predecessor's private office could have provided and from the wise counsel that a long-established principal private secretary might have offered. But with her wish to see Cameron's staff removed, she had virtually none of that support. Case, her principal private secretary, had only been in post since January 2016 and was to leave the post soon after, some ten months after she became Prime Minister.

In addition, the joint chiefs of staff – whom May had appointed to replace Llewellyn, on the suggestion of Heywood – appeared to have complete authority in No. 10. Heywood recommended that, rather than have a single figure as her chief of staff, she should, very unusually, use two of her trusted lieutenants from the Home Office – Fiona Hill[*] and Nick Timothy[†] – to fill the role jointly. May jumped at the proposed solution, although sharing power in such an important and high-profile post was high risk, to put it mildly. Heywood must have realised that risk. Talented as they undoubtedly were, Hill and Timothy did not seek consensus with many of the civil servants with whom they had to work. Indeed, quite the opposite. Their former civil service head at the Home Office, the Permanent Secretary, was Mark Sedwill.[‡] He commented, while still at the Home Office, that his main performance objective at that time was, put simply, trying to control Hill and Timothy and the way they engaged with, and at times irritated and frustrated, Home Office employees.[28] Timothy and, in particular, Hill often

---

[*]   Fiona Hill (1973–); joint chief of staff to the Prime Minister (Theresa May) 2016–17.

[†]   Nicholas Timothy (1980–); joint chief of staff to the Prime Minister (Theresa May) 2016–17.

[‡]   Mark Sedwill (1964–); civil servant; Permanent Secretary Home Office 2013–17; national security adviser 2017–20; Cabinet Secretary 2018–20.

sought to antagonise civil servants rather than seek common cause. In Seldon's view, 'not since the Blair team arrived in 1997 had an incoming administration held such suspicion of the civil service'.[29] He continued:

> [Timothy and Hill] were two of the most controversial, driven and brilliant figures to have served at the heart of Downing Street in recent times. But they were young and inexperienced. To achieve the best out of them, and to mitigate their downsides in No. 10 – over-zealousness, secrecy and belligerence – they needed a powerful figure above them to shape them and, when necessary, put them in their place. No one did.[30]

In fact, a more profound change in the workings of the No. 10 private office, including in terms of the working relationships between private secretaries and special advisers, was beginning to emerge at around this time. It was mirrored to a lesser extent in some government departmental private offices. Specifically, the tasks associated with dealing with Brexit – including the cross-departmental challenges and the negotiations with the European Union – were inevitably developing into some of the most technically complex and politically sensitive matters for decades. Simultaneously, the Prime Minister was under attack on many fronts, and all at a time when there was a lack of consistent leadership, especially at the heart of Downing Street. Case, and his successor as principal private secretary, Peter Hill* from the Foreign Office, while both able civil servant administrators, were not political deal-makers. Neither was Fiona Hill nor Nick Timothy as joint chiefs of staff. More

---

* Peter Hill; Foreign Office diplomat, principal private secretary to the Prime Minister (Theresa May and Boris Johnson) 2017–19.

and more decisions were being handled on the special adviser and political network – and often controversial issues were simply not being sorted out effectively. The power of private office was on the wane. On what became the most important challenge for government as a whole – the Brexit deal – the civil service and specifically those in the most influential posts within private office and at the centre of government were not well skilled or adept enough. This led to a vacuum which was filled by special advisers and some more unusual civil service appointments such as Olly Robbins, the chief Brexit negotiator, who was simultaneously trying to serve both the Prime Minister and the Brexit Secretary of State, David Davis. The net effect of all this was to weaken the role and influence of private office and that of the civil service. There was no commanding figure from the civil service who could make things happen. Heywood had fulfilled that position for almost ten years since Brown had enticed him back from his private sector role in 2007. Since then, he had shaped the centre of government, serving first as head of domestic policy in the Cabinet Office, then as principal private secretary to the Prime Minister and Permanent Secretary at No. 10 and, by the time May was Prime Minister, as her Cabinet Secretary. But as Cabinet Secretary, he was obviously less able to spend time running the Prime Minister's office and, additionally, the first signs of his cancer – from which he would die two years later – were becoming apparent to his very close friends and colleagues. It would, in due course, sap his prodigious energy and massive appetite for work. The commanding, powerful presence that Heywood had exhibited so well over the past decade was finally beginning to fade.

Politically, too, May was soon in further trouble. On the back of what – with hindsight – turned out to be the misjudged calling of another general election in 2017, the Conservatives lost their overall majority in the House of Commons.* Hill and Timothy were forced to resign, not least because they had fallen out with so many senior Cabinet ministers, including the Chancellor of the Exchequer, Philip Hammond. As one well-informed journalist commented: 'Hill and Timothy were required to fall on their swords in the immediate aftermath of the election debacle. That was the price demanded by senior Tories in exchange for granting May a reprieve from being sent to the chopping block herself.'[31] It was a fate which they had unnecessarily brought upon themselves by their conduct in supporting May and in not seeking to build up sufficient personal allies, over the previous year, especially with the civil service and private office.

May appointed in their place, as her chief of staff, Gavin Barwell. Barwell had been a middle-ranking minister before the election and, having lost his seat, was immediately available to work at No. 10. He started with one distinct advantage over the Hill–Timothy duo, namely that he was not widely disliked by many politicians and civil servants. But May had emerged from the general election severely weakened and was, by now, reliant on the Northern Ireland Democratic Unionist Party to stay in power. May's continuing difficulty in securing a Brexit deal led to the high-profile resignations of Boris Johnson and David Davis in July 2018, and the remainder of her premiership was dominated by Brexit, which she never did 'get done'. Barwell, in reflecting on the failure of the May government, commented perceptively that his experience made him conclude that 'political [by which he means special] advisers are too influential ... There has been an explosion in the number of political advisers. They are the people ministers spend most of their

---

* In the 2017 general election, the Conservatives won 317 seats, Labour 262, the SNP thirty-five, the Liberal Democrats twelve and others twenty-four. No overall majority.

time with, and that's a mistake.'[32] Barwell argued that his experience
of being chief of staff left him with a far greater respect for the 'quality
and integrity of our senior civil servants' and that, with hindsight, he
should have 'urged the Prime Minister to invest more time in her relationships with her senior colleagues [i.e. politicians]'.[33] If politicians
do not trust their closest of civil servants, such as those in their private office, they will not get any of the benefits that such officials may
be able to offer them and the support and loyalty that an effective private office can provide. Barwell's observation would have been wise
advice, had it also been offered to May's successor, Boris Johnson. But
it likely would not have been heeded, even if it had been offered.

PRIME MINISTER JOHNSON AND PRIVATE OFFICE

Boris Johnson finally achieved his lifelong ambition to become
Prime Minister on 24 July 2019, having been elected leader of the
Conservative Party the day before. He inherited a private office
whose reputation had not been enhanced over recent years. In the
previous three years, there had been four different people with the
title 'chief of staff' and three different principal private secretaries.
Jeremy Heywood had died in 2018 and been replaced as Cabinet
Secretary by Mark Sedwill. There was certainly a lack of continuity and, also tellingly, of corporate knowledge of the centre, at a
time when even the most ardent Johnson supporters might have
recognised the value of having access to such qualities – given his
idiosyncratic style and personality and the volatile politics of the
time, including the enduring issue of Brexit. Johnson, for reasons
which are not entirely clear, did not even initially appoint anyone
to the role of chief of staff. The combative Dominic Cummings was

appointed as a No. 10 special adviser with the title of 'chief adviser to the Prime Minister'. He did not have line management responsibilities over the Downing Street private office but was remarkably influential with both the Prime Minister and other special advisers across Whitehall. What was to happen over the next three years was that the system of private office, certainly as it operated in No. 10, simply broke down. The principles of integrity and good governance at the heart of the Prime Minister's office failed. The principal cause of that failure was Johnson himself, although others, including some senior civil servants, were complicit. The Prime Minister should have been responsible for upholding the Ministerial Code, which governs the behaviour of all ministers, up to and including the Prime Minister. He failed in that basic task. His private office was either unable or unwilling to ensure that, as Prime Minister, he acted with due propriety in that role.

Johnson inherited, on arrival in office, May's principal private secretary, Peter Hill. Hill was able and well liked, although, unlike most of his predecessors in that position, he did not have a Treasury background, having mainly worked at the Foreign Office. He stayed on at No. 10 for only a few months to oversee the prime ministerial transition and then returned to the Foreign Office. His successor was Martin Reynolds, another Foreign Office diplomat, who, at the time of Partygate three years later, was to be nicknamed by the media 'Party Marty'. Reynolds had been Johnson's principal private secretary when Johnson was Foreign Secretary and, on the back of that experience, Johnson recruited him to work for him again at No. 10. The two men had got on well and, while they were at the Foreign Office, Reynolds was able to make some order out of the unusual and inefficient style of Johnson's operation. Reynolds explained what his political master – the Foreign Secretary – wished to do in ways which the civil service and others could understand. However, his appointment to the more senior and stretching No. 10 principal private secretary role highlighted three associated failures in the system. First, as already mentioned, the rapid turnover of senior staff in No. 10, coupled with the absence of any Heywood-type figure, meant the overall leadership cadre was weak. There was no strong chief of staff able to bring a coherence to the office, notwithstanding the appointment in late 2020 of Dan Rosenfield (formerly principal private secretary to Alistair Darling when he was Chancellor at the end of the Brown government), which was a belated attempt to strengthen the top team. Second, and perhaps inevitably, more powerful advisers such as Cummings (with his roving but ill-defined role) or even Johnson's wife-to-be, Carrie (who was not appointed to any role but was certainly influential), began to carry more clout and disproportionate influence within the building and beyond. The role of the private office was compromised. The authority of the private secretaries was diminished. But third, the appointment of Reynolds based on the fact that his main qualification was to have been principal private secretary in Johnson's former Cabinet position created an extraordinary and unhelpful precedent, which Johnson's two successors as Prime Minister were both to follow and to exploit. There is no evidence that either Mark Sedwill or Simon Case sought to prevent this and yet, in many ways, it undermined the role and responsibilities of the principal private secretary to the Prime Minister in a most egregious manner. If the principal private secretary could be replaced almost on the whim of the Prime Minister because he preferred the person who had fulfilled that role when the Prime Minister was a departmental Cabinet minister, then the benefits that accrued from having a figure of experience and absolute integrity in that central No. 10 position would be lost.

The major failings of the Johnson era, though, stemmed more from the Prime Minister's laxness of approach, his unwillingness to obey rules consistently and his general lack of respect for due propriety. His private office – and indeed that of the Cabinet Secretary – should have tried harder to compensate for all three of these shortcomings, but they failed, or more likely, were simply unable to do so. Three glaring case studies illustrate this.

PROROGATION

The first example was the decision by Johnson to prorogue the House of Commons early in August 2019 – as a means of avoiding scrutiny of the government's proposed Brexit legislation. Reynolds could take none of the blame for this, since he had not yet arrived in the No. 10 private office. However, Johnson's then 'director of legislative affairs', Nikki da Costa, was responsible for the advice. And it is relevant and important to understand da Costa's position and role in this context. The post of 'director of legislative affairs' had no real historical provenance within No. 10. It was a new concept, and da Costa was not a permanent civil servant or a member of private office but rather a political appointee. The history of the prorogation of Parliament in the summer of 2019 has been detailed in several places.[34] Anthony Seldon and Raymond Newell, in particular, provide a detailed chronology of events and summarise that

Da Costa wrote her fateful memo on prorogation to the Prime Minister on 15 August [2019], with a recommendation of the timetable and emphasizing that MPs would need to return by the time of the EU October Council in order to pass a deal. Johnson's response in the margin was '✔ YES'. He was not 100 per cent enthused.[35]

The fact that Johnson approved such a profound constitutional decision merely by ticking a piece of paper and saying 'yes' without any further advice is not in itself improper. Many prime ministerial and ministerial decisions may be signed off in this or a similar way. That said, it appears that the official civil service machine – including the private office – did not fully know what was going on. According to Seldon and Newell, the Cabinet Secretary Mark Sedwill was only copied into the plan at the last minute, with Johnson's team having 'taken advantage of his absence on holiday to push it through'.[36] So, on an issue of supreme relevance to the constitution and to the Crown, No. 10 was not fully sharing what they were doing. There appears to have been no time or scope for a formal process of seeking proper authority from the Treasury Solicitor or any other legal experts. That should have been an issue on which the principal private secretary should have insisted that such proper processes of scrutiny were essential and unavoidable. Private office was not working as it should have been, because it was not – and perhaps for the first time since 1945 – in any meaningful sense, fully in control of events.

PARTYGATE

Johnson, aided by the impressive campaigning and organisational skills of Cummings and others, led the Conservative Party to a massive eighty-seat majority at the general election held on 12

December 2019.* It represented the pinnacle of his political career. But even as he celebrated his victory, far away in China a number of people were just beginning to suffer the symptoms of a new flu-like disease. Within months, the Covid pandemic was sweeping across the globe. The government introduced stringent measures to control the pandemic, which, at times, were clearly flouted by No. 10.

The government had to introduce stringent restrictions on the freedom of movement of the public, with several 'lockdowns' being imposed. It was in this climate that the second fundamental failing of No. 10 under Johnson occurred over what became known as 'Partygate'. These events have been scrutinised and well documented elsewhere and, most significantly, from the government's point of view, in Sue Gray's report into the events.[37] It is not, therefore, necessary to chronicle here the multiple shortcomings at the centre but rather to seek to capture the reasons for this widespread systemic failure which meant that private office was, once again, not operating effectively as it should. Private office and in particular the principal private secretary – working, as necessary, with the Cabinet Secretary – had a constitutional duty to maintain due propriety in the way in which the Prime Minister operated and so ensure that Johnson complied with the restrictions he had imposed on the population at large. Yet this they failed to do. Reynolds, as had been seen in the notorious extract from his email – cited in the Introduction to this book – drove a coach and horses through the guidance by encouraging No. 10 staff to break the law on 20 May 2020. Belatedly, when the story became public, Johnson claimed that, with the benefit of hindsight, he should have told staff to return to work.

---

* In the 2019 general election, the Conservatives won 365 seats, Labour 202, the SNP forty-eight, the Liberal Democrats eleven and others twenty-four. A Conservative overall majority of eighty.

As a defence, it sounded hollow and a feeble excuse. Reynolds had invited the Prime Minister, his wife and up to 200 staff to an illegal gathering, and many duly turned up. Johnson attended more than one such gathering in lockdown. But he was unable to abide by the strict guidance and regulations that his government had put in place. Reynolds even commented afterwards, 'We seem to have got away with it.' As Andrew Blick and that wise observer of the constitution, Peter Hennessy, have commented on this event: 'It might seem a relatively trivial remark in itself. But we must attach wider significance to it, prompting as it should the realisation that a person in such a position could regard ... activities that might be illegal as something to be "got away with".'[38]

If Reynolds failed to enforce proper controls on the Prime Minister – as was surely his constitutional duty as principal private secretary – why did the chief of staff at that time not do so? Because at that point, the post was vacant and there was something of a revolving door. Power lay somewhere between Reynolds and Cummings, neither of whom was playing the due propriety card. In the three years of Johnson's premiership, there were no fewer than four full or acting chiefs of staff.[*] The best chiefs of staff (whether in the United Kingdom or the USA) earn their authority, to some extent at least, on account of their integrity and their longevity in post. Under Johnson, the tenures of his chiefs of staff lasted between two and thirteen months.

The reason for the failures at the centre were more acute, as Anthony Seldon and Raymond Newell detail:

Because [Johnson] had banished rule-minded figures from No. 10

---

[*]   Baron Lister, Dan Rosenfield, Steve Barclay and Baroness Finn (acting).

and appointed those who found it difficult to stand up to him, there was no one to say 'we have to be the absolute model of what we're enforcing on others' ... Once the first post-lockdown gatherings had been tolerated ... the precedent had been set ... The response was bungled, with the weak shouldering the blame rather than the two leaders, himself and Case [by now Cabinet Secretary]. Longer-serving staff look back to the Ed Llewellyn and Gavin Barwell regimes as chiefs of staff in the 2010s, or to Gus O'Donnell and Jeremy Heywood as Cabinet Secretaries, and say they would have handled it properly, and that is no doubt true.[39]

THE FINAL NAIL IN JOHNSON'S COFFIN

The third major failing of the Johnson era as Prime Minister was his failure and that of his private office to ensure due propriety in the way it performed its constitutional functions in respect of providing accurate statements to the House of Commons. This was only fully exposed in the written and the oral evidence Johnson finally presented in 2023, after he had left office, during his appearance before the House of Commons Privileges Committee. That committee was investigating whether Johnson, during his time as Prime Minister, had deliberately lied to the House and failed properly to correct the inaccuracies as had appeared in his parliamentary statements. Johnson, as Prime Minister, had had to make many such statements to the House of Commons on Partygate and its implications.[40] One example serves to illustrate the tone and flavour of parliamentary events by the spring of 2022 and the effect it was having on the Prime Minister's authority, documented by Sebastian Payne:

From the government Despatch Box on Wednesday 25 May 2022, Johnson corrected the record on Partygate. 'When I came to this House and said in all sincerity that the rules and guidance had been followed at all times, it was what I believed to be true. But clearly that was not the case for some of those gatherings after I had left, and at other gatherings when I was not even in the building.' His statement was followed by more jeers from MPs who believed he was once again avoiding responsibility and trying to create a narrative that took himself out of the picture.[41]

It is one of the tasks of any private office to ensure that ministers give accurate information to the House of Commons and that, in cases where this has not happened, any inadvertent errors are corrected as soon as possible. Private office was very busy in this respect during the Johnson era. However, as the end approached, many ministers became concerned by the conduct of the Prime Minister and refused to serve. Resignations built up rapidly and by 6 July 2022, it seemed as if it might not even be possible to appoint enough ministers to establish a working government. According to Payne, 'Number 10 also [even] asked the Cabinet Office just how small a government could be and still function.'[42]

As the Prime Minister's lies and inaccuracies reflected badly on him, so too, they affected his closest advisers in private office. Part of their role was to persuade the Prime Minister to tell the truth, especially to Parliament. If they really had tried hard – and failed – it is perhaps surprising that none of the civil servants involved resigned. However, and this is constitutionally significant, Johnson had come to a point where he failed to recognise (deliberately or not) the constitutional differences between the civil servants in his private office and his political advisers. This represented a further breakdown in the workings of the No. 10 private office. Even the so-called golden triangle of advisers (the Cabinet Secretary, the private secretary to the monarch and the principal private secretary to the Prime Minister) did not appear to be operating in the way it had done during past crises. One of the concerns of senior officials in the Cabinet Office was that Johnson might go for the 'nuclear option' and seek to call a general election. The 'Lascelles principles' (named after King George VI's private secretary) set out the three criteria for when a prime ministerial request to the monarch to hold a general election could be rejected. These principles were discussed, and agreement was reached, to ensure that the Queen was not to be put in a position where she might have to respond to a request to dissolve Parliament. Sebastian Payne refers to discussions between officials in the Cabinet Office and the palace in the final days of the Boris Johnson government as being between a 'magic triangle' of the Cabinet Secretary (Simon Case), the Queen's private secretary (Edward Young) and Sir Graham Brady (the chairman of the 1922 Committee, representing the parliamentary Conservative Party).[43] So, Hennessy's 'golden triangle' had been replaced by the 'magic triangle', with the Prime Minister's principal private secretary no longer at the heart of constitutional debate.

When Johnson finally gave oral evidence to the House of Commons Committee on Privileges on 22 March 2023 – over six months after he ceased to be Prime Minister – he continued to defend his actions. Even then, he still claimed that he and his office has done nothing wrong. Despite the body of evidence which showed that he had knowingly been untruthful to Parliament, he argued in his written evidence that 'I did not intentionally or recklessly mislead the House on 1 December 2021, 8 December 2021, or on any other date. I would never have dreamed of doing so.'[44] He also commented that it was 'my honest belief that it was within the rules ... based on what I was told by senior advisers'.[45] Johnson carefully and cleverly elided the advice of civil servant officials (his private office) with those of his other advisers, and specifically his communications adviser Jack Doyle, whom Johnson cited in his evidence. Doyle was then Johnson's head of communications, not a private secretary official. If Doyle did so advise, it was also incumbent on the private office to ascertain whether that advice was accurate. It turned out that it was not.

In the report published in June 2023, the committee pointed out that, while Johnson had claimed no senior civil servant raised any concerns with him about the rules and guidance in No. 10 not being followed, it found that some officials, including Reynolds, did in fact question Johnson, but to little or no effect.[46] The committee added that, while it was not accusing civil servants of lying, it recognised that 'it would have been difficult, if not impossible, for many staff members, especially junior ones, to express concerns about the Prime Minister's behaviour or the behaviour of others in No. 10 as this would have been potentially career-damaging criticism of senior staff or the head of government'.[47] However, in one of the most damning criticisms of a Prime Minister, and by extension the private office staff who supported him, the committee concluded that 'when he [Johnson] told the House and this Committee that the Rules and Guidance were being complied with, his own knowledge was such that he deliberately misled the House and this Committee'.[48] The game was up for Johnson. The committee's report was published on 15 June 2023. Three days previously, Johnson had already resigned from the House of Commons.

By the time the report was published, there had been two more

Prime Ministers in post. And while the No. 10 private office returned to a somewhat more normal method of functioning, its power and authority was diminished. The major reason for this was that, once again, the new Prime Ministers both brought in their former departmental private secretaries to head the No. 10 private office. Both also brought in new chiefs of staff. There was no continuity of civil service leadership at No. 10.

Liz Truss had previously fallen out with some of her private secretaries in her previous ministerial posts and she was not always popular with her officials. According to Harry Cole and James Heale, 'many officials, though, did impress Truss: her Principal Private Secretary Nick Catsaras would accompany her from [the Foreign, Commonwealth and Development Office] to No. 10, as would some senior officials with intelligence backgrounds'.[49] Catsaras even began to morph into a more political role 'merging the traditional Principal Private Secretary job with responsibilities that might usually fall to a Chief of Staff. "Nick is in everything and all seeing," said a colleague'.[50] However, as has been seen before, when private secretaries seek to perform a more overtly political role, the impartiality of the civil service comes into question. Catsaras never got to play a significant role because Truss was ousted by the parliamentary Conservative Party, after only forty-nine days in office, and replaced by Rishi Sunak on 25 October 2022.

Again, it was all change in the No. 10 private office. Catsaras was replaced by Sunak's former principal private secretary at the Treasury, Elizabeth Perelman. Perelman had the honour of becoming the first woman in history to occupy that position, but again she had to start from scratch in No. 10. The rate of turnover in this post had become, by this stage, remarkably high – with no fewer than seven occupants of the post in seven years. Perelman and the private office managed to bring something of a greater sense of calm to the operation of No. 10 following the chaotic final days of the Johnson era and the equally tense brief tenure of Liz Truss. But the damage had already been done. The notion that the No. 10 private office which had loyally served one Prime Minister would then remain unchanged and, equally loyally and impartially, serve the incoming Prime Minister, as had happened, for example, during the Brown–Cameron transition little over a decade previously, no longer existed.

CONCLUSION

When David Cameron described his private office as being like a family, he was following in a long tradition of politicians paying tribute to the close-knit nature of their private office and their private secretaries. In 1974, Robert Armstrong had been close to tears when Ted Heath lost office, and Heath later described him as almost like a son. Harold Macmillan relied so much on his small private office team that his biographer was to describe how a 'highly intimate relationship was built up between Prime Minister and private secretaries'.[1] Hugh Gaitskell, the outgoing Chancellor of the Exchequer, on the day after the Labour Party's defeat in the 1951 general election, had reflected – and not without some sense of personal surprise – that it was 'rather remarkable what close and intimate relations one manages to develop' with the private office.[2] And, famously, Disraeli had said that the closeness of his relationship with his private secretary was second only to that with his wife.

The ways in which a minister and their private secretary work together has been at the core of this book; how private office plays a critical role for any minister, especially the Prime Minister, and how some private secretaries have become almost indispensable to their political masters. Private office is one of the central elements – an essential building block – of our unwritten constitution. This body and its power, purpose, influence and, at times, shortcomings matter.

Private office, and in particular the No. 10 private office, has always represented a largely invisible element of the hidden wiring of the British state. It is the one institution at the heart of government that has received no sustained historical enquiry. This book has concentrated on the work of the most powerful private office of all – that of the Prime Minister at No. 10 – but the analysis includes the wider role of all private offices. A good private office can help to make a good minister better. Equally, it can help to make a poor minister not as bad as they might otherwise be.

In short, the private office is the central junction box of government, at the heart of Whitehall. It is the critical link between a Prime Minister, or any minister, and the administrative machine. And, so long as there has been a Prime Minister at No. 10, so too there has always been a private secretary. Any historian seeking to understand a Prime Minister must first understand their character and their competence. But they must then understand the ecology and the environment within which that Prime Minister and their private office operated – because that too is revealing of the nature of each premiership. And the historian should remember also that a principal private secretary to the Prime Minister will carry to their grave more secrets than any other official, apart from the Cabinet Secretary.

Every private office performs two vital and fundamental roles. First, it ensures that the business of government is transacted quickly, accurately and efficiently. That role includes assuring due propriety in the conduct of business, in accordance with the requirements of the Ministerial Code. In its simplest form, that is its central purpose. But second, private office must be able to offer the flexibility to serve any political master loyally and impartially – whatever their personal style and idiosyncrasies – so long as their minister works with due probity. Private office supports any minister of whatever political party, without fear or favour. If the minister changes, private office offers that same commitment to the new minister as they did to the previous one.

Private office is not some optional bureaucratic extra. Rather, it is the essential junction box that helps to guide the power of government and underpin the work of the Prime Minister and ministers. It is an indispensable element of our unwritten constitution. Private office makes the connections, carries out ministers' and Prime Ministers' wishes and (usually) gets things done.

However, some commentators have questioned the role and value of private office in its current structure and form, because over the past half-century, the job of private office has become far harder. All ministerial jobs, including that of the Prime Minister, have become more complex and stretched. Consequently, the work of private offices has similarly been stretched, due to five broad reasons.

First, the speed of transactions and decision-making has had an immediate impact on private office. The power of the markets means that political decisions today have to be made ever more rapidly. Jim Callaghan, Denis Healey and their private offices in late 1976 could spend three months handling the financial crisis and negotiating the IMF loan. Gordon Brown, Alistair Darling and their private offices had only three hours to bail out the failing RBS in 2008. Private office therefore needs to be far more agile than it ever was and with systems that can operate swiftly and flexibly.

Second, the enormous growth in the volume of work private office now handles has put far more pressure on the system overall. Fifty years ago, some policy areas – such as artificial intelligence, climate change, migration or globalisation – simply did not exist as issues with which ministers had to grapple. Certainty, there were great military and defence challenges in the post-war era, but, taken together, the workload facing any Prime Minister today is far greater and more varied – while the tools available to tackle it have not kept pace. It is now not sufficient for a Prime Minister to rely on their private secretary to read the overnight diplomatic telegrams and report back what has been happening around the world. Similarly, the range of domestic tasks that fall to government has increased. The past is indeed another country.

Third, changes in technology have (for good and bad) transformed the operation of private office. The IT revolution has given all ministers access to a level of data and information unheard of half a century ago. Today, No. 10 can speak to their counterparts anywhere in the world, whenever they so wish. Information and facts are available in seconds. Yet, on the other hand, the internet can promulgate fake news stories and provide challenges to any minister, just as they can to the public at large. It is not just a one-way benefit. Clement Attlee reluctantly agreed to the installation of a news agency tape at No. 10 in the late 1940s. Tony Blair, almost proudly, boasted that he never sent a work email or text in his decade in power. By way of contrast, today's ministers, and by extension all private secretaries, are effectively on call and online twenty-four hours a day, seven days a week.

Fourth, the growth in the scope and reach of modern communications and the media has put massive pressure on the traditional mode of operation of private office. Individuals and opposition politicians can now know things before ministers do. Social media has transformed the speed at which a story can spread. When Harold Wilson became Prime Minister in 1964, there were only two terrestrial television channels, neither of which broadcast for twenty-four hours a day. Government was a five-day-a-week operation with weekend working a rarity for private offices. Today, the media never sleeps in a 'nessun dorma' world.

Finally, the rise of political operators and the growth in the number of special advisers has brought a fundamentally new dimension to the work of private office. The centre of government is today a much more politicised environment than it ever was in the past. Harold Macmillan had the equivalent of one special adviser when he was Prime Minister in the early 1960s. Now there are forty-one.[3]

Since Prime Minister Walpole appointed Henry Bilson-Legge as his secretary – the equivalent of a modern-day private secretary – all holders of the prime ministership have been supported by a private secretary and, since the late nineteenth century, private office has become a part of the constitutional arrangements for every minister of the Crown. In the aftermath of the First World War, when the structure of modern Cabinet government was firmly established, private office developed into an institution, providing support and continuity, especially when the minister or Prime Minister changed. That model and structure survived practically unchanged during the twentieth century. Throughout all the upheavals of that century – including world wars, the creation of the welfare state, Suez, devaluation, entry into the European Community, the Thatcher 'revolution', the Falklands, Westland, Black Wednesday and the arrival of New Labour – private office was an ever-present, if rarely seen, part of the British constitutional settlement. A kind of Butskellite mechanism that operated whatever party was in power. Such a description is, of course, over-simplistic. It does not take into account some of the fundamental long-term changes in British government, the type of people who become ministers and civil servants and the societal and technological changes which have affected the development of the traditional private office model and stretched its capacity to the limit.

The distinctive relationship between a minister and their private secretary is qualitatively different from many of the transactions a minister may have with other civil servants. While, at the most basic level, it has always been simply a business relationship, in practice the relationship has often proved more profound and far closer. As has been seen, some private secretaries have built deep relationships with their ministers based upon genuine admiration and mutual respect – as the testimonies at the start of this chapter bear witness. A century ago, Lloyd George's private secretary A. J. Sylvester observed that, by the time of Lloyd George's resignation in 1922, he had 'grown to admire and love [Lloyd George] and his work'.[4] Jock Colville became a personal favourite private secretary to Churchill during the war, such that Churchill summonsed him back to No. 10 in 1951 to reprise that role during his final premiership. From the late 1950s, Tim Bligh, Macmillan's most senior aide for most of his premiership, played a vital part in helping defend the Conservative government from attacks by Wilson's opposition. Bligh was something of a cavalier character and one who, in practice, undoubtedly over-politicised his role. And yet politicisation is fundamentally contrary to the principles of political impartiality dating back to the Northcote–Trevelyan report published in 1854.

The vast majority of private secretaries to the Prime Minister have not succumbed to any element of party politicisation. Most have adhered to the strict impartiality of the civil service. Robert Armstrong served Heath throughout his premiership and was so devoted to him that, twenty years later, he acted as the executor of his will. Yet there is no suggestion that Armstrong was politicised. In common with some senior civil servants of his time, he did not conceal his personal support for entering what was then called the Common Market. He may, therefore, have been what might be termed 'policy politicised' over this one critical issue of Europe, but he was not 'party politicised' more generally. (The same might well have been said of more recent civil servants, such as Lord McDonald,* the former head of the Foreign Office, and his views on Brexit nowadays.†) Armstrong's pro-Europeanism alone could have explained why Marcia Williams wanted him removed from the private office when Wilson returned to No. 10 after the February 1974 general election. But Wilson insisted that Armstrong should remain as principal private secretary between 1974 and 1975, testament to Armstrong's undoubted capabilities as well as to his wider political impartiality. By way of comparison, a decade later, Charles Powell, one of the most able, charismatic and controversial of private secretaries to have served at No. 10 in the post-war era, was arguably politicised, particularly by the end of his tenure at No. 10. Powell is the only private secretary in the history of the job for whom the Prime Minister of the day (Thatcher) threatened to resign if he were moved to a different position in the civil service.[5] Powell, like Bligh and Colville before him, did not return to the civil service on leaving No. 10, preferring to work in the private sector.

The most distinctive professional quality of the outstanding private secretary is that they can serve – with equal loyalty and equal integrity – ministers and Prime Ministers from different political

---

* Lord McDonald (1961–); British diplomat; Permanent Secretary FCO 2015–20.

† In September 2023, McDonald admitted that, in 2016, he had told fellow staff that he had voted to remain in the European Union at the referendum. This was an exceptionally unusual statement for an impartial civil servant to make, given that he was then the head of the Foreign Office.

parties, with often fundamentally different policies. In the modern era, that marks out people such as Robert Armstrong, Robin Butler, Ken Stowe, Alex Allan and Jeremy Heywood. Arguably, Charles Powell, for all his many skills, did not have such qualities.

Some critics of the private office model (mostly, but not exclusively, from the left) have claimed that it has been dominated for much of this time by questions of class and that embedded at the heart of government has been a non-partisan, unelected governing elite. They have argued that its membership was recruited, in the main, from a fairly narrow social spectrum, which tended to support the status quo. Until recently, recruitment of private secretaries did indeed come from a narrow section of the civil service, reflecting the male dominance of the service in the post-war years and the social groupings which tended to enter the civil service fast stream. So, there is some truth in that criticism. For while private office has not become party political, it may well have been more comfortable with certain forms of politics and certain types of politicians. In the 1970s, civil servants (such as Armstrong) tended to be more at ease with pro-Europeans such as Heath, rather than anti-Common-Market politicians such as Tony Benn. The private office of the 1960s and 1970s, with its narrow band of recruitment, may well have felt more comfortable working with a 'good chap' political adviser like Douglas Hurd rather than a 'difficult woman' like Marcia Williams. Indeed, there have been similar criticisms levied against today's private office. For example, during the hearings of the Covid public inquiry in October 2023, the former Deputy Cabinet Secretary, Helen MacNamara, made a powerful critique of No. 10 saying that, even in the 2020s, the office of the Prime Minister retained a strongly macho culture.

However, regardless of the culture of private office, it is at the time of general elections and prime ministerial transitions that it is tested to its maximum extent. Between 1945 and 2020, there were twenty-one general elections, eight of which resulted in a change of party of government. In addition, there have been ten separate occasions when prime ministerial transitions took place in between general elections. In such circumstances, the principal private secretary is the civil servant responsible for managing the No. 10 transition and for welcoming the new Prime Minister into the job. In February and March 1974, Armstrong assisted Heath throughout the four days of detailed negotiations, following the inconclusive general election, and then immediately prepared to serve Wilson. In November 1990, when Thatcher resigned, Andrew Turnbull recorded the outcome of every meeting Thatcher held with her Cabinet colleagues, the majority of whom urged her to step down. Turnbull was then responsible for welcoming the new Prime Minister, John Major, after he won the subsequent leadership election. Fortunately for historians, both Armstrong and Turnbull provided detailed narratives of the events and decisions made by the respective Prime Ministers, ministers and advisers.

At such times, the principal private secretary, while not being involved in the political negotiations, is essential to ensuring the smooth transfer of power and the continuity of government. Yet, during the equivalent ousting of Boris Johnson from No. 10 in 2022, the private office and the principal private secretary were virtually absent. Negotiations about the future of his premiership were handled by special advisers, working in liaison with senior Conservative backbenchers from the 1922 Committee, not by civil servants. This represented a serious weakness in the transition process. And, critically, after Johnson's departure, there was no continuity in terms of the support that the principal private secretary could have provided to the new Prime Minister, Liz Truss. Why? Because a fundamental principle of the No. 10 private office – that of continuity of the No. 10 principal private secretary in a transition – had been lost. Johnson had brought in his own principal private secretary from the Foreign Office (Martin Reynolds). Similarly, Truss imported her former principal private secretary (Nick Catsaras) from the Foreign Office. And more recently still, Rishi Sunak was to do the same with his former principal private secretary from the Treasury (Elizabeth Perelman). All these decisions were profound errors – however accomplished the individuals concerned. The continuity, ballast and source of advice that an experienced principal private secretary could have been able to bring was lost. The management of the transitions was inevitably less smooth.

The increasing churn in the turnover of private secretaries at No. 10 has not been good for the oversight of governance at the centre of government. Between 1964 and 2010, there were fifteen different principal private secretaries to the Prime Minister, each serving on average just under four years. Between 2010 and 2022, there were eight different principal private secretaries in No. 10, each serving on average eighteen months. Such change in staff has only been matched by the increasingly rapid turnover of ministers and Prime Ministers. Yet continuity in government matters.

Throughout history, private office has normally been able to adapt to the political context in which it operates. In 1964, Wilson entered No. 10 committed to major reform of Whitehall. He wanted to increase the political input at the centre of government and to achieve that by positioning his powerful adviser, Marcia Williams, at the heart of his governmental operation. Yet her personality – bordering at times on hysterical – and her concerns about plots against Wilson (both genuine and imagined) did little to support the private office.

Wilson introduced the first formal special advisers into government, particularly to seek to influence economic policy. At the end of his first term, he also brought in a political appointee, Joe Haines, as his chief press secretary. In these ways, Wilson made powerful political statements about the way in which he intended to govern. By comparison, Heath's three and a half years of government were marked by a more managerial atmosphere, with fewer special advisers and the press secretary function restored to the civil service. Private office reasserted its central role. When Heath needed advice, he tended to use Robert Armstrong or Douglas Hurd as his two main advisers, who worked closely together in No. 10. Hurd was a political appointee and so could shape the political positioning of No. 10 and the Prime Minister, but he did it in a more subtle way than did Williams, and thus made fewer enemies in the process.

During Wilson's second premiership, Williams and Haines were unable to assert themselves in the way they had done during his first period in office, as economic pressures, the lack of a strong parliamentary majority and the onset of Wilson's failing health took their toll. Under James Callaghan, the civil service influence was dominant. Ken Stowe, Callaghan's principal private secretary, was in no sense a political animal. Nor did he have aspirations to be one. He was a loyal operator from the civil service who saw his task as solely to run No. 10 as efficiently as possible. Callaghan had great respect and affection for Stowe. That style was replicated under the first phase of Margaret Thatcher's term of office. The private office worked effectively, with the business of No. 10 and its relationships with Whitehall departments, perhaps, at their most smooth and efficient.

However, from 1983, Thatcher grew in confidence and her government brought in its most radical legislation which later became defined as Thatcherism. She was more dominant, did not tolerate criticism and asserted more vigorously her political beliefs on issues such as the economy and Europe. She was aided in this not by her political special advisers but by Charles Powell, her foreign affairs private secretary who, for seven years, loyally supported her and, in Armstrong's words, at times even 'egged her on'.[6] Powell worked closely with Thatcher's chief press secretary, Bernard Ingham (also a civil servant), who, by their own admission, formed a *'cabinet à deux'* that sustained the Prime Minister. Such hubris and overconfidence eventually contributed to her fall. When Thatcher was forced to resign, her successor John Major ushered in a far more measured and conciliatory form of government, and the civil service was once again central to the operation of No. 10. Under New Labour, Tony Blair increased the number of special advisers in No. 10 from six to twenty-eight and gave special authority to his two most senior aides – Jonathan Powell (brother of Charles), his chief of staff, and Alastair Campbell, who was in charge of the government's communications strategy. Yet, although this was one of the most political phases of the past half-century, there was no suggestion that civil servants in the No. 10 private office were politicised. There was no suggestion that Powell or Campbell sought to politicise civil servants.* Blair may have expressed his frustrations at times at the pace of reform, but he remained a supporter of the impartial civil service and of the need for strong, well-run private offices.[7] In retirement from the premiership, he extolled their virtues to other world leaders. David Cameron, too, had nothing but praise for the operation and impartiality of his private office during his premiership.

All Prime Ministers have, understandably, relied on those aides

---

* Had there been, they would have been raised with the Cabinet Secretary who was responsible for questions of propriety. No complaints were ever raised.

they most trust to manage business and to influence politics. Different advisers have become engaged in that political dimension of government in different ways and on a spectrum of levels of engagement. Of the civil servants, at one end was Ken Stowe, who did not involve himself in political issues. At the other end was Charles Powell, who involved himself deeply in such matters. Other private secretaries fit in somewhere between these two extremes. Robert Armstrong could perform the interventionist role he did because he did not overstep the mark and had Douglas Hurd available to act politically if needed. Jeremy Heywood similarly could turn to Jonathan Powell, Alastair Campbell or any of the special advisers at No. 10 if there were political tasks to perform. Charles Powell had no such political adviser to whom he could turn and so usually relied on his own judgement. As he himself admitted, he did, on occasion, overstep the mark and act in a party political manner for Thatcher.[8]

Despite the attractions of some politicians to the Continental *cabinet* model, and the failed attempt to develop extended ministerial offices under the Cameron government, the private office model has remained and survived, in part because no one has ever devised a better model. Usually, in No. 10 and within ministerial private offices, civil servants work well alongside special advisers. Combining the administrative and non-political role of private office with the tasks of providing party political input to the policy-making process – including, at times, criticism of political opponents – would make a private office far more of a political function. There is no evidence that special advisers in No. 10 or those working for departmental ministers have had any difficulty in gaining access to their ministers or in challenging departmental advice should they have wished to do so. Possibly the opposite is true, as the power and influence of private office has declined in recent years. Political advisers now intervene routinely on a range of issues which, in the past, would have been the sole domain and responsibility of the civil service, such as public appointments or even, during the Covid pandemic, the provision of independent scientific advice to government.

One argument in favour of a *cabinet*-type system could be that it might provide for independent policy-making resources within a minister's office, rather than relying solely on departmental advice. Yet to have two different sources of advice within the private office is a recipe for conflict, if not chaos, unless there is a person or a process capable of weighing up those options, before they reach the minister. The former special adviser and Cabinet minister Ed Balls observed that, while he was at the Treasury, the special advisers – although robust and generally interventionist – never issued an instruction on behalf of the Chancellor. He saw that, fundamentally, as the job of the private office. He said that he and his fellow Treasury special advisers 'never wrote an alternative piece of advice to the Chancellor from that provided by the Treasury officials. It was our principle, from the very beginning that, at the point advice went up to the Chancellor of the Exchequer, it should always be collectively agreed.'9

The stretching of private office sits within the wider framework of the history of civil service reform. This was a priority for Wilson, when he commissioned the Fulton report, and during Heath's period of managerial reforms following publication of the White Paper on 'The Reorganisation of Central Government'. Later Prime Ministers sought limited reforms of the civil service but with less sense of strategic vision and less vigour than Wilson's and Heath's attempts. The introduction by the Blair government of the post of chief of staff was broadly a success. The model, which had been designed by Jonathan Powell (himself a former diplomat) in

1997, meant that, at the apex of No. 10, there was a senior political appointee but one who understood well the workings of the civil service and worked closely with the private office. Every subsequent Prime Minister has retained the post and with a broadly similar remit. Under Cameron, Ed Llewellyn performed the role in much the same way as did Powell. The role can offer a conduit between the permanent civil servants in the No. 10 private office, the other special advisers across government as well as other external political figures. But, once again, the far too rapid turnover of chiefs of staff – with nine in post in the eight years since 2016 – has damaged their credibility, at a time when they could have provided a semblance of stability, working with private secretaries as a central point in No. 10, straddling the political and official sides and reporting direct to the Prime Minister.

Over the post-war period, the No. 10 private office has flourished and operated best when it has met four conditions. First, when it has been well managed, with a strong personality as principal private secretary to the Prime Minister and operating with efficient systems. Second, when the private office has been given the authority to act, with clear political leadership from the Prime Minister. Third, when the quality of the team of private secretaries has been consistently high, with effective working between the civil service and political appointees in No. 10. Finally, the Prime Minister's private office has been at its most powerful when it has been widely respected across all of Whitehall. But, while these are the conditions for a successful private office, these do not, of course, guarantee political success for the government, which is judged by the electorate and according to a different yardstick. These are the necessary, but far from sufficient, elements for political success, as measured by a party being returned at a general election.

The most egregious failings of No. 10 and its private office came in 2022 when the Prime Minister, Boris Johnson, undermined the essential integrity expected of the occupants of his office. In the absence of any long-standing principal private secretary, there was no one to wave a metaphorical red flag at Johnson. Private office could not manage, contain or constrain Johnson. While the blame for that must lay squarely with Johnson himself, his private office should and could have done more to try to install order rather than chaos at the centre of government.

In future, there needs to be a reset of how private office works. Not to return to some mythical golden age which never existed. But rather to a system that builds on the best traditions of the civil service and recognises the political context in which all ministers and civil servants now operate. In Appendix 3, I offer a way forward for whichever party wins the next general election. The draft document I have prepared will help the Prime Minister restate to both the private office in No. 10 and every private office across Whitehall what their core purpose and activities should be. Many new ministers will be appointed with no prior experience of government or its workings. This note, which sets out the ten main functions of any private office, should operate as a broad guide to the purposes for which ministers should and should not use their private offices.

Private office matters. Private office can still reclaim its former status and, once again, play a powerful role as the central junction box of government. It has evolved and will continue to do so as the nature of politics, policy-making, public administration and communications – all driven by technology – develop. Within a constitutional democracy, there will always be a need for the functions that the private office fulfils to ensure that ministers' wishes are communicated and carried out, and that the government of the day is supported as effectively as possible. The private office, and especially the private office of the Prime Minister, has always attracted high-quality civil servants and will continue to do so. The greatest virtue of the private office has been that it has normally been well equipped to deliver for governments of all political persuasions on the sound principles of political impartiality and integrity. The shortcomings of private office have been exposed when it has either failed to respond to the political aspirations of incoming Prime Ministers or when it could not adapt quickly enough to the new demands of new administrations.

Private office has worked best when ministers are not suspicious of it and it is given the flexibility to work closely with political appointees drawing on the strengths of both parts of the system – on the one hand, the politicians and special advisers, and on the other hand, the politically aware, but impartial, civil servants. Prime Ministers and ministers have acknowledged the strengths and value of their private offices. Politicians may have waxed and waned like the phases of the moon, but the private office has always been constant as the North Star. Historians, too, have often neglected its contribution, yet it has always been there. It has, for the most part, been of benefit to the British political system. With flexibility, change and a recognition of the nature of today's politics, it can remain so for many years to come.

APPENDIX 1: GLOSSARY

Cabinet Secretary: The most senior civil servant; traditionally, the Prime Minister's principal official policy adviser and head of the Cabinet Office secretariats. The post has existed since 1916. The Cabinet Secretary attends all meetings of Cabinet and is the head of the home civil service.

'*Cabinet*' system: The Continental form of private office which contains both permanent civil servants and political appointees, working in a joint ministerial support unit. *Cabinets* tend to be larger than the equivalent British private office and more business will be transacted directly via the *cabinet*. They will also make and initiate policy on behalf of their minister or commissioner. They exist in many European governments and are used routinely throughout the European Commission.

Central Policy Review Staff (CPRS): A unit, based in the Cabinet Office, which existed between 1970 and 1983. It was established as a result of a proposal in the 'Reorganisation of Central Government' White Paper published in October 1970. It was responsible for advising the Prime Minister on long-term strategic planning and cross-government policy-making.

Chief of staff: In the UK, the overall head of the Prime Minister's support team (private office, special advisers and support staff) and, in the EU Commission, the head of the *cabinet*. The title 'chief of staff' has existed in the White House since 1952. Between 1979 and 1985, Margaret Thatcher had a chief of staff but he did not run the private office. However, in Britain since 1997, the post has existed in No. 10 and has usually been held by a political appointee responsible for the overall leadership of the No. 10 office, reporting directly to the Prime Minister.

Chief press secretary: The chief adviser to the Prime Minister on press, media and communications. This post has sometimes been held by a civil servant (such as Bernard Ingham, from 1979 to 1997) and sometimes by a political appointee (such as Alastair Campbell, from 1997 to 2003). The chief press secretary works closely with the Prime Minister and the private office.

Diary secretary: The official within the private office responsible for management of the Prime Minister's (or any minister's) diary and appointments. They may often also play a gatekeeper role.

Expert adviser: A term used for an adviser who is brought into government because of their specific expertise in a particular area of policy. Such appointments have to be agreed by the Prime Minister. While they are usually political appointees, expert advisers do not count against the number of special advisers which Cabinet ministers are eligible to appoint. One of the best-known expert advisers was Professor Sir Michael Barber, who was head of the Prime Minister's Delivery Unit (PMDU) from 2001 to 2005.

Fast stream: A shorthand term for the recruitment and accelerated promotion scheme within the civil service. Entrants via this scheme are known, colloquially, as 'fast-streamers'. Many will serve in the private office as part of their career development.

Fulton report: The report commissioned by Harold Wilson and published in 1968. It was an inquiry into the future organisation and management of the civil service. It was chaired by Lord Fulton.

Gatekeeper: An informal term for someone who manages, in close liaison with the diary secretary (and who may even be the diary secretary), access to the Prime Minister or to a minister. Examples of powerful gatekeepers were Marcia Williams (for Harold Wilson); Anji Hunter (for Tony Blair); Sue Nye (for Gordon Brown) and Kate Fall (for David Cameron).

Northcote–Trevelyan system: The foundation of the British system of an impartial civil service. The title refers to the system of civil service recruitment based on merit and competitive examinations. It was named after Stafford Northcote and Charles Trevelyan who jointly wrote the report which was published in 1854, advocating the establishment of such a system.

Parliamentary private secretary: A Member of Parliament appointed by the Prime Minister or a Cabinet minister to be their contact with Parliament and political matters. They are an unpaid political appointment who helps keep their minister fully informed about political developments and their implications. The parliamentary private secretary (PPS) should not be confused with the civil service principal private secretary (also referred to as the PPS) in a ministerial private office. The parliamentary private secretary is often regarded as the first rung on the ministerial ladder.

Permanent Secretary: The permanent civil service head, and accounting officer, of a government department. There are others of Permanent Secretary rank who do not head departments, such as some senior ambassadors, the chief scientific adviser and the chief medical officer. There are also people at this rank who head non-ministerial government departments. Permanent Secretaries are appointed by the Prime Minister, normally following a competition and from a list of appointable candidates, recommended by the First Civil Service Commissioner.

Personal secretary: A minister's personal secretary, who is normally their administrative assistant. They may combine the role with that of diary secretary. They may be departmentally based or based in the minister's constituency. They should not be confused with the private secretary. They would usually be appointed personally by the minister.

Policy Unit (No. 10): The unit, based at No. 10 since it was established in 1974, comprising a combination of outside special advisers and civil servants, to advise the Prime Minister directly on policy matters. Increasingly, over time, it has become staffed predominantly by special advisers and other political appointees.

Prime Minister's Delivery Unit (PMDU): A unit, which existed from 2001 to 2010, based jointly in the Cabinet Office and Treasury and reporting directly to the Prime Minister, responsible for ensuring delivery of the Labour government's major public service

Edward Heath (1970–74)

Principal private secretary
Sandy Isserlis   1970
Robert Armstrong   1970–74

Chief press secretary
Donald Maitland   1970–73
Robin Haydon   1973–74

Cabinet Secretary
Burke Trend   1970–73
John Hunt   1973–74

Harold Wilson (1974–76)

Principal private secretary
Robert Armstrong   1974–75
Kenneth Stowe   1975–76

Personal and political secretary
Marcia Williams   1974–76

Chief press secretary
Joe Haines   1974–76

Cabinet Secretary
John Hunt   1974–76

James Callaghan (1976–79)

Principal private secretary
Kenneth Stowe   1976–79

Chief press secretary
Tom McCaffery   1976–79

Cabinet Secretary
John Hunt   1976–79

Margaret Thatcher (1979–90)

Chief of staff
David Wolfson   1979–85

Principal private secretary
Kenneth Stowe   1979
Clive Whitmore   1979–82
Robin Butler   1982–85
Nigel Wicks   1985–88
Andrew Turnbull   1988–90

Chief press secretary
Henry James   1979
Bernard Ingham   1979–90

Cabinet Secretary
John Hunt   1979

Robert Armstrong   1979–88
Robin Butler   1988–90

John Major (1990–97)

Principal private secretary
Andrew Turnbull   1990–92
Alex Allan   1992–97

Chief press secretary
Gus O'Donnell   1990–94
Christopher Meyer   1994–96
Jonathan Haslam   1996–97

Cabinet Secretary
Robin Butler   1990–97

Tony Blair (1997–2007)

Chief of staff
Jonathan Powell   1997–2007

Principal private secretary
Alex Allan   1997
John Holmes   1997–99
Jeremy Heywood   1999–2003
Ivan Rogers   2003–06
Oliver Robbins   2006–07

Chief press secretary/director of communications
Alastair Campbell   1997–2003
David Hill   2003–07

Cabinet Secretary
Robin Butler   1997–98
Richard Wilson   1998–2002
Andrew Turnbull   2002–05
Gus O'Donnell   2005–07

Gordon Brown (2007–10)

Chief of staff
Tom Scholar   2007–08
Stephen Carter   2008
('chief of strategy and principal adviser')

Principal private secretary
Oliver Robbins   2007–08
Tom Scholar   2008
Jeremy Heywood   2008–10
(from 2010, Permanent Secretary No. 10)
James Bowler   2010

Director of communications
Michael Ellam   2007–09
Simon Lewis   2009–10

Cabinet Secretary
Gus O'Donnell   2007–10

David Cameron (2010–16)

Chief of staff
Ed Llewellyn   2010–16

Permanent Secretary, No. 10
Jeremy Heywood   2010–12

Principal private secretary
James Bowler   2010–11
Chris Martin   2011–15
Simon Case   2015–16

Director of communications
Andy Coulson   2010–11
Craig Oliver   2011–16

Cabinet Secretary
Gus O'Donnell   2010–11
Jeremy Heywood   2012–16

Theresa May (2016–19)

Chief of staff
Fiona Hill   (joint) 2016–17
Nick Timothy   (joint) 2016–17
Gavin Barwell   2017–19

Principal private secretary
Simon Case   2016–17
Peter Hill   2017–19

Director of communications
Katie Perrior   2016–17
Robbie Gibb   2017–19

Cabinet Secretary
Jeremy Heywood   2016–18
Mark Sedwill   2018–19

Boris Johnson (2019–22)

Chief of staff
Dominic Cummings   2019–20
('chief adviser to the Prime Minister')
Edward Lister   2020–21
Dan Rosenfield   2021–22
Steve Barclay   2022
Simone Finn   2022

Permanent Secretary, No. 10
Simon Case   2020

Principal private secretary
Peter Hill   2019
Martin Reynolds   2019–22
Peter Wilson   2022

Director of communications
Lee Cain   2019–20
James Slack   2021
Jack Doyle   2021–22
Guto Harri   2022

Cabinet Secretary
Mark Sedwill   2019–20
Simon Case   2020–22

Cabinet Secretary
Simon Case   2022

Rishi Sunak (2022–)

Chief of staff
Liam Booth-Smith   2022–

Principal private secretary
Elizabeth Perelman 2022–

Director of communications
Amber de Botton   2022–23
Nerissa Chesterfield 2023–

Cabinet Secretary
Simon Case   2022–

Liz Truss (2022)

Chief of staff
Mark Fulbrook   2022

Principal private secretary
Nick Catsaras   2022

Director of communications
Adam Jones   (joint) 2022
Simon McGee   (joint) 2022

APPENDIX 3: A SUBMISSION TO THE PRIME MINISTER ON THE ROLE OF PRIVATE OFFICE

To: Prime Minister   **From: Principal private secretary**
                                       to the Prime Minister

cc: Cabinet Secretary
Chief of staff, No. 10
All private secretaries, No. 10
Director of communications
Chief press secretary

Congratulations on winning the general election.

As you know, the Cabinet Secretary has made clear that the full resources of the civil service are now at your and your ministers' disposal to deliver your agenda. As principal private secretary to the Prime Minister, and head of your No. 10 private office, I know that I speak for all Downing Street staff in saying that we will all serve you as effectively as we can. I also wish to work as closely as possible with your political team and ensure your special advisers are fully supported and integrated within the overall No. 10 operation.

The reputation of private office – including here at No. 10 – was damaged by the experience of 'Partygate'. We have already taken steps to address some of the causes, but, if you agree, I think it would be well worth restating the core purpose of private office, given its central role in ensuring the effective and efficient operation of the government. That should be particularly helpful to your colleagues who have never previously served as a minister. You can set out the key principles of an effective private office and the ways in which you wish private office to operate both at No. 10 and, equally importantly, in all government departments.

I have therefore drafted the attached short note on what constitutes an effective private office and summarising the key characteristics. I would welcome your views. In particular, would you like me to circulate this in No. 10 and then, also, to members of your Cabinet, asking them to share it widely with their ministerial private offices?

I am happy to discuss over the weekend.

Signed: Principal private secretary.

WHAT IS PRIVATE OFFICE FOR? A GUIDE FOR MINISTERS
This note summarises the characteristics of an effective private office. It is intended to help a minister build a good working relationship with their private office and get the best from their close team. The key attributes are as follows:

Overview
Ministers should rely on their private office to support them in all official work. Close working with private office pays dividends by ensuring ministers can progress their priorities promptly. A well-functioning private office will make a minister's work that

much more efficient. All government activities should be pursued via civil service channels. In particular, government business should never be transacted other than via government secure IT systems.

Staffing

The principal private secretary is the most senior manager in the Secretary of State's office and is the most confidential adviser on all policy and organisation matters. They will wish to ensure that any ministerial concerns are addressed promptly and properly. If a minister has concerns about the capability or competence of the principal private secretary – or if there is a personality clash (which can occasionally happen) – the matter should be raised immediately with the departmental Permanent Secretary.

Observation of political boundaries

An effective private office works best when private secretaries work in close collaboration with special advisers. Ministers should look to build and encourage good relationships, and the sharing of information, to mutual benefit. However, private office should not be a personal 'cheerleader' for the Secretary of State. That is not their role. Any party political activity must be carried out solely via special advisers or under the auspices of party officials, not civil servants in private office.

Effective communications and media work

Good communications are vital for an effective private office. Private secretaries, special advisers and departmental communications staff should work closely together and share information. They must be clear about their respective roles, reporting lines and their relationship with communications staff at No. 10. Again, civil servants should not cross the party political divide or run anything that might be construed as a separate media operation.

Work–life balance

The effective operation of a private office should not require a permanent long-hours culture and should not adversely impact the personal or family life of staff. Private offices demonstrate considerable personal loyalty to their minister, but this should not routinely involve late nights and weekend working. Ministers should encourage staff to leave work at a reasonable time, when possible, and encourage the principal private secretary to manage late working effectively.

Proactivity

An effective private office should be proactive in seeking out advice on issues which are of particular interest to their minister and ensuring that their priorities are progressed rapidly. Private secretaries should be encouraged to make suggestions on departmental submissions. However, they should not become an alternative or rival source of ministerial advice. If ministers are not satisfied with the advice they receive from departmental officials, they should raise the matter with their principal private secretary or their Permanent Secretary.

Financial matters and appointments

An effective private office is based on a good understanding of the Ministerial Code and a clear commitment to observe its provisions. This is particularly important in regard to financial issues and public appointment. If in doubt, ministers should look to their principal private secretary and Permanent Secretary (or, if necessary, the Cabinet Office propriety and ethics team) for advice on such issues.

Planning for contingencies

Crises happen in government and most ministers are likely to have to deal with some form of crisis during their tenure. The private office is an essential support mechanism in such circumstances. To ensure the most effective response to crises, thorough preparation is essential. Training and exercising for such eventualities, by both ministers and private secretaries, are vital.

Probity

An effective private office should demonstrate awareness that the conduct of any minister and the operation of their office may be the subject of intense scrutiny, especially in the media. Great care must be taken to avoid giving the impression of taking advantage of 'perks' and favours. This extends, for example, to the use of departmental transport, hospitality and communication resources. Again, if ministers have doubts about any of the rules, they should discuss them with their principal private secretary or Permanent Secretary.

Dignity and respect

An effective private office should be characterised by courtesy and high levels of mutual respect. In particular, ministers should never engage in behaviour that could be construed, in any way, as bullying or harassment.

NOTES

INTRODUCTION

1   As quoted in the 'Findings of the Second Permanent Secretary's Investigation into Alleged Gatherings on Government Premises during COVID Restrictions' ('Sue Gray report') (London: Cabinet Office, 2022), p. 11.

2   Ibid., p. 13.

3   Peter Hennessy, *The Hidden Wiring* (London: Victor Gollancz, 1995).

4   Fabian Tract 355, *The Administrators: The Reform of the Civil Service* (London: The Fabian Society, 1964).

5   Andrew Blick and Peter Hennessy, *Good Chaps No More? Safeguarding the Constitution in Stressful Times* (London: Constitution Society, 2019).

6   House of Commons Library note, 24 September 2019.

7   Hennessy, *The Hidden Wiring*.

8   Nicholas Henderson, *The Private Office Revisited* (London: Profile Books, 2001).

9   R. A. W. Rhodes, *Everyday Life in British Government* (Oxford: Oxford University Press, 2011), pp. 137–65.

10 George Jones, 'The Prime Minister's Aides', in Anthony King (ed.), *The British Prime Minister* (London: Macmillan, 1988), pp. 72–95.

11 Ibid. p. 76.

12 The main work on the prime ministership is Peter Hennessy, *The Prime Minister: The Office and its Holders Since 1945* (London: Penguin, 2001), which includes reference throughout to the work of the private offices of all Prime Ministers from Attlee to Blair. For more specific studies on the work of the Prime Minister and the No. 10 private office, see Andrew Blick and George Jones, *Premiership: The Development, Nature and Power of the Office of the British Prime Minister* (Exeter: Imprint Academic, 2010); Peter Hennessy, *Whitehall* (London: Secker & Warburg, 1989); Andrew Holt and Warren Dockter (eds), *Private Secretaries to the Prime Minister: Foreign Affairs from Churchill to Thatcher* (London: Routledge, 2017); George Jones, 'The Prime Minister's secretaries: politicians or administrators?', in J. Griffith (ed.), *From Policy to Administration* (London: Allen & Unwin, 1976); Dennis Kavanagh and Anthony Seldon, *The Powers Behind the Prime Minister* (London: HarperCollins, 1999); King (ed.), *The British Prime Minister*; J. M. Lee, G. W. Jones and J. Burnham, *At the Centre of Whitehall: Advising the Prime Minister and Cabinet* (Basingstoke: Macmillan, 1998); and Kevin Theakston, *Leadership in Whitehall* (Basingstoke: Macmillan, 1999).

13 Kevin Theakston, *The Civil Service Since 1945* (Oxford: Blackwell, 1995), pp. 34–55.

14 Blick and Jones, *Premiership*.

15 Kavanagh and Seldon, *The Powers Behind the Prime Minister*, Appendix 1, pp. 327–44.

16 See, for example, Andrew Rawnsley, *Servants of the People* (London: Penguin, 2000) and Andrew Rawnsley, *The End of the Party* (London: Penguin, 2010); James Naughtie, *The Rivals: The Intimate Story of a Political Marriage* (London: HarperCollins, 2001); and Anthony Seldon and Guy Lodge, *Brown at 10* (London: Biteback, 2010).

17 Anthony Seldon, *Blair* (London: Simon & Schuster, 2004); Anthony Seldon, *Blair Unbound* (London: Simon & Schuster, 2008); Seldon and Lodge, *Brown at 10*; Anthony Seldon and Peter Snowden, *Cameron at 10* (London: HarperCollins, 2015); and Anthony Seldon, *May at 10* (London: Biteback, 2019).

18 Jonathan Powell, *The New Machiavelli: How to Wield Power in the Modern World* (London: Bodley Head, 2010).

19 Ibid., p. 97.

20 Holt and Dockter (eds), *Private Secretaries to the Prime Minister*.

21 Anthony Seldon, 'The Prime Minister's Private Office from John Martin to Chris Martin', in Holt and Dockter, *Private Secretaries to the Prime Minister*, pp. 187–207.

22 Gerald Kaufman, *How to Be a Minister* (London: Sidgwick & Jackson, 1980).

23 Ibid., pp. 33–4.

24 John Hutton and Leigh Lewis, *How to Be a Minister: A 21st-Century Guide* (London: Biteback, 2014).

25 Ibid., p. 117.

26 Ibid., p. 118.

27 Ibid., p. 121.

28 Hennessy, *Whitehall*, in particular, pp. 380–92.

29 Hennessy, *The Prime Minister*. For his analysis of the functions of the Prime Minister, see pp. 53–101.

30 See, for example, Jon Davis, *Prime Ministers and Whitehall* (London: Hambledon Continuum, 2007); Gavin Drewry and Tony Butcher, *The Civil Service Today* (London: John Wiley and Sons, 1991), Nevil Johnson, 'Change in the Civil Service', *Public Administration*, 63 (Winter 1985), pp. 415–33; Rodney Lowe, *The Official History of the British Civil Service, Volume 1: The Fulton Years, 1966–81* (Abingdon: Routledge, 2011); Theakston, *The Civil Service Since 1945*; and Kevin Theakston, *The Labour Party and Whitehall* (London: Routledge, 1992).

31 Andrew Blick, *People Who Live in the Dark* (London: Politico's, 2004), pp. 63–122.

32 Blick and Hennessy, *Good Chaps No More?*, p. 3.

1. THE JUNCTION BOX OF GOVERNMENT: WHAT IS PRIVATE OFFICE AND WHAT DOES IT DO?

1 Robert Blake, *Disraeli* (London: Faber and Faber, 2010), p. 449.

2 Susan Crosland, *Tony Crosland* (London: Jonathan Cape, 1982), p. 269.

3 Dominic Cummings, 'The Hollow Men II: Some reflections on Westminster and Whitehall dysfunction', https://dominiccummings.com/2014/10/30/the-hollow-men-ii-some-reflections-on-westminster-and-whitehall-dysfunction/.

4 R. A. W. Rhodes, *Everyday Life in British Government* (Oxford: Oxford University Press, 2011), pp. 137–65.

5 Catherine Haddon, Tim Durrant, Daniel Devine and Tess Kidney Bishop, *Becoming Secretary of State* (Institute for Government Insight Briefing, 2019). See also Peter Riddell, *15 Minutes of Power: The Uncertain Life of British Ministers* (London: Profile Books, 2019).

6 David Cameron, Hansard, *House of Commons Debates*, column 1346, 25 November 2015.

7 Martin Stanley, *How to Be a Civil Servant* (London: Biteback, 2016). See also Stanley's website which covers the role of the private office: https://www.civilservant.org.uk/private_offices.html.

8 https://www.politics.co.uk/reference/private-office.

9 *Report on the Organisation of the Permanent Civil Service* (London: HMSO, 1854). See also Lowe, *The Official History of the British Civil Service*, pp. 17–41; and Hennessy, *Whitehall*, pp. 17–51.

10 See, for example, A. Dutheillet de Lamothe, 'Ministerial Cabinets in France', *Public Administration* 43/4 (1965), pp. 365–81.

11 Hennessy, *The Hidden Wiring*, pp. 12–13.

12 Interview with Andrew Cahn, 14 December 2022.

13 These issues are discussed in Blick, *People Who Live in the Dark*, pp. 1–29.

14 Material on current civil service policy-making procedures and other relevant documents can be found on the website Understanding the Civil Service, https://www.civilservant.org.uk. The website includes a section on policy-making in government, https://www.policy-making.org.uk/index.html.

15 The Ministerial Code, Cabinet Office, 22 December 2022, https://www.gov.uk/government/publications/ministerial-code.

16 For the history of the Ministerial Code see Amy Baker, *Prime Ministers and the Rule Book* (London: Politico's, 2000).

17 The Ministerial Code.

18 Ibid., paragraph 8.14.

19 Ibid., paragraph 10.5.

20 Interview with Lord Butler, 29 September 2010.

21 See Akash Paun, *Supporting Ministers to Lead* (London: Institute for Government, 2013), p. 7.

22 *The British Imperial Calendar and Civil Service List*, 1964.

23 Stanley, *How to Be a Civil Servant*, pp. 8–9.

24 *The Administrators*.

25 See Paun, *Supporting Ministers to Lead*, pp. 8–20.

26 House of Lords Written Answer, Lord Young of Cookham, 8 February 2018.

27 David Willetts, cited by Nicola Hughes in her Institute for Government blog, https://www. instituteforgovernment.org.uk/blog/scrapping-extended-ministerial-offices-mistake.

28 Christopher Jary, *Working with Ministers*, https://www.civilservant.org.uk/library/2015_Working_with_ Ministers.pdf, first published in 2004 and updated regularly ever since.

29 Hennessy, *The Prime Minister*, pp. 57–101.

30 Ibid., p. 60.

31 For the most up-to-date full list, see Peter Hennessy, *Distilling the Frenzy: Writing the History of One's Own Times* (London: Biteback, 2012), pp. 102–23. A few of the forty-seven functions were specific to the role of the Prime Minister during a coalition. See also Peter Hennessy, 'What Are Prime Ministers For?', *Journal of the British Academy*, 2 (2014), pp. 213–29.

32 Darling, *Back from the Brink*, p. 167.

33 See Jary, *Working with Ministers*.

34 Interview with David Cameron, 23 April 2018.

35 Kenneth Clarke interviewed by Michael Cockerell, BBC2, *The Secret World of Whitehall*, Episode 3, 'The Network'.

36 Michael Jago, *Robin Butler: At the Heart of Power from Heath to Blair* (London: Biteback, 2017), p. 144.

37 Jonathan Powell, *Great Hatred, Little Room* (London: Bodley Head, 2008), pp. 60–61.

38 Private information.

39 Interview with Roger Dawe.

40 Interview with Lord Butler.

41 Interview with David Cameron.

42 Institute for Government, *Strengthening Private Office* (London: Institute for Government, 2023).

43 The Ministerial Code, paragraph 2.5.

44 Sherard Cowper-Coles, *Ever the Diplomat* (London: HarperPress, 2012), p. 85.

45 For more information on the process see: https://www.parliament.uk/about/how/business/questions.

46 See House of Commons Library Parliamentary Information List, *Number of Urgent Questions in the House of Commons since 1997*, CBP 08344, 29 May 2020.

47 For more information see: https://www.parliament.uk/about/how/business/urgent-questions.

48 Interview with Andrew Cahn.

49 Charles Moore, *Margaret Thatcher: The Authorized Biography, Volume 2: Everything She Wants* (London: Allen Lane, 2016), p. 603.

50 Private information.

51 Private information.

52 Private information.

53 Interview with Lord Armstrong, 22 July 2014.

54 Interviews with Tony Blair and David Cameron.

55 See Suzanne Heywood, *What Does Jeremy Think?* (London: William Collins, 2021).

56 Interview with Joe Haines, 4 April 2018.

57 See Ian Kennedy, *Cleaning Up the Mess* (London: Biteback, 2019). See also, Gavin Little and David Stopforth, 'The Legislative Origins of the MPs' Expenses Scandal', *Modern Law Review*, 76/1 (2013), pp. 83–108.

58 Haddon et al., *Becoming Secretary of State*, p. 5.

59 The Ministerial Code (updated version December 2022).

60 Blick, *People Who Live in the Dark*, pp. 223–7.

61 Roy Jenkins, as quoted in John Campbell, *Roy Jenkins: A Well-Rounded Life* (London: Jonathan Cape, 2014), p. 264.

62 Robin Butler, 'Police inquiry into Edward Heath has been a disgrace', *The Times*, 3 October 2017.

63 Historical figures on public appointments, 'Annual Report of the Commissioner for Public Appointments', 2011–12, p. 21.

64 'Annual Report of the Commissioner for Public Appointments', 2018–19.

65 John Colville, *The Fringes of Power: Downing Street Diaries 1939–1955* (London: Hodder & Stoughton, 1985), p. 708.

66 Gordon Brown, *My Life, Our Times* (London: Bodley Head, 2017), p. 113.

67 Interview with James Bowler, 5 September 2018.

68 Ibid.

69 Interview with Tony Blair.

70 Darling, *Back from the Brink*, p. 2 and p. 157.

71 Interview with Roger Dawe.

72 These figures are from: Cabinet Office Annual Report on Special Advisers, 2019.

2. A MIXTURE OF LEPORELLO AND MEPHISTOPHELES: WHO ARE THE PRIVATE SECRETARIES AND WHERE DO THEY COME FROM?

1   Farewell letter from Healey to Nairne on the latter's appointment as assistant under-secretary of state (logistics), 10 August 1967. (Private papers of Sir Patrick Nairne, shared with the author.)
2   Ibid.
3   Interview with Denis Healey, 12 January 2015.
4   Denis Healey, *The Time of My Life* (London: Michael Joseph, 1989), p. 268. See also the obituary of Sir Patrick Nairne, *The Guardian*, 5 June 2013.
5   The data in this table is based on Kevin Theakston, *The Civil Service Since 1945* (Oxford: Blackwell, 1995), Table 2.1, 'Permanent Secretaries and their experience', p. 37, and has been updated for 2010 and 2020 from *Who's Who* (London: A & C Black, 2020).
6   This was certainly the view of Henderson in *The Private Office Revisited*, p. 185, as well as Hennessy in *The Hidden Wiring*, pp. 123–4 and p. 129.
7   For more details of the fast stream competition and its nature, see the Institute of Government's description of the scheme, https://www.instituteforgovernment.org.uk/explainers/civil-service-fast-stream. For a historical description of how the scheme operated, see Peter Kellner and Lord Crowther-Hunt, *The Civil Servants* (London: Macdonald Futura, 1980), esp. pp. 103–73.
8   For Hurd's description, see Stanley, *How to Be a Civil Servant*, pp. 13–14.
9   Interview with Lord Powell.
10 Institute for Government, *Strengthening Private Office*, p. 12.
11 Ibid.
12 Private information.
13 Interview with Tony Blair, 18 January 2018. See also Powell, *The New Machiavelli*, pp. 80–81.
14 For a near-complete list of all principal private secretaries to the Prime Minister since 1868, see: https://en.wikipedia.org/wiki/Principal_Private_Secretary_to_the_Prime_Minister.
15 See Caroline Slocock, *People Like Us* (London: Biteback, 2018).
16 Ibid., p. 20.
17 The data in this table is based on *Who's Who* and *Who Was Who*, https://www.ukwhoswho.com (London: A & C Black).
18 Hennessy, *Whitehall*, pp. 655–7.

3. GENESIS OF AN INSTITUTION: THE ORIGINS AND GROWTH OF PRIVATE OFFICE

1   Andrew Blick and George Jones, *At Power's Elbow: Aides to the Prime Minister from Robert Walpole to David Cameron* (London: Biteback, 2013), p. 160.
2   See Robert Latham, *The Shorter Pepys* (London: Unwin Hyman, 1990) and Claire Tomalin, *Samuel Pepys: The Unequalled Self* (London: Penguin, 2012).
3   Blick and Jones, *At Power's Elbow*, p. 51.
4   Ibid.
5   Ibid.
6   Ibid.
7   Iain Dale (ed.), *The Prime Ministers* (London: Hodder & Stoughton, 2020), p. 50.
8   Roy Jenkins, *The Chancellors* (London: Macmillan, 1998), p. 7.
9   Kavanagh and Seldon, *The Powers Behind the Prime Minister*, p. 35.
10 West, as quoted in Charles Petrie, *The Powers Behind the Prime Ministers* (London: Macgibbon and Kee, 1958), p. 34.
11 Ibid. p. 44.
12 Roy Jenkins, *Gladstone* (London: Pan Macmillan, 2018), p. 390.
13 Christopher Hibbert, *Disraeli: A Personal History* (London: Harper Perennial, 2005), p. 252.
14 Petrie, *The Powers Behind the Prime Ministers*, p. 12.
15 Douglas Hurd and Edward Young, *Disraeli* (London: Phoenix, 2014), p. 286.
16 Petrie, *The Powers Behind the Prime Ministers*, p. 15.
17 Hurd and Young, *Disraeli*, p. 12.
18 See Anthony Seldon, *The Cabinet Office 1916–2016* (London: Biteback, 2016), pp. 25–39.
19 Peter Hennessy, *Cabinet* (London: Basil Blackwell, 1986), p. 16, and quoting Lloyd George's biographer, John Grigg.
20 Roger Mortimore and Andrew Blick, *Butler's British Political Facts* (Basingstoke: Palgrave Macmillan, 2018), pp. 8–11.

21 See Blick and Jones, *Premiership*, p. 130 on the development of the convention that 'the Private Office as a whole should comprise only, or almost entirely, permanent Whitehall staff'.

22 A. J. Sylvester, *The Real Lloyd George* (London: Cassel, 1947), pp. 99–100.

23 Philip Snowden, Hansard, *House of Commons Debates*, column 977, 6 March 1928.

24 Ibid.

25 Blick and Jones, *At Power's Elbow*, p. 160.

26 See Hennessy, *Whitehall*, pp. 85–86, on his closeness to Chamberlain.

27 G. C. Peden, 'Sir Horace Wilson and Appeasement', *Historical Journal*, 53/4 (2010), pp. 983–1,014 and Adrian Phillips, *Fighting Churchill, Appeasing Hitler: How a British Civil Servant Helped Cause the Second World War* (London: Biteback, 2019).

28 Blick and Jones, *At Power's Elbow*, p. 164.

29 Ibid., pp. 165–7.

30 'Intelligence files: Edward VIII bugged by own Government as he prepared to abdicate', *The Daily Telegraph*, 22 May 2013.

31 Richard J. Aldrich and Rory Cormac, *The Secret Royals: Spying and the Crown from Victoria to Diana* (London: Atlantic Books, 2021), p. 219.

32 Tim Bouverie, *Appeasing Hitler* (London: Vintage, 2019), p. 217.

33 Peden, 'Sir Horace Wilson and Appeasement', p. 983.

34 Hennessy, *Whitehall*, p. 85.

35 Peden, 'Sir Horace Wilson and Appeasement', p. 986.

36 Ibid.

37 Ibid., p. 990.

38 Ibid.

39 Ibid.

40 Ibid., p. 86.

41 Simon Heffer (ed.), *Henry 'Chips' Channon: The Diaries, Vol. 1 1918–1938* (London: Hutchinson, 2021), footnote p. 933.

42 Kenneth Harris, *Attlee* (London: Weidenfeld & Nicolson, 1982), p. 180.

43 John Bew, *Citizen Clem* (London: Riverrun, 2016), p. 267.

44 Dan Todman, '"Zealous ferret" to national saviour: Churchill in 1940', *The Historian*, 12 June 2017.

45 Peden, 'Sir Horace Wilson and Appeasement', p. 984.

4. GOVERNING IN WAR AND PEACE: PRIVATE OFFICE 1940–64

1   Harold Macmillan, as quoted in Andrew Boyle, *Poor Dear Brendan* (London: Hutchinson & Co., 1974), p. 250.

2   Colville, *The Fringes of Power*, p. 39.

3   Ibid.

4   John Martin, *Downing Street: The War Years* (London: Bloomsbury, 1991), p. 11.

5   Colville, *The Fringes of Power*, p. 39.

6   Ibid., p. 65.

7   Ibid.

8   Colville, quoted in Bew, *Citizen Clem*, p. 364.

9   Leo McKinstry, *Attlee and Churchill* (London: Atlantic Books, 2019), p. 449.

10 Kavanagh and Seldon, *The Powers Behind the Prime Minister*, p. 55.

11 Philip M. Williams (ed.), *The Diary of Hugh Gaitskell 1945–1956* (London: Jonathan Cape, 1983), p. 305.

12 Colville, *The Fringes of Power*, p. 632.

13 Ibid., pp. 667–80. See also Roy Jenkins, *Churchill* (London: Macmillan, 2001), pp. 862–8 and Hennessy, *The Prime Minister*, pp. 196–7.

14 Jenkins, *Churchill*, p. 861.

15 Martin Gilbert, *Never Despair, Churchill 1945–65* (London: Minerva, 1990), p. 849.

16 Jenkins, *Churchill*, pp. 862–3.

17 Gilbert, *Never Despair*, p. 849.

18 See Hennessy, *The Hidden Wiring*, pp. 52–3.

19 Ibid., p. 858.

20 Kavanagh and Seldon, *The Powers Behind the Prime Minister*, p. 299.

21 Kevin Theakston, *After Number 10: Former Prime Ministers in British Politics* (Basingstoke: Palgrave Macmillan, 2010), p. 166.

22 Lord Egremont, *Wyndham and Children First* (London: Macmillan, 1968), pp. 161–2.
23 Ibid.
24 Ibid., p. 162.
25 Ibid., pp. 168–9.
26 See Peter Hennessy, *Having It So Good* (London: Allen Lane, 2006), pp. 602–3 on how Bligh briefed the media, dropping hints on Macmillan's tour of Africa and in advance of his 'Winds of Change' speech.
27 See David Profumo, *Bringing the House Down* (London: John Murray, 2007), p. 177.
28 H. Montgomery Hyde, *A Tangled Web* (London: Futura, 1986), p. 260.
29 See for example, TNA PREM 5/374, 'Ministerial Appointments. Ministry of Harold Macmillan (Conservative) Part 6', Minute from Bligh to Macmillan, 19 April 1962. See also Peter Hennessy, *Winds of Change* (London: Allen Lane, 2019, p. 160), which includes the notes that Bligh wrote for Macmillan to use when sacking seven Cabinet ministers.
30 Hennessy, *Whitehall*, p. 183; and Peter Riddell and Catherine Haddon, *Transitions: Preparing for Changes of Government* (London: Institute for Government, 2010), pp. 18–20.
31 Interview with Roger Dawe, 22 January 2010.
32 Marcia Williams, *Inside Number 10*, p. 20.
33 Kavanagh and Seldon, *The Powers Behind the Prime Minister*, p. 64.
34 Williams, *Inside Number 10*, p. 20.
35 Ibid., p. 21.
36 Ibid.
37 Obituary of Sir Derek Mitchell, *The Times*, 21 August 2009. This incident is also described in more detail in Kavanagh and Seldon, *The Powers Behind the Prime Minister*, pp. 62–3.
38 Obituary of Sir Timothy Bligh, *The Times*, 13 March 1969.

5. REFORM AND THE ARRIVAL OF SPECIAL ADVISERS: PRIVATE OFFICE 1964–70

1   'The Civil Service: Report of the Committee 1966–68' ('Fulton report'), Cmnd 3638 (London: HMSO, 1968).
2   For general political histories of the period and the Prime Ministers, see, in particular, Hennessy, *The Prime Minister*, pp. 286–396; Hennessy, *Winds of Change*, esp. on the run-up to the general election of 1964; Peter Hennessy and Anthony Seldon (eds), *Ruling Performance: British Governments from Attlee to Thatcher* (Oxford: Blackwell, 1987); Brian Lapping, *The Labour Government 1964–70* (London: Penguin Books, 1970); Kenneth O. Morgan, *Britain Since 1945* (Oxford: Oxford University Press, 2001); Clive Ponting, *Breach of Promise: Labour in Power 1964–70* (London: Hamish Hamilton, 1989); Dominic Sandbrook, *White Heat: A History of Britain in the Swinging Sixties* (London: Little, Brown, 2006); Dominic Sandbrook, *State of Emergency: The Way We Were: Britain 1970–74* (London: Allen Lane, 2010); Dominic Sandbrook, *Seasons in the Sun: The Battle for Britain, 1974–79* (London: Allen Lane, 2012); and John Young, *The Labour Governments 1964–70* (Manchester: Manchester University Press, 2003). On the general elections of the period, see David Butler and Anthony King, *The British General Election of 1964* (London: Macmillan, 1965); David Butler and Anthony King, *The British General Election of 1966* (London: Macmillan, 1966); David Butler and Michael Pinto-Duschinsky, *The British General Election of 1970* (London: Macmillan, 1971); David Butler and Dennis Kavanagh, *The British General Election of February 1974* (London: Macmillan, 1974); and David Butler and Dennis Kavanagh, *The British General Election of October 1974* (London: Macmillan, 1975).
3   On UK relative economic decline, see, for example, Wilfred Beckerman (ed.), *The Labour Government's Economic Record 1964–1970* (London: Duckworth, 1972); Sam Brittan, *Steering the Economy: The Role of the Treasury* (London: Secker & Warburg, 1969); Alec Cairncross, *Managing the British Economy in the 1960s: A Treasury Perspective* (London: Palgrave Macmillan, 1996); Edmund Dell, *The Chancellors* (London: HarperCollins, 1996); Jim Tomlinson, *The Labour Governments 1964–1970, Vol. 3: Economic Policy* (Manchester: Manchester University Press, 2004); Jim Tomlinson, *The Politics of Decline* (Harlow: Pearson Education, 2000); and Jim Tomlinson, 'Inventing "Decline": the falling behind of the British economy in the post-war years', *Economic History Review*, 49/4 (1996), pp. 731–57.
4   On the civil service, Fulton and machinery of government issues, see, in particular, Andrew Blick, 'Harold Wilson, Labour and the Machinery of Government', *Contemporary British History*, 20/3 (2006), pp. 343–62; Davis, *Prime Ministers and Whitehall*; Lowe, *The Official History of the British Civil Service*; and Theakston, *The Civil Service Since 1945*.
5   On outsiders, experts and the first special advisers, see Blick and Jones, *At Power's Elbow*; Blick, *People Who Live in the Dark*; Kavanagh and Seldon, *The Powers Behind the Prime Minister*; and Theakston, *Leadership in Whitehall*.

6   Harold Wilson, *The Labour Government 1964-70* (London: Weidenfeld & Nicolson, 1971); Harold Wilson, *Final Term: The Labour Government 1974-76* (London: Weidenfeld & Nicolson, 1979); and Harold Wilson, *The Governance of Britain* (London: Weidenfeld & Nicolson, 1976).

7   Ben Pimlott, *Harold Wilson* (London: HarperCollins, 1992); Nick Thomas-Symonds, *The Winner* (London: Weidenfeld & Nicolson, 2022); and Philip Ziegler, *Wilson: The Authorised Life of Lord Wilson of Rievaulx* (London: Weidenfeld & Nicolson, 1993). See also Andrew Crines and Kevin Hickson (eds), *Harold Wilson: The Unprincipled Prime Minister* (London: Biteback, 2016).

8   Relevant autobiographies and memoirs include George Brown, *In My Way* (London: Victor Gollancz, 1971); James Callaghan, *Time and Chance* (London: Collins, 1987); Healey, *The Time of My Life*; Roy Jenkins, *A Life at the Centre* (London: Macmillan, 1991); and David Owen, *Time to Declare* (London: Penguin Books, 1992).

9   Tony Benn, *Out of the Wilderness: Diaries 1963-67* (London: Hutchinson, 1987), *Office Without Power: Diaries 1968-72* (London: Hutchinson, 1988) and *Against the Tide: Diaries 1973-77* (London: Hutchinson, 1989); Barbara Castle, *The Castle Diaries 1964-70* (London: Weidenfeld & Nicolson, 1974) and *The Castle Diaries 1974-76* (London: Weidenfeld & Nicolson, 1980); Richard Crossman, *The Diaries of a Cabinet Minister: Volume 1: Minister of Housing 1964-66* (London: Hamish Hamilton and Jonathan Cape, 1975), *The Diaries of a Cabinet Minister: Volume 2: Lord President of the Council and Leader of the House of Commons 1966-68* (London: Hamish Hamilton and Jonathan Cape, 1976) and *The Diaries of a Cabinet Minister: Volume 3: Secretary of State for Social Services 1968-70* (London: Hamish Hamilton and Jonathan Cape, 1977).

10 Bernard Donoughue, *Prime Minister: The Conduct of Policy Under Harold Wilson and James Callaghan* (London: Jonathan Cape, 1987), *The Heat of the Kitchen: An Autobiography* (London: Politico's, 2004), *Downing Street Diary: Volume 1 - With Harold Wilson in No. 10* (London: Jonathan Cape, 2004) and *Downing Street Diary: Volume 2 - With James Callaghan in No. 10* (London: Pimlico, 2009); Joe Haines, *The Politics of Power* (London: Jonathan Cape, 1977), *Glimmers of Twilight* (London: Politico's, 2003) and *Kick 'Em Back* (Tolworth: Grosvenor House Publishing, 2019); and David Lipsey, *In the Corridors of Power* (London: Biteback, 2012). Several of these volumes cover the Wilson governments and the Callaghan government. See also Williams, *Inside Number 10* and *Downing Street in Perspective* (London: Weidenfeld & Nicolson, 1983).

11 Edward Heath, *The Course of My Life* (London: Hodder & Stoughton, 1998). John Campbell, *Edward Heath: A Biography* (London: Jonathan Cape, 1993) and Philip Ziegler, *Edward Heath: The Authorized Biography* (London: HarperCollins, 2010). See also Michael McManus, *Edward Heath: A Singular Life* (London: Elliott and Thompson Limited, 2016).

12 Stuart Ball and Anthony Seldon (eds), *The Heath Government 1970-74* (London: Longman, 1990); Dennis Kavanagh, 'The Heath Government 1970-74', in Hennessy and Seldon (eds), *Ruling Performance*; and John Ramsden, *The Winds of Change: Macmillan to Heath 1957-1975* (London: Longman, 1996). See also Douglas Hurd, *Memoirs* (London: Abacus, 2004) and *An End to Promises: Sketch of a Government* (London: Collins, 1979).

13 Callaghan, *Time and Chance*; and Kenneth O. Morgan, *Callaghan: A Life* (Oxford: Oxford University Press, 1997).

14 See Pimlott, *Harold Wilson*, pp. 60-87 and Ziegler, *Harold Wilson*, pp. 30-40.

15 Hennessy, *The Prime Minister*, p. 293.

16 Thomas Balogh, 'The Apotheosis of the Dilettante', in Hugh Thomas (ed.), *The Establishment* (London: Anthony Blond, 1959), pp. 83-128. See p. 104 on the greater use of experts.

17 Ibid., p. 124.

18 Pimlott, *Harold Wilson*, p. 515.

19 Tony Benn, quoted in Ziegler, *Harold Wilson*, p. 170.

20 Balogh to Wilson, 6 February 1964, Wilson Archives, Bodleian Library, Oxford.

21 On the work of the group, see Hennessy, *Whitehall*, pp. 172-3.

22 *The Administrators*, pp. 41-2.

23 Ibid., pp. 39-41.

24 Ibid., p. 40.

25 See Lowe, *The Official History of the British Civil Service*, p. 91, citing Samuel Brittan, *The Treasury Under the Tories* (London: Secker & Warburg, 1964).

26 Pimlott, *Harold Wilson*, p. 275.

27 Lowe, *The Official History of the British Civil Service*, p. 93.

28 Davis, *Prime Ministers and Whitehall*, p. 7.

29 1964 Labour Party manifesto, *The New Britain* (London: Labour Party, 1964).

30 Hennessy, *The Prime Minister*, p. 293.
31 Donoughue, *Prime Minister, The Heat of the Kitchen, Downing Street Diary: Volume 1* and *Downing Street Diary: Volume 2*; Haines, *The Politics of Power, Glimmers of Twilight* and *Kick 'Em Back*; and Lipsey, *In the Corridors of Power*. Several of these volumes cover the Wilson governments and the Callaghan government. See also Williams, *Inside Number 10* and *Downing Street in Perspective*.
32 See, for example, Ben Pimlott, 'When Harold met Marcia', *The Independent*, 18 October 1992. See also Pimlott, *Harold Wilson*, pp. 199–211, Ziegler, *Wilson*, pp. 118–22 and Haines, *The Politics of Power*, especially pp. 157–97.
33 Pimlott, 'When Harold met Marcia'.
34 Hennessy, *The Prime Minister*, pp. 297–8.
35 Williams, *Inside Number 10*, p. 21.
36 Davis, *Prime Ministers and Whitehall*, p. 38.
37 Hennessy, *The Prime Minister*, p. 299.
38 Haines, *The Politics of Power*, p. 155.
39 Pimlott, 'When Harold met Marcia'.
40 Interview with Roger Dawe.
41 Ibid.
42 Interview with Joe Haines.
43 See Hennessy, *The Prime Minister*, p. 299.
44 Interview with Roger Dawe.
45 Ibid.
46 Ibid.
47 Ibid.
48 Pimlott, *Harold Wilson*, p. 347, quoting an unnamed No. 10 official.
49 Interview with Roger Dawe.
50 Ibid.
51 Pimlott, *Harold Wilson*, p. 347.
52 See Ziegler, *Wilson*, p. 184 and Hennessy, *The Prime Minister*, p. 307.
53 Ziegler, *Wilson*, p. 184.
54 Interview with Roger Dawe.
55 *The Times*, 20 January 1967.
56 Interview with Roger Dawe.
57 Ibid.
58 Wigg to Wilson, 17 July 1966, Wilson Archives, Bodleian Library, Oxford.
59 See Jane Burnham and George Jones, 'Innovators at 10 Downing Street', in Kevin Theakston (ed.), *Bureaucrats and Leadership* (Basingstoke: Macmillan, 2000), p. 85.
60 See Haines, *The Politics of Power, Glimmers of Twilight* and *Kick 'Em Back*.
61 Pimlott, *Harold Wilson*, pp. 323–47.
62 Blick, *People who Live in the Dark*, pp. 63–75 and pp. 90–122.
63 Blick, 'Harold Wilson, Labour and the Machinery of Government', pp. 343–62.
64 Blick, *People Who Live in the Dark*, pp. 74–5.
65 Ziegler, *Wilson*, p. 94.
66 Blick, *People Who Live in the Dark*, p. 64.
67 Ibid., p. 88.
68 Ibid., p. 89. *Annual Report on Special Advisers* (Cabinet Office, 2019).
69 Blick, 'Harold Wilson, Labour and the Machinery of Government', pp. 350–51.
70 Statement by the Prime Minister, Hansard, *House of Commons Debates*, columns 209–10, 8 February 1966.
71 Fulton report.
72 Lowe, *The Official History of the British Civil Service*, p. 92.
73 Fulton rejected the French *cabinet* model. See Fulton report, para. 285, p. 94.
74 Ibid.
75 Ibid., p. 95.
76 Wilson, *The Labour Government 1964–1970*, pp. 539–41.
77 See Lowe, *The Official History of the British Civil Service*, pp. 114–28 and Hennessy, *Whitehall*, pp. 190–208.
78 Healey, *The Time of My Life*, p. 268.
79 Ibid.
80 Ibid.
81 Ibid.
82 Interview with Denis Healey.

83 Richard Crossman, quoted in the obituary of George Moseley, *Daily Telegraph*, 12 December 2011.

84 Crossman, *Diaries: Volume 1*, p. 184.

85 Ibid., p. 618.

86 Tam Dalyell, *New Scientist*, 23 November 1972.

87 Pimlott, *Harold Wilson*, p. 403.

88 Campbell, *Roy Jenkins*, pp. 262–3.

89 Interview with Roger Dawe.

90 Ibid.

91 Philip Allen, 'A Young Home Secretary', in Andrew Adonis and Keith Thomas (eds), *Roy Jenkins: A Retrospective* (Oxford: Oxford University Press, 2004), p. 81.

92 Roy Jenkins, obituary of David Dowler, *The Times*, 13 January 1970.

93 Jenkins, *A Life at the Centre*, p. 170.

94 Campbell, *Roy Jenkins*, p. 264.

95 Ziegler, *Wilson*, p. 213 and Hennessy, *The Prime Minister*, p. 298.

96 Davis, *Prime Ministers and Whitehall*, p. 62, citing correspondence between Helsby and Wilson.

97 Ziegler, *Wilson*, p. 214.

98 TNA, BA 7/40, Details of the legal case subsequently brought by Halls's widow, Marjorie, against the civil service department, 1973.

99 Interview with Roger Dawe.

100 Correspondence with Lord Armstrong, 15 November 2019.

101 Pimlott, *Harold Wilson*, p. 519.

102 Interview with Roger Dawe.

103 TNA, BA 7/40, Marjorie Halls's evidence to the High Court of Justice, 4 March 1974.

104 Davis, *Prime Ministers and Whitehall*, pp. 62–8.

105 Wilson, *The Labour Government 1964–1970*, p. 774.

106 Ziegler, *Wilson*, p. 315.

107 Wilson, *The Labour Government 1964–1970*, p. 774.

108 See Butler and King, *The British General Election of 1966*.

109 See, for example, his obituaries in *The Times*, 6 April 2020 and the *Daily Telegraph*, 6 April 2020.

110 Interview with Lord Armstrong.

111 Ibid.

112 Jenkins, *A Life at the Centre*, p. 221.

113 Ibid.; and Campbell, *Roy Jenkins*, p. 473.

6. GOVERNING IN HARD TIMES: PRIVATE OFFICE 1970–79

1 See Mortimore and Blick, *Butler's British Political Facts*, pp. 425 and 604.

2 See, for example, his interview with Anthony Barker, 'Heath on Whitehall Reform', *Parliamentary Affairs*, 31/4 (1978), pp. 363–90.

3 Anthony King, 'Overload: Problems of Governing in the 1970s', *Political Studies*, 23/2 (1975), pp. 284–96; and Anthony King (ed.), *Why is Britain becoming so hard to govern?* (London: BBC, 1976).

4 Heath, *The Course of My Life*, p. 314.

5 Hennessy, *Cabinet*, p. 74.

6 Obituary of Sir Edward Heath, *Daily Telegraph*, 18 July 2005.

7 Campbell, *Edward Heath*, p. 291.

8 See Kevin Theakston, 'The Heath Government, Whitehall and the Civil Service', in Ball and Seldon (eds), *The Heath Government*, pp. 75–106.

9 Kavanagh and Seldon, *The Powers Behind the Prime Minister*, pp. 73–4. See also Lowe, *The Official History of the British Civil Service*, pp. 162–4. Barker and Heath interview, 'Heath on Whitehall Reform', pp. 363–90.

10 Campbell, *Edward Heath*, p. 19.

11 1970 Conservative Party manifesto, *A Better Tomorrow* (London: Conservative Party, 1970).

12 Hennessy, *Cabinet*, p. 74.

13 Heath, *The Course of My Life*, p. 314.

14 'The Reorganisation of Central Government', Cmnd 4506 (London: HMSO, 1970).

15 Hennessy, *Cabinet*, p. 75.

16 'The Reorganisation of Central Government'. The key elements are summarised in Hennessy, *The Prime Minister*, pp. 339–40.

17 On the machinery of government changes, see Christopher Pollitt, *Manipulating the Machine: Changing the Pattern of Ministerial Departments, 1960–83* (London: Allen and Unwin, 1984).

18 On Heath's machinery of government changes, see Campbell, *Edward Heath* pp. 314–27; Davis, *Prime Ministers and Whitehall*, esp. pp. 113–43; Hennessy, *The Prime Minister*, pp. 331–56; Kavanagh and Seldon, *The Powers Behind the Prime Minister*, pp. 95–102 and pp. 167–9; Lowe, *The Official History of the British Civil Service*, pp. 162–92; Pollitt, *Manipulating the Machine*; and Theakston, *The Civil Service Since 1945*, esp. pp. 108–19. For Heath's personal views on machinery of government issues, see Barker and Heath interview, 'Heath on Whitehall Reform'.

19 Campbell, *Edward Heath*, p. 313.

20 Davis, *Prime Ministers and Whitehall*, p. 157.

21 Theakston, *The Civil Service Since 1945*, p. 113.

22 Lowe, *The Official History of the British Civil Service*, pp. 162–92.

23 There is a wide body of literature on the CPRS: Tessa Blackstone and William Plowden, *Advising the Cabinet 1971–1983* (London: Heinemann, 1988) was written by two former members of the CPRS and is a history of its role and the studies it carried out. For analysis of its effectiveness, see Davis, *Prime Ministers and Whitehall*, pp. 116–32; Hennessy, *Whitehall*, pp. 221–35; Peter Hennessy, Susan Morrison and Richard Townsend, *Routine Punctuated by Orgies: The Central Policy Review Staff, 1970–83*, Strathclyde papers on government and politics, no. 31 (Glasgow: University of Strathclyde, 1985); Simon James, 'The Central Policy Review Staff 1970–1983', *Political Studies*, 34/3 (1986), pp. 423–40; Lowe, *The Official History of the British Civil Service*, pp. 165–70; and Theakston, *The Civil Service Since 1945*, pp. 109–13. Jago, *Robin Butler*, pp. 49–65 looks at the CPRS from Butler's perspective as one of its first members.

24 Davis, *Prime Ministers and Whitehall*, p. 110.

25 Theakston, *The Civil Service Since 1945*, p. 114.

26 Kavanagh and Seldon, *The Powers Behind the Prime Minister*, pp. 98–102; Lewis Baston and Anthony Seldon, 'Number 10 Under Edward Heath', in Ball and Seldon (eds), *The Heath Government 1970–74*, pp. 47–74.

27 Baston and Seldon, 'Number 10 Under Edward Heath', p. 71.

28 Ibid., p. 74.

29 Heath, *The Course of My Life*, esp. pp. 312–18.

30 Ibid., p. 313.

31 Ibid.

32 Theakston, 'The Heath Government, Whitehall and the Civil Service', p. 86.

33 Hennessy, *The Prime Minister*, p. 340.

34 Personal correspondence with Lord Butler.

35 Heath, *The Course of My Life*, p. 312.

36 Ibid, pp. 308–9.

37 Jon Davis, *Prime Ministers and Whitehall*, p. 99.

38 *The Times*, 11 July 1970.

39 Ibid.

40 Interview with Lord Armstrong.

41 Ibid.

42 Correspondence with Lord Armstrong, subsequent to interview.

43 Campbell, *Edward Heath*, p. 489.

44 Theakston, *Leadership in Whitehall*, pp. 203–4.

45 Personal correspondence with Lord Butler.

46 Campbell, *Edward Heath*, p. 489.

47 Interview with Lord Armstrong.

48 Ibid.

49 Obituary of Robert Armstrong, *Daily Telegraph*, 6 April 2020.

50 Heath, *The Course of My Life*, p. 311.

51 Interview with Lord Butler, 29 September 2010.

52 Ziegler, *Edward Heath*, p. 244.

53 Interview with Lord Armstrong.

54 Ibid.

55 Ibid.

56 Personal correspondence with Lord Butler.

57 Hennessy, *The Prime Minister*, p. 337.

58 Lowe, *The Official History of the British Civil Service*, p. 165.

59 Davis, *Prime Ministers and Whitehall*, pp. 106–7.

60 Jago, *Robin Butler*, pp. 72–7.

61 Heath, *The Course of My Life*, p. 311.
62 Personal correspondence with Lord Butler.
63 Interview with Lord Armstrong.
64 Hurd, *An End to Promises*, p. 32.
65 Ibid., p. 35.
66 Barker and Heath interview, 'Heath on Whitehall Reform', p. 388.
67 Obituary of Sir Donald Maitland, *Daily Telegraph*, 25 August 2010.
68 Theakston, *Leadership in Whitehall*, p. 204.
69 Interview with Lord Armstrong.
70 Blick and Jones, *At Power's Elbow*, p. 244.
71 Heath, *The Course of My Life*, p. 365.
72 Ibid.
73 Uwe Kitzinger, *Diplomacy and Persuasion: How Britain Joined the Common Market* (London: Thames & Hudson, 1973) pp. 115–16, and cited in Campbell, *Edward Heath*, p. 356.
74 Heath, *The Course of My Life*, p. 364.
75 TNA PREM 15/62, Minute from W. A. Neild (Cabinet Office) to the Prime Minister, 19 June 1970.
76 Alan Campbell, 'Anglo-French Relations a Decade Ago: A new Assessment (2)', *International Affairs*, 58/3 (1982), pp. 329–446.
77 Ibid. p. 432.
78 Interview with Lord Armstrong.
79 Seldon, *The Cabinet Office 1916–2016*, p. 178.
80 Campbell, *Edward Heath*, p. 491.
81 For the detailed history of the final negotiations, see Stephen Wall, *The Official History of Britain and the European Community, Vol. II: From Rejection to Referendum 1963–75* (London: Routledge, 2013), pp. 405–56.
82 TNA PREM 15/1507, Note for the record, Robert Armstrong meeting with Michel Jobert, 9 and 10 April 1973.
83 Ibid.
84 Ibid., Comment from Heath on Armstrong's note of his meetings with Jobert, 21 April 1973.
85 TNA PREM 15/1507, Note for the record, Armstrong to Heath, 17 September 1973.
86 Ibid.
87 Ibid.
88 Campbell, *Edward Heath*, p. 552.
89 For the complete analysis of the election, see Butler and Kavanagh, *The British General Election of February 1974*.
90 Correspondence with Lord Armstrong, 15 November 2019.
91 Comment by Robin Butler. Queen Mary University of London seminar on the February 1974 election, 28 February 2024.
92 TNA PREM 16/231, Note for the record, Armstrong, 16 March 1974. This note is also available via the Margaret Thatcher Foundation archives: https://www.margaretthatcher.org/document/110605.
93 Ibid.
94 Ibid.
95 Heath, *The Course of My Life*, p. 518. See also Jeremy Thorpe, *In My Own Time* (London: Politico's, 1999).
96 TNA PREM 16/231, Note for the record, Armstrong, 16 March 1974.
97 Private correspondence with Lord Armstrong.
98 Ibid.
99 Ibid.
100 Ibid.
101 Margaret Thatcher Foundation archives (MTA THCR 1/9/18A/17 f12).
102 Butler and Kavanagh, *The British General Election of February 1974*, p. 95.
103 Donoughue, *Downing Street Diary: Volume 1*, p. 56.
104 Donoughue, *Prime Minister*, p. 20.
105 Ibid.
106 Wilson, *The Governance of Britain*, p. 246.
107 Interview with Lord Donoughue.
108 Donoughue, *Prime Minister*, p. 19.
109 Ibid., pp. 51–78.
110 Private correspondence with Lord Butler.

111 Interview with Lord Butler.
112 Private correspondence with Lord Armstrong.
113 Pimlott, *Harold Wilson*, p. 622.
114 Haines, *Glimmers of Twilight*, p. 95. See also Jago, *Robin Butler*, p. 90.
115 Personal correspondence with Lord Butler.
116 Ibid.
117 Interview with Lord Armstrong.
118 Obituary of Sir Kenneth Stowe, *The Times*, 11 September 2015.
119 Obituary of Sir Kenneth Stowe, *The Guardian*, 16 September 2015.
120 Interview with Bernard Donoughue.
121 Donoughue, *Prime Minister*, p. 18.
122 Interview with Joe Haines.
123 Interview with Lord Lipsey, 5 February 2018.
124 See Donoughue, *Prime Minister*, esp. pp. 79–88 and Donoughue, *Downing Street Diary: Volume 1*, pp. 560–616.
125 Seldon, *The Cabinet Office 1916–2016*, p. 183.
126 Interview with Joe Haines.
127 Ibid.
128 Ibid.
129 Ibid.
130 Lipsey, *In the Corridors of Power*, p. 117.
131 Kenneth O. Morgan, 'A Comparative Case Study of Labour Prime Ministers Attlee, Wilson, Callaghan and Blair', *Journal of Legislative Studies*, 10/2–3 (2006), pp. 38–52.
132 Ibid.
133 Hennessy, *The Prime Minister*, p. 391.
134 See, for example: Kathleen Burk and Alec Cairncross, *Goodbye, Great Britain: The 1976 IMF Crisis* (London: Yale University Press, 1992); Ben Clift and Jim Tomlinson, 'Negotiating Credibility: Britain and the International Monetary Fund 1956–1976', *Contemporary European History*, 17/4 (2008), pp. 545–66; Edmund Dell, *A Hard Pounding: Politics and Economic Crisis 1974–76* (Oxford: Oxford University Press, 1991); William Keegan, *Nine Crises* (London: Biteback, 2019), pp. 97–114; Richard Rogers, *When Britain Went Bust* (London: OMFIF, 2016); and Douglas Wass, *Decline to Fall: The Making of British Macro-Economic Policy and the 1976 IMF Crisis* (Oxford: Oxford University Press, 2008).
135 Hennessy, *The Prime Minister*, p. 385.
136 Donoughue, *Prime Minister*, p. 85.
137 PREM 16/798, Wright to Stowe, 24 August 1976.
138 Roberts, *When Britain Went Bust*, p. 53.
139 Ibid., p. 7.
140 Healey, *The Time of My Life*, p. 431.
141 TNA PREM 16/799, Note for the record, Prime Minister's meeting with Chancellor Schmidt, 11 October 1976.
142 Morgan, *Callaghan*, p. 547.
143 Donoughue, *Downing Street Diary: Volume 2*, p. 102.
144 Ibid.
145 TNA PREM 16/802, Stowe to Hunt, 19 November 1976.
146 Morgan, *Callaghan*, p. 665.
147 Peter Hennessy, *Muddling Through: Power, Politics and the Quality of Government in Post-War Britain* (London: Victor Gollancz, 1996).

7. PERSONALITIES AND WARS: PRIVATE OFFICE 1979–90

1 Margaret Thatcher, *The Downing Street Years* (London: HarperCollins, 1993), p. 435.
2 Geoffrey Howe, *Conflict of Loyalty* (London: Macmillan, 1994), p. 471; Charles Moore, *Margaret Thatcher, Volume 2*, p. 485.
3 Moore, *Margaret Thatcher, Volume 2*, p. 485.
4 There is a wealth of literature on Thatcher and on what later became known as 'Thatcherism'. The online resources at the Margaret Thatcher Foundation at Churchill College, Cambridge, are the richest source of archive documentation: www.margaretthatcher.org. Government records belonging to her time in office can be found in the PREM 19 series of files at the National Archives (TNA). There is also an excellent series of interviews produced by the King's College Policy Institute on 'Margaret Thatcher and No. 10' at www.

thatcherandnumberten.com. See also, on the 1979 election, David Butler and Dennis Kavanagh, *The British General Election of 1979* (London: Macmillan, 1980).

5   See, for example, Dennis Kavanagh, *Thatcherism and British Politics* (Oxford: Oxford University Press, 1990); Peter Riddell, *The Thatcher Era and Its Legacy* (Oxford: Blackwell, 1989); and Hugo Young, *One of Us* (London: Macmillan, 1989).

6   Notably the authorised biography by Charles Moore, *Volume 1: Not for Turning* (London: Allen Lane, 2013), *Volume 2: Everything She Wants* (London: Allen Lane, 2016) and *Volume 3: Herself Alone* (London: Allen Lane, 2019). Other biographies include John Campbell's two-volume work, *Margaret Thatcher: The Grocer's Daughter* (London: Random House, 2001) and *Margaret Thatcher: The Iron Lady* (London, Jonathan Cape, 2003). David Cannadine, *Margaret Thatcher: A Life and Legacy* (Oxford: Oxford University Press, 2017) is a shorter volume based on the *Dictionary of National Biography* entry. Thatcher's two-volume autobiography is: Thatcher, *The Downing Street Years* and *The Path to Power* (London: HarperCollins, 1995). Memoirs include: Kenneth Baker, *The Turbulent Years: My Life in Politics* (London: Faber and Faber, 1993); John Biffen, *Semi-Detached* (London: Biteback, 2013); Lord Carrington, *Reflect on Things Past* (London: Collins, 1988); Kenneth Clarke, *Kind of Blue* (London: Macmillan, 2016); Norman Fowler, *Ministers Decide* (London: Chapmans Publishing, 1991); Ian Gilmour, *Dancing With Dogma* (London: Simon & Schuster, 1992); Lord Hailsham, *A Sparrow's Flight* (London: Collins, 1990); Michael Heseltine, *Life in the Jungle* (London: Hodder & Stoughton, 2000); Howe, *Conflict of Loyalty*; Hurd, *Memoirs*; Nigel Lawson, *The View from No. 11* (London: Bantam Press, 1992); John Nott, *Here Today, Gone Tomorrow* (London: Politico's, 2002); Cecil Parkinson, *Right at the Centre* (London: Weidenfeld & Nicolson, 1992); James Prior, *Balance of Power* (London: Hamish Hamilton, 1986); Francis Pym, *The Politics of Consent* (London: Hamish Hamilton, 1984); Nicholas Ridley, *My Style of Government: The Thatcher Years* (London: Hutchinson, 1991); Malcolm Rifkind, *Power and Pragmatism* (London: Biteback, 2016); Norman Tebbit, *Upwardly Mobile* (London: Weidenfeld & Nicolson, 1988); Peter Walker, *An Autobiography* (London: Bloomsbury, 1991); William Whitelaw, *The Whitelaw Memoirs* (London: Arum Press, 1989); and Lord Young, *The Enterprise Years* (London: Headline, 1990).

7   See, for example: Richard Vinen, *Thatcher's Britain: The Politics and Social Upheaval of the 1980s* (London: Simon & Schuster, 2009); Tim Bale, *The Conservative Party from Thatcher to Cameron* (Cambridge: Polity Press, 2010); and Ben Jackson and Rob Saunders (eds), *Making Thatcher's Britain* (Cambridge: Cambridge University Press, 2012).

8   Kavanagh and Seldon, *The Powers Behind the Prime Minister* contains the most comprehensive analysis of support available to the Prime Minister from private office, special advisers, political advisers and others. Moore and Young both analyse the role of Charles Powell in particular. In addition, Jago's *Robin Butler* is a biography of another of Thatcher's key private office members.

9   Sir Percy Cradock (Thatcher's foreign affairs policy adviser) quoted in Jago, *Robin Butler*, p. 179.

10 Moore, *Margaret Thatcher, Volume 1*, p. 419.

11 Ibid., p. 420.

12 Ibid.

13 Thatcher, *The Downing Street Years*, p. 18.

14 A full list of all the members of the No. 10 private office from 1945 to 1999 is contained in Kavanagh and Seldon, *The Powers Behind the Prime Minister*, pp. 327–44.

15 Interview with Lord Powell, 3 November 2010.

16 Bernard Ingham, in conversation with Charles Moore, www.thatcherandnumberten.com#ingham.

17 Kavanagh and Seldon, *The Powers Behind the Prime Minister*, p. 148.

18 Anonymous quote from one of Thatcher's private secretaries, quoted in ibid., p. 149.

19 John Hoskyns, *Just in Time: Inside the Thatcher Revolution* (London: Aurum Press, 2000), p. 99.

20 Interview with Peter Riddell, 20 October 2017, and subsequent correspondence.

21 Ibid.

22 TNA PREM 19/248 F183, Stowe to all Cabinet ministers' private secretaries, 7 May 1979.

23 Moore, *Margaret Thatcher, Volume 1*, p. 432.

24 Kavanagh and Seldon, *The Powers Behind the Prime Minister*, p. 162.

25 Private information.

26 See MTA INGH 2/1/1, No. 10 lobby briefing, 9 May 1979.

27 Interview with Lord Turnbull, 22 December 2011.

28 Ibid.

29 Ibid.

30 Ibid.

31 See Mortimore and Blick, *Butler's British Political Facts*, p. 433.

32 The definitive guide to the Falklands War is the official history: Lawrence Freedman, *The Official History of the Falklands Campaign: Volume 1 – The Origins of the Falklands War* (Abingdon: Routledge Press, 2005) and *Volume 2 – War and Diplomacy* (Abingdon: Routledge Press, 2005). The official report into the war, chaired by Lord Franks, is 'Falkland Islands Review: Report of a Committee of Privy Counsellors' ('Franks review') (London: HMSO, 1983). In addition, many of the politicians in Thatcher's Cabinet have written about the Falklands War in their memoirs, as did Bernard Ingham. On the operation of the War Cabinet, see Freedman, *The Official History of the Falklands Campaign: Volume 2*, pp. 21–8, and Hennessy, *The Prime Minister*, pp. 416–20.

33 Freedman, *The Official History of the Falklands Campaign: Volume 2*, p. 16.

34 Interview with David Omand, 30 July 2015.

35 Ibid.

36 Freedman, *The Official History of the Falklands Campaign: Volume 1*, p. 208; Moore, *Margaret Thatcher, Volume 1*, pp. 666–67; and Nott, *Here Today, Gone Tomorrow*, p. 257.

37 Moore, *Margaret Thatcher, Volume 1*, p. 667.

38 Ibid.

39 Freedman, *The Official History of the Falklands Campaign: Volume 1*, p. 210.

40 Freedman, *The Official History of the Falklands Campaign: Volume 2*, p. 14.

41 Ibid.

42 For the full speech, see Hansard, *House of Commons Debates*, columns 633–68, 3 April 1982.

43 Interview with David Omand.

44 Ibid.

45 TNA CAB 292/47, Franks Committee Falkland Islands Review Committee, Note of oral evidence session with the Prime Minister, 25 October 1982.

46 John Coles interviewed by the BBC, *Thatcher: Part 3*, 3 June 2019.

47 John Coles interviewed by Malcolm McBain, British Diplomatic Oral History Programme (BDOHP), Churchill College Archives, Cambridge, 2 November 1999.

48 Mortimore and Blick, *Butler's British Political Facts*, p. 433.

49 ONS data: https://www.ons.gov.uk/economy/grossdomesticproductgdp/timeseries/ihyq/pn2.

50 MTA, John Coles, 'An Appreciation of Margaret Thatcher', released 2014, p. 4.

51 Jago, *Robin Butler*. See Tony Blair, *A Journey* (London: Hutchinson, 2010), p. 16.

52 Jago, *Robin Butler*, p. 120.

53 Interview with Lord Butler.

54 Ibid.

55 Ibid.

56 See Jago, *Robin Butler*, p. 133.

57 Butler, as quoted in Jago, pp. 143–4.

58 See TNA PREM19/578 f278 Heseltine to Thatcher, 13 August 1981.

59 The full story of the Brighton bombing is told in Rory Carroll, *Killing Thatcher: The IRA, the Manhunt and the Long War on the Crown* (London: HarperCollins, 2023).

60 Butler, quoted in Jago, *Robin Butler*, p. 144.

61 Butler interviewed by the BBC, *Thatcher: Part 3*, 3 June 2019.

62 Correspondence with Lord Butler, 3 December 2019.

63 Ibid.

64 Interview with Lord Powell, 3 November 2010.

65 Vinen, *Thatcher's Britain*, pp. 265–7 and pp. 313–15.

66 See, for example, Patrick Dunleavy, 'Reinterpreting the Westland Affair: Theories of the State and Core Executive Decision Making', *Public Administration*, Volume 68/1 (1990), pp. 29–60; Lawrence Freedman, 'The Case of Westland and the Bias to Europe', *International Affairs*, 63/1 (1986/87), pp. 1–19; Peter Hennessy, 'Helicopter Crashes into Cabinet: Prime Minister and Constitution Hurt', *Law and Society*, 13/3 (1986), pp. 423–32; and Dawn Oliver and Rodney Austin, 'Political and Constitutional Aspects of the Westland Affair', *Parliamentary Affairs*, 40/1 (1987), pp. 20–40. For a journalistic account of the Westland Affair, see Magnus Linklater and David Leigh, *Not with Honour: The Inside Story of the Westland Scandal* (London: Sphere Books, 1986).

67 Thatcher, *The Downing Street Years*, pp. 423–37 and Heseltine, *Life in the Jungle*, pp. 293–333. Thatcher refers to Powell only once in this section, while Heseltine mentions Mottram (his principal private secretary) twice in passing.

68 Moore, *Margaret Thatcher, Volume 2*, especially pp. 449–98.

69 Young, *One of Us*, pp. 439–46.

70 Vinen, Richard, 'The Iron Lady & The Little Men', *Literary Review*, Issue 481, November 2019.

71 Moore, *Margaret Thatcher, Volume 2*, p. 453.

72 See, for example, Michael Crick, *Michael Heseltine* (London: Penguin, 1997), p. 55.

73 Crick, *Michael Heseltine*; Julian Critchley, *Heseltine: The Unauthorised Biography* (London: Andre Deutsch, 1987); and Heseltine, *Life in the Jungle*.

74 See Hennessy, *Whitehall*, pp. 607–8 and Crick, *Michael Heseltine*, pp. 205–9, for a description of how MINIS operated in the Department of the Environment.

75 Interview with Mark Gibson (Heseltine's principal private secretary at DTI and the Cabinet Office), 7 November 2011.

76 Heseltine, *Life in the Jungle*, p. 189.

77 Ibid.

78 Ibid.

79 Interview with Mark Gibson.

80 Heseltine, *Life in the Jungle*, p. 240.

81 Interview with Richard Mottram, 20 December 2016.

82 Ibid.

83 Ibid.

84 Interview with Lord Powell.

85 Moore, *Margaret Thatcher, Volume 2*, p. 456.

86 Ibid.

87 Interview with Richard Mottram.

88 Heseltine describes this episode in *Life in the Jungle*, pp. 277–9. Moore also refers to it in *Margaret Thatcher, Volume 2*, p. 452.

89 Interview with Lord Powell, 26 November 2010.

90 Interviews with Lord Powell and Richard Mottram.

91 Interview with Richard Mottram.

92 Ibid.

93 Ibid.

94 Ibid.

95 Ibid.

96 Moore, *Margaret Thatcher, Volume 3*, p. 102.

97 For the full chronology of events, see Moore, *Margaret Thatcher, Volume 2*, pp. 464–72.

98 Interview with Richard Mottram.

99 *The Times*, 4 January 1986.

100 Moore, *Margaret Thatcher, Volume 2*, p. 466.

101 Ibid.

102 Ibid., pp. 466–7.

103 TNA PREM 19/1667, Powell to Thatcher, 4 January 1986. Also cited in Moore, *Margaret Thatcher, Volume 2*, p. 467.

104 Moore, *Margaret Thatcher, Volume 2*, p. 468.

105 Ibid., p. 491.

106 Interview with Lord Powell.

107 Bernard Ingham, *Kill the Messenger* (London: HarperCollins, 1991), p. 335.

108 Moore, *Margaret Thatcher, Volume 2*, p. 468.

109 Clarke, *Kind of Blue*, p. 153.

110 Thatcher, *The Downing Street Years*, p. 42.

111 Private information.

112 TNA PREM 19/1668, Handwritten note by Amanda Ross (Downing Street clerk), 15 January 1986.

113 Private information.

114 Interview with Richard Mottram.

115 Ibid.

116 Interview with Lord Armstrong.

117 Armstrong, as cited in Jago, *Robin Butler*, p. 165.

118 Owen, *Time to Declare*, p. 637.

119 Interview with Lord Butler.

120 Charles Powell, quoted in Moore, *Margaret Thatcher, Volume 2*, p. 494.

121 Young, *One of Us*, p. 456.

122 See, for example, *The Times*, 6 February 1986, p. 1.

123 'Westland plc: The Government's Decision-making, Fourth Report from the Select Committee on Defence', HC 519, published 23 July 1986.
124 Ibid., pp. lxii–lxiii.
125 *The Times*, 25 July 1986, p. 13.
126 Interview with Richard Mottram.
127 Seldon and Kavanagh first used the phrase in *The Powers Behind the Prime Minister*, p. 18, but they did not elaborate on the implications.
128 Thatcher, *The Downing Street Years*, p. 20 and p. 747.
129 Moore, *Margaret Thatcher, Volumes 2 and 3* and Campbell, *Margaret Thatcher*.
130 Kavanagh and Seldon, *The Powers Behind the Prime Minister*; Hennessy, *The Prime Minister*; and David Richards, 'The Conservatives, New Labour and Whitehall: A Biographical Examination of the Political Flexibility of the Mandarin Cadre', in Theakston (ed.), *Bureaucrats and Leadership*, pp. 91–117.
131 Young, *One of Us*, p. 445.
132 Ibid., p. 446.
133 Percy Cradock, *In Pursuit of British Interests: Reflections on Foreign Policy under Margaret Thatcher and John Major* (London: John Murray, 1997), p. 15.
134 Jago, *Robin Butler*, p. 180; and Moore, *Margaret Thatcher, Volume 3*, pp. 306–12.
135 Interviews with Lord Armstrong, Lord Butler and Lord Turnbull.
136 Moore, *Margaret Thatcher, Volume 1*, p. 440.
137 Interview with Lord Powell.
138 Young, *One of Us*, p. 496.
139 Hennessy, *The Hidden Wiring*, p. 124.
140 See, for example, *The Times*, 21 September 1988.
141 Who's Who Online: http//www.ukwhoswho.com.
142 Interview with Lord Powell.
143 Seminar on Germany, 24 March 1990, summary record 25 March 1990, released to the MTA.
144 Ibid.
145 Ibid.
146 Slocock, *People Like Us*, p. 49.
147 Cowper-Coles, *Ever the Diplomat*, p. 85.
148 Interview with Lord Butler.
149 Moore, *Margaret Thatcher, Volume 2*, p. 603.
150 Private information from various sources.
151 See Moore, *Margaret Thatcher, Volumes 2 and 3*, and John Dickie, *Inside the Foreign Office* (London: Chapmans, 1992), esp. pp. 267–87.
152 Moore, *Margaret Thatcher, Volume 3*, p. 102.
153 Interview with Lord Butler.
154 Interviews with Lord Armstrong and Lord Butler.
155 Charles Powell, quoted in Kavanagh and Seldon, *The Powers Behind the Prime Minister*, p. 184.
156 Young, *One of Us*, pp. 456–7.
157 Lawson, *The View from No. 10*, p. 680.
158 Charles Powell, interviewed by Sir Kevin Tebbit, www.thatcherandnumberten.com#powell.
159 Ibid.
160 As reported by Powell to Moore in correspondence and as footnoted in Moore, *Margaret Thatcher, Volume 2*, p. 700.
161 Interview with Lord Powell.
162 MTA, Powell letter to Thatcher, 13 June 1987, THCR 1/3/23 f28.
163 Charles Powell interviewed by the BBC, *Thatcher: Part 4*, 10 June 2019.
164 Interview with Lord Turnbull.
165 Interview with Lord Armstrong.
166 Ibid.
167 Hennessy, *The Prime Minister*, pp. 405–6.
168 Moore, *Margaret Thatcher, Volume 3*, p. 307.
169 This is certainly Moore's view. See Moore, *Margaret Thatcher, Volume 3*, p. 308.
170 Turnbull's note for the record of a meeting between Thatcher and Butler, 13 June 1989. Quoted in Moore, *Margaret Thatcher, Volume 3*, p. 308.
171 Ibid.
172 Interview with Lord Powell.

173 Interview with Lord Turnbull.
174 See Alan Clark, *Diaries* (London: Phoenix, 1994), p. 226.
175 See ibid., pp. 122–52, and Hugo Young, *This Blessed Plot* (London: Papermac, 1999), pp. 346–52 on Powell's role in drafting the speech.
176 For the full text of the Bruges speech, delivered on 20 September 1988, see MTA, https://www.margaretthatcher.org/document/107332.
177 Interview with Lord Powell.
178 Ibid.
179 Ibid.
180 Ibid.
181 MTA, Minute from John Kerr to the private secretary to the Foreign Secretary, 16 September 1988.
182 Interview with Lord Powell.
183 Moore, *Margaret Thatcher, Volume 3*, p. 149.
184 Ibid., p. 150.
185 Ibid., pp. 324–5.
186 PREM 19/3000, Powell to Thatcher, 18 March 1990.
187 Moore, *Margaret Thatcher, Volume 3*, pp. 297–8.
188 Ibid., pp. 314–22.
189 MTA, George Younger, 'Post-mortem meeting notes', 6 December 1989.
190 Ibid.
191 See Howe's resignation speech, Hansard, *House of Commons Debates*, columns 461–5, 13 November 1989.
192 Interview with Lord Powell.
193 Ibid.
194 Ibid.
195 Interview with Lord Turnbull.
196 Ibid.
197 See Slocock, *People Like Us*, pp. 291–323. See also Moore, *Margaret Thatcher, Volume 3*, pp. 676–726 and Alan Watkins, *A Conservative Coup: The Fall of Margaret Thatcher* (London: Duckworth, 1991).
198 Slocock, *People Like Us*.
199 Interview with Lord Turnbull.
200 Baker, *The Turbulent Years*, p. 397.
201 Ibid.
202 Richards, 'The Conservatives, New Labour and Whitehall', p. 101.
203 Sir Percy Cradock quoted in Hennessy, *The Prime Minister*, p. 406.
204 Interview with Lord Powell.
205 Lawson, *The View from No. 11*, p. 680.
206 Interview with Lord Powell.
207 See Moore, *Margaret Thatcher, Volume 3*, p. 742.
208 Private information.

8. BACK TO BASICS? PRIVATE OFFICE 1990–97

1 Major, *The Autobiography*, p. 209.
2 Clarke, *Kind of Blue*, p. 252.
3 Heseltine, *Life in the Jungle*, p. 488.
4 Interview with John Major, 13 October 2022.
5 Interview with Lord Turnbull.
6 Interview with John Major.
7 Interview with Alex Allan, 26 March 2010.
8 Lawson, *The View from No. 11*, p. 385.
9 Major, *The Autobiography*, pp. 319–20.
10 Interview with John Major.
11 Private information.
12 Interview with John Major.
13 Ibid.
14 Ibid.
15 Norman Lamont, *In Office* (London: Warner Books, 2000), p. 37.
16 Ibid., p. 194.
17 Clarke, *Kind of Blue*, p. 319.

18 Interview with David Cameron, 23 April 2018.

19 See Heywood, *What Does Jeremy Think?*, pp. 517–23.

20 Anthony Seldon, *Major: A Political Life* (London: Weidenfeld & Nicolson, 1997), p. 270.

21 Interview with Lord Heywood, 10 December 2010.

22 Ibid.

23 Interview with Alex Allan.

24 Interview with Lord Heywood.

25 TNA, T449/810, Minute from Jeremy Heywood, principal private secretary to the Chancellor of the Exchequer, to Treasury officials, 23 June 1992.

26 Interview with Lord Heywood.

27 Heywood, *What Does Jeremy Think?*, p. 7.

28 Interview with Lord Heywood.

29 Lamont, *In Office*, photo caption between pp. 280–81.

30 Heywood, *What Does Jeremy Think?*, p. 44.

31 See Blick and Mortimore, *Butler's British Political Facts*, pp. 435–7.

32 See Seldon, *Major*, pp. 572–90. Major also chronicles these events in detail in his *Autobiography*, pp. 608–47.

33 See Seldon, *Major*, pp. 600–602.

34 See Heseltine, *Life in the Jungle*, p. 488.

35 Ibid., p. 483.

36 Interview with Mark Gibson.

37 Ibid.

38 Heseltine, *Life in the Jungle*, pp. 496–7.

39 Hennessy, *The Prime Minister*, p. 473.

40 Simon Jenkins, 'No Mirror for Ministers', *The Times*, 3 July 1996.

41 Hennessy, *The Prime Minister*, p. 474.

42 Major, *The Autobiography*, p. 725.

43 Interview with Alex Allan.

44 Kavanagh and Seldon support this view, see *The Powers Behind the Prime Minister*, p. 181.

45 See Hennessy, *The Hidden Wiring*.

9. NEW LABOUR, NEW PRIVATE OFFICE? PRIVATE OFFICE 1997–2010

1 James Callaghan as quoted (inaccurately) in *The Sun*, 11 January 1979, and Harold Macmillan's speech at Bedford football ground, 20 July 1957, as quoted in Hennessy, *Having It So Good*, p. 1.

2 *New York Times*, 18 May 1997.

3 Interview with Alex Allan. Interview with Alastair Campbell, 20 March 2012. Campbell also describes the episode in Alastair Campbell, *The Alastair Campbell Diaries, Volume 2* (London: Arrow Books, 2011), p. 12.

4 For example, Naughtie, *The Rivals* and Rawnsley, *Servants of the People*.

5 See Nicholas Jones, *Sultans of Spin: The Media and the New Labour Government* (London: Weidenfeld & Nicolson, 1999); Nicholas Jones, *The Control Freaks: How New Labour Gets its Own Way* (London: Politico's, 2001); A. Mughan, *Media and the Presidentialization of Parliamentary Elections* (Basingstoke: Macmillan, 2000); Peter Oborne, *Alastair Campbell: New Labour and the Rise of the Media Class* (London: Aurum, 1999); Peter Oborne and Simon Walters, *Alastair Campbell* (London: Aurum, 2004); Lance Price, *Where Power Lies: Prime Ministers v the Media* (London: Simon & Schuster, 2011); and Colin Seymour-Ure, *Prime Ministers and the Media: Issues of Power and Control* (Oxford: Blackwell, 2003).

6 Jon Davis and John Rentoul, *Heroes or Villains?* (Oxford: Oxford University Press, 2019) pp. 160–64; Peter Hennessy, 'Command and Control: Tony Blair', in Hennessy, *The Prime Minister*, pp. 476–538; Peter Hennessy, 'The Blair Style and the Requirements of the Twenty-First Century Premiership', *Political Quarterly*, 71/4 (2000), pp. 386–95; Peter Hennessy, 'The Blair government in historical perspective: An analysis of the power relationships within New Labour', *History Today*, 52/1 (2002); Seldon, *Blair*; and Anthony Seldon (ed.), *The Blair Effect: The Blair Government 1997–2001* (London: Little, Brown, 2001).

7 See Davis and Rentoul, *Heroes or Villains?*, and Michael Barber, *Instruction to Deliver: Tony Blair, Public Services and the Challenge of Targets* (London: Politico's, 2007).

8 Blair, *A Journey*. For biographies, see, John Rentoul, *Tony Blair: Prime Minister* (London: Little, Brown, 2001); Peter Riddell, *The Unfulfilled Prime Minister* (London: Politico's, 2005); Seldon, *Blair*; and Philip Stephens, *Tony Blair: The Price of Leadership* (London: Politico's 2004). For a more journalistic account, see Adam Boulton, *Tony's Ten Years* (London: Pocket Books, 2009).

9 Ed Balls, *Speaking Out* (London: Arrow Books, 2016); David Blunkett, *The Blunkett Tapes* (London: Bloomsbury, 2006); Brown, *My Life, Our Times*; Darling, *Back from the Brink*; Peter Hain, *Outside In* (London: Biteback, 2012); Harriet Harman, *A Woman's Work* (London: Penguin, 2018); John Prescott, *Prezza: My Story: Pulling No Punches* (London: Headline Review, 2008); Peter Mandelson, *The Third Man* (London: HarperPress, 2010); and Jack Straw, *Last Man Standing: Memoirs of a Political Survivor* (London: Macmillan, 2012). For advisers' accounts, see: Powell, *The New Machiavelli*; Powell, *Great Hatred, Little Room*; Barber, *Instruction to Deliver*; and Derek Scott, *Off Whitehall: A View from Downing Street* (London: I. B. Taurus, 2004).

10 Alastair Campbell, *The Alastair Campbell Diaries, Volume 1* (London: Arrow Books, 2011), *Volume 2* (London: Arrow Books, 2011), *Volume 3* (London: Arrow Books, 2012), *Volume 4* (London: Arrow Books, 2013). See also Alastair Campbell, *The Blair Years: Extracts from the Alastair Campbell Diaries* (London: Arrow Books, 2008).

11 See, for example, Seldon (ed.), *The Blair Effect* and Anthony Seldon and Dennis Kavanagh (eds), *The Blair Effect II: The Blair Government 2001–2005* (Cambridge: Cambridge University Press, 2005).

12 Tom Bower, *Gordon Brown: Prime Minister* (London: Harper Perennial, 2007); William Keegan, *The Prudence of Mr Gordon Brown* (London: John Wiley & Sons, 2004); Robert Peston, *Brown's Britain* (London, Short Books, 2005); Steve Richards, *Whatever it Takes: The Real Story of Gordon Brown and New Labour* (London: Fourth Estate, 2010); Paul Routledge, *Gordon Brown: The Biography* (London: Simon & Schuster, 1998); Seldon and Lodge, *Brown At 10*. On the global financial crisis, see Keegan, *Nine Crises*, pp. 169–90, William Keegan, *Saving the World?* (London: Searching Finance, 2012). See also Brown, *My Life, Our Times*, pp. 295–363.

13 See Seldon, *Blair*; Seldon (ed.), *The Blair Effect*; Seldon and Kavanagh (eds), *The Blair Effect II*; Seldon and Lodge, *Brown at 10*; and Seldon and Kavanagh, *The Powers Behind the Prime Minister*. See also Davis and Rentoul, *Heroes or Villains?*, Chapter 2 pp. 54–109.

14 Powell, *The New Machiavelli*, p. 6.

15 Iraq Inquiry, evidence from Jonathan Powell, https://webarchive.nationalarchives.gov.uk/20171123122517/http://www.iraqinquiry.org.uk/the-evidence/witnesses/p/mr-jonathan-powell/, pp. 8–9.

16 Correspondence with Alastair Campbell, 30 June 2020.

17 Davis and Rentoul, *Heroes or Villains?*, p. 109.

18 Interview with Jonathan Powell, 27 May 2020.

19 Interview with Tony Blair, 18 January 2018.

20 Mortimer and Blick, *Butler's British Political Facts*, pp. 436–7.

21 Blair, *A Journey*, p. 4.

22 See, for example, Seldon, *Blair*, p. 261, and Riddell, *The Unfulfilled Prime Minister*, pp. 56–7.

23 Interview with Tony Blair.

24 Campbell, *The Alastair Campbell Diaries, Volume 1*, p. 462.

25 Interview with Lord Wilson, 19 May 2020.

26 Campbell, *The Alastair Campbell Diaries, Volume 1*, p. 734.

27 See, for example, Boulton, *Tony's Ten Years*, pp. 265–300; Gould, *The Unfinished Revolution*, esp. pp. 183–200; Richard Heffernan, 'Tony Blair as Labour Party Leader', in Seldon (ed.), *Blair's Britain*, pp. 143–63; Naughtie, *The Rivals*, pp. 54–75; and Seldon, *Blair*, pp. 157–63. See also Mandelson's own description of his relationship with Brown in Mandelson, *The Third Man*, pp. 158–73.

28 Mandelson, *The Third Man*, pp. 178–9.

29 Campbell, *The Alastair Campbell Diaries, Volume 1*, pp. 45–6.

30 Campbell, *The Alastair Campbell Diaries, Volume 2*, p. 306.

31 Mandelson, *The Third Man*, p. 223.

32 Jago, *Robin Butler*, pp. 266–8.

33 These included Anthony Giddens, *The Third Way* (Oxford: Blackwell, 1998) and Will Hutton, *The State We're In* (London: Jonathan Cape, 1995).

34 Rentoul, *Blair*, p. 172.

35 Peter Riddell, cited in Seldon, *Blair*, p. 380.

36 Peter Mandelson and Roger Liddle, *The Blair Revolution: Can New Labour Deliver?* (London: Faber and Faber, 1996).

37 Ibid., pp. 232–55.

38 Ibid., p. 240.

39 Ibid., p. 241.

40 Ibid., p. 249.

41 Ibid., p. 242.

42 1997 Labour Party manifesto, *Britain Deserves Better* (London: Labour Party, 1997).
43 Correspondence with Alastair Campbell, 30 June 2020.
44 Rentoul, *Tony Blair*, p. 277.
45 See Powell, *The New Machiavelli*, p. 22.
46 Blair, *A Journey*, pp. 19–20.
47 Interview with Jonathan Powell, 26 November 2010.
48 For details of the seminars and the process, see Riddell and Haddon, *Transitions*, pp. 15–16.
49 Interview with Jonathan Powell, 27 May 2020.
50 Peter Hennessy, Rosaleen Hughes and Jean Seaton, *Ready, Steady, Go! New Labour and Whitehall* (London: Fabian Society, 1997).
51 Interview with Rosaleen Hughes, 7 July 2020.
52 Hennessy et al., *Ready, Steady, Go!*, pp. 30–32.
53 Ibid., pp. 35–6.
54 See Barber, *Instruction to Deliver*. See also Michelle Clement, *The Art of Delivery: Sir Michael Barber and the Prime Minister's Delivery Unit 2001 to 2005* (unpublished PhD thesis, King's College London, 2020).
55 Interviews with Lord Butler and Lord Wilson.
56 See also Riddell and Haddon, *Transitions*, p. 19.
57 Interview with Jonathan Powell, 27 May 2020.
58 Interview with Jonathan Powell.
59 Powell, *The New Machiavelli*, p. 14.
60 Ibid.
61 Interview with Alex Allan.
62 Interview with Jonathan Powell.
63 Ibid.
64 Ibid. Campbell, *The Alastair Campbell Diaries, Volume 1*, p. 740, also relates how Blair and Brown argued about ministerial appointments on the afternoon of 1 May.
65 Interview with Jonathan Powell.
66 Interview with Alex Allan.
67 Interview with Lord Butler.
68 Riddell and Haddon, *Transitions*, pp. 28–32 describes this meeting and Blair's indifference to such questions of civil service procedure.
69 Ibid. See also Jago, *Robin Butler*, p. 264.
70 Jago, *Robin Butler*, p. 264.
71 Interview with Jonathan Powell.
72 Interview with Lord Butler.
73 Campbell, *The Alastair Campbell Diaries, Volume 1*, pp. 743–4.
74 Interviews with Jonathan Powell and Tony Blair, respectively.
75 Interview with Jonathan Powell.
76 Interview with Alex Allan.
77 Interview with Jonathan Powell.
78 Private information. See also: https://www.theguardian.com/uk/2000/nov/18/politics.dome.
79 Interview with Alex Allan.
80 Campbell, *The Alastair Campbell Diaries, Volume 2*, p. 5.
81 See https://www.bbc.co.uk/news/uk-politics-43808651.
82 Private information.
83 Interview with Alex Allan.
84 Interview with Ed Balls, 16 March 2020.
85 Ibid.
86 Ibid.
87 Interviews with Lord Macpherson and Ed Balls.
88 Interview with Ed Balls.
89 Balls, *Speaking Out*, p. 141, which describes Burns as being 'taken aback' by the news.
90 Ibid.
91 Ibid., p. 142.
92 Rawnsley, *Servants of the People*, p. 32.
93 Brown, *My Life, Our Times*, p. 117.
94 Ibid., p. 118.
95 Campbell, *The Alastair Campbell Diaries, Volume 2*, p. 93.

96 Interview with Lord Heywood.
97 Interview with Jonathan Powell.
98 Interview with Tony Blair.
99 Interview with Jonathan Powell.
100 Powell, quoted in Davis and Rentoul, *Heroes or Villains?*, p. 158.
101 Interview with Lord Wilson. See also Davis and Rentoul, *Heroes or Villains?*, pp. 157–60.
102 Davis and Rentoul, *Heroes or Villains?*, p. 102, citing Powell.
103 Blair, *A Journey*, p. 294.
104 Campbell, *The Alastair Campbell Diaries, Volume 3*, p. 396.
105 Powell, *The New Machiavelli*, p. 44.
106 Foot and Mouth Disease: Lessons to be Learned Inquiry Report, Meeting notes from interview with Jonathan Powell, Jeremy Heywood and David North, 17 May 2002, HC888, TNA, https://webarchive. nationalarchives.gov.uk/20100809105008/http://archive.cabinetoffice.gov.uk/fmd/fmd_report/report/ index.htm. (The author of this book was the secretary to the Lessons to be Learned Inquiry.)
107 Ibid.
108 Ibid., pp. 100–102.
109 Private information.
110 Private information.
111 Blair, *A Journey*, p. 311.
112 Ibid., p. 351.
113 'The Iraq Inquiry: Report of a Committee of Privy Counsellors' ('Chilcot report'), HC 264, 6 July 2016.
114 Campbell, *The Alastair Campbell Diaries, Volume 4*.
115 Davis and Rentoul, *Heroes or Villains?*, p. 282.
116 Ibid.
117 Chilcot report, para. 390, p. 54.
118 Ibid., para. 399, p. 56.
119 Iraq Inquiry, evidence from Matthew Rycroft, https://webarchive.nationalarchives.gov.uk/20171123123736/ http://www.iraqinquiry.org.uk/the-evidence/witnesses/r/mr-matthew-rycroft/, p. 21.
120 Ibid.
121 Ibid., question from Sir Roderick Lyne.
122 Iraq Inquiry, evidence from Jonathan Powell, https://webarchive.nationalarchives.gov.uk/20171123122517/ http://www.iraqinquiry.org.uk/the-evidence/witnesses/p/mr-jonathan-powell/, p. 9.
123 Davis and Rentoul, *Heroes or Villains?*, pp. 274–5.
124 'Review of Intelligence on Weapons of Mass Destruction: Report of a Committee of Privy Counsellors' ('Butler review'), HC 898, 14 July 2004.
125 See Barber, *Instruction to Deliver*.
126 See Jill Rutter and Josh Harris, *The Special Ones: How to make central government units work* (London: Institute for Government, 2014).
127 Barber, *Instruction to Deliver*, p. 58.
128 Ibid.
129 Interview with Lord Heywood, 10 December 2010.
130 Ibid.
131 Josh Harris and Jill Rutter, *Centre Forward* (London: Institute for Government, 2014). See pp. 21–2 on the Policy Directorate.
132 Barber, *Instruction to Deliver*, p. 156.
133 Interview with Tony Blair.
134 Private information.
135 See Balls, *Speaking Out*, p. 134.
136 Interview with Jonathan Powell.
137 Private information.
138 Interview with Jonathan Powell.
139 Interview with James Bowler, 5 September 2018.
140 See, for example, Seldon and Lodge, *Brown at 10*, pp. 1–14, which describes the many changes Brown introduced to distinguish his administration from Blair's.
141 Interview with Gordon Brown, 16 May 2018.
142 Balls, *Speaking Out*, p. 209.
143 Brown, *My Life, Our Times*, p. 200.
144 Ibid., p. 198.

145 Ibid., pp. 198–9.
146 Seldon and Lodge, *Brown at 10*, p. 12.
147 Private information.
148 Interview with Jonathan Powell.
149 Seldon and Lodge, *Brown at 10*, p. 31.
150 See Seldon and Lodge, *Brown at 10*, p. 31, and Balls, *Speaking Out*, pp. 208–13. The latter explains the pressure Brown put on him to become his chief of staff, and oversee the Cabinet Office, in late 2007.
151 Seldon and Lodge, *Brown at 10*, p. 70.
152 Ibid., p. 71.
153 Private information.
154 Interview with Gordon Brown.
155 Of the massive literature, see, in particular, Martin Wolf, *The Shifts and the Shock: What we've learned – and have still have to learn – from the financial crisis* (London: Penguin, 2015). See also Eleanor Hallam, *HM Treasury and the Financial Crisis 2007-2009* (unpublished PhD, King's College London, 2020).
156 Brown, *My Life, Our Times*, p. 296.
157 Interview with Lord Darling, 3 September 2020.
158 Ibid.
159 Darling, *Back from the Brink*, p. 145.
160 Ibid., pp. 153–4.
161 Interview with Lord Darling.
162 Darling, *Back from the Brink*, p. 162.
163 Interview with Lord Darling.
164 Ibid.
165 Darling, *Back from the Brink*, p. 167.
166 Interview with Gordon Brown.
167 Interview with Tony Blair.
168 Ibid.
169 Tony Blair, 'Tips for an Incoming President', *African Business Magazine*, 23 January 2020.

10. AN INSTITUTION IN DECLINE: PRIVATE OFFICE 2010–22

1 See Dennis Kavanagh and Philip Cowley, *The British General Election of 2010* (Basingstoke: Palgrave Macmillan, 2010), p. 128.
2 Mortimore and Blick, *Butler's British Political Facts*, pp. 439–40.
3 The Cabinet Manual (London: Cabinet Office), first published October 2011.
4 Interview with David Cameron.
5 Ibid.
6 David Cameron, *For the Record* (London: William Collins, 2019), p. 135.
7 Interview with David Cameron.
8 Ibid.
9 See, for example, Chris Whipple, *The Gatekeepers* (New York: Broadway Books, 2018) and Peter Baker and Susan Glasser, *The Man Who Ran Washington* (New York: Doubleday, 2020).
10 Kate Fall, *The Gatekeeper* (London: HQ Books, 2021), p. 123.
11 Interview with James Bowler.
12 Private information.
13 Heywood, *What Does Jeremy Think?*, p. 335.
14 Interview with David Cameron.
15 Akash Paun and Stuart Hallifax, *A game of two halves: How coalition governments renew in mid-term and last the full term* (London: Institute for Government, 2012), p. 17.
16 See, for example, the BBC profile of Cummings, 20 July 2021, https://www.bbc.co.uk/news/uk-politics-49101464.
17 See 'Civil Service Reform Plan', June 2012, www.civilservice.gov.uk/reform.
18 'Civil Service Reform Plan: One Year On Report', July 2013.
19 Ibid., p. 31.
20 See Paun, *Supporting Ministers to Lead*, pp. 8–20.
21 See, for example, Nicola Hughes, 'Is scrapping Extended Ministerial Office a mistake?', Institute for Government, 6 January 2017.
22 House of Lords Written Answer, Lord Young of Cookham, 8 February 2018.

23 Willetts, cited by Hughes, https://www.instituteforgovernment.org.uk/blog/scrapping-extended-ministerial-offices-mistake.

24 Fall, *The Gatekeeper*, p. 87.

25 Interview with David Cameron.

26 Seldon and Snowdon, *Cameron at 10*, p. 542.

27 Seldon, *May at 10*, p. xi.

28 Private information.

29 Seldon, *May at 10*, p. 49.

30 Ibid.

31 Andrew Rawnsley review of *Betting the House* and *Fallout*, *The Guardian*, 10 December 2017.

32 Gavin Barwell, *Chief of Staff* (London: Atlantic Books, 2021), p. 419.

33 Ibid., pp. 418–19.

34 See, for example, Tim Bale, *The Conservative Party After Brexit* (Cambridge: Polity, 2023), pp. 116–19; and Anthony Seldon and Raymond Newell, *Johnson at 10: The Inside Story* (London: Atlantic Books, 2023), pp. 72–89.

35 Seldon and Newell, *Johnson at 10*, p. 81.

36 Ibid.

37 Sue Gray report.

38 Andrew Blick and Peter Hennessy, *The Bonfire of the Decencies* (London: Haus, 2022), p. 40.

39 Seldon and Newell, *Johnson at 10*, pp. 541–2.

40 For a full journalistic narrative of these events, see Sebastian Payne, *The Fall of Boris Johnson* (London: Pan Books, 2023).

41 Ibid., p. 123.

42 Ibid., p. 203.

43 Ibid. pp. 206–10.

44 Written submission by the Rt Hon. Boris Johnson in the matter referred to the House of Commons Committee on Privileges on 21 April 2022, published by the committee, 21 March 2023.

45 Ibid., p. 9.

46 'Final report of the House of Commons Committee on Privileges, Fifth Report of Session 2022–23, Matter referred on 21 April 2022 (conduct of Rt Hon. Boris Johnson): Final Report', HC 564 (London: House of Commons, 2023), p. 34.

47 Ibid., p. 35.

48 Ibid., p. 37.

49 Harry Cole and James Heale, *Out of the Blue: The inside story of the unexpected rise and rapid fall of Liz Truss* (London: HarperCollins, 2022), p. 226.

50 Ibid. p. 276.

CONCLUSION

1 Alistair Horne, *Macmillan, Volume 2* (London: Macmillan, 1988), p. 162.

2 Williams (ed.), *The Diary of Hugh Gaitskell 1945–1956*, p. 305.

3 Cabinet Office, Annual Report on Special Advisers, 2023.

4 Sylvester, *The Real Lloyd George*, p. 99.

5 See Moore, *Margaret Thatcher, Volume 3*, p. 308.

6 Interview with Lord Armstrong.

7 Interview with Tony Blair.

8 Interview with Lord Powell. See also various references in Moore, *Margaret Thatcher, Volumes 2 and 3*.

9 Interview with Ed Balls.

APPENDIX 2: NO. 10 PRIVATE OFFICE AND SENIOR OFFICIALS: 1945–2024

1 The information in this appendix is based on: the updated tables from Kavanagh and Seldon, *The Powers Behind the Prime Minister*, pp. 331–44; Seymour-Ure, Colin, *Memorandum submitted to the House of Commons Select Committee on Public Administration, 6th Report, Appendix 8*, 1998; *Dod's Parliamentary Companion*, 1964–2023; *The Civil Service Year Book*, 1973–2023; *The Imperial Calendar*, 1964–72; https://www.ukwhoswho.com.

BIBLIOGRAPHY

PRIMARY SOURCES

ARCHIVES

The National Archives (TNA), Kew:

 Cabinet Office Papers (CAB).

 Prime Minister's Papers (PREM):

  PREM 13 for 1964–70 (Wilson).

  PREM 15 for 1970–74 (Heath).

  PREM 16 for 1974–79 (Wilson/Callaghan).

  PREM 19 for 1979 onwards (Thatcher/Major).

 Treasury Papers (T).

The Bodleian Library, Oxford:

 Papers of Harold Wilson.

Churchill Archives Centre, Cambridge:

 Papers of Baroness Thatcher.

ONLINE RESOURCES

Archive of Sir John Major, www.johnmajorarchive.org.uk.

Hansard, https://hansard.parliament.uk.

King's College, 'Margaret Thatcher and No. 10',
 www.thatcherandnumberten.com.

Who's Who online, www.ukwhoswho.com.

PRIVATE PAPERS

Private papers of Sir Patrick Nairne (courtesy of Lord Hennessy).
Private papers of Joe Haines.

PUBLISHED DOCUMENTS

'The Civil Service: Report of the Committee 1966–68' ('Fulton report'), Cmnd 3638 (London: HMSO, 1968).

'The Iraq Inquiry: Report of a Committee of Privy Counsellors' ('Chilcot report'), HC 264 (London: HMSO, 2016).

'Falkland Islands Review: Report of a Committee of Privy Counsellors' ('Franks review') (London: HMSO, 1983).

'Findings of the Second Permanent Secretary's Investigation into Alleged Gatherings on Government Premises during COVID Restrictions' ('Sue Gray report') (London: Cabinet Office, 2022).

'The Reorganisation of Central Government', Cmnd 4506 (London: HMSO, 1970).

'Review of Intelligence on Weapons of Mass Destruction: Report of a Committee of Privy Counsellors' ('Butler review'), HC 898 (London: HMSO, 2004).

'Special Advisers in the thick of it: Sixth Report of the House of Commons Public Administration Select Committee', HC 134 (London: HMSO, 2012–13).

'Westland plc: The Government's Decision-making: Fourth Report from the Select Committee on Defence', HC 519 (London: HMSO, 1985–86).

AUTOBIOGRAPHIES, DIARIES AND MEMOIRS

Baker, Kenneth, *The Turbulent Years* (London: Faber and Faber, 1993).

Balls, Ed, *Speaking Out* (London: Arrow Books, 2016).

Barber, Michael, *Instruction to Deliver: Tony Blair, Public Services and the Challenge of Targets* (London: Politico's, 2007).

Barwell, Gavin, *Chief of Staff: Notes from Downing Street* (London: Atlantic Books, 2021).

Benn, Tony, *Against the Tide: Diaries, 1973–1977* (London: Hutchinson, 1989).

Benn, Tony, *Office Without Power: Diaries, 1968–1972* (London: Hutchinson, 1988).

Benn, Tony, *Out of the Wilderness: Diaries, 1963–1967* (London: Hutchinson, 1987).

Blair, Tony, *A Journey* (London: Hutchinson, 2010).

Blunkett, David, *The Blunkett Tapes* (London: Bloomsbury, 2006).

Brown, Gordon, *My Life, Our Times* (London: Bodley Head, 2017).

Callaghan, James, *Time and Chance* (London: Politico's, 2006).

Cameron, David, *For the Record* (London: William Collins, 2019).

Campbell, Alastair, *The Alastair Campbell Diaries, Volume 1: Prelude to Power 1994–1997* (London: Arrow Books, 2011).

Campbell, Alastair, *The Alastair Campbell Diaries, Volume 2: Power and the People 1997–1999* (London: Arrow Books, 2011).

Campbell, Alastair, *The Alastair Campbell Diaries, Volume 3: Power and Responsibility 1999–2001* (London: Arrow Books, 2012).

Campbell, Alastair, *The Alastair Campbell Diaries, Volume 4: The Burden of Power: Countdown to Iraq* (London: Arrow Books, 2013).

Campbell, Alastair, *The Blair Years* (London: Arrow Books, 2008).

Castle, Barbara, *The Castle Diaries 1964–70* (London: Weidenfeld & Nicolson, 1974).

Castle, Barbara, *The Castle Diaries 1974–76* (London: Weidenfeld & Nicolson, 1980).

Clark, Alan, *Diaries* (London: Phoenix, 1994).

Clarke, Kenneth, *Kind of Blue* (London: Macmillan, 2016).

Cole, John, *As it Seemed to Me* (London: Weidenfeld & Nicolson, 1995).

Colville, John, *The Fringes of Power: Downing Street Diaries 1939–1955* (London: Hodder & Stoughton, 1985).

Cowper-Coles, Sherard, *Ever the Diplomat* (London: HarperPress, 2012).

Cradock, Percy, *In Pursuit of British Interests: Reflections on Foreign Policy under Margaret Thatcher and John Major* (London: John Murray, 1997).

Crossman, Richard, *The Diaries of a Cabinet Minister: Volume 1* (London: Cape, 1975).

Crossman, Richard, *The Diaries of a Cabinet Minister: Volume 2* (London: Cape, 1976).

Crossman, Richard, *The Diaries of a Cabinet Minister: Volume 3* (London: Hamilton, 1977).

Donoughue, Bernard, *Downing Street Diary: Volume 1 – With Harold Wilson in No. 10* (London: Jonathan Cape, 2004).

Donoughue, Bernard, *Downing Street Diary: Volume 2 – With James Callaghan in No. 10* (London: Pimlico, 2009).

Donoughue, Bernard, *The Heat of the Kitchen* (London: Politico's, 2003).

Donoughue, Bernard, *Prime Minister: The Conduct of Policy Under Harold Wilson and James Callaghan* (London: Jonathan Cape, 1987).

Egremont, Lord, *Wyndham and Children First* (London: Macmillan, 1968).

Gould, Philip, *The Unfinished Revolution* (London: Little, Brown, 1998).

Haines, Joe, *Glimmers of Twilight* (London: Politico's, 2003).

Haines, Joe, *Kick 'Em Back* (Tolworth: Grosvenor House Publishing, 2019).

Haines, Joe, *The Politics of Power* (London: Jonathan Cape, 1977).

Healey, Denis, *The Time of My Life* (London: Michael Joseph, 1989).

Heath, Edward, *The Course of My Life* (London: Hodder & Stoughton, 1998).

Heseltine, Michael, *Life in the Jungle* (London: Hodder & Stoughton, 2000).

Hoskyns, John, *Just in Time: Inside the Thatcher Revolution* (London: Aurum Press, 2000).

Hurd, Douglas, *An End to Promises: Sketch of a Government* (London: Collins, 1979).

Hurd, Douglas, *Memoirs* (London: Abacus, 2004).

Ingham, Bernard, *Kill the Messenger* (London: HarperCollins, 1991).

Lamont, Norman, *In Office* (London: Warner Books, 2000).

Lawson, Nigel, *The View from No. 11* (London: Bantam Press, 1992).

Lipsey, David, *In the Corridors of Power* (London: Biteback, 2012).

Major, John, *An Autobiography* (London: HarperCollins, 1999).

Mandelson, Peter, *The Third Man* (London: HarperPress, 2010).

Martin, John, *Downing Street: The War Years* (London: Bloomsbury, 1991).

Powell, Jonathan, *Great Hatred, Little Room* (London: Bodley Head, 2008).

Powell, Jonathan, *The New Machiavelli* (London: Bodley Head, 2010).

Profumo, David, *Bringing the House Down* (London: John Murray, 2007).

Shephard, Gillian, *Shephard's Watch* (London: Politico's, 2000).

Slocock, Caroline, *People Like Us* (London: Biteback, 2018).

Sylvester, A. J., *The Real Lloyd George* (London: Cassell, 1947).

Thatcher, Margaret, *The Downing Street Years* (London: HarperCollins, 1995).

Thatcher, Margaret, *The Path to Power* (London: HarperCollins, 1995).

Thorpe, Jeremy, *In My Own Time* (London: Politico's, 1999).

Waldegrave, William, *A Different Kind of Weather* (London: Constable, 2015).

Williams, Marcia, *Downing Street in Perspective* (London: Weidenfeld & Nicolson, 1983).

Williams, Marcia, *Inside No. 10* (London: Weidenfeld & Nicolson, 1971).

Wilson, Harold, *Final Term: The Labour Government 1974–76* (London: Weidenfeld & Nicolson, 1979).

Wilson, Harold, *The Governance of Britain* (London: Weidenfeld & Nicolson, 1976).

Wilson, Harold, *The Labour Government 1964–70* (London: Weidenfeld & Nicolson, 1971).

INTERVIEWS

Debbie Ailes, 30 June 2010.

Sir Alex Allan, 26 March 2010.

The Rt Hon. Lord Armstrong of Ilminster, 20 July 2014 and 27 July 2014 (and subsequent correspondence).

The Rt Hon. Ed Balls, 16 March 2020.

The Rt Hon. Tony Blair, 17 January 2018.

James Bowler, 5 September 2018.

The Rt Hon. Gordon Brown, 16 May 2018.

The Rt Hon. Lord Butler of Brockwell, 29 September 2010 (and subsequent correspondence).

Sir Andrew Cahn, 14 December 2022.

The Rt Hon. David Cameron, 23 April 2018.

Alastair Campbell, 20 March 2012 (and subsequent correspondence).

Simon Case, 15 June 2018.

The Rt Hon. Lord Darling of Roulanish, 3 September 2020.

Roger Dawe, 22 January 2010 and 12 January 2016 (and subsequent correspondence).

Lord Donoughue of Ashton, 12 February 2018.

Mark Gibson, 7 November 2011.

Joe Haines, 4 April 2018.

The Rt Hon. Lord Healey, 12 January 2015.

Lord Heywood of Whitehall, 10 December 2010.

Rosaleen Hughes, 7 July 2020.

The Rt Hon. Lord Lansley of Orwell, 30 April 2013.

Lord Lipsey of Tooting Bec, 5 February 2018.

Lord Macpherson of Earl's Court, 3 December 2010.

The Rt Hon. Sir John Major, 13 October 2022.

Sir Richard Mottram, 20 December 2016.

Sir David Omand, 30 July 2015.

Jonathan Powell, 26 November 2010 and 27 May 2020.

Lord Powell of Bayswater, 3 November 2010.

The Rt Hon. Peter Riddell, 20 October 2017.

Jill Rutter, 26 May 2011.

Caroline Slocock, 8 September 2020.

Lord Turnbull of Enfield, 22 December 2011.

Lord Wilson of Dinton, 19 May 2020.

SECONDARY SOURCES

NEWSPAPERS AND PERIODICALS

African Business Magazine
Civil Service World
Daily Telegraph
The Economist
Financial Times
The Guardian
The Independent
Literary Review
New Scientist
New Statesman
New York Times
The Observer
Prospect
The Scotsman
The Spectator
Sunday Times
The Times

BOOKS AND PAMPHLETS

Adonis, Andrew and Thomas, Keith (eds), *Roy Jenkins: A Retrospective* (Oxford: Oxford University Press, 2004).

Baker, Amy, *Prime Ministers and the Rule Book* (London: Politico's, 2000).

Baker, Peter and Glasser, Susan, *The Man Who Ran Washington* (New York: Doubleday, 2020).

Bale, Tim, *The Conservative Party After Brexit* (Cambridge: Polity, 2023).

Bew, John, *Citizen Clem* (London: Riverrun, 2016).

Blackstone, Tessa and Plowden, William, *Inside the Think Tank: Advising the Cabinet 1971–83* (London: Mandarin Paperbacks, 1990).

Blick, Andrew, *People who Live in the Dark* (London: Politico's, 2004).

Blick, Andrew and Jones, George, *Premiership* (Exeter: Imprint Academic, 2010).

Blick, Andrew and Hennessy, Peter, *The Bonfire of the Decencies* (London: Haus, 2022).

Blick, Andrew and Hennessy, Peter, *Good Chaps No More? Safeguarding the Constitution in Stressful Times* (London: Constitution Society, 2019).

Boulton, Adam, *Tony's Ten Years* (London: Pocket Books, 2009).

Bower, Tom, *Gordon Brown: Prime Minister* (London: Harper Perennial, 2007).

Bruce-Gardyne, Jock, *Ministers and Mandarins* (London: Sidgwick & Jackson, 1986).

Buckley, Stephen, *The Prime Minister and Cabinet* (Edinburgh: Edinburgh University Press, 2006).

Burnham, Jane and Pyper, Robert, *Britain's Modernised Civil Service* (Basingstoke: Palgrave Macmillan, 2008).

Butler, David and King, Anthony, *The British General Election of 1964* (London: Macmillan, 1965).

Butler, David and King, Anthony, *The British General Election of 1966* (London: Macmillan, 1966).

Butler, David and Pinto-Duschinsky, Michael, *The British General Election of 1970* (London: Macmillan, 1971).

Butler, David and Kavanagh, Dennis, *The British General Election of February 1974* (London: Macmillan, 1974).

Butler, David and Kavanagh, Dennis, *The British General Election of October 1974* (London: Macmillan, 1975).

Butler, David and Kavanagh, Dennis, *The British General Election of 1979* (London: Macmillan, 1979).

Butler, David and Kavanagh, Dennis, *The British General Election of 1983* (London: Macmillan, 1984).

Butler, David and Kavanagh, Dennis, *The British General Election of 1987* (Basingstoke: Palgrave Macmillan, 1988).

Butler, David and Kavanagh, Dennis, *The British General Election of 1992* (Basingstoke: Palgrave Macmillan, 1992).

Butler, David and Kavanagh, Dennis, *The British General Election of 1997* (Basingstoke: Palgrave Macmillan, 1997).

Butler, David and Kavanagh, Dennis, *The British General Election of 2001* (Basingstoke: Palgrave Macmillan, 2001).

Butler, David and Kavanagh, Dennis, *The British General Election of 2005* (Basingstoke: Palgrave Macmillan, 2005).

Campbell, John, *Edward Heath: A Biography* (London: Jonathan Cape, 1993).

Carroll, Rory, *Killing Thatcher: The IRA, the Manhunt and the Long War on the Crown* (London: HarperCollins, 2023).

Crick, Michael, *Michael Heseltine* (London: Penguin, 1997).

Critchley, Julian, *Heseltine: The Unauthorised Biography* (London: Andre Deutsch, 1987).

Crosland, Susan, *Tony Crosland* (London: Jonathan Cape, 1982).

Dale, Iain (ed.), *The Prime Ministers* (London: Hodder & Stoughton, 2020).

d'Ancona, Matthew, *In it Together* (London: Penguin, 2014).

Davenport-Hines, Richard, *An English Affair* (London: William Collins, 2013).

Davis, Jon, *Prime Ministers and Whitehall 1960–74* (London: Hambledon Continuum, 2007).

Davis, Jon and Rentoul, John, *Heroes or Villains?* (Oxford: Oxford University Press, 2019).

Diamond, Patrick, *New Labour's Old Roots: Revisionist Thinkers in Labour's History* (Exeter: Academic Imprint, 2004).

Dickie, John, *Inside the Foreign Office* (London: Chapmans, 1992).

Drewry, Gavin and Butcher, Tony, *The Civil Service Today* (London: John Wiley and Sons, 1991).

Fabian Tract 355, *The Administrators: The Reform of the Civil Service* (London: Fabian Society, 1964).

Foley, Michael, *The British Presidency: Tony Blair and the politics of public leadership* (Manchester: Manchester University Press, 2000).

Freedman, Lawrence, *The Official History of the Falklands Campaign: Volume 1 – The Origins of the Falklands War* (Abingdon: Routledge Press, 2005).

Freedman, Lawrence, *The Official History of the Falklands Campaign: Volume 2 – War and Diplomacy* (Abingdon: Routledge Press, 2005).

Green, E. E. H., *Thatcher* (London: Hodder Arnold, 2006).

Hague, William, *William Pitt the Younger* (London: Harper Perennial, 2005).

Harris, Josh and Rutter, Jill, *Centre Forward: Effective Support for the Prime Minister at the Centre of Government* (London: Institute for Government, 2014).

Harris, Josh and Rutter, Jill, *The Special Ones: How to make central government units work* (London: Institute for Government, 2014).

Henderson, Nicholas, *The Private Office Revisited* (London: Profile Books, 2001).

Hennessy, Peter, *Cabinet* (Oxford: Blackwell, 1986).

Hennessy, Peter, *Distilling the Frenzy: Writing the History of One's Own Times* (London: Biteback, 2012).

Hennessy, Peter, *Having It So Good: Britain in the Fifties* (London: Allen Lane, 2006).

Hennessy, Peter, *The Hidden Wiring* (London: Indigo Books, 1996).

Hennessy, Peter, *The Prime Minister: The Office and its Holders Since 1945* (London: Penguin, 2001).

Hennessy, Peter, *Whitehall* (London: Secker & Warburg, 1989).

Hennessy, Peter, *Winds of Change: Britain in the Early Sixties* (London: Allen Lane, 2019).

Hennessy, Peter, Hughes, Rosaleen and Seaton, Jean, *Ready, Steady, Go! New Labour and Whitehall* (Fabian Society: London, 1997).

Hennessy, Peter, Morrison, Susan, and Townsend, Richard, *Routine Punctuated by Orgies: The Central Policy Review Staff, 1970–83*, Strathclyde papers on government and politics, no. 31 (Glasgow: University of Strathclyde, 1985).

Hibbert, Christopher, *Disraeli: A Personal History* (London: Harper Perennial, 2005).

Hogg, Sarah and Hill, Jonathan, *Too Close to Call* (London: Little, Brown, 1995).

Holt, Andrew and Dockter, Warren (eds), *Private Secretaries to the Prime Minister: Foreign Affairs from Churchill to Thatcher* (London: Routledge, 2017).

Hurd, Douglas and Young, Edward, *Disraeli* (London: Phoenix, 2014).

Hutton, John and Lewis, Leigh, *How to Be a Minister – A 21st-Century Guide* (London: Biteback, 2014).

Jackson, Ben and Saunders, Robert (eds), *Making Thatcher's Britain* (Cambridge: Cambridge University Press, 2012).

Jago, Michael, *Robin Butler: At the Heart of Power from Heath to Blair* (London: Biteback, 2017).

Jones, Nicholas, *The Control Freaks: How New Labour Gets its Own Way* (London: Politico's, 2002).

Jones, Nicholas, *Sultans of Spin: The Media and the New Labour Government* (London: Weidenfeld & Nicolson, 1999).

Kaufman, Gerald, *How to Be a Minister* (London: Sidgwick & Jackson, 1980).

Kavanagh, Dennis, *Thatcherism and British Politics* (Oxford: Oxford University Press, 1990).

Kavanagh, Dennis and Cowley, Philip, *The British General Election of 2010* (Basingstoke: Palgrave Macmillan, 2010).

Kavanagh, Dennis and Seldon, Anthony, *The Major Effect* (London: Macmillan, 1994).

Kavanagh, Dennis and Seldon, Anthony, *The Powers Behind the Prime Minister* (London: HarperCollins, 1999).

Keegan, William, *Nine Crises* (London: Biteback, 2019).

Keegan, William, *Saving the World?* (London: Searching Finance, 2012).

Keegan, William, *The Prudence of Mr Gordon Brown* (London: John Wiley & Sons, 2004).

Kellner, Peter and Lord Crowther-Hunt, *The Civil Servants* (London: Macdonald Futura, 1980).

Kennedy, Ian, *Cleaning Up the Mess* (London: Biteback, 2019).

King, Anthony, *The British Constitution* (Oxford: Oxford University Press, 2007).

King, Anthony (ed.), *The British Prime Minister* (London: Macmillan, 1985).

King, Anthony and Crewe, Ivor, *The Blunders of Our Governments* (London: One World, 2013).

Kitzinger, Uwe, *Diplomacy and Persuasion: How Britain Joined the Common Market* (London: Thames & Hudson, 1973).

Latham, Robert, *The Shorter Pepys* (London: Unwin Hyman, 1990).

Lee, J. M., Jones, G. W. and Burnham, J., *At the Centre of Whitehall: Advising the Prime Minister and Cabinet* (Basingstoke: Macmillan, 1998).

Linklater, Magnus and Leigh, David, *Not with Honour: The Inside Story of the Westland Scandal* (London: Sphere Books, 1986).

Lowe, Rodney, *The Official History of the British Civil Service, Volume 1: The Fulton Years, 1966–81* (Abingdon: Routledge, 2011).

McDougall, Linda, *Marcia Williams: The Life and Times of Baroness Falkender* (London: Biteback, 2023).

Mandelson, Peter and Liddle, Roger, *The Blair Revolution: Can New Labour Deliver?* (London: Faber and Faber, 1996).

Montgomery Hyde, H., *A Tangled Web* (London: Futura, 1987).

Moore, Charles, *Margaret Thatcher: The Authorized Biography, Volume 1: Not for Turning* (London: Allen Lane, 2013).

Moore, Charles, *Margaret Thatcher: The Authorized Biography, Volume 2: Everything She Wants* (London: Allen Lane, 2016).

Moore, Charles, *Margaret Thatcher: The Authorized Biography, Volume 3: Herself Alone* (London: Allen Lane, 2019).

Morgan, Kenneth O., *Callaghan: A Life* (Oxford: Oxford University Press, 1997).

Morgan, Kenneth O., *Michael Foot: A Life* (London: Harper Perennial, 2008).

Mortimore, Robin and Blick, Andrew (eds), *Butler's British Political Facts* (Palgrave Macmillan, 2018).

Oakley, Robin, *Inside Track* (London: Corgi Books, 2001).

Oborne, Peter and Walters, Simon, *Alastair Campbell* (London: Aurum, 2004).

Omand, David, *How Spies Think* (London: Penguin Viking, 2020).

Paun, Akash, *Supporting Ministers to Lead* (London: Institute for Government, 2013).

Payne, Sebastian, *The Fall of Boris Johnson* (London: Pan Books, 2023).

Petrie, Charles, *The Powers Behind the Prime Ministers* (London: Macgibbon and Kee, 1958).

Phillips, Adrian, *Fighting Churchill, Appeasing Hitler: How a British Civil Servant Helped Cause the Second World War* (London: Biteback, 2019).

Pollitt, Christopher, *Manipulating the Machine: Changing the Pattern of Ministerial Departments, 1960–83* (London: Allen and Unwin, 1984).

Profumo, David, *Bringing the House Down* (London: John Murray, 2007).

Pyper, Robert and Robins, Lynton (eds), *Governing the UK in the 1990s* (London: Palgrave, 1995).

Rawnsley, Andrew, *The End of the Party* (London: Penguin, 2010).

Rawnsley, Andrew, *Servants of the People: The Inside Story of New Labour* (London: Penguin, 2001).

Rhodes, R. A. W., *Everyday Life in British Government* (Oxford: Oxford University Press, 2015).

Rhodes, R. A. W. and Dunleavy, Patrick, *Prime Minister, Cabinet and Core Executive* (London: Macmillan, 1995).

Richard, David, *New Labour and the Civil Service: Reconstituting the Westminster Model* (Basingstoke: Palgrave Macmillan, 2008).

Riddell, Peter, *Fifteen Minutes of Power: The Uncertain Life of British Ministers* (London: Profile Books, 2019).

Riddell, Peter, *The Thatcher Era and its Legacy* (London: Blackwell, 1991).

Riddell, Peter and Haddon, Catherine, *Transitions: Preparing for*

Changes of Government (London: Institute for Government, 2009).

Roberts, Richard, *When Britain Went Bust* (London: OMFIF, 2016).

Seldon, Anthony, *Blair* (London: Simon & Schuster, 2004).

Seldon, Anthony, *Blair Unbound* (London: Simon & Schuster, 2008).

Seldon, Anthony, *The Cabinet Office 1916–2016* (London: Biteback, 2016).

Seldon, Anthony, *The Impossible Office? The History of the British Prime Minister* (Cambridge: Cambridge University Press, 2021).

Seldon, Anthony, *Major: A Political Life* (London: Weidenfeld & Nicolson, 1997).

Seldon, Anthony, *May at 10* (London: Biteback, 2019).

Seldon, Anthony and Lodge, Guy, *Brown at 10* (London: Biteback, 2010).

Seldon, Anthony and Newell, Raymond, *Johnson at 10: The Inside Story* (London: Atlantic Books, 2023).

Seldon, Anthony and Snowden, Peter, *Cameron at 10* (London: HarperCollins, 2016).

Stanley, Martin, *How to Be a Civil Servant* (London: Biteback, 2016).

Theakston, Kevin, *After Number 10: Former Prime Ministers in British Politics* (Basingstoke: Palgrave Macmillan, 2010).

Theakston, Kevin (ed.), *Bureaucrats and Leadership* (Basingstoke: Macmillan, 2000).

Theakston, Kevin, *The Civil Service Since 1945* (Oxford: Blackwell, 1995).

Theakston, Kevin, *Junior Ministers in British Government* (Oxford: Basil Blackwell, 1987).

Theakston, Kevin, *The Labour Party and Whitehall* (London: Routledge, 1992).

Theakston, Kevin, *Leadership in Whitehall* (Basingstoke: Macmillan, 1999).

Theakston, Kevin and Connelly, Philip, *William Armstrong and British Policy Making* (Basingstoke: Palgrave Macmillan, 2017).

Todman, Daniel, *Britain's War: Into Battle 1937–1941* (London: Penguin, 2017).

Tomalin, Claire, *Samuel Pepys: The Unequalled Self* (London: Penguin, 2012).

Tomlinson, Jim, *The Labour Governments 1964–70, Volume 3: Economic Policy* (Manchester: Manchester University Press, 2004).

Tomlinson, Jim, *The Politics of Decline* (Harlow: Longman, 2000).

Vinen, Richard, *Thatcher's Britain: The Politics and Social Upheaval of the Thatcher Era* (London: Simon & Schuster, 2009).

Wall, Stephen, *The Official History of Britain and the European Community, Vol II: From Rejection to Referendum, 1963–75* (London: Routledge, 2013).

Wass, Douglas, *Decline to Fall: The Making of British Macro-Economic Policy and the 1976 IMF Crisis* (Oxford: Oxford University Press, 2008).

Watkins, Alan, *A Conservative Coup* (London: Duckworth, 1991).

Whipple, Chris, *The Gatekeepers* (New York: Broadway Books, 2018).

Wolf, Martin, *The Shifts and the Shock: What we've learned – and have still have to learn – from the financial crisis* (London: Penguin, 2015).

Yong, Ben and Hazell, Robert, *Special Advisers* (London: Hart Publishing, 2014).

Young, Hugo, *One of Us* (London: Macmillan, 1989); updated version (London: Pan, 1993).

Young, Hugo, *This Blessed Plot* (London: Papermac, 1999).

Ziegler, Philip, *Edward Heath: The Authorized Biography* (London: HarperCollins, 2010).

Ziegler, Philip, *Wilson: The Authorised Life of Lord Wilson of Rievaulx* (London: Weidenfeld & Nicolson, 1993).

ARTICLES, CHAPTERS IN EDITED BOOKS AND PAPERS

Balogh, Thomas, 'The Apotheosis of the Dilettante', in Thomas, Hugh (ed.), *The Establishment* (London: Anthony Blond, 1959), pp. 83–128.

Bevir, Mark and Rhodes, R. A. W., 'Prime Ministers, Presidentialism and Westminster Smokescreens', *Political Studies*, 54 (2006), pp. 671–90.

Blick, Andrew, 'Harold Wilson, Labour and the Machinery of Government', *Contemporary British History*, 20/3 (2006), pp. 343–62.

Bowles, Edward, 'The Role of the Private Secretary', https://www.civilservant.org.uk/library/2010_Bowles-The_Role_Of_The_Private_Secretary.pdf.

Burch, Martin and Holliday, Ian, 'The Blair Government and the Core Executive', *Government and Opposition*, 39/1 (2004), pp. 1–21.

Butcher, Tony, 'A New Civil Service? The Next Steps Agencies', in Pyper, Robert and Robins, Lynton (eds), *Governing the UK in the 1990s* (London: Palgrave, 1995).

Campbell, Alan, 'Anglo-French Relations a Decade Ago: A New Assessment (2)', *International Affairs*, 58/3 (1982), pp. 429–46.

Davis, Jon, 'Enduring continuity and endless change in the British Civil Service', *Political Quarterly*, 76/1 (2005), pp. 131–3.

Davis, Jon, 'Meritocracy in the Civil Service 1853–1970', *Political Quarterly*, 71/s1 (2000), pp. 27–35.

Davis, Jon, 'How Tony Blair's Special Advisers changed government', https://blog.oup.com/2019/03/how-tony-blair-advisers-changed-government.

De Lamothe, A. Dutheillet, 'Ministerial Cabinets in France', *Public Administration*, 43/4 (1965), pp. 365–81.

Fielding, Steven, 'Rethinking Labour's 1964 Campaign', *Contemporary British History*, 21/3 (2007), pp. 309–24.

Freedman, Lawrence, 'The Case of Westland and the Bias to Europe', *International Affairs*, 63/1 (1986/87), pp. 1–19.

Haddon, Catherine, Durrant, Tim, Devine, Daniel and Kidney Bishop, Tess *Becoming Secretary of State* (Institute for Government Insight Briefing, 2019).

Heffernan, R., 'Exploring (and Explaining) the British Prime Minister', *British Journal of Politics and International Relations*, 7/4 (2005), pp. 605–20.

Hennessy, Peter, 'The Blair government in historical perspective: An analysis of the power relationships within New Labour', *History Today*, 52/1 (2002).

Hennessy, Peter, 'The Blair Style and the Requirements of Twenty-First Century Premiership', *Political Quarterly*, 71/4 (2000), pp. 386–95.

Hennessy, Peter, 'The Blair Style of Government', *Government and Opposition*, 33/1 (1998), pp. 3–10.

Hennessy, Peter, 'Helicopter Crashes into Cabinet: Prime Minister and Constitution Hurt', *Law and Society*, 13/3 (1986), pp. 423–32.

Hennessy, Peter, 'Rulers and Servants of the State: The Blair Style of Government 1997–2004', *Parliamentary Affairs*, 58/1 (2005), pp. 6–16.

Hennessy, Peter, 'What Are Prime Ministers For?' *Journal of the British Academy*, 2014, pp. 213–29.

House of Commons Library Research Paper, *The Centre of Government – No. 10: The Cabinet Office and HM Treasury*, 05/92 (2005).

James, Simon, 'The Central Policy Review Staff 1970–1983', *Political Studies*, 34/3 (1986), pp. 423–40.

Johnson, Nevil, 'Change in the Civil Service', *Public Administration*, 63/4 (1985), pp. 415–33.

Jones, George, 'The Prime Minister's secretaries: politicians or administrators?', in Griffith, J. (ed.), *From Policy to Administration* (London: Allen & Unwin, 1976).

Little, Gavin and Stopforth, David, 'The Legislative Origins of the MPs' Expenses Scandal', *Modern Law Review*, 76/1 (2013), pp. 83–108.

Morgan, Kenneth O., 'A Comparative Case Study of Labour Prime Ministers Attlee, Wilson, Callaghan and Blair', *Journal of Legislative Studies*, 10/2–3 (2006).

Oliver, Dawn and Austin, Rodney, 'Political and Constitutional Aspects of the Westland Affair', *Parliamentary Affairs*, 40/1 (1987), pp. 20–40.

Peden, G. C., 'Sir Horace Wilson and Appeasement', *Historical Journal*, 53/4 (2010), pp. 983–1,014.

Rhodes, Rod, 'The Court Politics of the Blair Presidency', Department of the Senate Occasional Lecture, 27 June 2005.

Richards, David, 'The Conservatives, New Labour and Whitehall: a Biographical Examination of the Mandarin Cadre', in Theakston, Kevin (ed.), *Bureaucrats and Leadership* (London: Macmillan, 2000), pp. 91–117.

Richards, David, 'Political memoirs and New Labour: Interpretations of Power and the "Club Rules"', *British Journal of Politics and International Relations*, 12/4 (2010), pp. 498–522.

Richards, David, Blunkett, David and Mathers, Helen, 'Old and New Labour Narratives of Whitehall: Radicals, Reactionaries and Defenders of the Westminster Model', *The Political Quarterly*, 79/4 (2008), pp. 488–98.

Sanders, David et al., 'Government Popularity and the Falklands War: A Reassessment', *British Journal of Political Science*, 17/3 (1987), pp. 281–313.

Sanders, David et al., 'Recapturing the Falklands – Models of Conservative Popularity, 1979–83', *British Journal of Political Science*, 20/1 (1990), pp. 83–90.

Seldon, Anthony, 'The Prime Minister's Private Office from John Martin to Chris Martin', in Holt, Andrew and Dockter, Warren (eds), *Private Secretaries to the Prime Minister* (London: Routledge, 2017), pp. 187–207.

Theakston, Kevin, *The 1964–70 Labour Governments and Whitehall Reform*, POLIS Working Paper No. 2, University of Leeds (2004).

Theakston, Kevin, 'Gordon Brown as prime minister: Political skills and leadership style', *British Politics*, 6 (2011), pp. 78–100.

Theakston, Kevin, 'New Labour, New Whitehall?', *Public Policy and Administration*, 13/1 (1998), pp. 13–34.

Theakston, Kevin and Fry, Geoffrey K. 'Britain's Administrative Elite', *Public Administration*, 67/2 (1989), pp. 129–47.

Vinen, Richard, 'The Iron Lady & The Little Men', *Literary Review*, Issue 481, November 2019.

ACKNOWLEDGEMENTS

This book has had a long genesis. The idea of writing about private office first came to me in a conversation with Peter Hennessy some twenty-five years ago when I was a principal private secretary in the Education Department. Peter encouraged me to turn my ideas into a PhD with him as supervisor. A decade later, I started on my research (part-time) at Queen Mary University of London. Since then, Peter has been my guide, mentor, critic and dear friend throughout this long journey. James Ellison succeeded Peter as my supervisor and was superb in the way in which he scrutinised and challenged my work. Via his thoughtful and thorough comments, James taught me to be far more analytical in my research and, as a result, a better historian. Beyond academia, two other people have been invaluable sources of help. Gerard Hetherington, friend and former civil servant for over thirty years, read all the chapters of the book in draft and much improved their readability. Similarly, Peter Riddell, the former political journalist, read much of the book in draft and made many helpful suggestions. I must also thank my great friend and regular lunch companion, the journalist Bill Keegan. Bill's memories of politicians and civil servants go back well over half a century. He was also responsible for organising three memorably long lunches with Denis Healey, Nigel Lawson and Ed Balls.

My wonderful agent Caroline Michel had faith in this project from the outset. Her support and guidance through to publication have been immense. At Biteback, the whole team has been a pleasure to work with. But, in particular, Ella Boardman has been a very supportive and efficient editor. While I was chief executive of the British Academy, my two presidents – Lord Stern and Sir David Cannadine – were both supportive of me continuing my research. Sir David read an early version of the Thatcher chapter and made a number of helpful comments. I am also very grateful to those members of the academy staff who helped with the recording and transcribing of some of my interviews with former Prime Ministers.

I am particularly grateful to all the people who agreed to give me interviews about their memories of private office, all of whom are listed in the Bibliography. Without their memories and honest accounts, the book would have been far less interesting. In addition, I would like to thank that much wider group of friends and colleagues who have supported and helped me over the years on this project in a wide range of ways. They are: Mark Allen, Iain Anderson, Andrew Arends, Chris Bartlett, Val Bartlett, Andrew Blick, Rupert Cazalet, Robert Chote, Michelle Clement, John Curtice, Camilla Darling, Paul Darling, Dawn Davidson, Euan Davidson, Jon Davis, Howard Ewing, Dominic Fagan, Charlie Falconer, Robert Fox, Jullien Gaer, Cath Haddon, Guy Heald, Simon Heffer, Suzanne Heywood (with particular thanks for her memories and photos of the late Jeremy Heywood), James Jinks, Bernadette Kelly, Steve Kerridge, the late Tony King, Matt Lyus, Jonathan McClory, Ruth Martin, Rupesh Mehta, Steve O'Neil, James Naughtie, Kieron Norris, Hilary Omissi, Akash Paun, Stuart Phillips, Michael Portillo, Chris Quirk, Emily Riddell, Martin Rogers, Rob Saunders, Martin Stolliday, Karl Sydow, Kevin Theakston, Alex Thomas, John

Turle, Sara Turle, Claire Tyler, George Walden and Kieron White. I hope I have not missed anyone. It goes without saying that any errors that remain in the book are mine and mine alone. If you do spot any errors, please do let me know.

Finally, I should like to thank my three elder brothers, David, Christopher and Robert, who have all helped and advised me, in a variety of ways, during the course of writing this book, not least with much-needed IT advice to make up for my poor technological skills.

Last, but not least, I could not have written this without the support of my two wonderful daughters, Charlotte and Harriet, to whom this book is dedicated. My late wife, Ingrid, made me promise before she died that I must finish my PhD and book. I am only sorry that she did not live to see it published – but I hope she would have liked the final product.

Alun Evans
Wanstead, Greenwich and La Salvetat-Peyralès
April 2024

INDEX

5353 6059

666.84

R319

20

5559

634 31142

Comp math server

1690

tЄ+

Sπ ξO